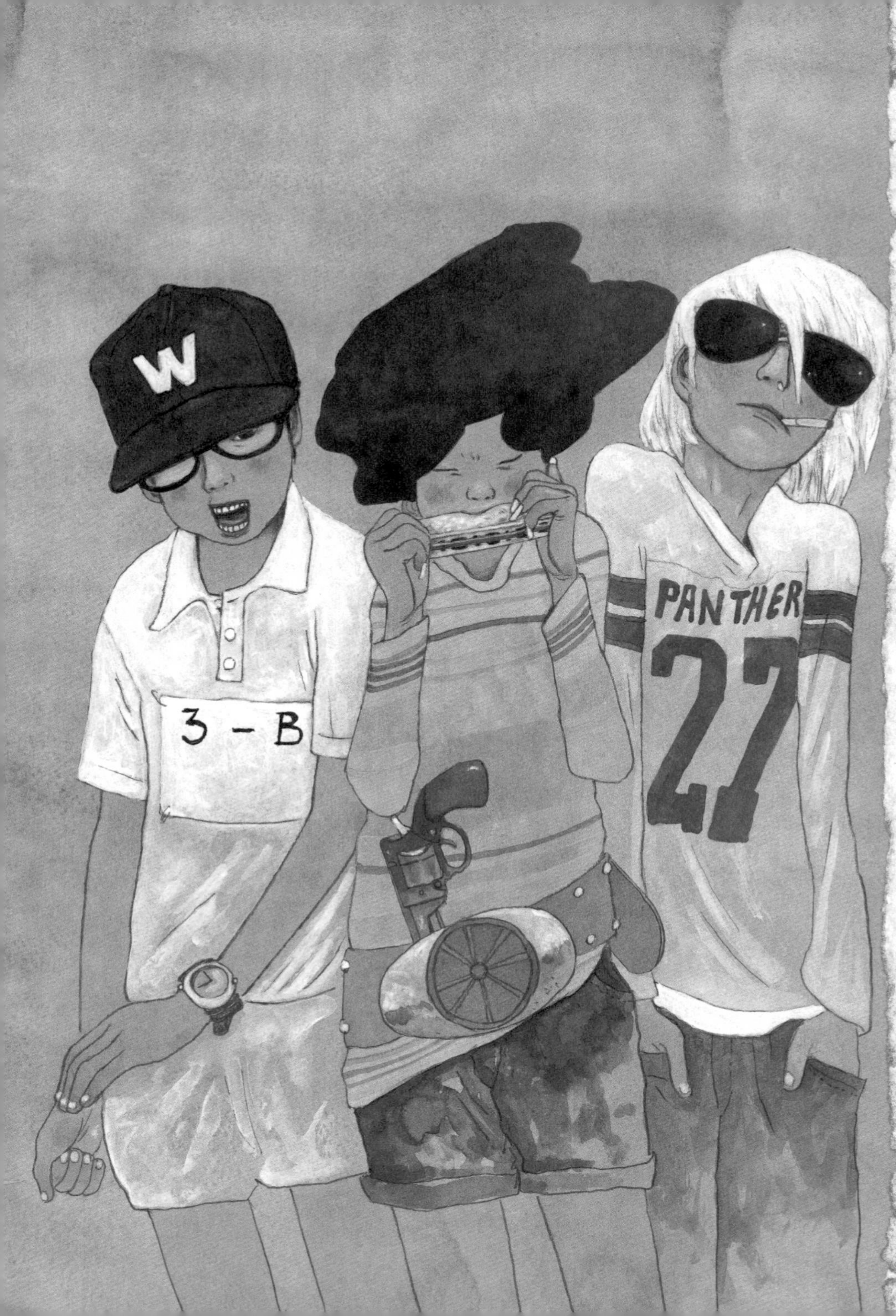
W
3 - B
PANTHER
27

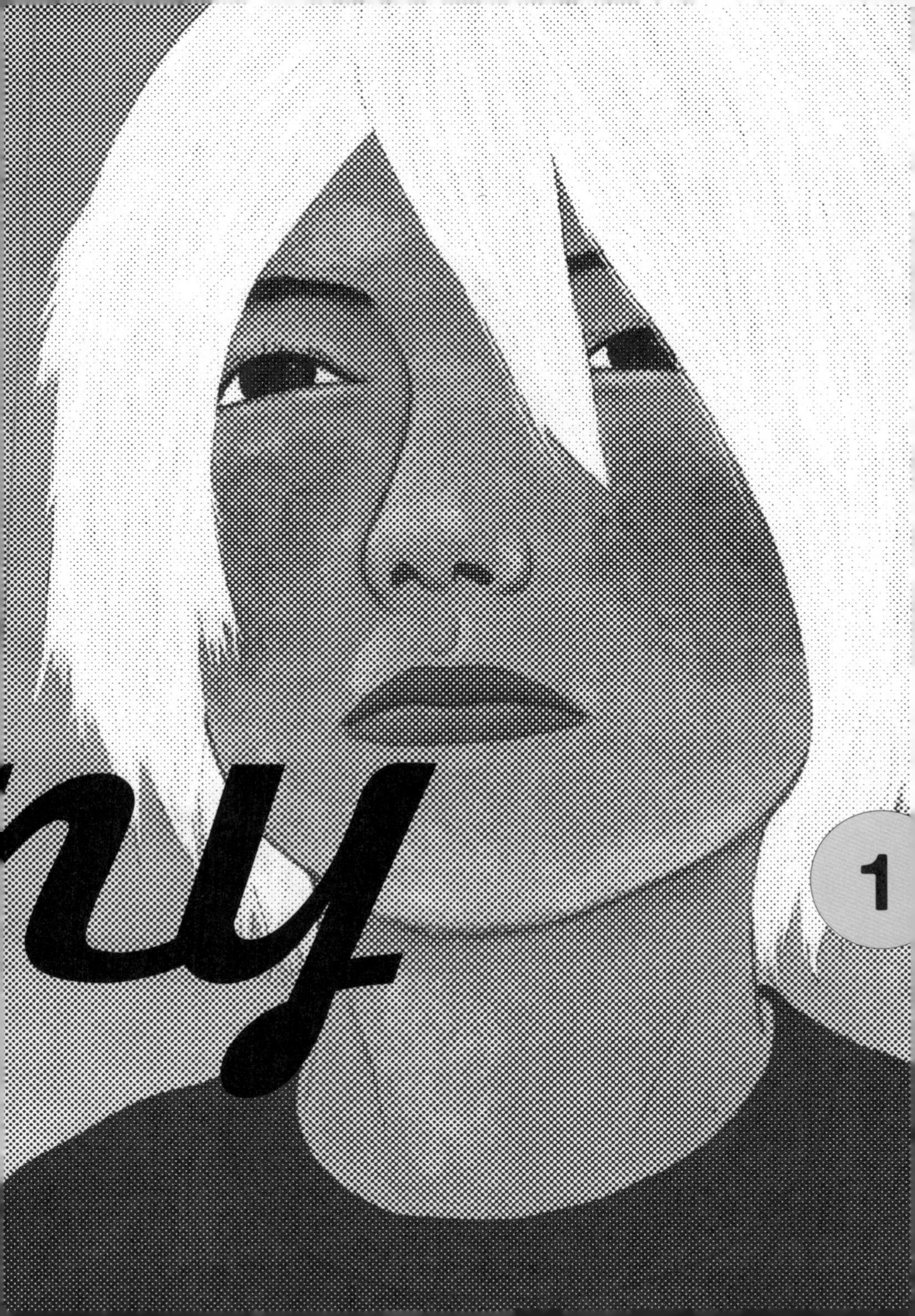
ny
1

Sun

T A I Y O M A T S U M O T O

CONTENTS

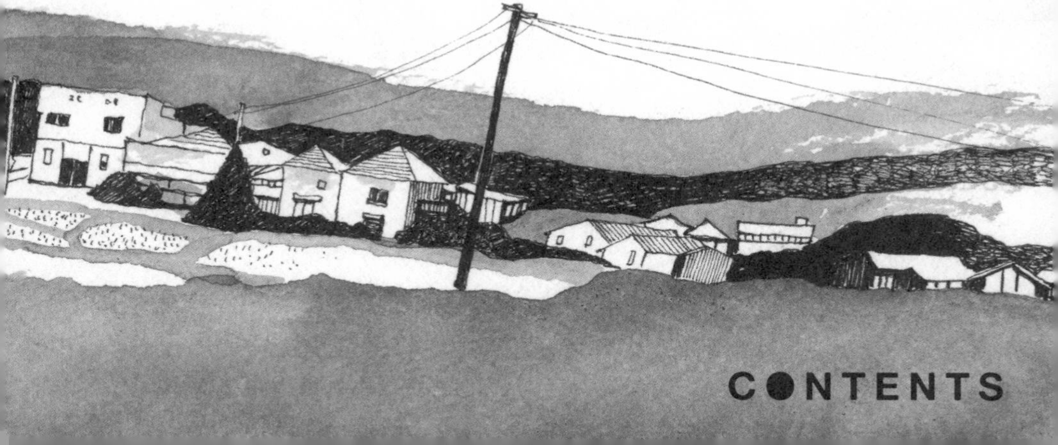

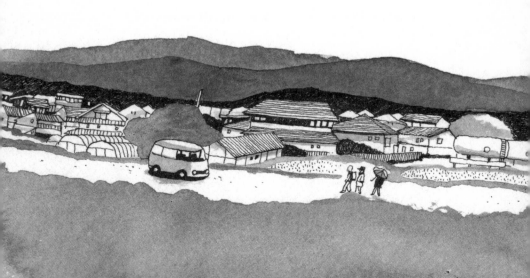

Sunny

(1)

CHAPTER 1

"Where's
Yokohama?"

"I dunno,
somewhere
'round
Tokyo?"

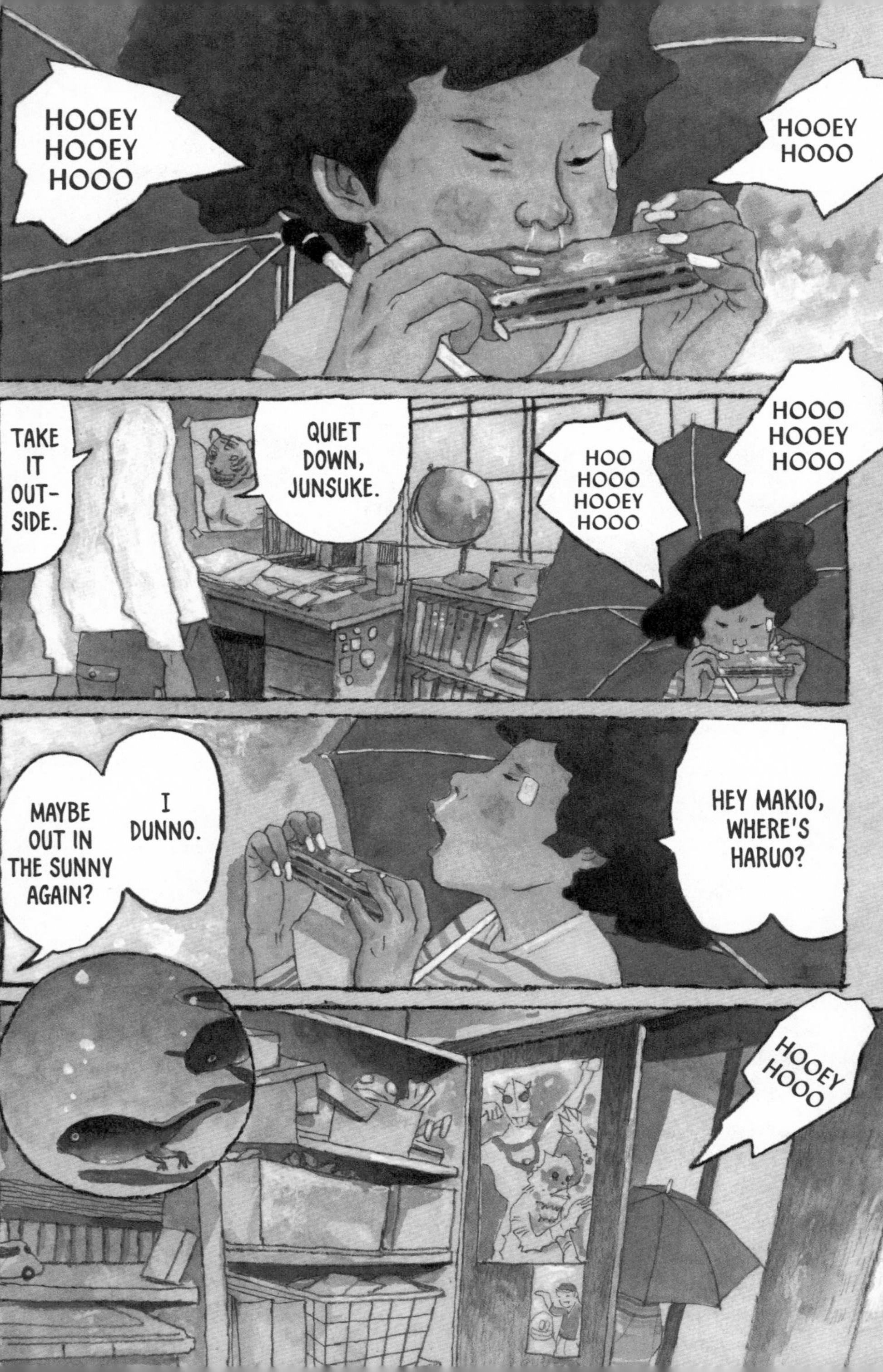
HOOEY HOOO
HOOEY HOOEY HOOO
HOOO HOOEY HOOO
HOO HOOO HOOEY HOOO
QUIET DOWN, JUNSUKE.
TAKE IT OUT-SIDE.
HEY MAKIO, WHERE'S HARUO?
I DUNNO.
MAYBE OUT IN THE SUNNY AGAIN?
HOOEY HOOO

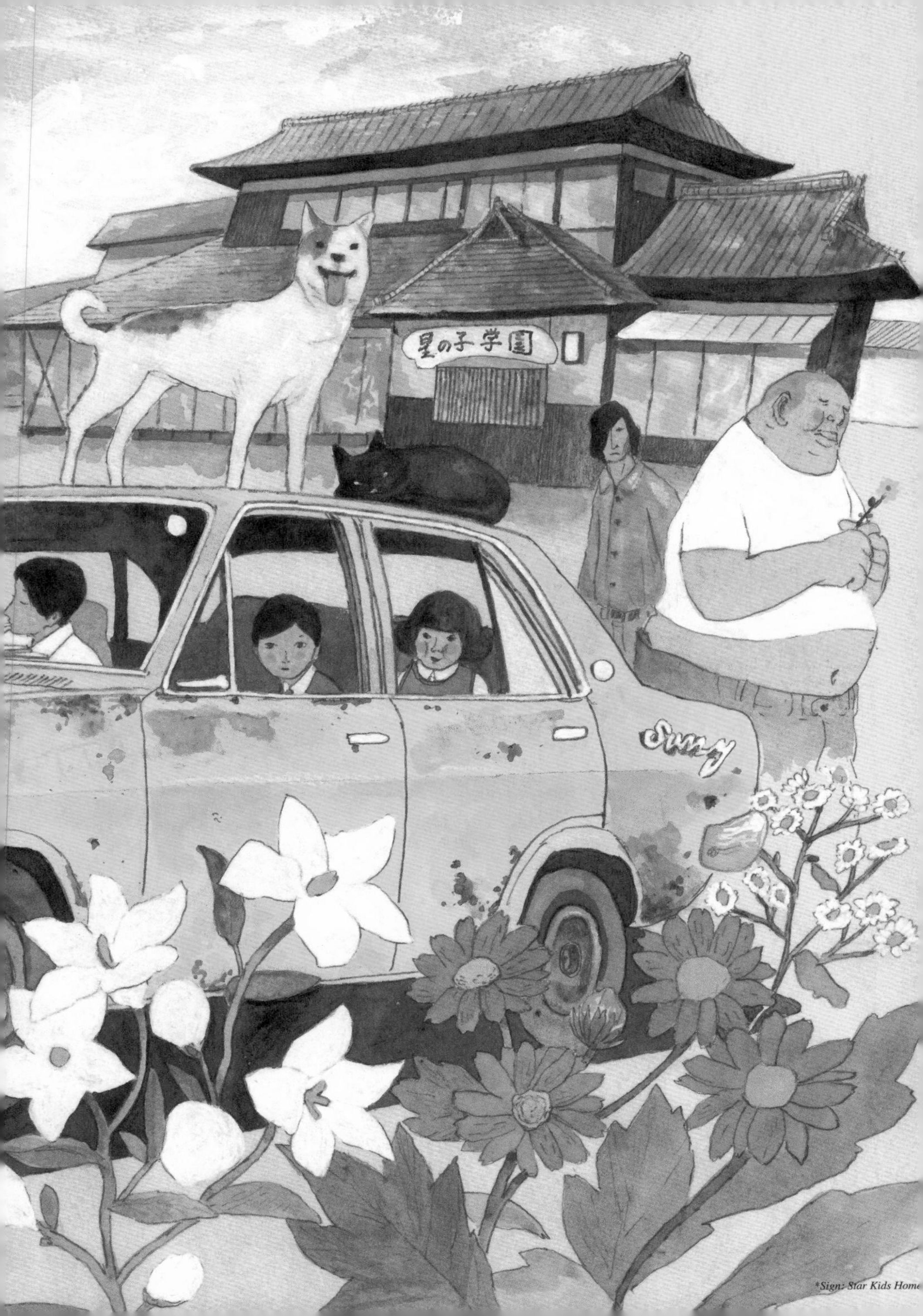
星の子学園
Suny

*Sign: Star Kids Home

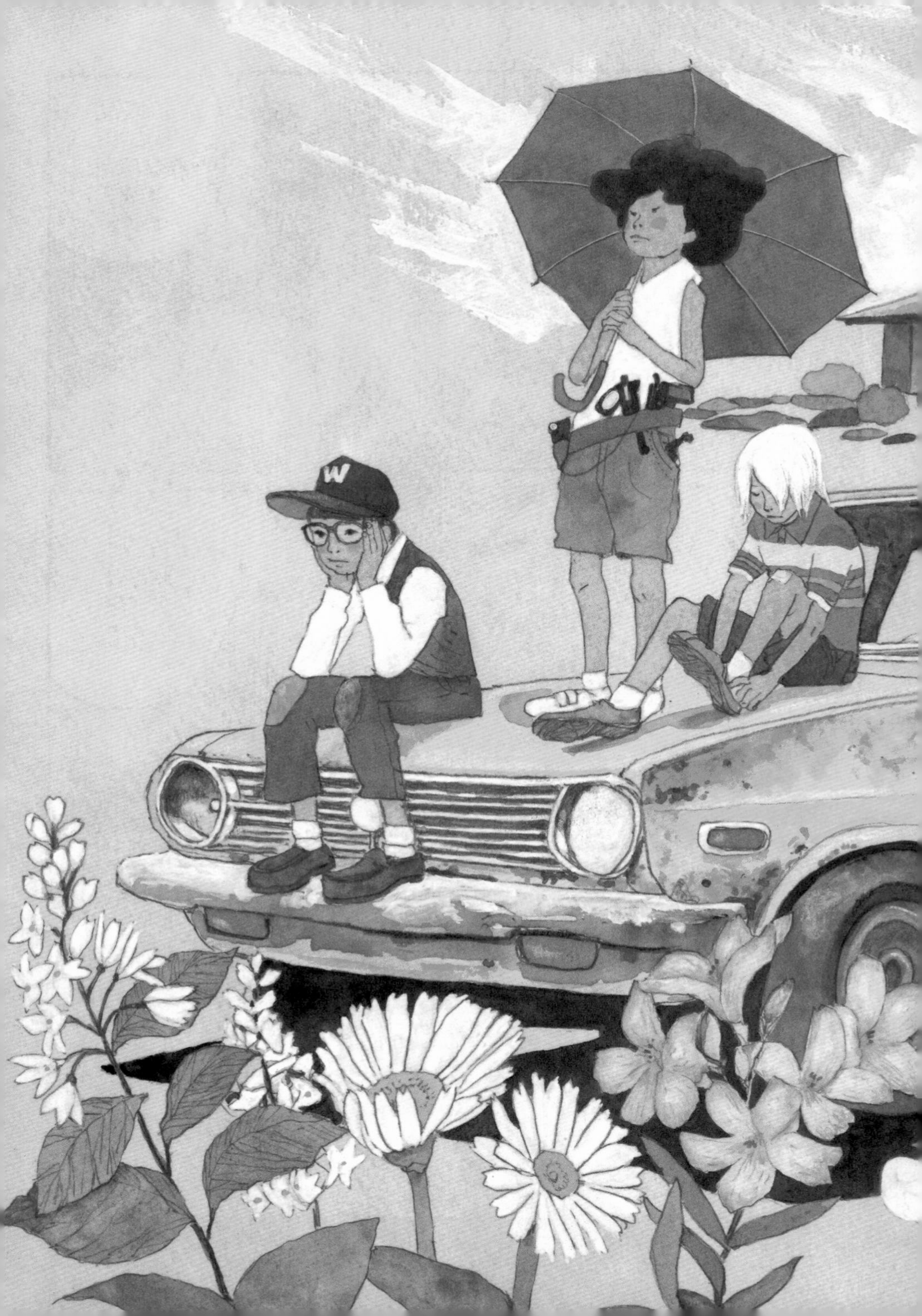

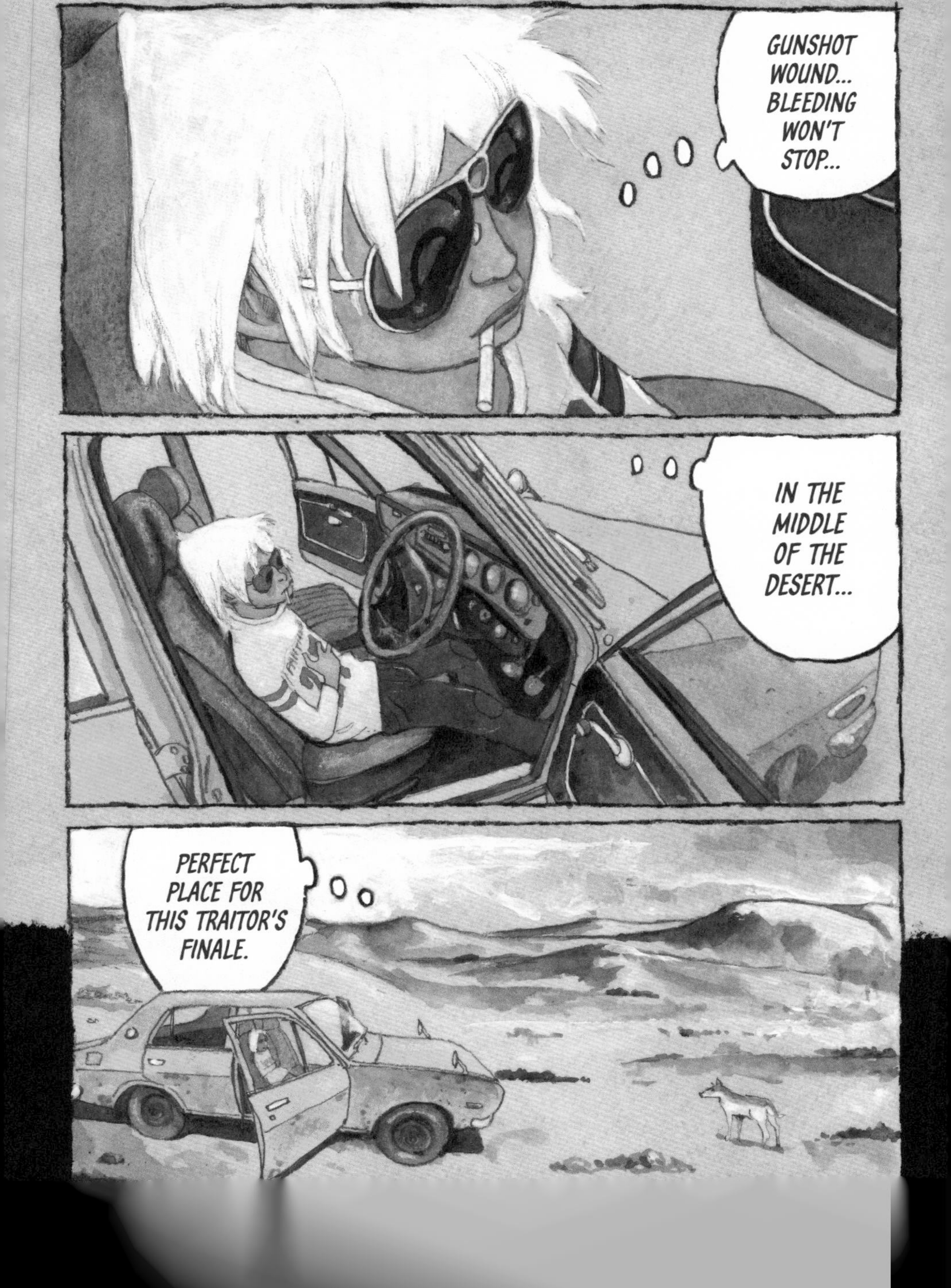
GUNSHOT WOUND... BLEEDING WON'T STOP...
IN THE MIDDLE OF THE DESERT...
PERFECT PLACE FOR THIS TRAITOR'S FINALE.

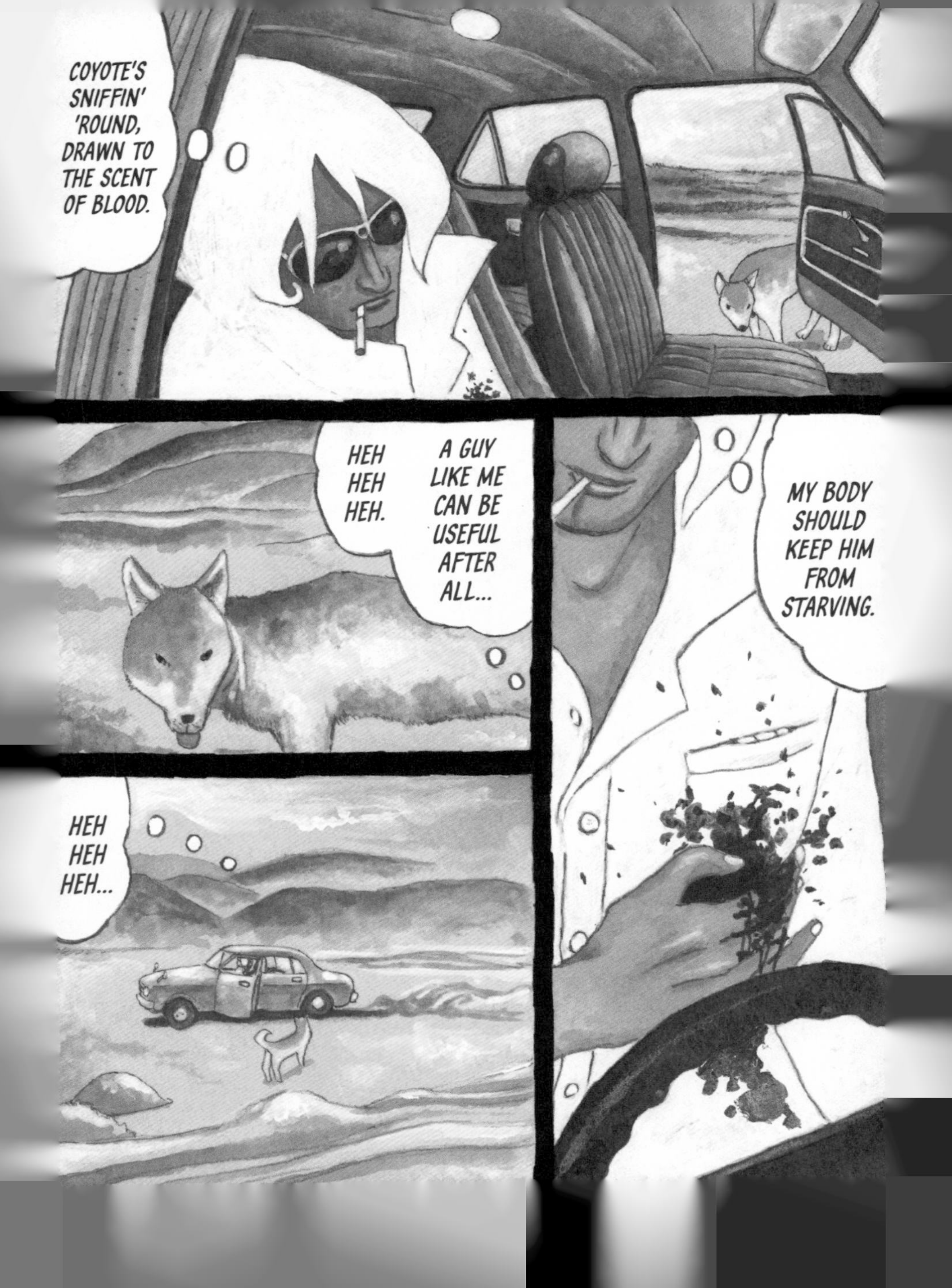
COYOTE'S SNIFFIN' 'ROUND, DRAWN TO THE SCENT OF BLOOD.
HEH HEH HEH. A GUY LIKE ME CAN BE USEFUL AFTER ALL...
MY BODY SHOULD KEEP HIM FROM STARVING.
HEH HEH HEH...

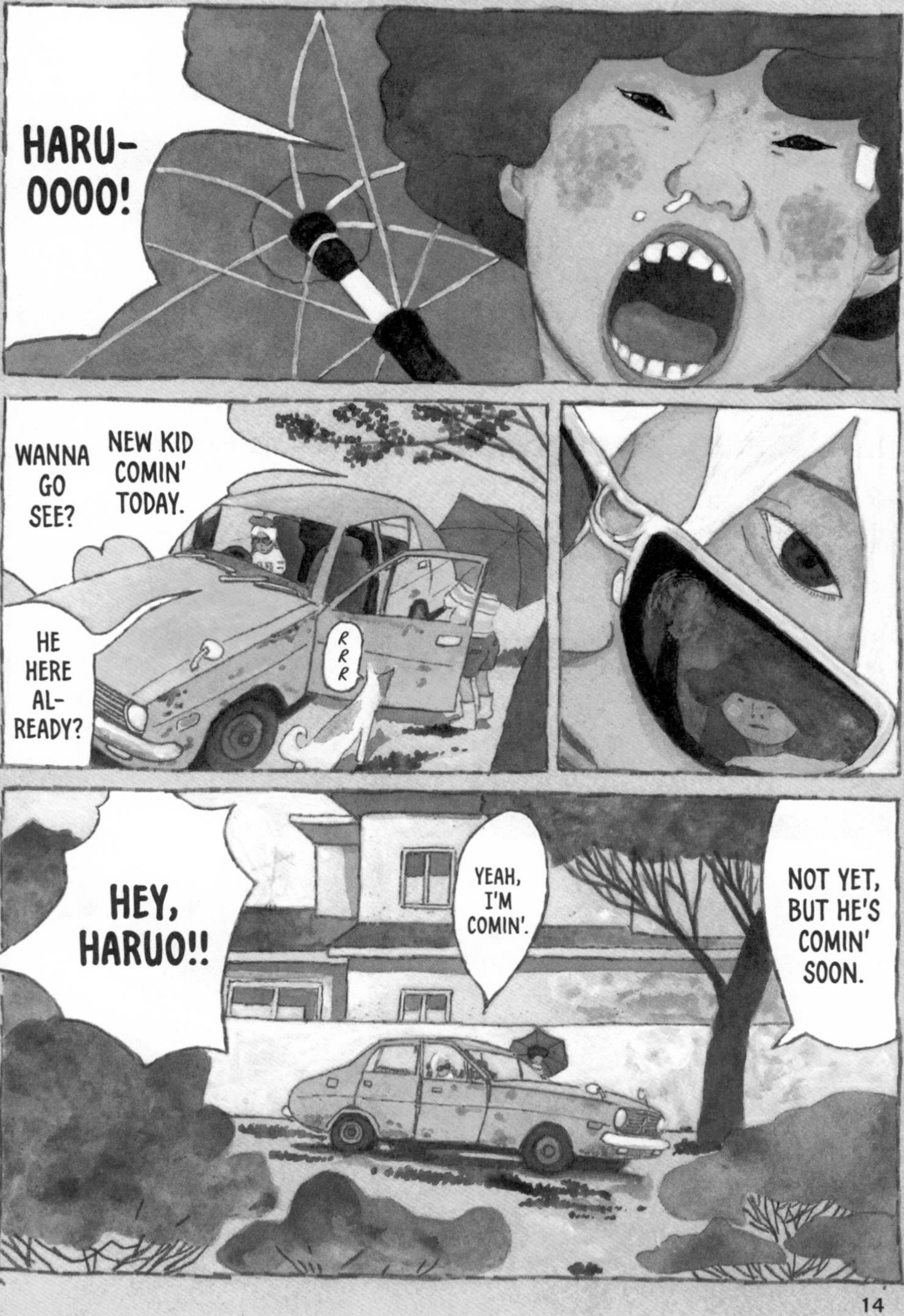
HARU-OOOO!
NEW KID COMIN' TODAY.
WANNA GO SEE?
HE HERE AL-READY?
RRR
NOT YET, BUT HE'S COMIN' SOON.
YEAH, I'M COMIN'.
HEY, HARUO!!

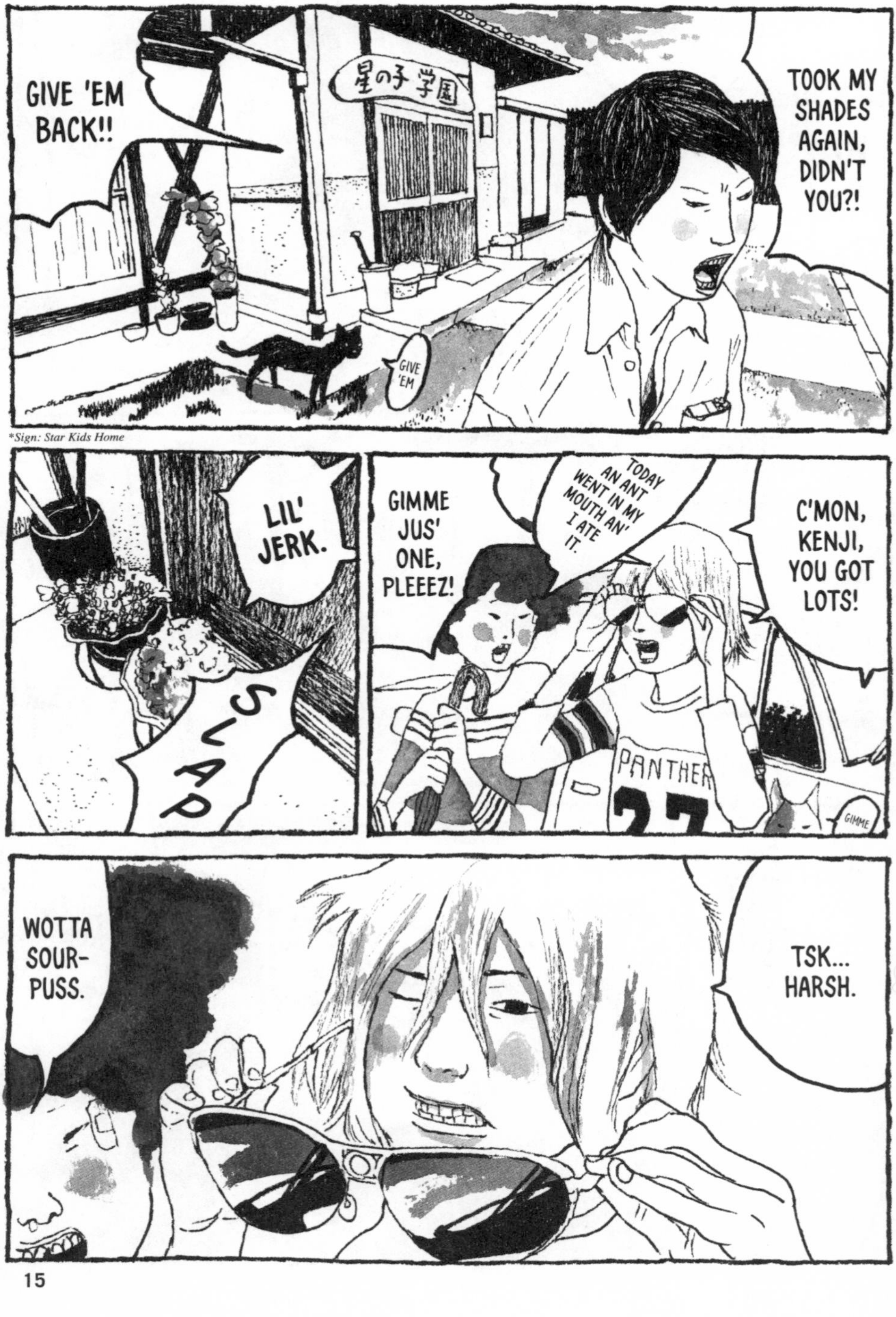
TOOK MY SHADES AGAIN, DIDN'T YOU?!
星の子学園
GIVE 'EM
GIVE 'EM BACK!!
C'MON, KENJI, YOU GOT LOTS!
TODAY AN ANT WENT IN MY MOUTH AN' I ATE IT.
GIMME JUS' ONE, PLEEEZ!
PANTHER
GIMME
LIL' JERK.
SLAP
TSK... HARSH.
WOTTA SOUR-PUSS.
*Sign: Star Kids Home

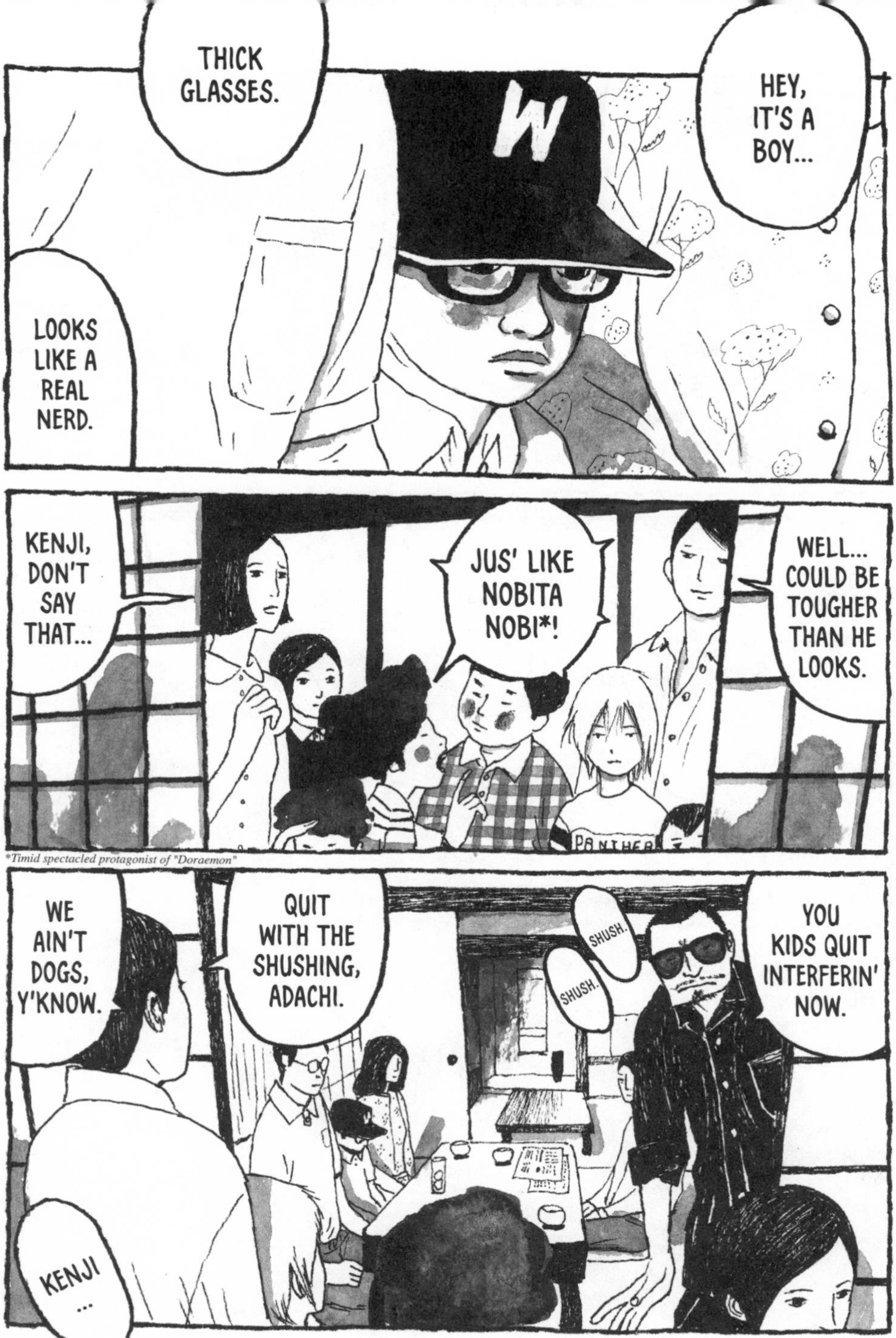
HEY, IT'S A BOY...
THICK GLASSES.
LOOKS LIKE A REAL NERD.
WELL... COULD BE TOUGHER THAN HE LOOKS.
JUS' LIKE NOBITA NOBI*!
KENJI, DON'T SAY THAT...
PANTHER
YOU KIDS QUIT INTERFERIN' NOW.
SHUSH.
SHUSH.
QUIT WITH THE SHUSHING, ADACHI.
WE AIN'T DOGS, Y'KNOW.
KENJI ...

*Timid spectacled protagonist of "Doraemon"

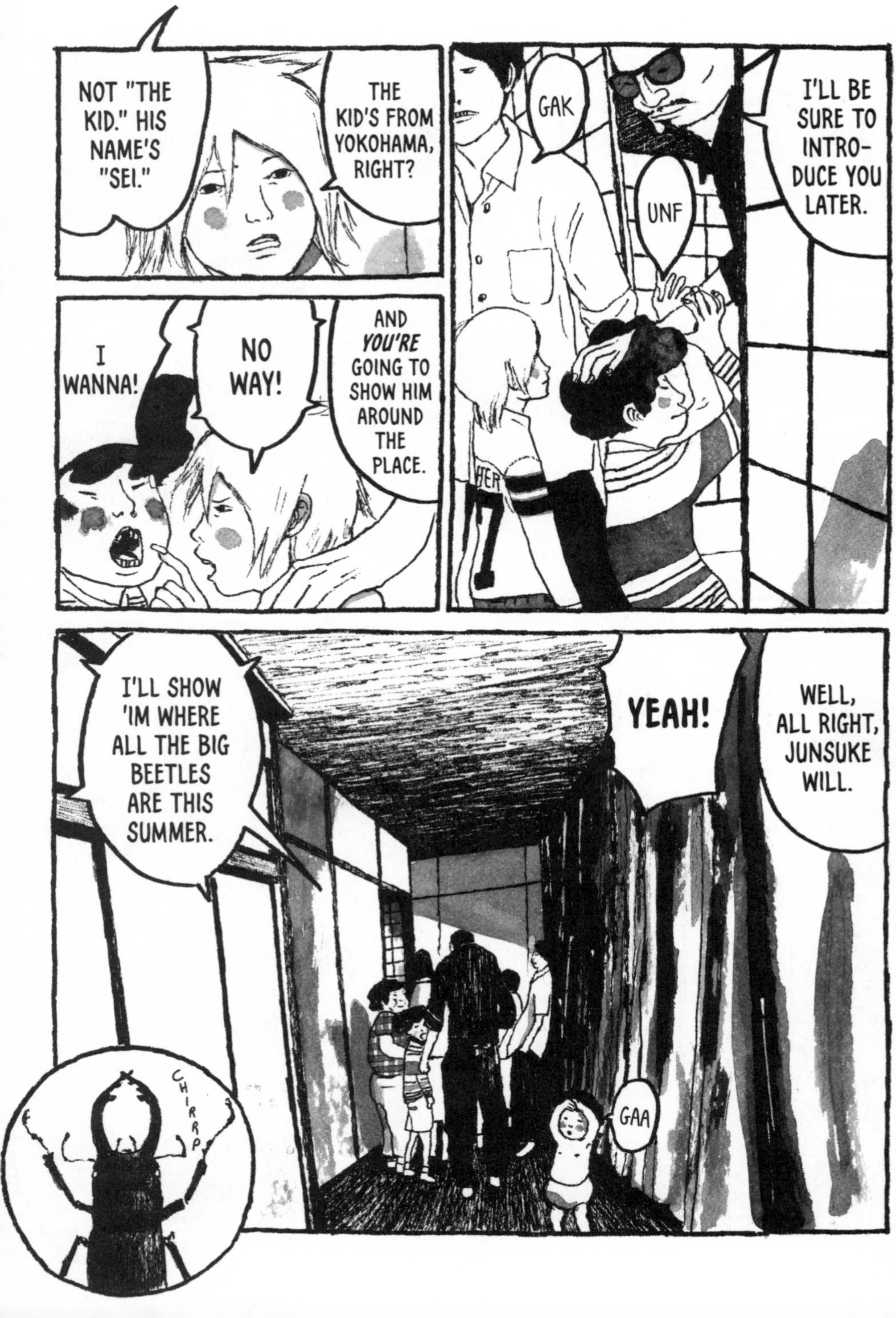
I'LL BE SURE TO INTRO- DUCE YOU LATER.
GAK
UNF
THE KID'S FROM YOKOHAMA, RIGHT?
NOT "THE KID." HIS NAME'S "SEI."
AND *YOU'RE* GOING TO SHOW HIM AROUND THE PLACE.
NO WAY!
I WANNA!
WELL, ALL RIGHT, JUNSUKE WILL.
YEAH!
I'LL SHOW 'IM WHERE ALL THE BIG BEETLES ARE THIS SUMMER.
GAA
CHIRRP

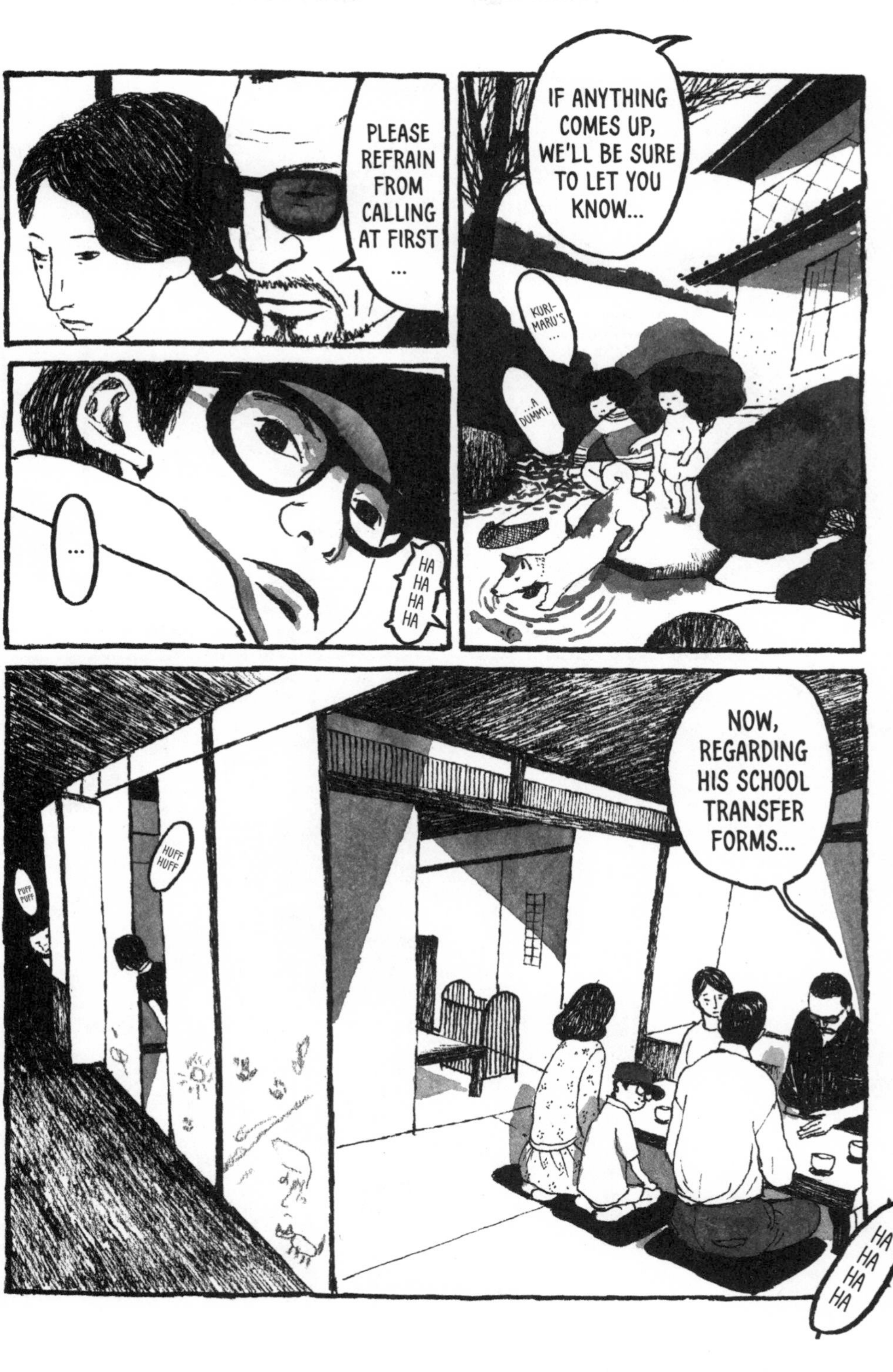
IF ANYTHING COMES UP, WE'LL BE SURE TO LET YOU KNOW...
KURI-MARU'S...
...A DUMMY.
PLEASE REFRAIN FROM CALLING AT FIRST...
HA HA HA HA
...
NOW, REGARDING HIS SCHOOL TRANSFER FORMS...
HUFF HUFF
PUFF PUFF
HA HA HA HA

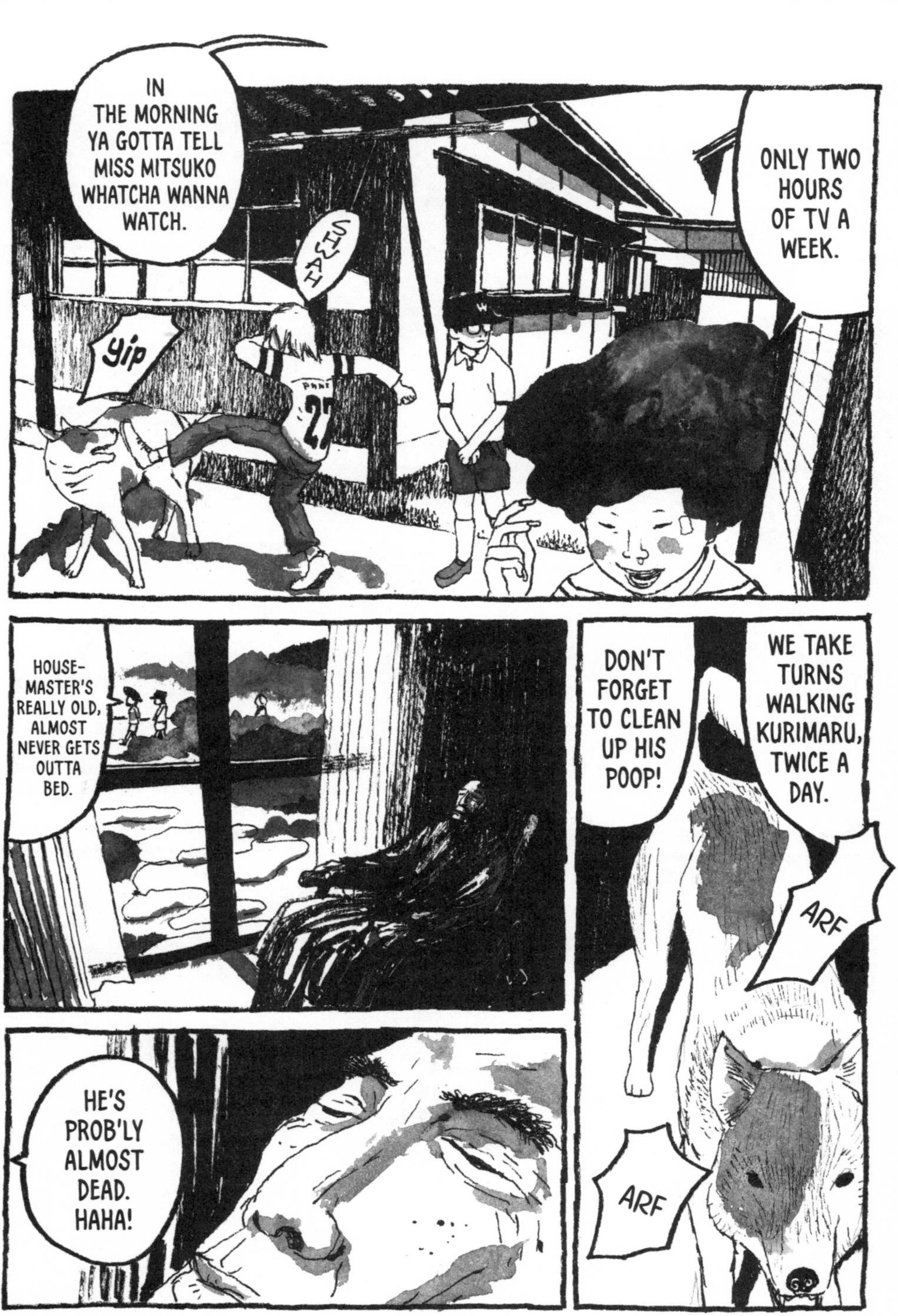
ONLY TWO HOURS OF TV A WEEK.
IN THE MORNING YA GOTTA TELL MISS MITSUKO WHATCHA WANNA WATCH.
SWAH
yip
WE TAKE TURNS WALKING KURIMARU, TWICE A DAY.
DON'T FORGET TO CLEAN UP HIS POOP!
ARF
ARF
HOUSE-MASTER'S REALLY OLD, ALMOST NEVER GETS OUTTA BED.
HE'S PROB'LY ALMOST DEAD. HAHA!

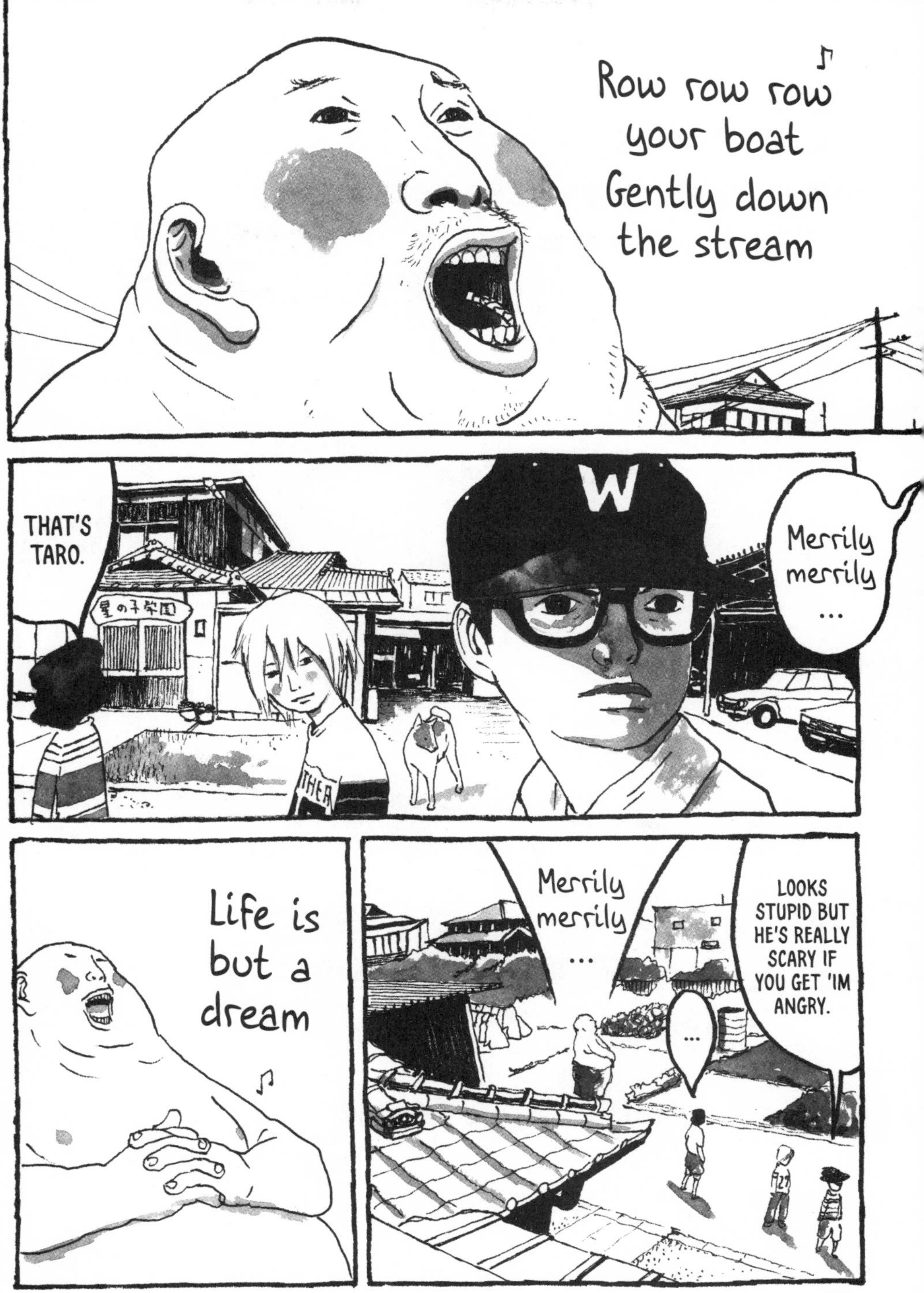
♪
Row row row your boat Gently down the stream
Merrily merrily ...
THAT'S TARO.
LOOKS STUPID BUT HE'S REALLY SCARY IF YOU GET 'IM ANGRY.
Merrily merrily ...
...
Life is but a dream
♪

HMPH.
KA-CHUNK
A SUNNY 1200.
HEY, YOU LIKE CARS?
DOES IT RUN?
TELEPATHY, YA MOVE IT WITH TELEPATHY!
SNIFF
SNIFF

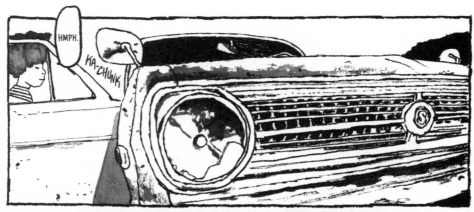

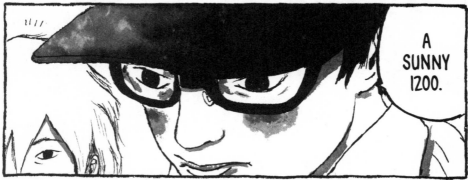

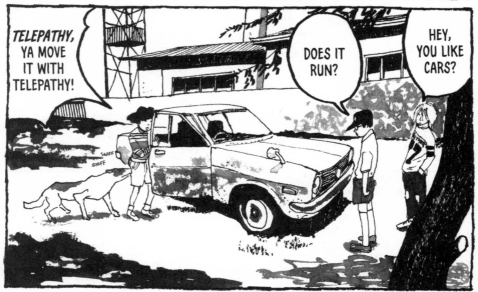

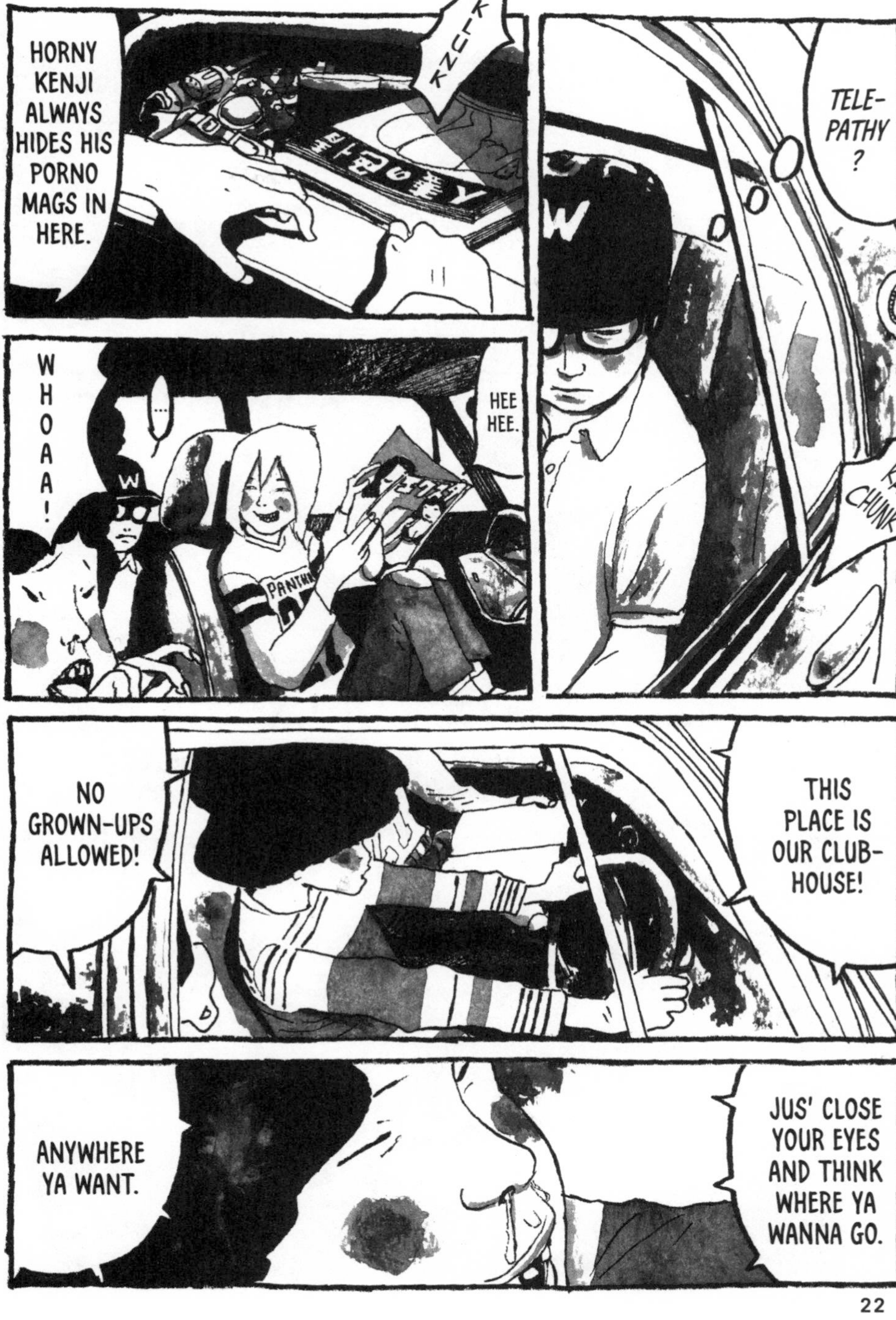
TELE-PATHY?
KA-CHUNK
KLUNK
HORNY KENJI ALWAYS HIDES HIS PORNO MAGS IN HERE.
HEE HEE.
...
WHOAAA!
THIS PLACE IS OUR CLUB-HOUSE!
NO GROWN-UPS ALLOWED!
JUS' CLOSE YOUR EYES AND THINK WHERE YA WANNA GO.
ANYWHERE YA WANT.

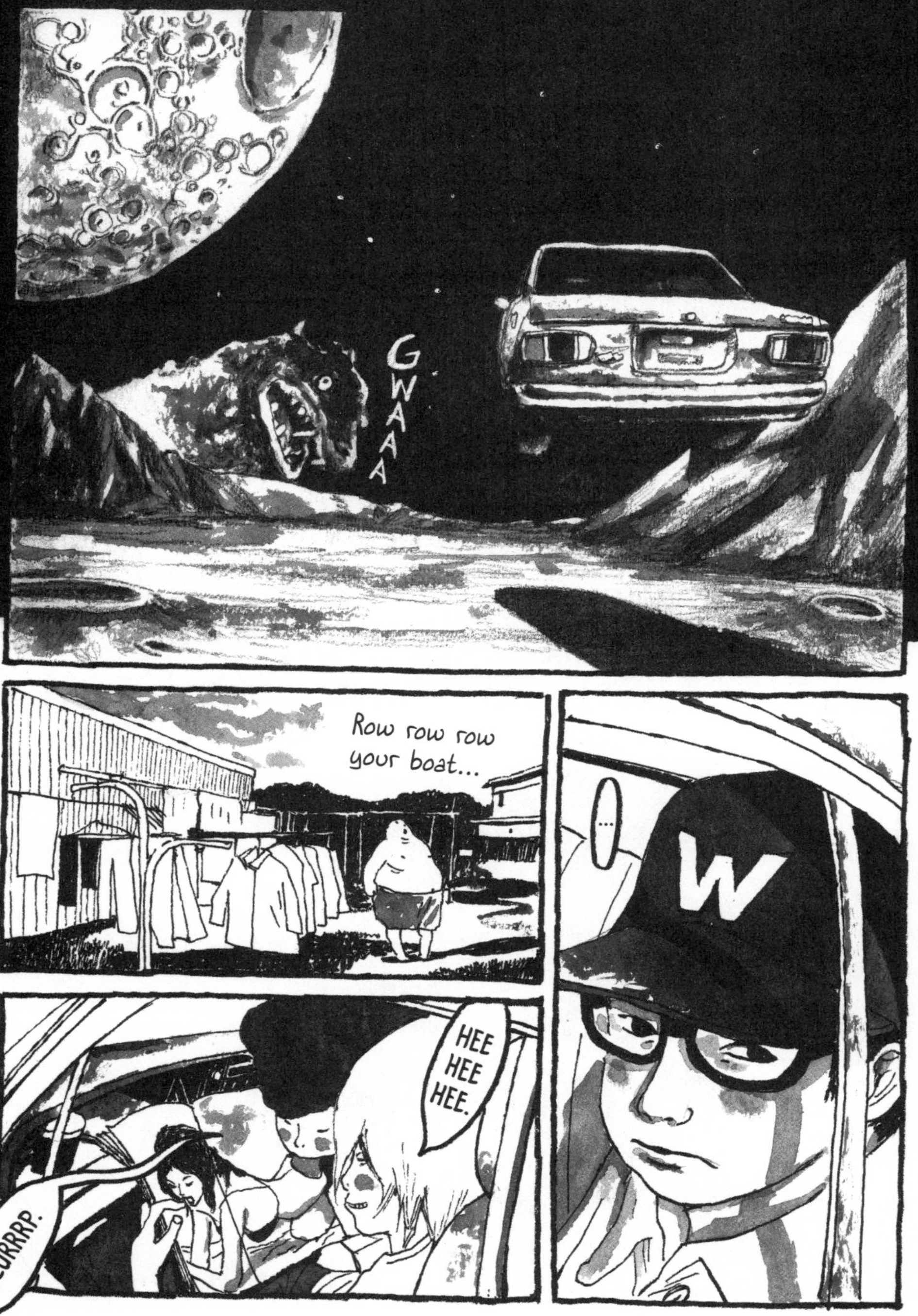
GWAAAA
...
Row row row your boat...
HEE HEE HEE.
SLURRRP.

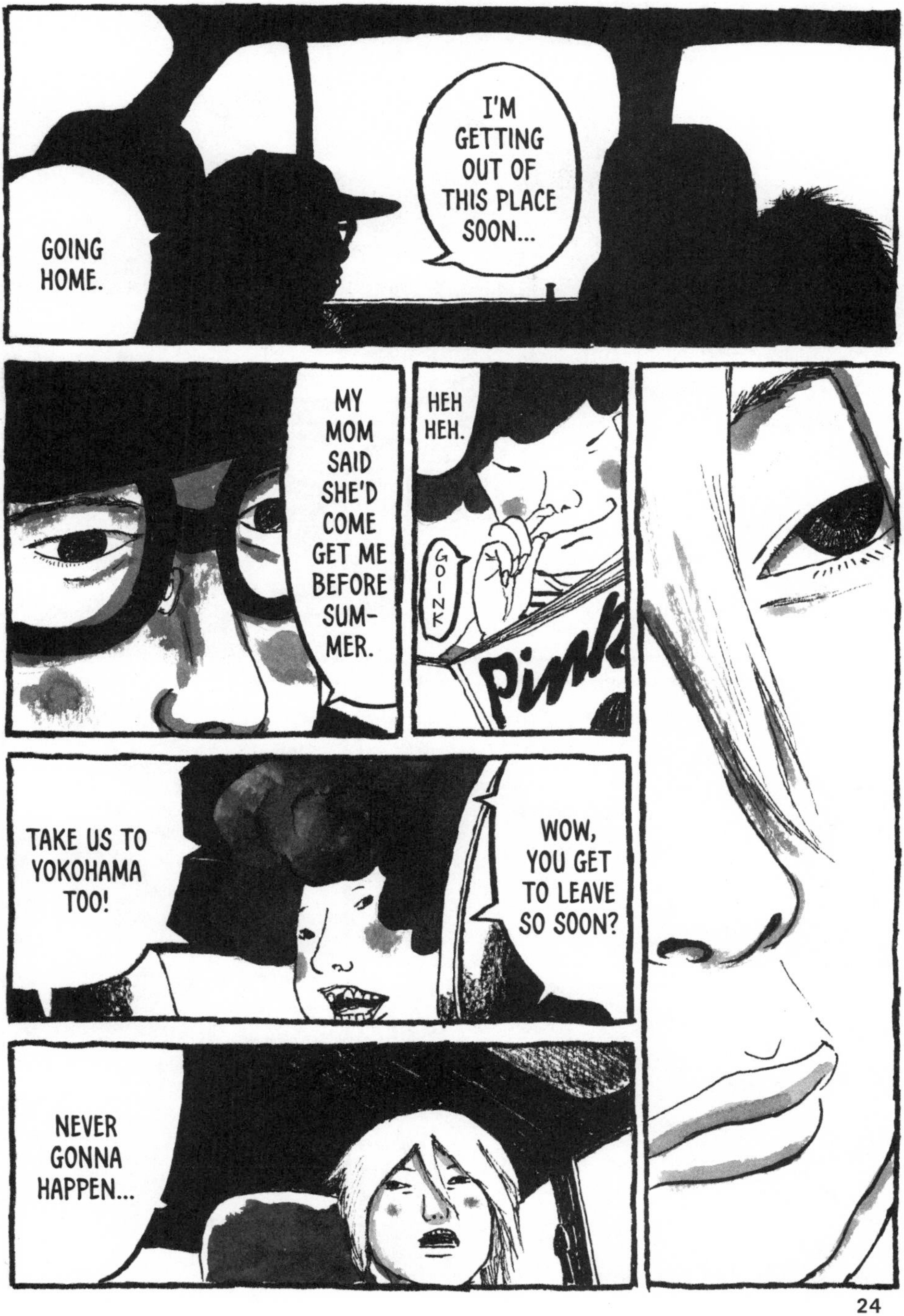
I'M GETTING OUT OF THIS PLACE SOON...
GOING HOME.
HEH HEH.
GOINK
PINK
MY MOM SAID SHE'D COME GET ME BEFORE SUM-MER.
WOW, YOU GET TO LEAVE SO SOON?
TAKE US TO YOKOHAMA TOO!
NEVER GONNA HAPPEN...

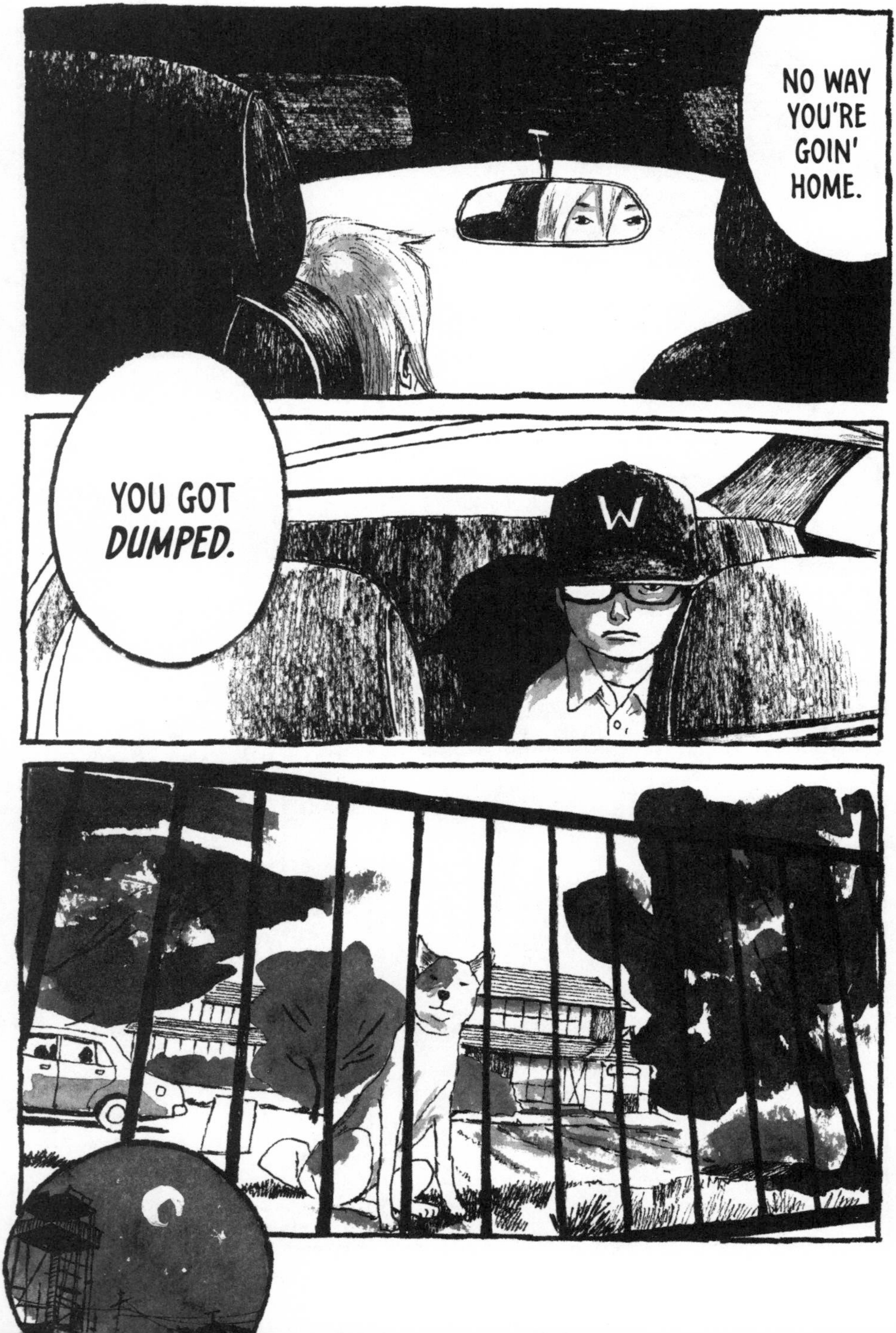
NO WAY YOU'RE GOIN' HOME.
YOU GOT *DUMPED.*

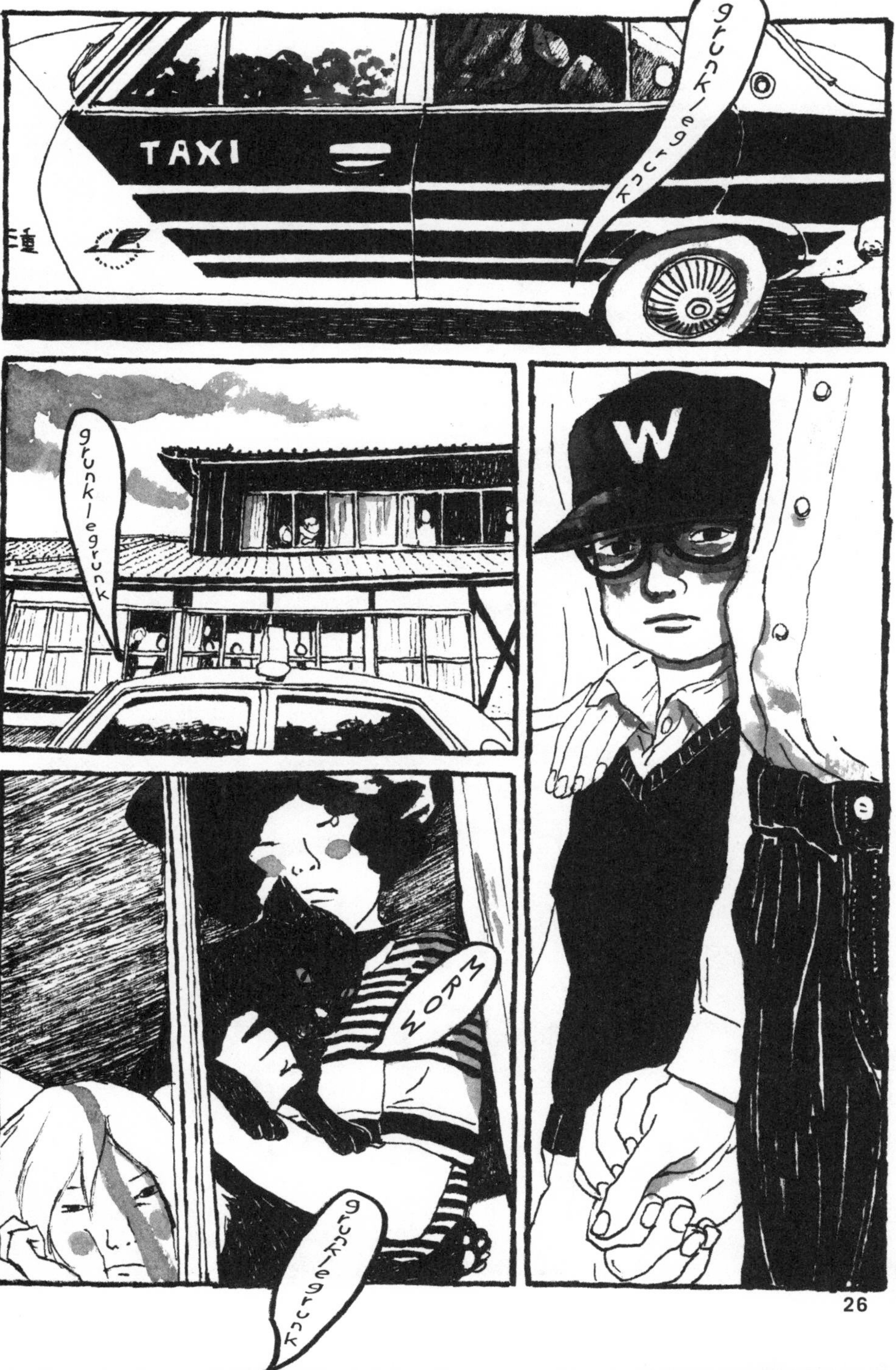
grunklegrunk
grunklegrunk
MROW
grunklegrunk

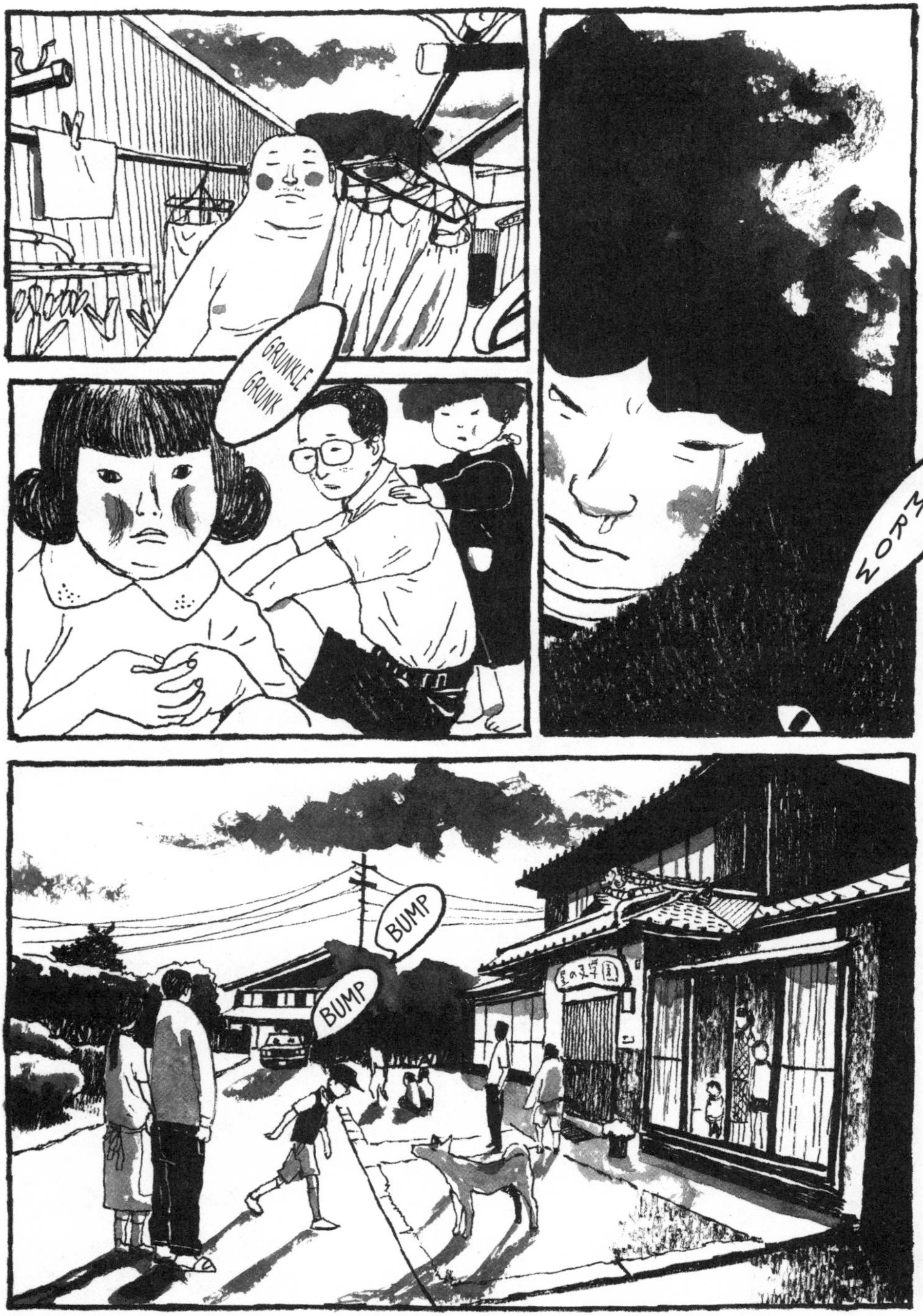
WORM
GRUNKLE GRUNK
BUMP
BUMP

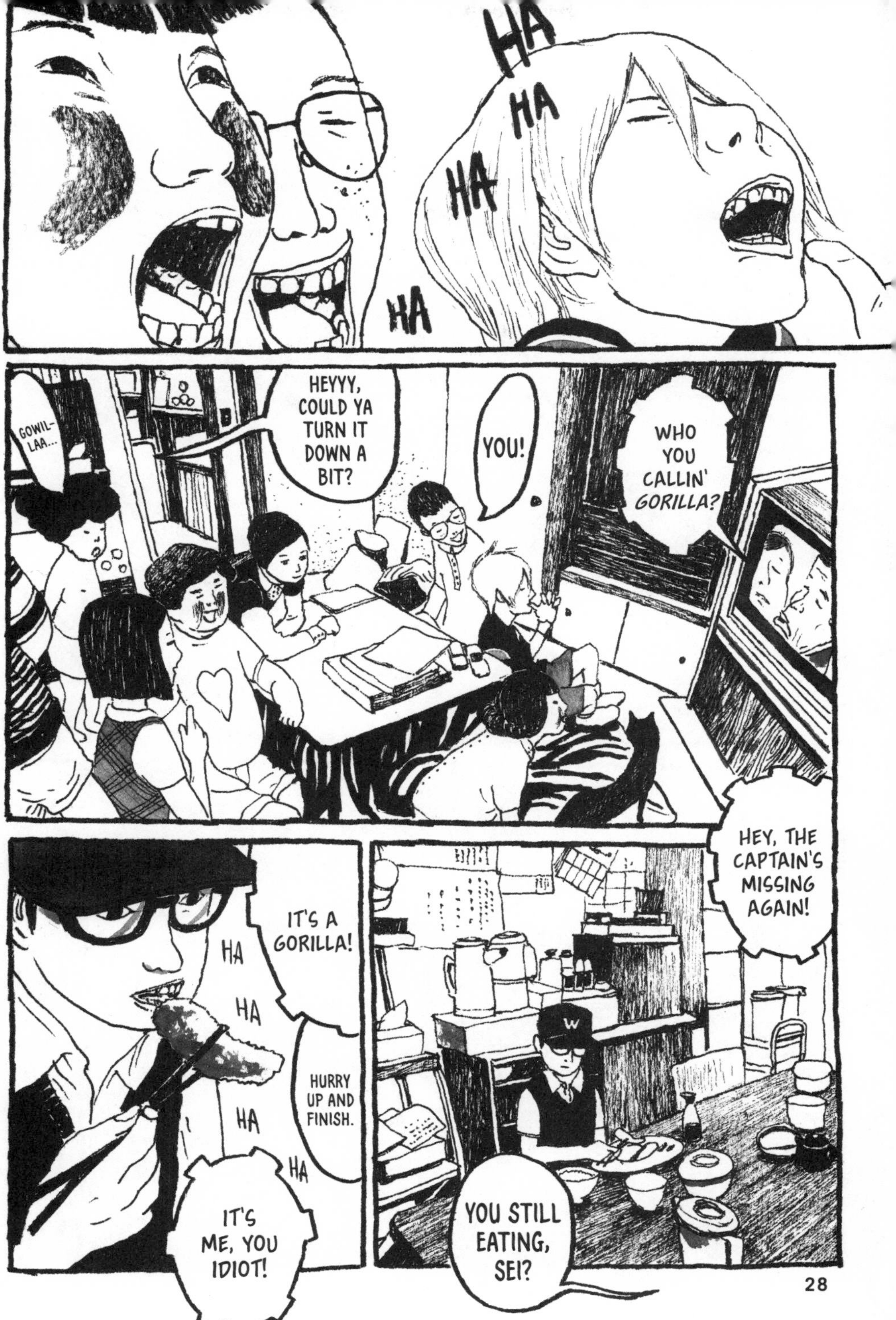
HA
HA
HA
HA
WHO YOU CALLIN' GORILLA?
YOU!
HEYYY, COULD YA TURN IT DOWN A BIT?
GOWIL-LAA...
HEY, THE CAPTAIN'S MISSING AGAIN!
YOU STILL EATING, SEI?
IT'S A GORILLA!
HA
HA
HA
HA
HURRY UP AND FINISH.
IT'S ME, YOU IDIOT!

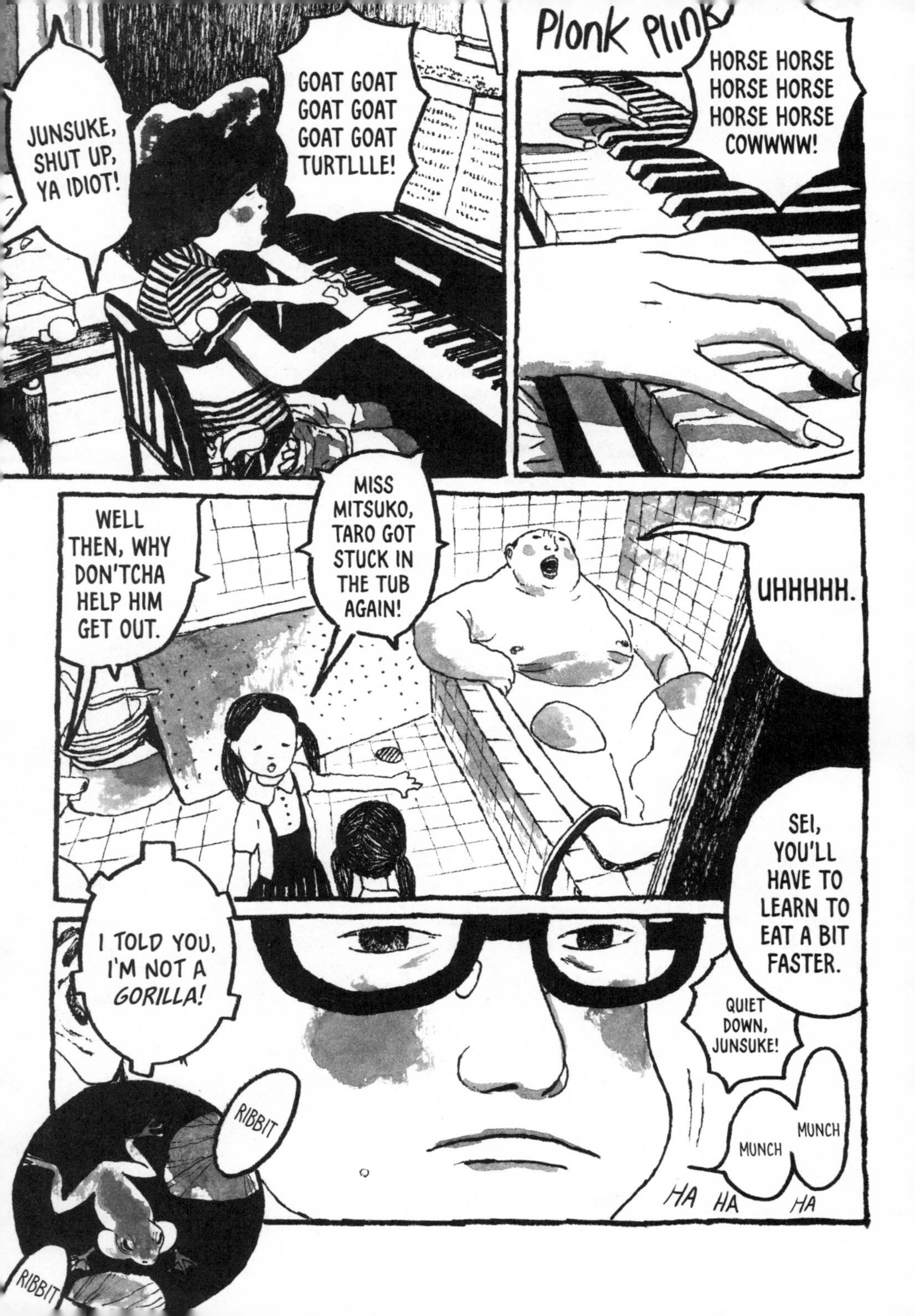
Plonk Plink
HORSE HORSE HORSE HORSE HORSE HORSE COWWWW!
GOAT GOAT GOAT GOAT GOAT GOAT TURTLLLE!
JUNSUKE, SHUT UP, YA IDIOT!
UHHHHH.
MISS MITSUKO, TARO GOT STUCK IN THE TUB AGAIN!
WELL THEN, WHY DON'TCHA HELP HIM GET OUT.
SEI, YOU'LL HAVE TO LEARN TO EAT A BIT FASTER.
QUIET DOWN, JUNSUKE!
MUNCH MUNCH
HA HA HA
I TOLD YOU, I'M NOT A *GORILLA*!
RIBBIT
RIBBIT

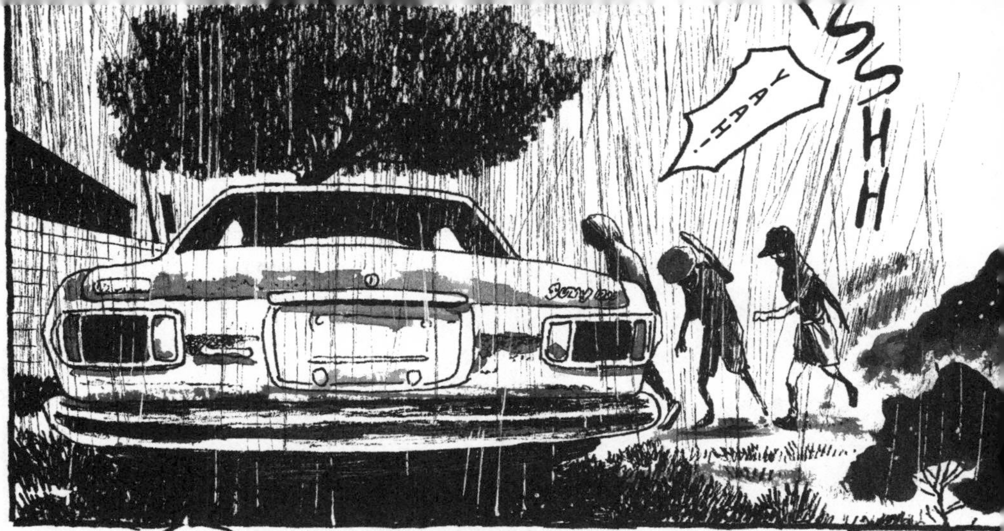
SSHH
YAAH!!
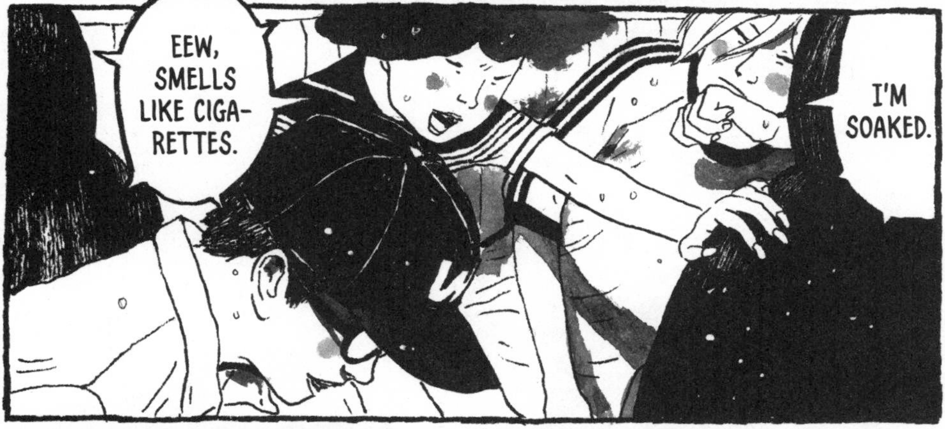
I'M SOAKED.
EEW, SMELLS LIKE CIGARETTES.
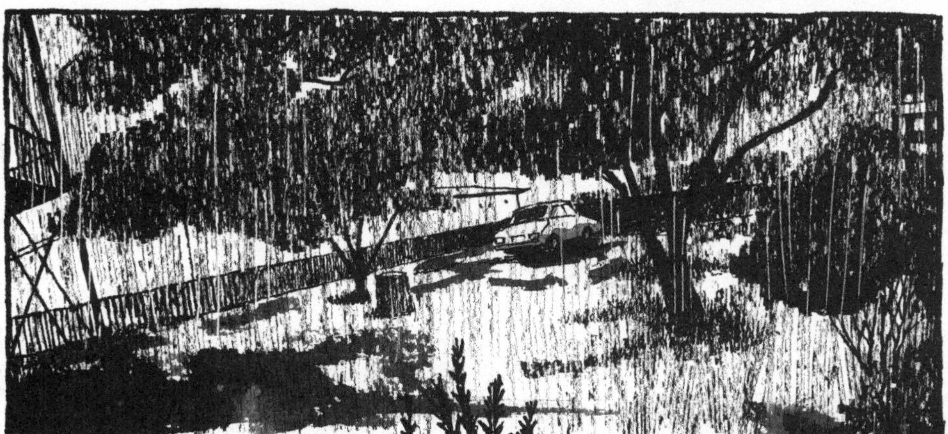

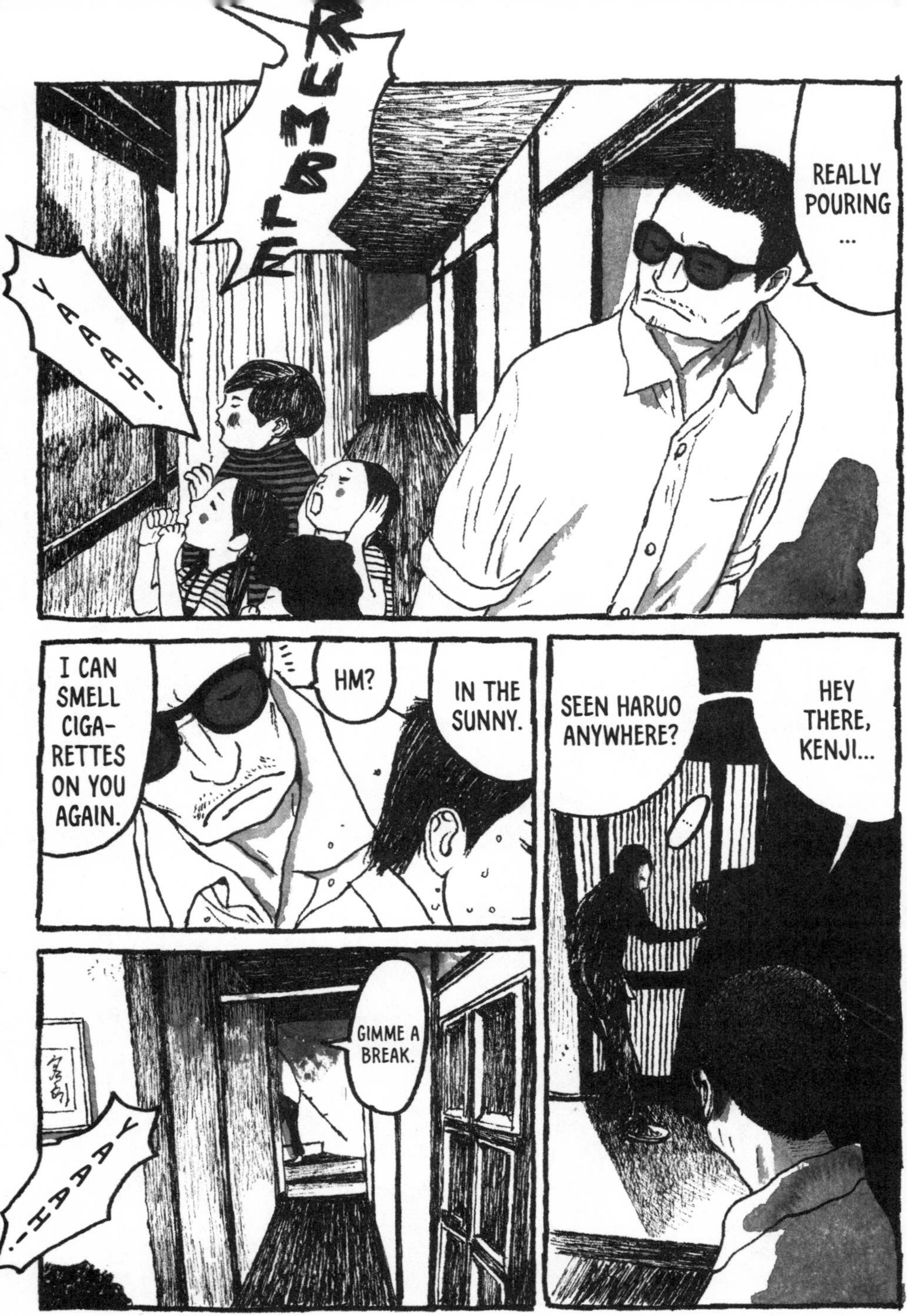
RUMBLE
REALLY POURING ...
YAAAAI--!
HEY THERE, KENJI...
SEEN HARUO ANYWHERE?
IN THE SUNNY.
HM?
I CAN SMELL CIGA-RETTES ON YOU AGAIN.
GIMME A BREAK.
YAAAAI--!

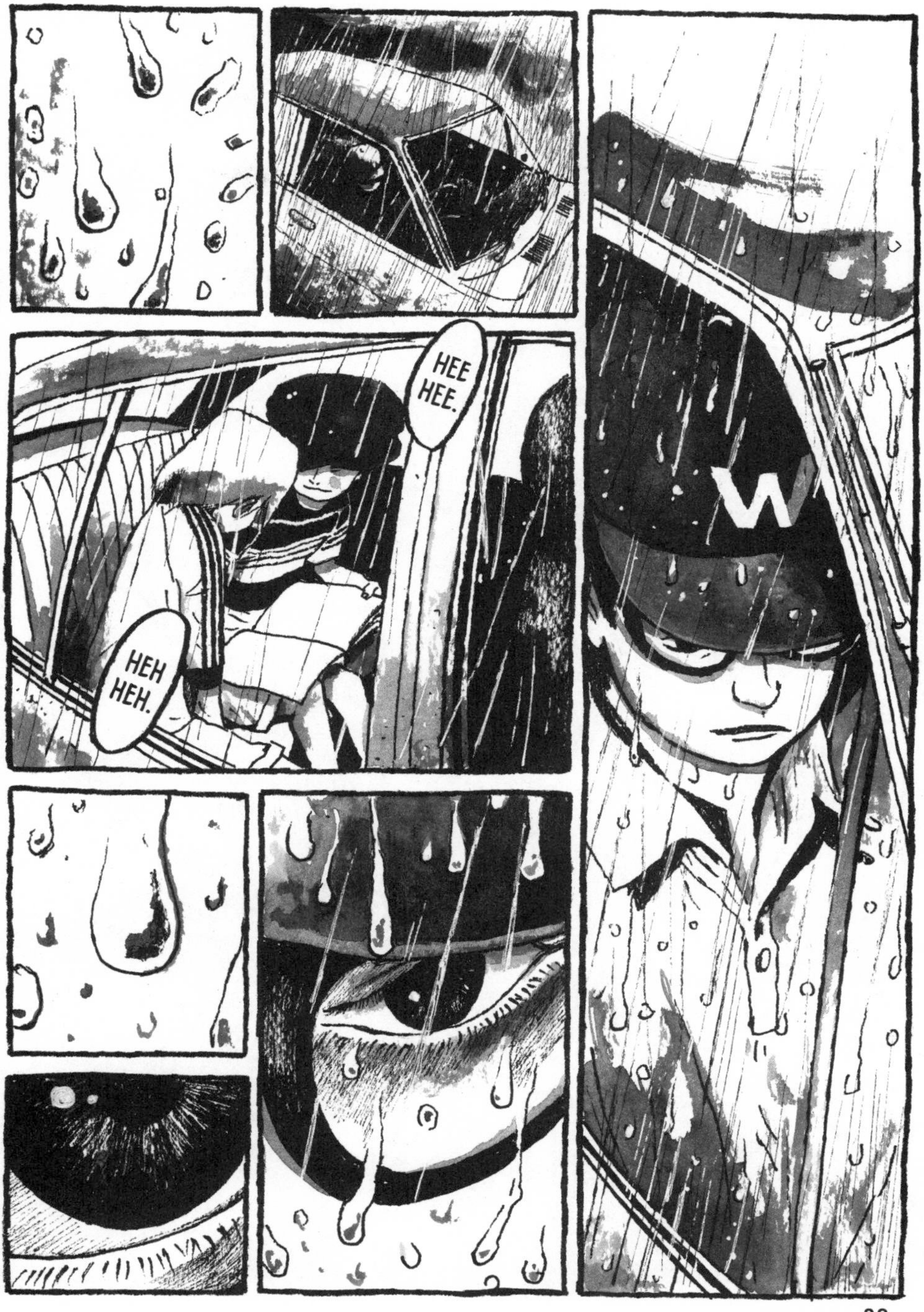
W
HEE HEE.
HEH HEH.

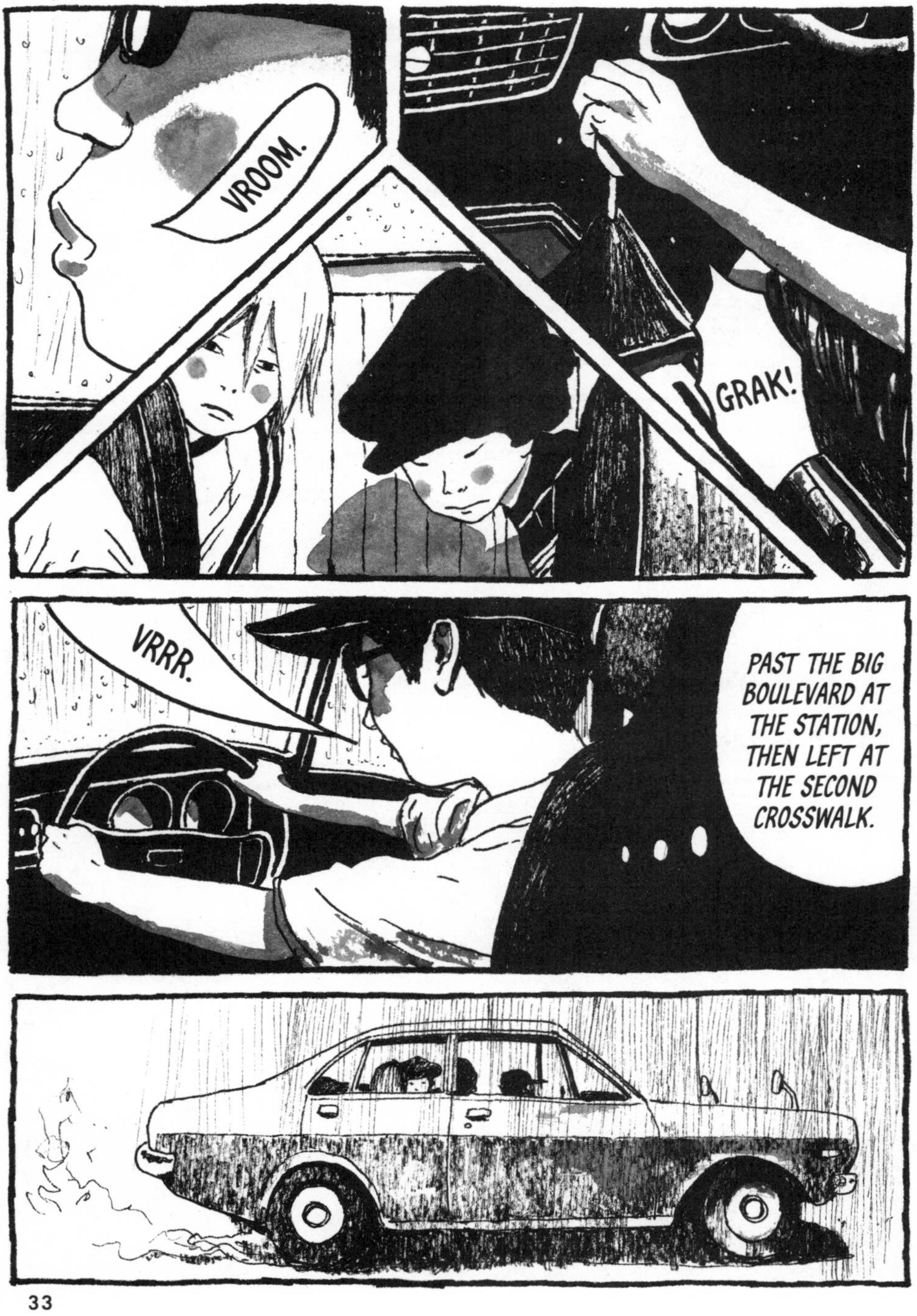
GRAK!
VROOM.
PAST THE BIG BOULEVARD AT THE STATION, THEN LEFT AT THE SECOND CROSSWALK.
VRRR.

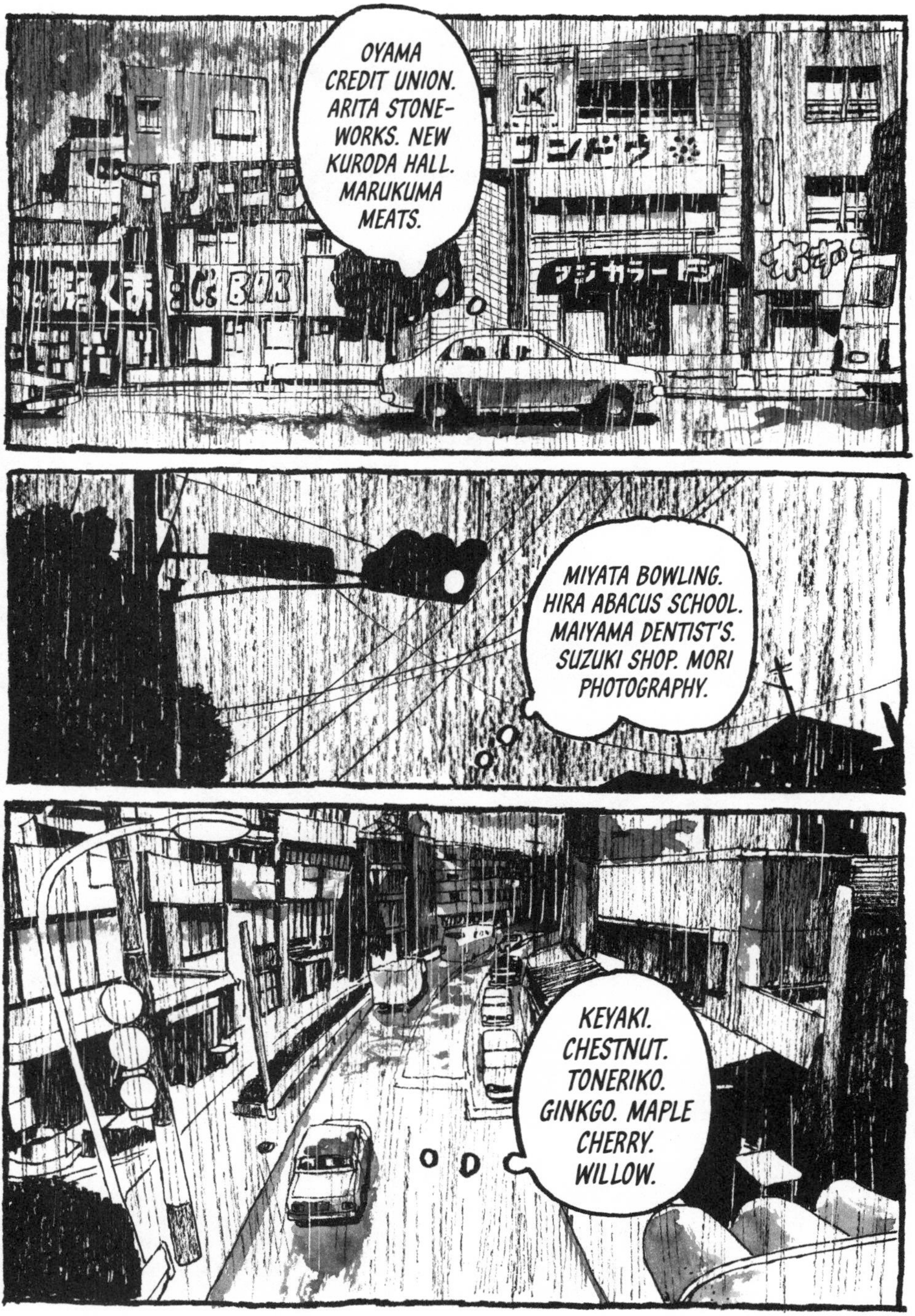
OYAMA CREDIT UNION. ARITA STONE-WORKS. NEW KURODA HALL. MARUKUMA MEATS.
MIYATA BOWLING. HIRA ABACUS SCHOOL. MAIYAMA DENTIST'S. SUZUKI SHOP. MORI PHOTOGRAPHY.
KEYAKI. CHESTNUT. TONERIKO. GINKGO. MAPLE CHERRY. WILLOW.

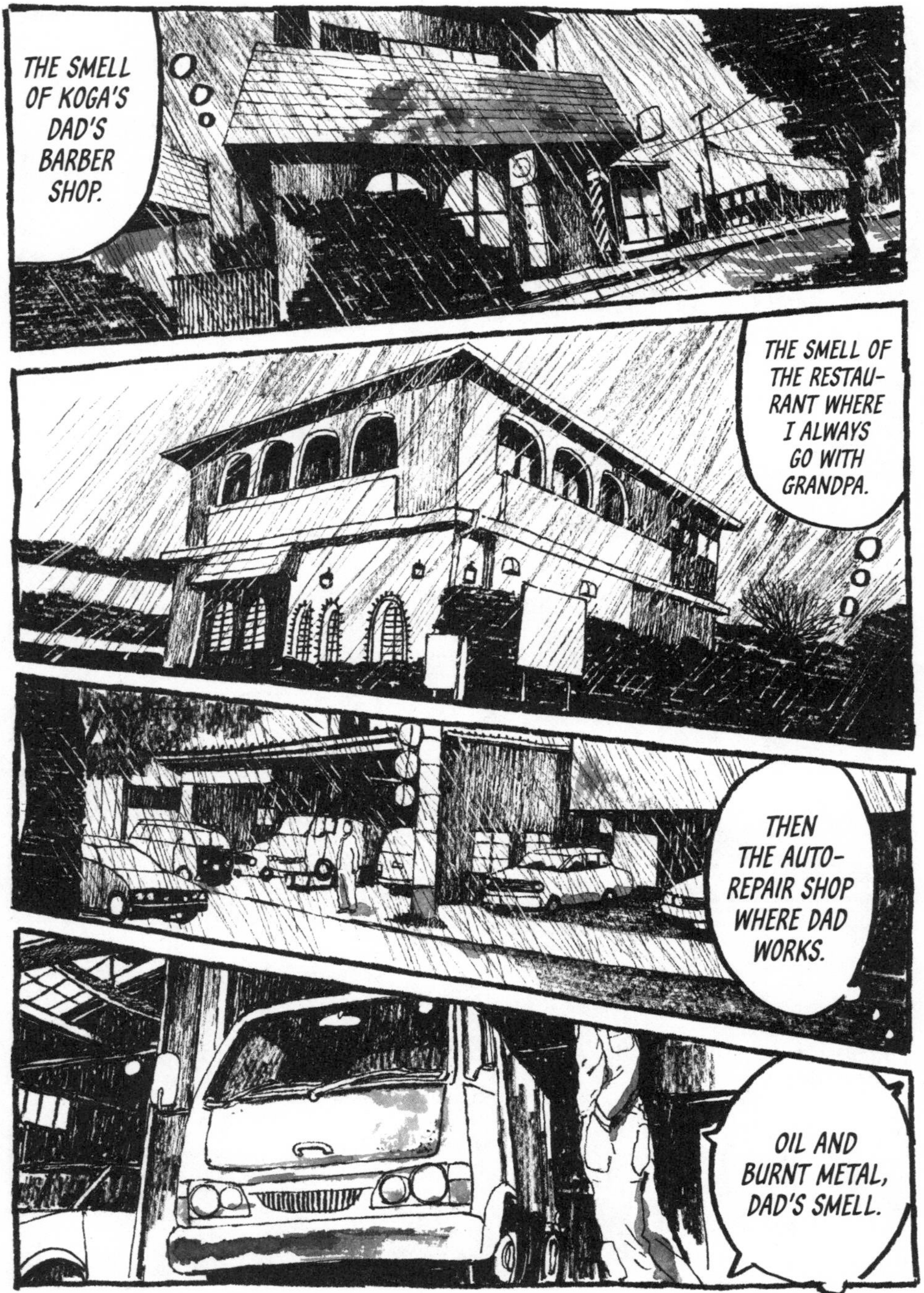
THE SMELL OF KOGA'S DAD'S BARBER SHOP.
THE SMELL OF THE RESTAU-RANT WHERE I ALWAYS GO WITH GRANDPA.
THEN THE AUTO-REPAIR SHOP WHERE DAD WORKS.
OIL AND BURNT METAL, DAD'S SMELL.

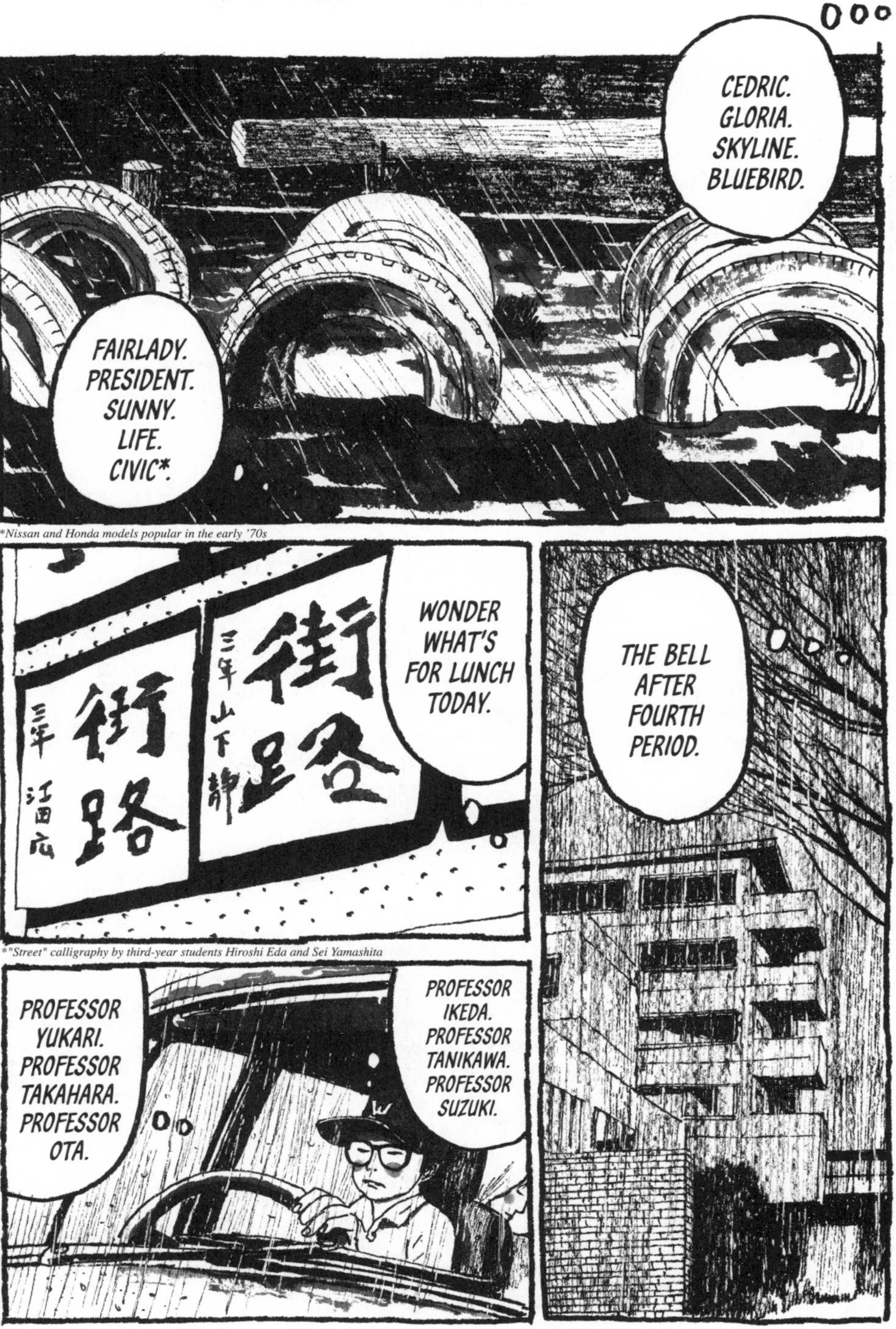
CEDRIC. GLORIA. SKYLINE. BLUEBIRD.
FAIRLADY. PRESIDENT. SUNNY. LIFE. CIVIC*.
THE BELL AFTER FOURTH PERIOD.
WONDER WHAT'S FOR LUNCH TODAY.
街路
三年 山下静
街路
三年 江田広
PROFESSOR IKEDA. PROFESSOR TANIKAWA. PROFESSOR SUZUKI.
PROFESSOR YUKARI. PROFESSOR TAKAHARA. PROFESSOR OTA.

*Nissan and Honda models popular in the early '70s

*"Street" calligraphy by third-year students Hiroshi Eda and Sei Yamashita

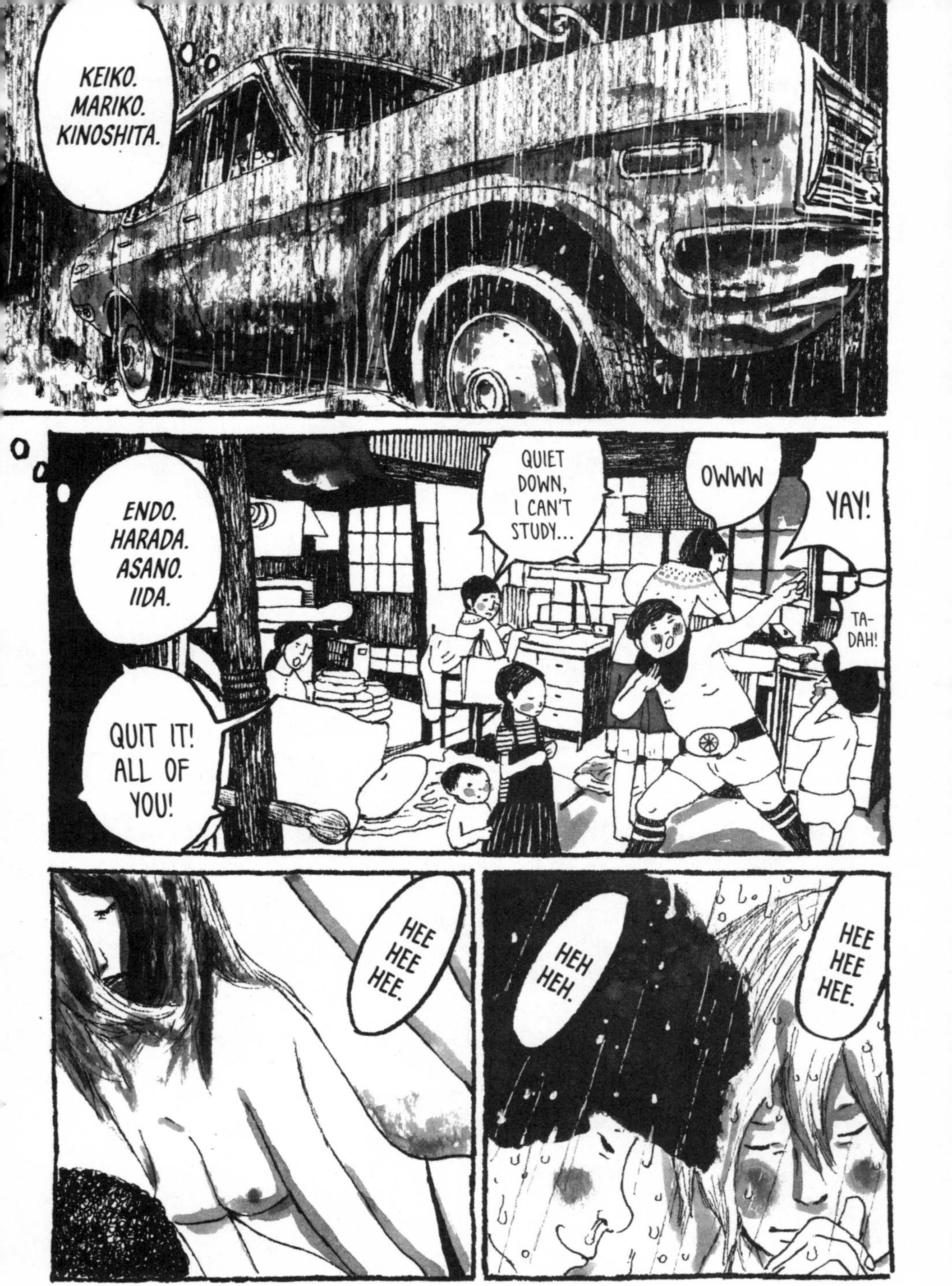
KEIKO. MARIKO. KINOSHITA.
YAY!
TA-DAH!
OWWW
QUIET DOWN, I CAN'T STUDY...
ENDO. HARADA. ASANO. IIDA.
QUIT IT! ALL OF YOU!
HEE HEE HEE.
HEH HEH.
HEE HEE HEE.

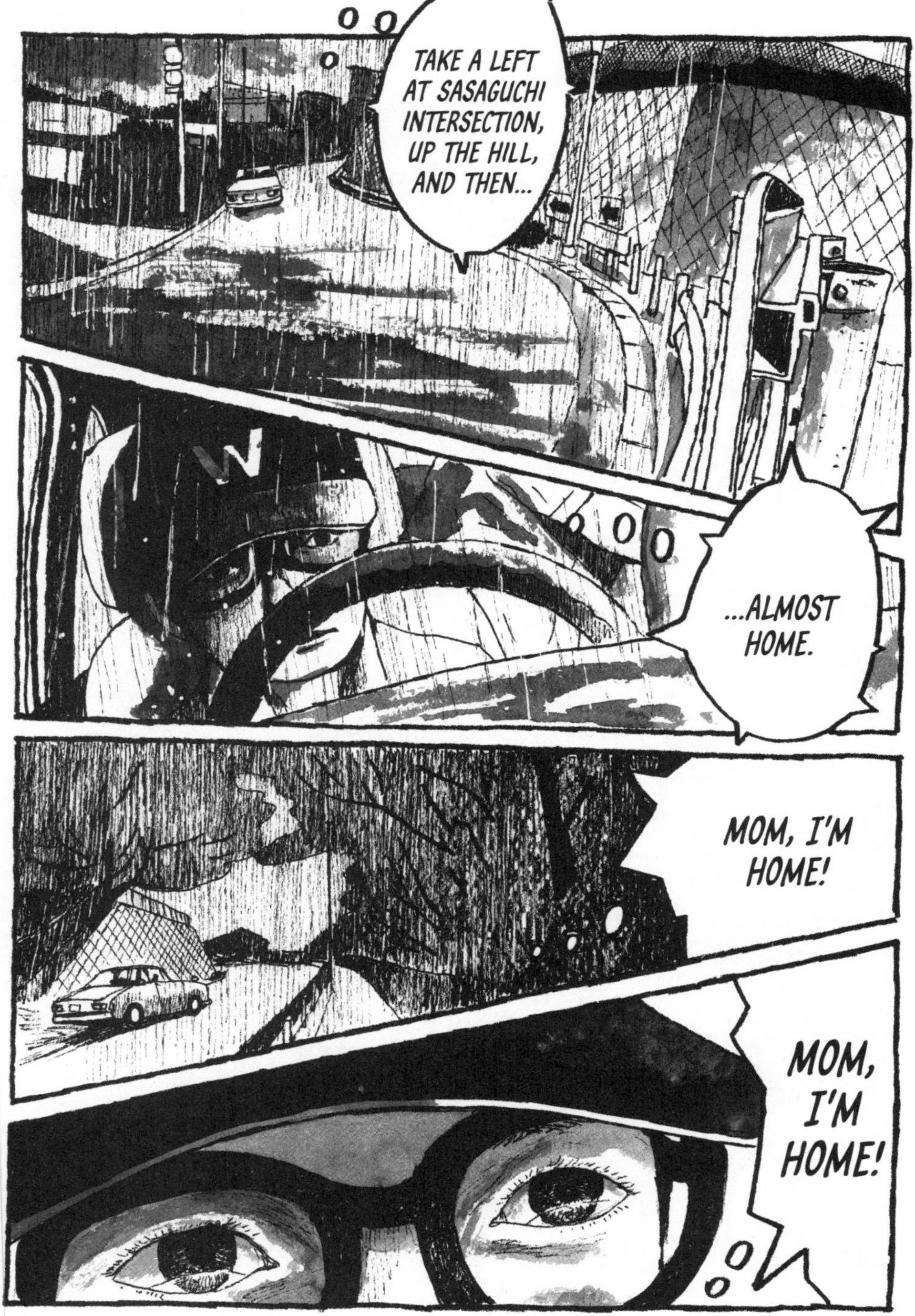
TAKE A LEFT AT SASAGUCHI INTERSECTION, UP THE HILL, AND THEN...
...ALMOST HOME.
MOM, I'M HOME!
MOM, I'M HOME!

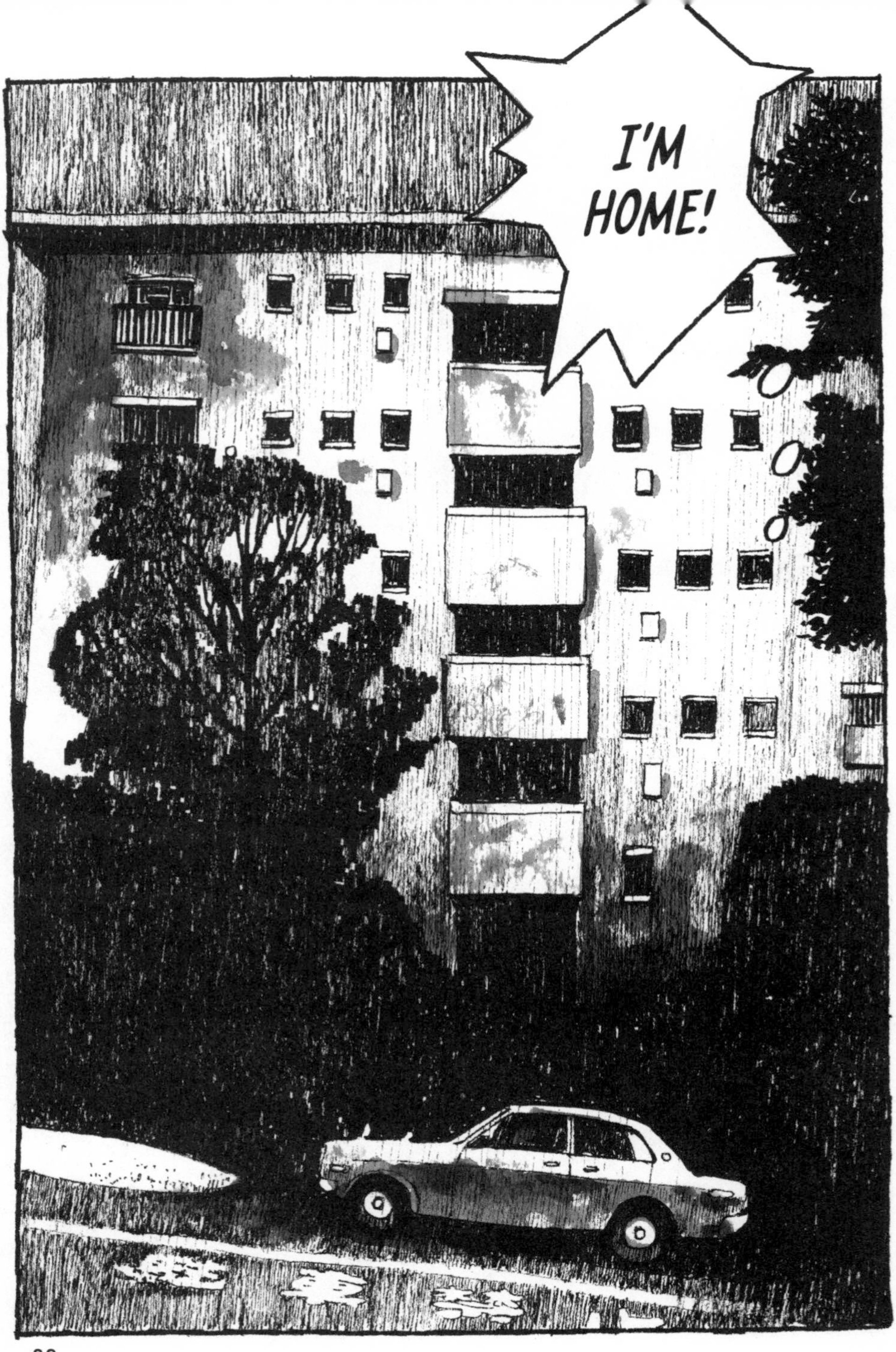
I'M HOME!

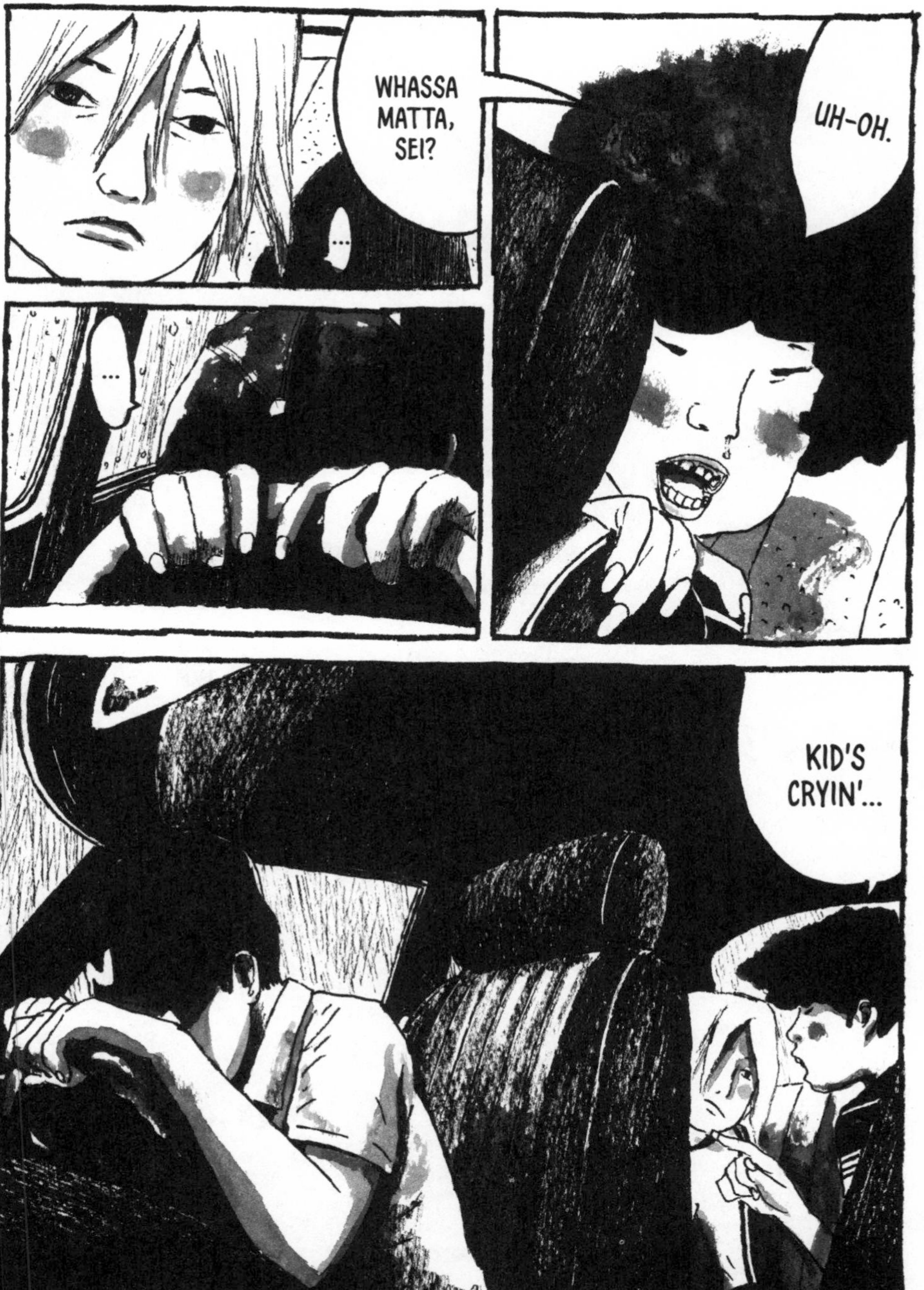

WHASSA MATTA, SEI?
...
...
UH-OH.
KID'S CRYIN'...

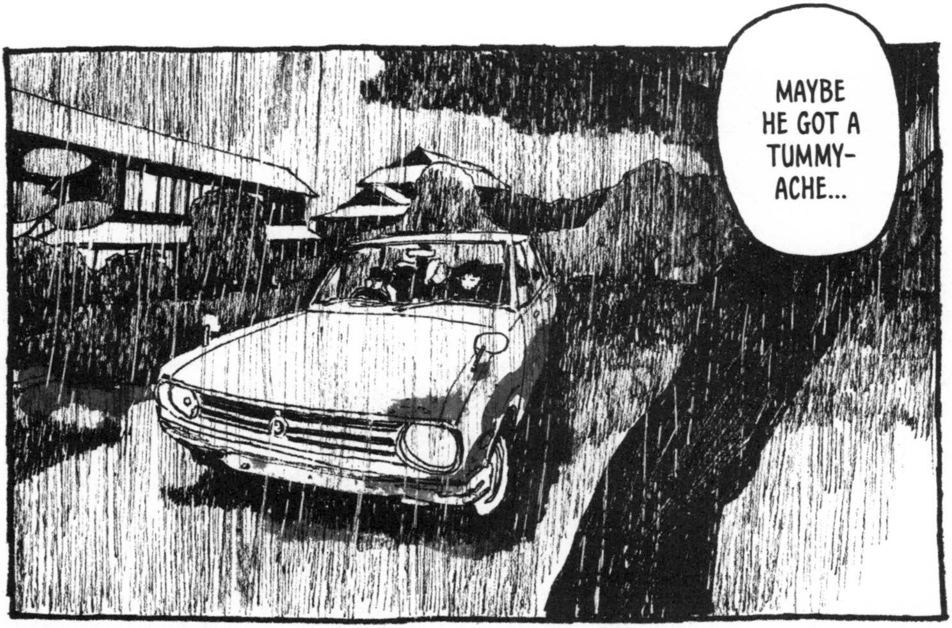
MAYBE HE GOT A TUMMY-ACHE...

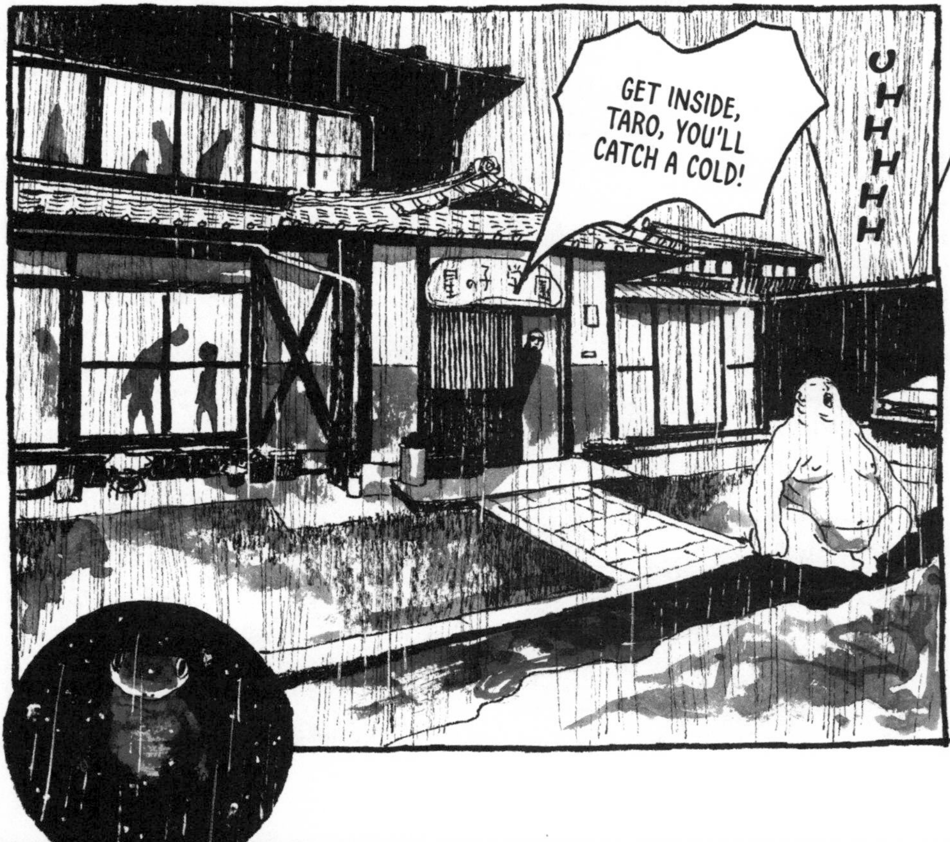
UHHHHH
GET INSIDE, TARO, YOU'LL CATCH A COLD!

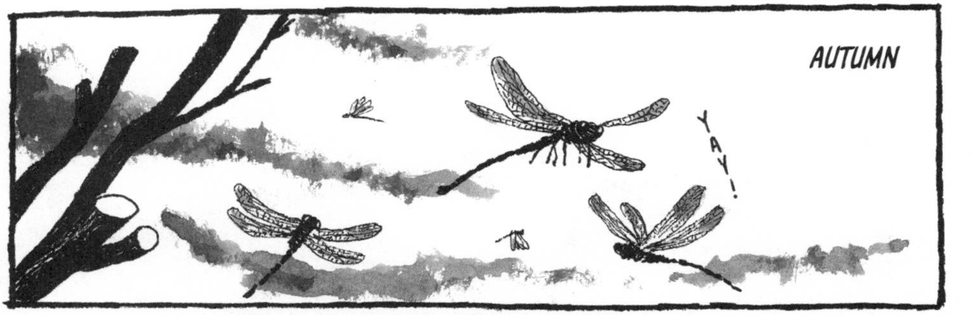
AUTUMN
YAY!

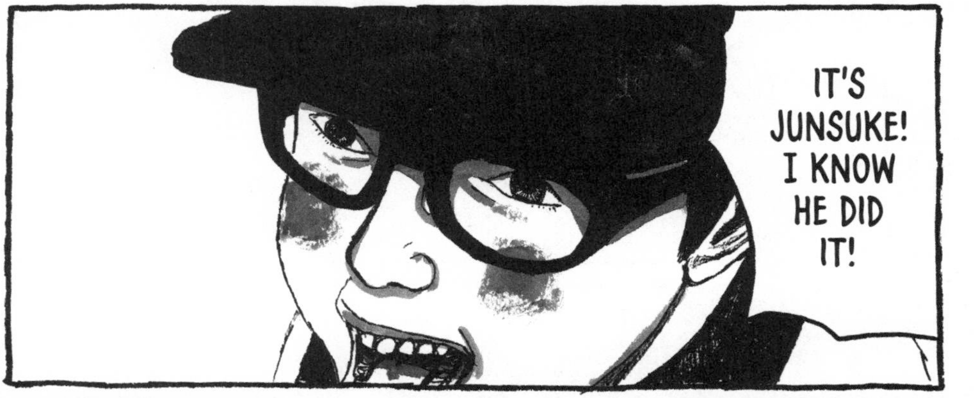
IT'S JUNSUKE! I KNOW HE DID IT!

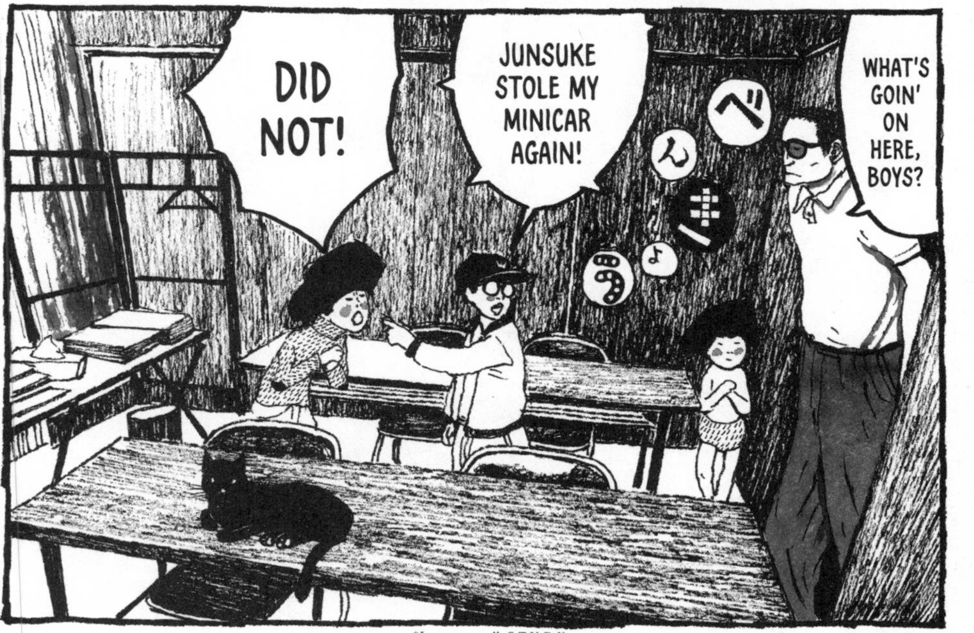
WHAT'S GOIN' ON HERE, BOYS?
JUNSUKE STOLE MY MINICAR AGAIN!
DID NOT!

*Letters on wall: S-T-U-D-Y

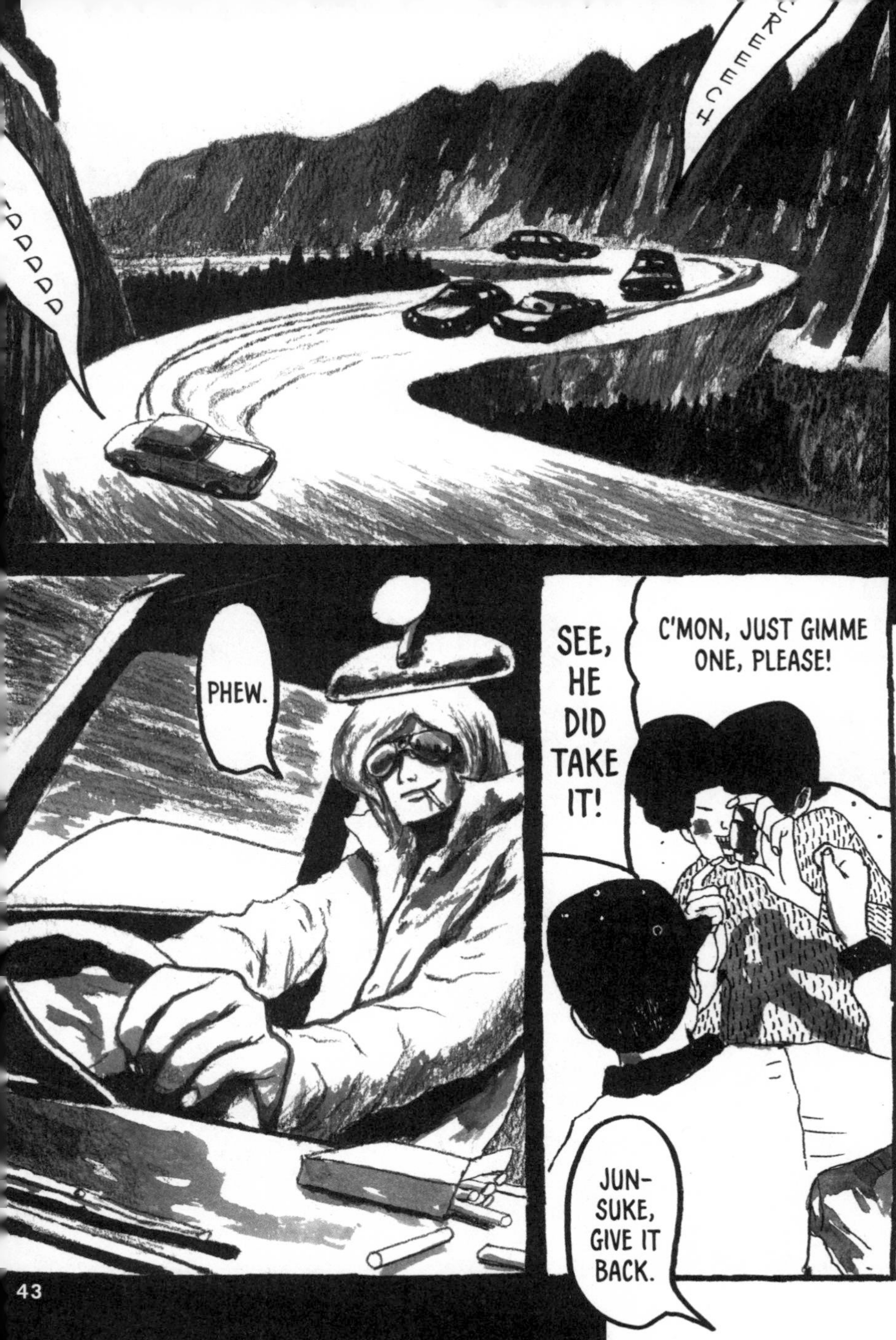
REEECH
DDDDDD
C'MON, JUST GIMME ONE, PLEASE!
SEE, HE DID TAKE IT!
JUN-SUKE, GIVE IT BACK.
PHEW.

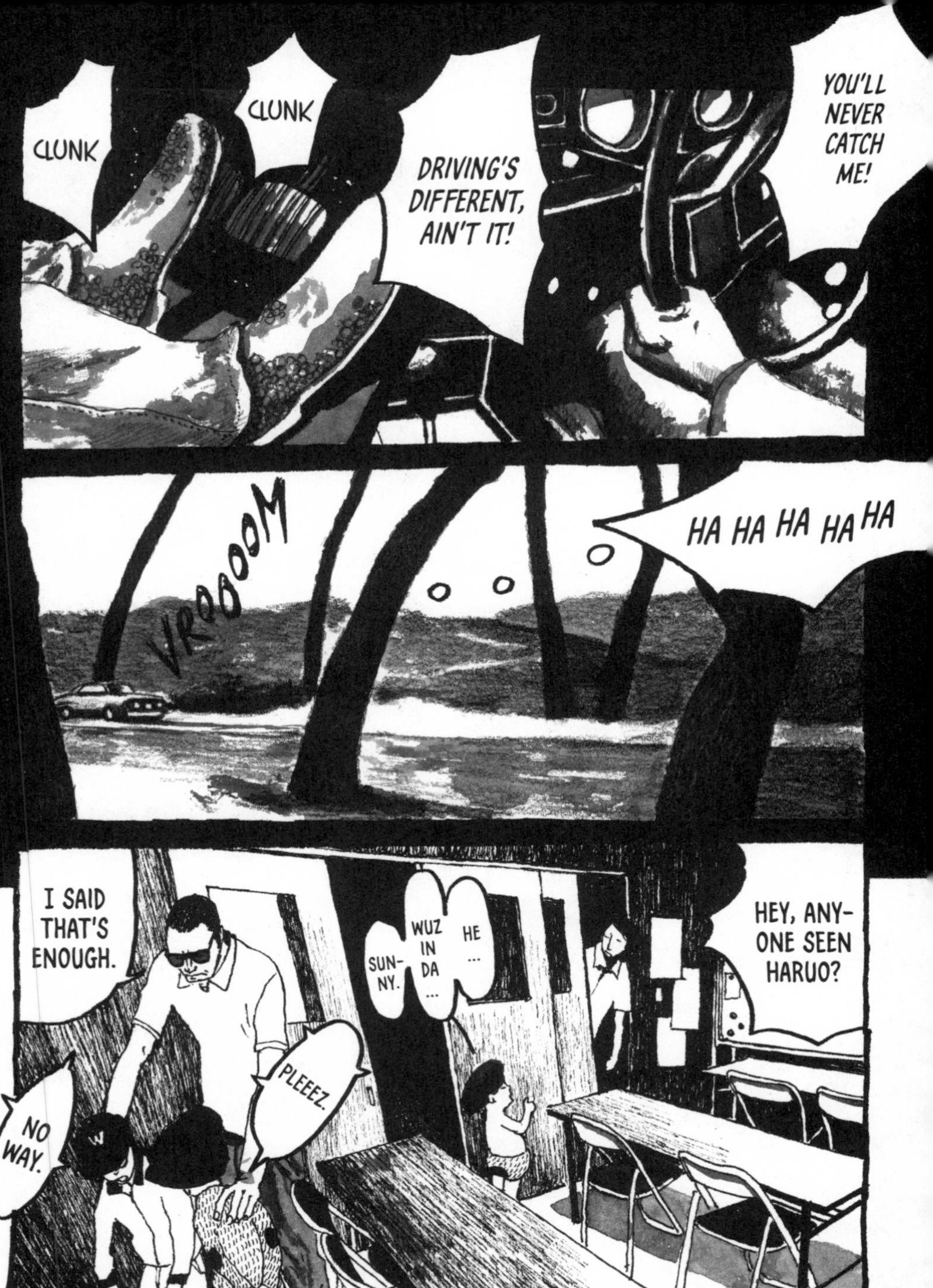
YOU'LL NEVER CATCH ME!
DRIVING'S DIFFERENT, AIN'T IT!
CLUNK
CLUNK
HA HA HA HA HA
VROOOOM
HEY, ANY-ONE SEEN HARUO?
HE ... WUZ IN DA ... SUN-NY.
I SAID THAT'S ENOUGH.
PLEEEZ.
NO WAY.

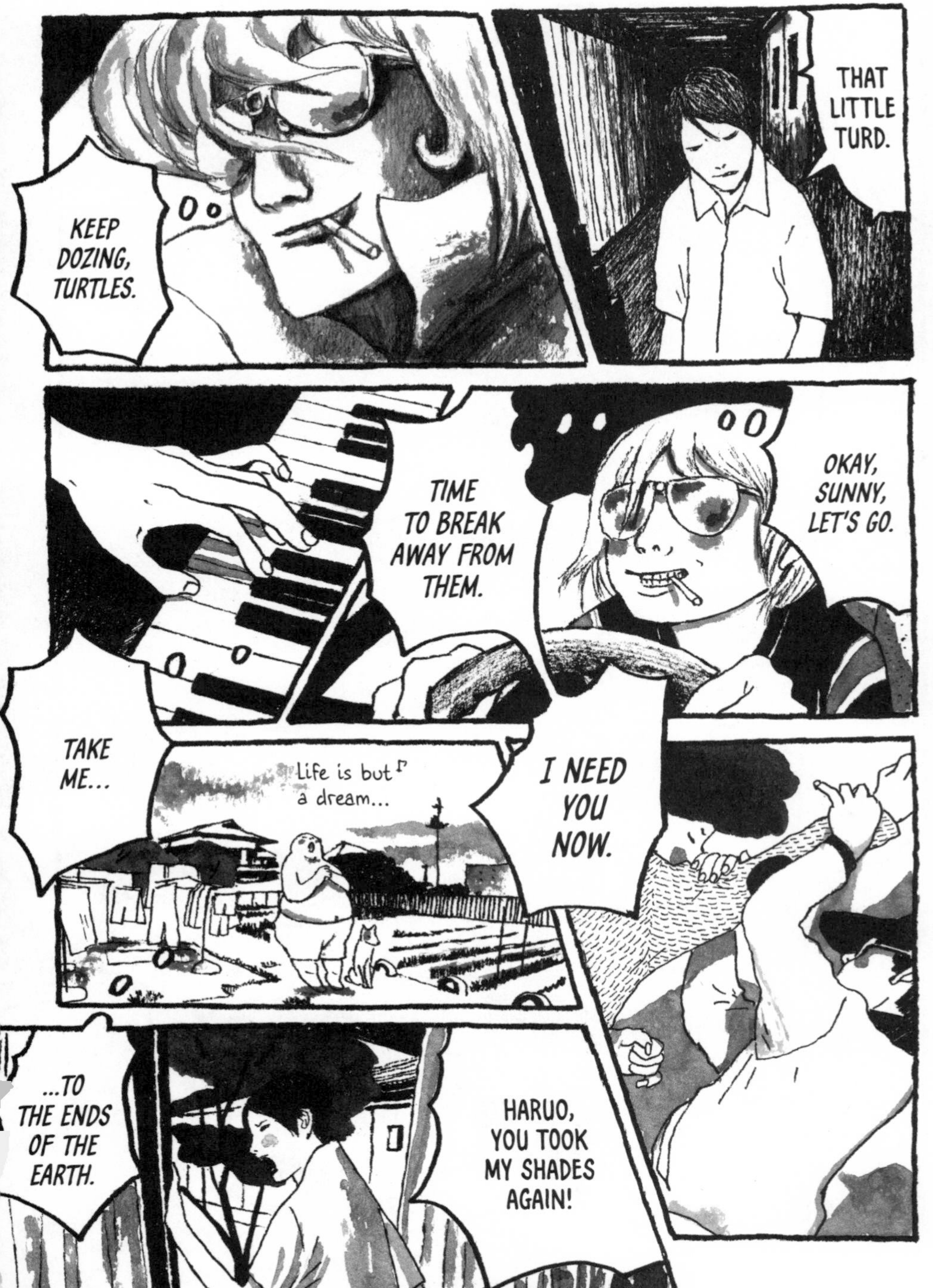
THAT LITTLE TURD.
KEEP DOZING, TURTLES.
OKAY, SUNNY, LET'S GO.
TIME TO BREAK AWAY FROM THEM.
TAKE ME...
I NEED YOU NOW.
Life is but a dream...
HARUO, YOU TOOK MY SHADES AGAIN!
...TO THE ENDS OF THE EARTH.

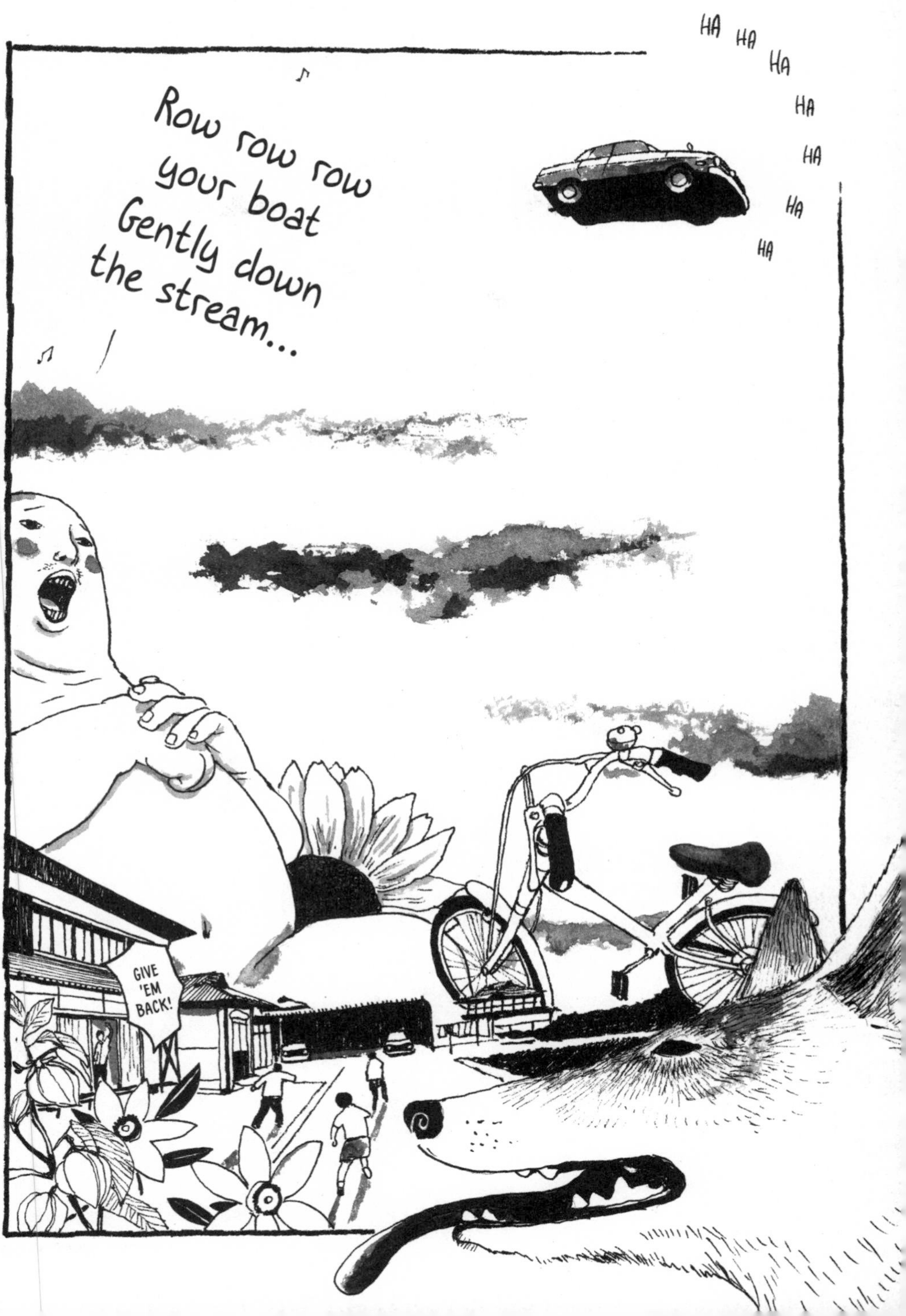
HA HA HA HA HA HA HA
♪ Row row row your boat Gently down the stream... ♪
GIVE 'EM BACK!

CHAPTER 2

"Why're
Dracula's
fingernails
so long?"

"'Cause
he doesn't
cut 'em."

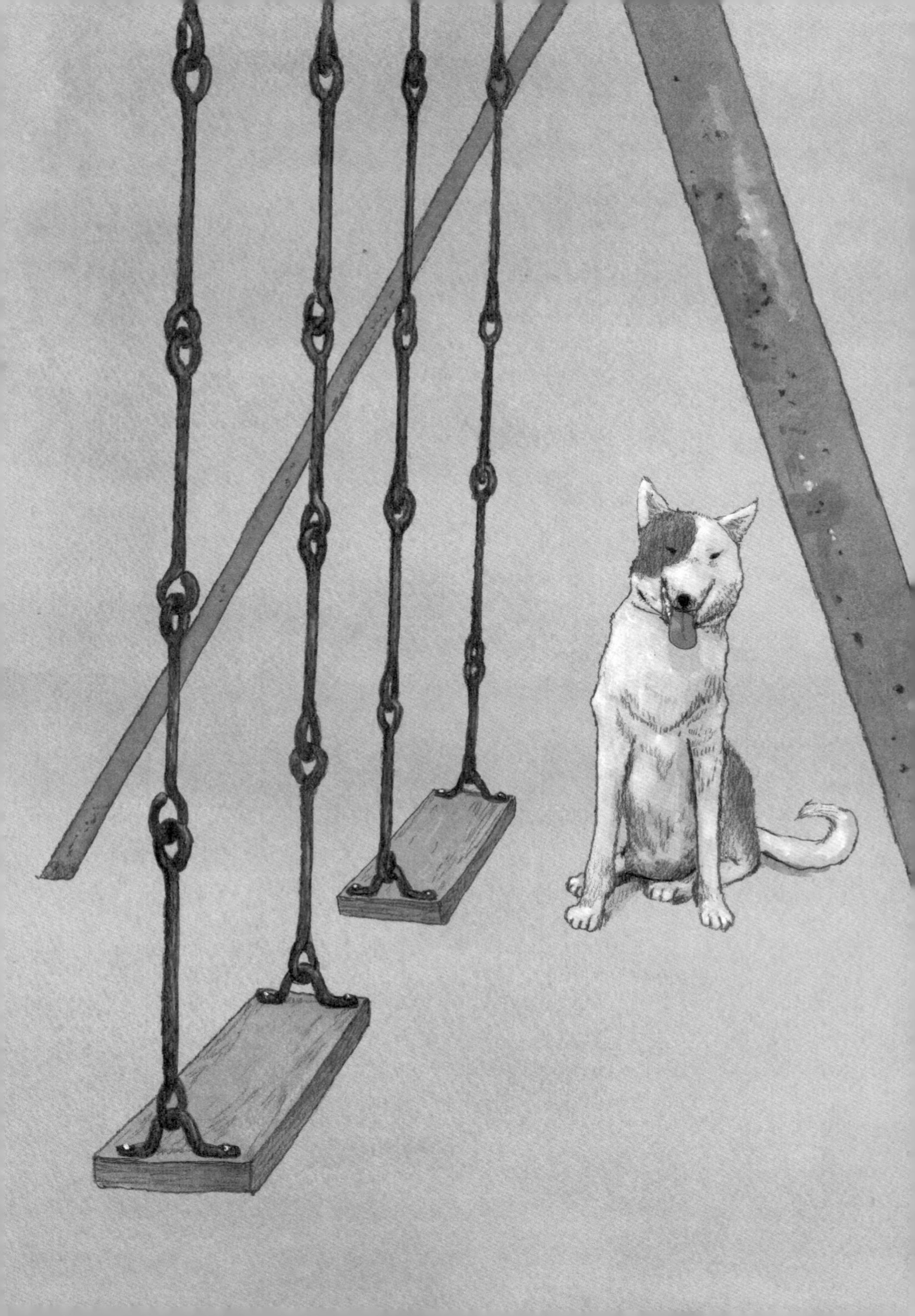

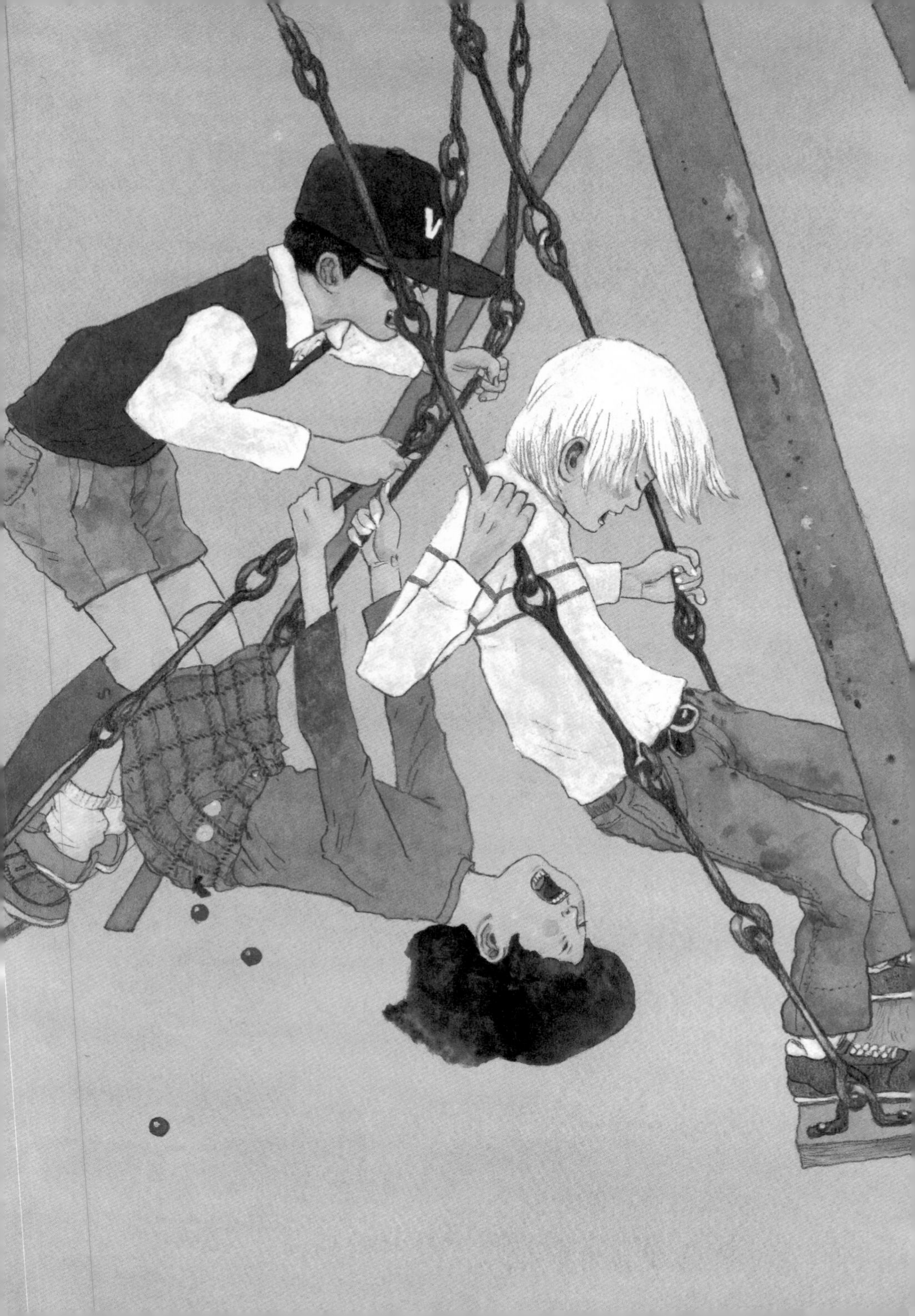

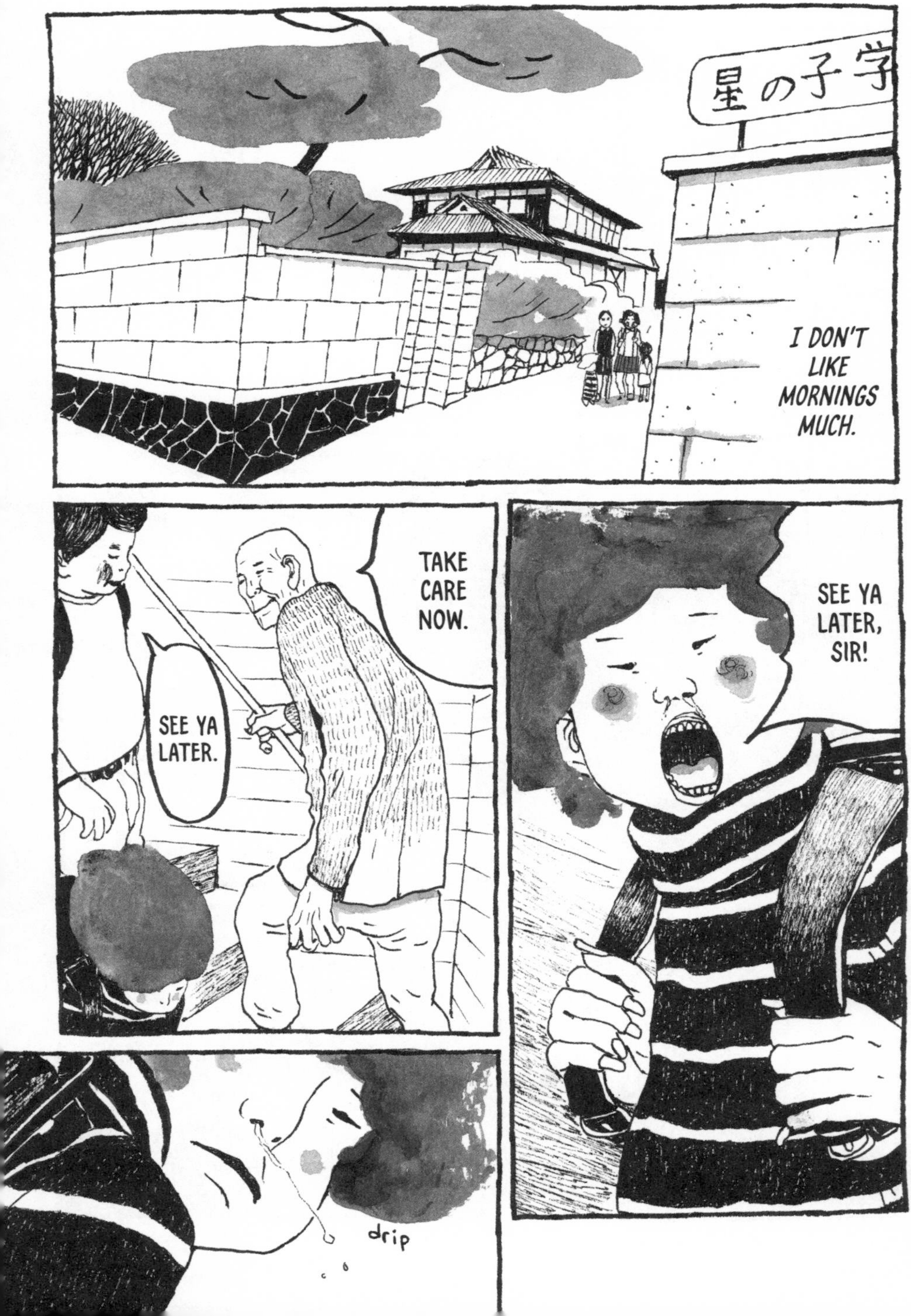

星の子学
I DON'T LIKE MORNINGS MUCH.
SEE YA LATER, SIR!
TAKE CARE NOW.
SEE YA LATER.
drip

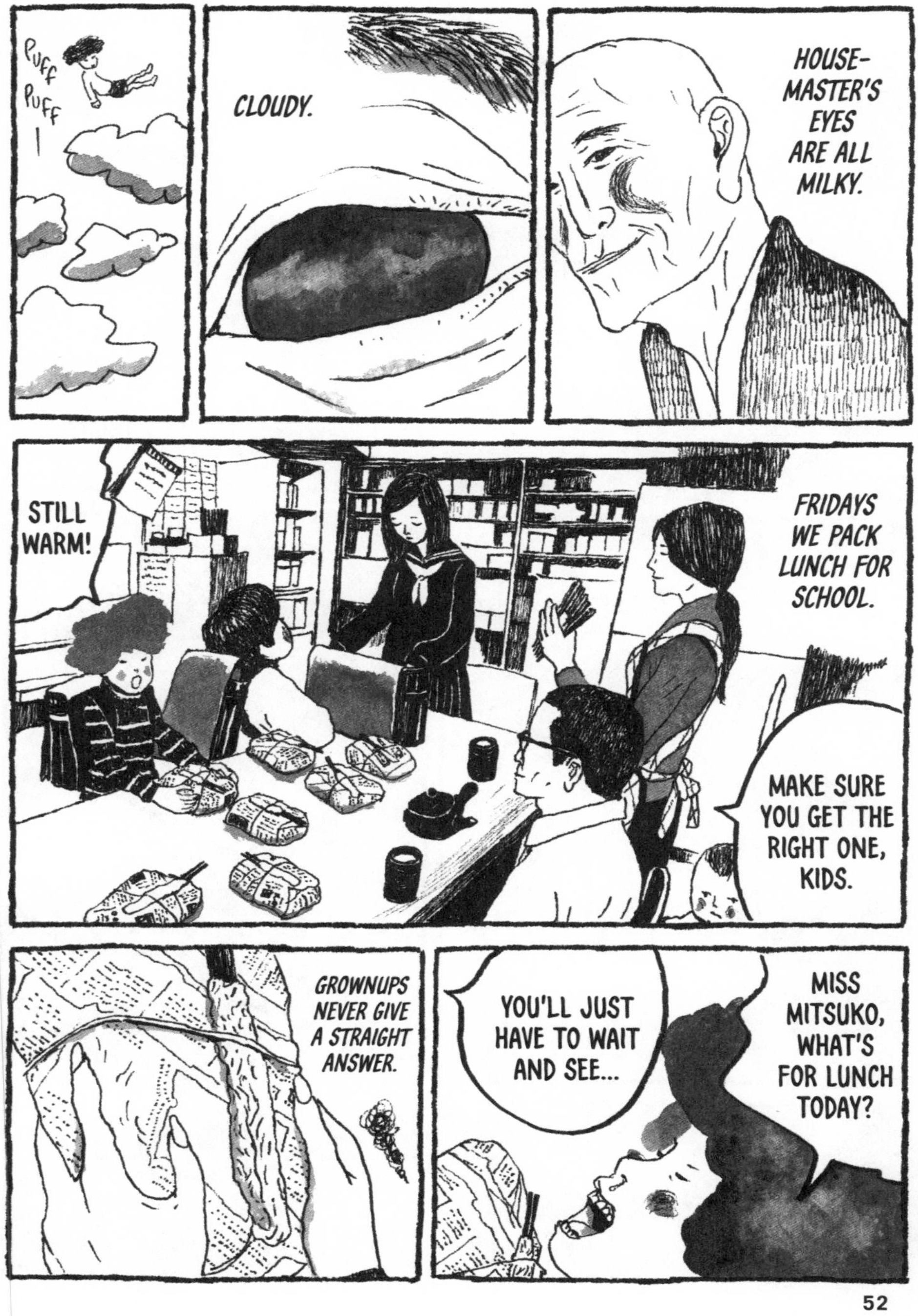
HOUSE-MASTER'S EYES ARE ALL MILKY.
CLOUDY.
PUFF PUFF
FRIDAYS WE PACK LUNCH FOR SCHOOL.
MAKE SURE YOU GET THE RIGHT ONE, KIDS.
STILL WARM!
MISS MITSUKO, WHAT'S FOR LUNCH TODAY?
YOU'LL JUST HAVE TO WAIT AND SEE...
GROWNUPS NEVER GIVE A STRAIGHT ANSWER.

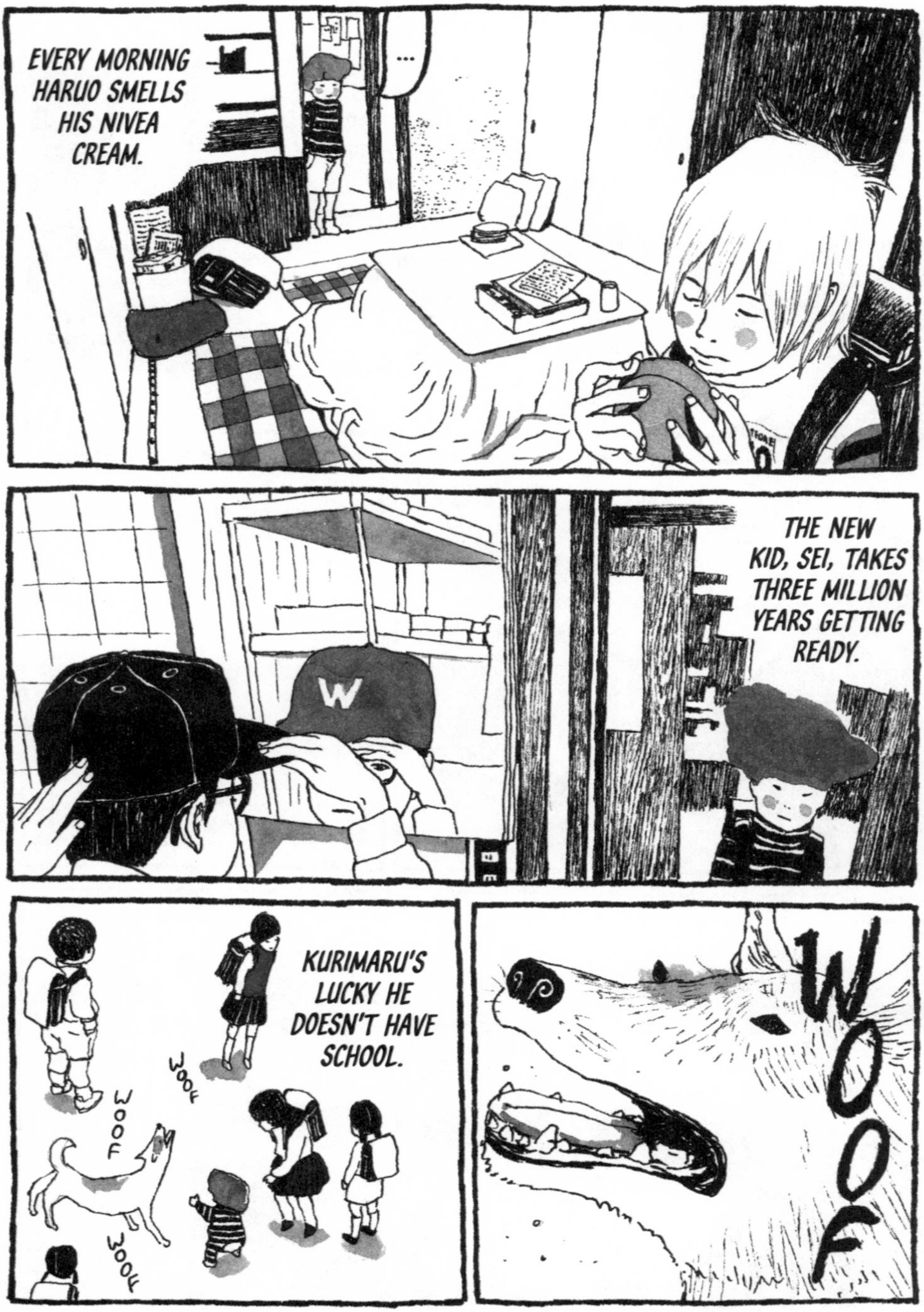
EVERY MORNING HARUO SMELLS HIS NIVEA CREAM.
...
THE NEW KID, SEI, TAKES THREE MILLION YEARS GETTING READY.
KURIMARU'S LUCKY HE DOESN'T HAVE SCHOOL.
WOOF
WOOF
WOOF
WOOF

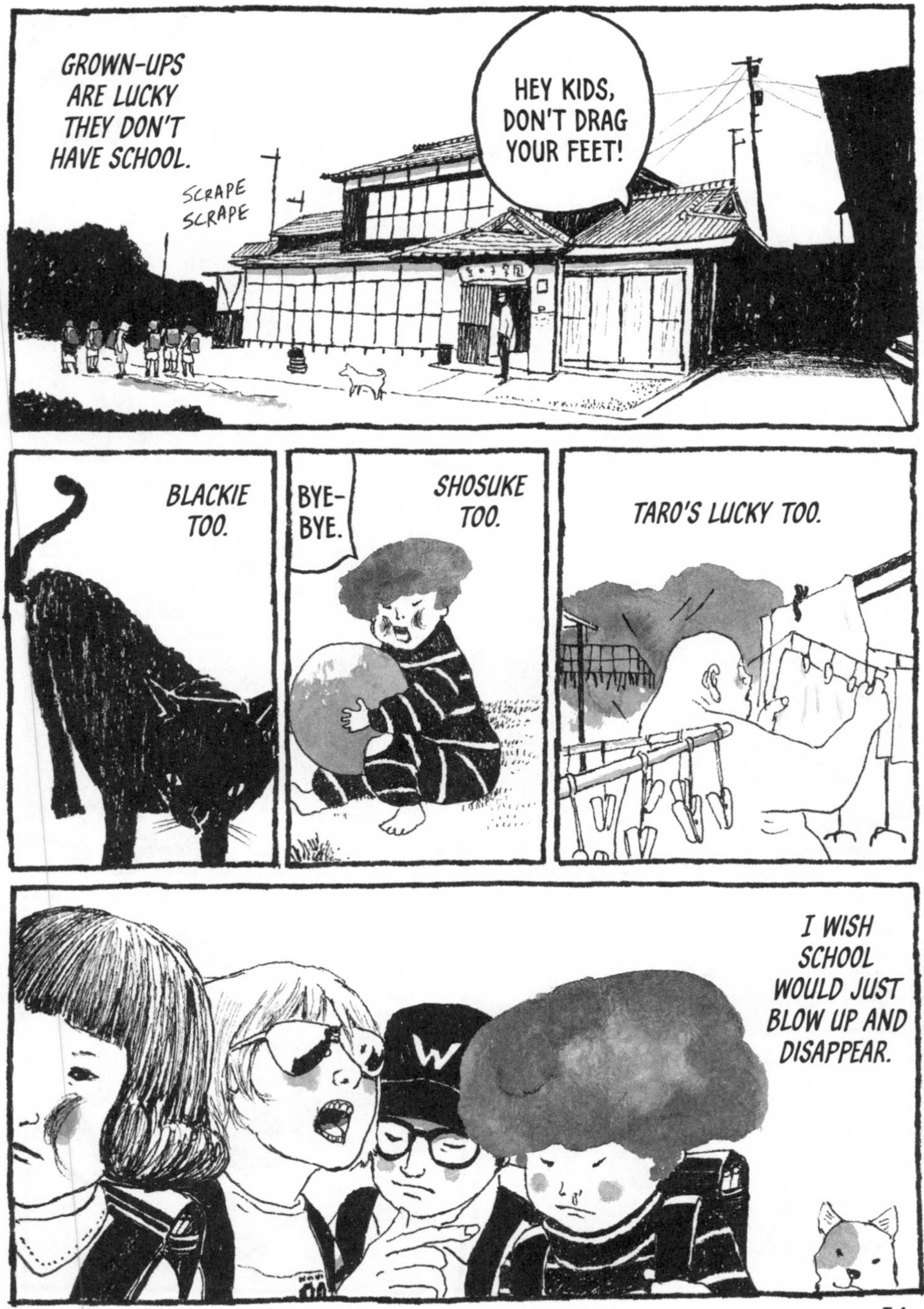
GROWN-UPS ARE LUCKY THEY DON'T HAVE SCHOOL.
SCRAPE SCRAPE
HEY KIDS, DON'T DRAG YOUR FEET!
BLACKIE TOO.
BYE-BYE.
SHOSUKE TOO.
TARO'S LUCKY TOO.
I WISH SCHOOL WOULD JUST BLOW UP AND DISAPPEAR.

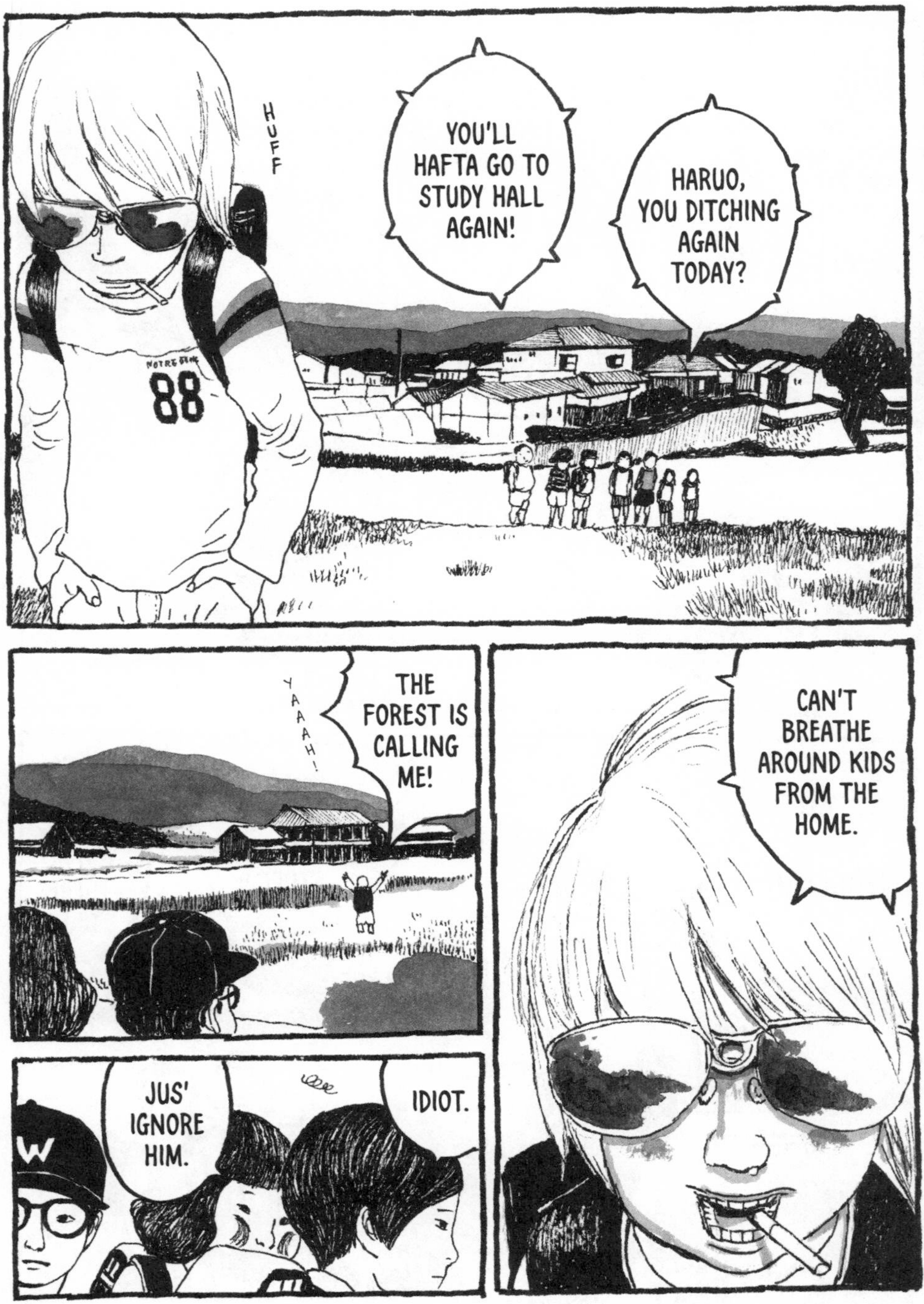
HUFF
HARUO, YOU DITCHING AGAIN TODAY?
YOU'LL HAFTA GO TO STUDY HALL AGAIN!
88
CAN'T BREATHE AROUND KIDS FROM THE HOME.
YAAAAH!
THE FOREST IS CALLING ME!
IDIOT.
JUS' IGNORE HIM.

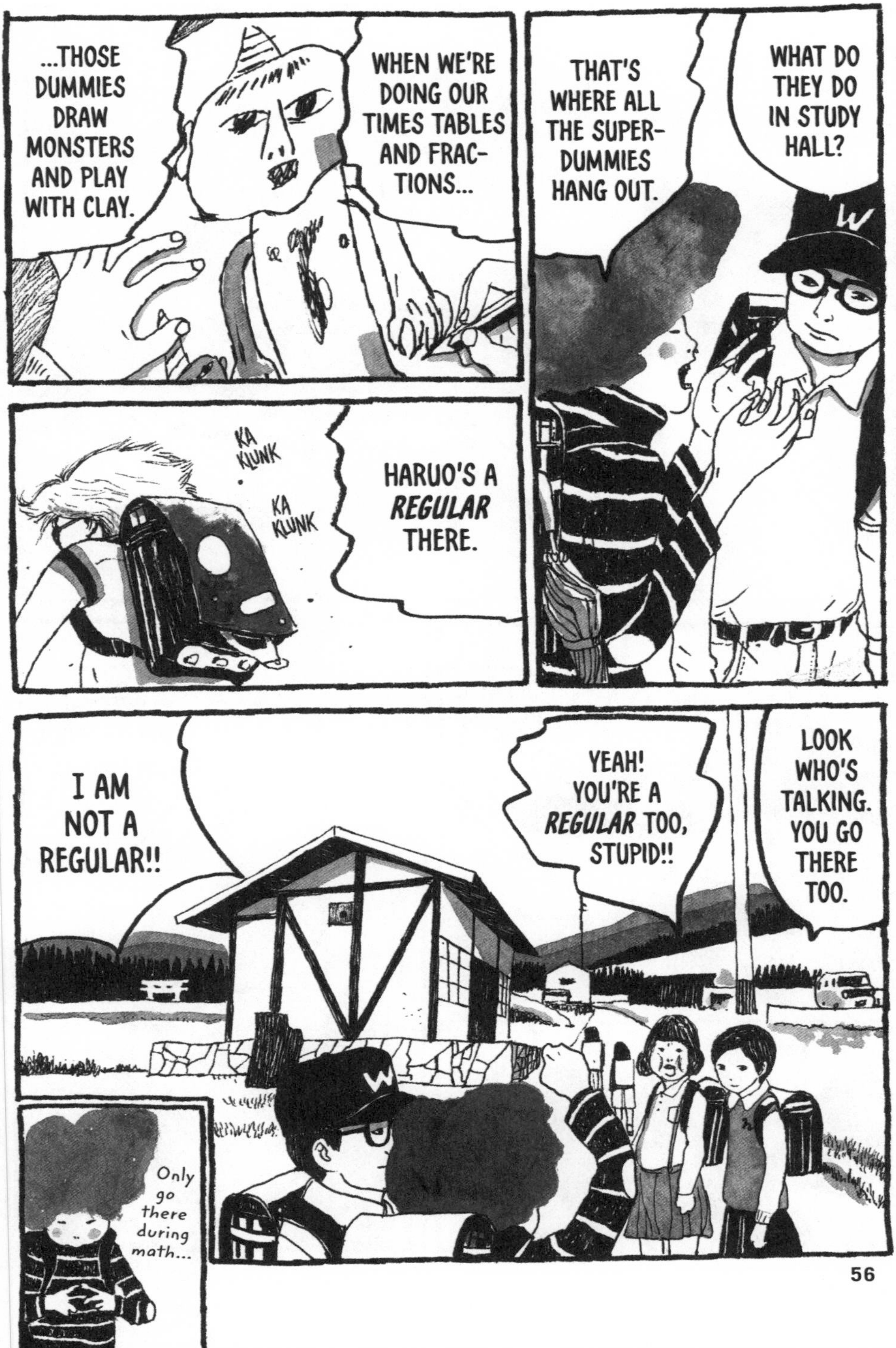
WHAT DO THEY DO IN STUDY HALL?
THAT'S WHERE ALL THE SUPER-DUMMIES HANG OUT.
WHEN WE'RE DOING OUR TIMES TABLES AND FRAC-TIONS...
...THOSE DUMMIES DRAW MONSTERS AND PLAY WITH CLAY.
HARUO'S A *REGULAR* THERE.
KA KLUNK
KA KLUNK
LOOK WHO'S TALKING. YOU GO THERE TOO.
YEAH! YOU'RE A *REGULAR* TOO, STUPID!!
I AM NOT A REGULAR!!
Only go there during math...

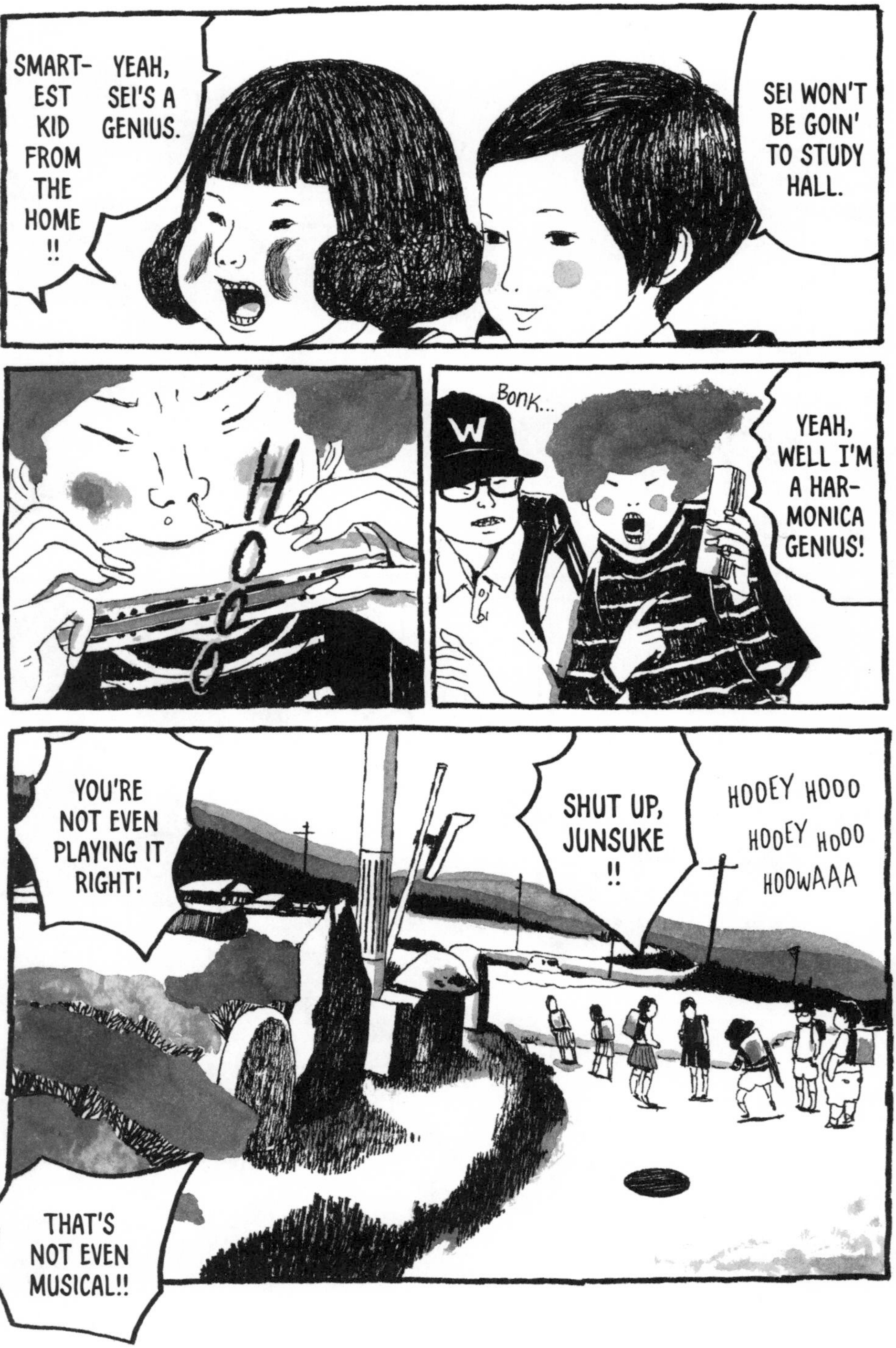
SEI WON'T BE GOIN' TO STUDY HALL.
YEAH, SEI'S A GENIUS. SMARTEST KID FROM THE HOME!!
Bonk...
YEAH, WELL I'M A HARMONICA GENIUS!
HOOO
HOOEY HOOO HOOEY HOOO HOOWAAA
SHUT UP, JUNSUKE!!
YOU'RE NOT EVEN PLAYING IT RIGHT!
THAT'S NOT EVEN MUSICAL!!

**From* Mochi Mochi no Ki, *a children's picture book by Yūsuke Saito and Shirō Takidaira, 1971*

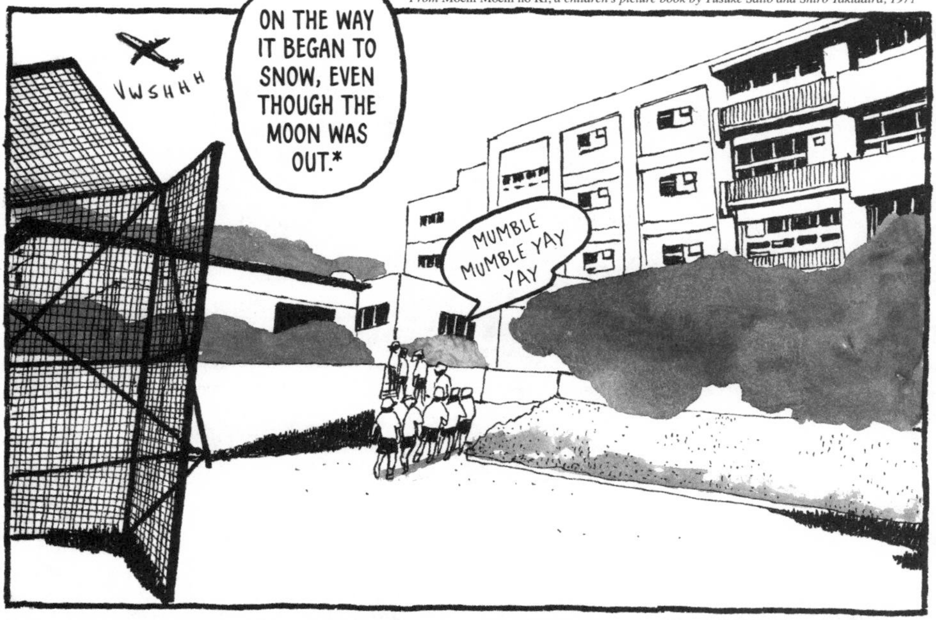
VWSHHH
MUMBLE MUMBLE YAY YAY
ON THE WAY IT BEGAN TO SNOW, EVEN THOUGH THE MOON WAS OUT.*

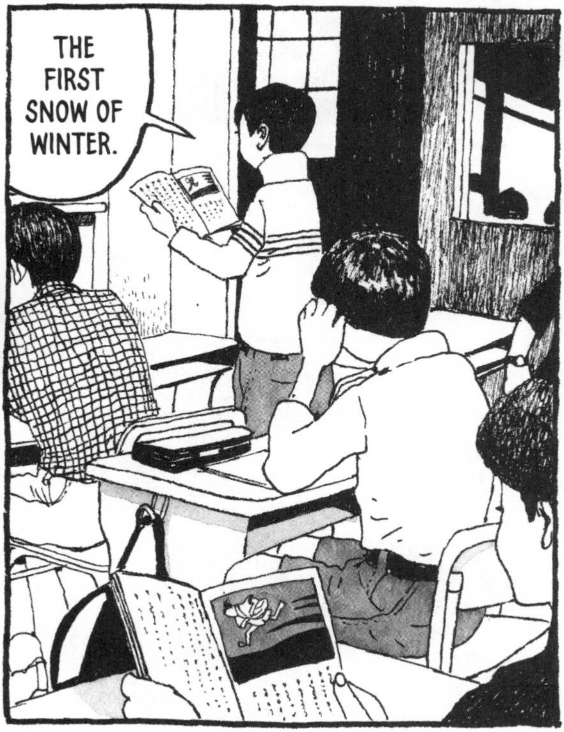
THE FIRST SNOW OF WINTER.

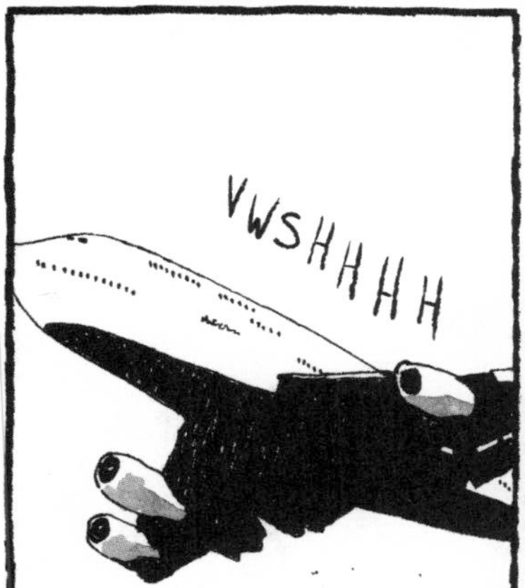
VWSHHHHH

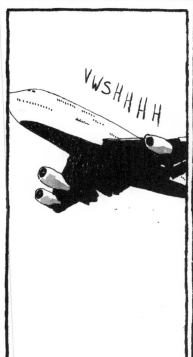

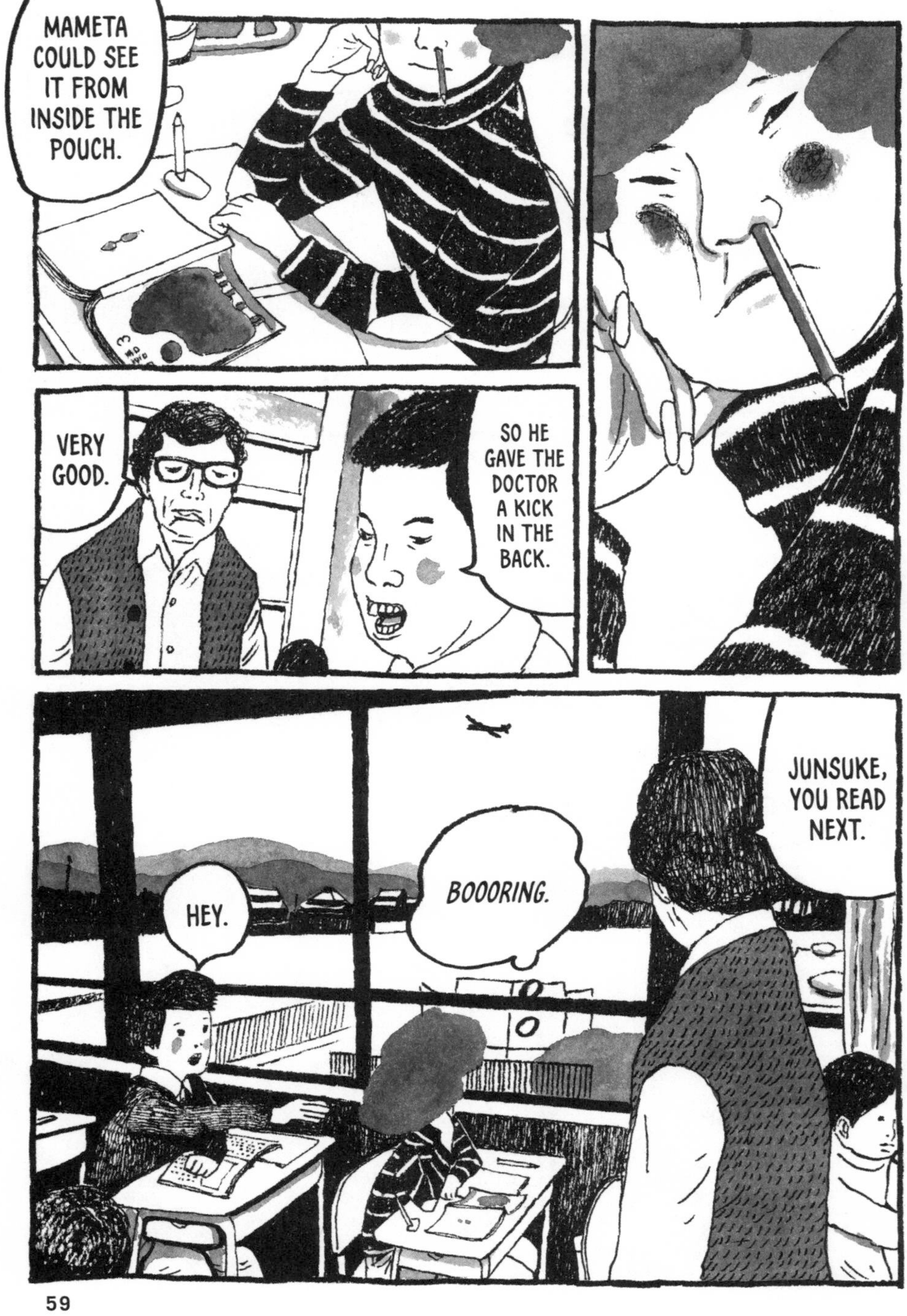
MAMETA COULD SEE IT FROM INSIDE THE POUCH.
SO HE GAVE THE DOCTOR A KICK IN THE BACK.
VERY GOOD.
JUNSUKE, YOU READ NEXT.
BOOORING.
HEY.

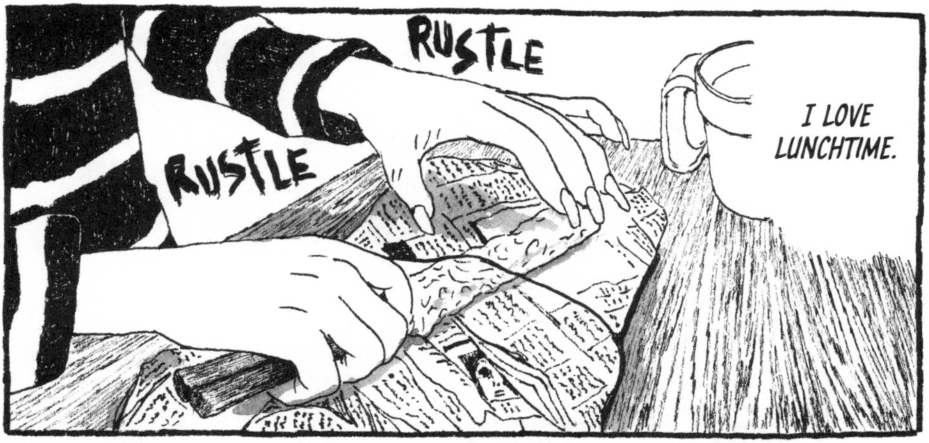
I LOVE LUNCHTIME.
RUSTLE
RUSTLE

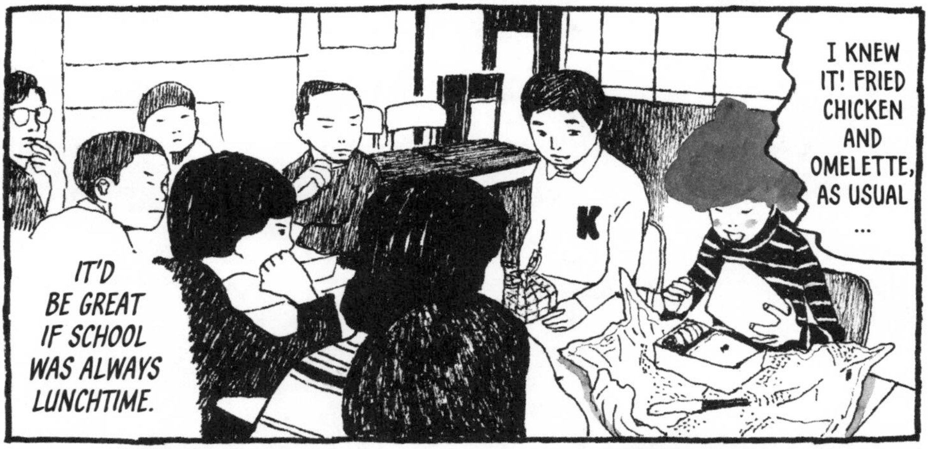
I KNEW IT! FRIED CHICKEN AND OMELETTE, AS USUAL ...
IT'D BE GREAT IF SCHOOL WAS ALWAYS LUNCHTIME.

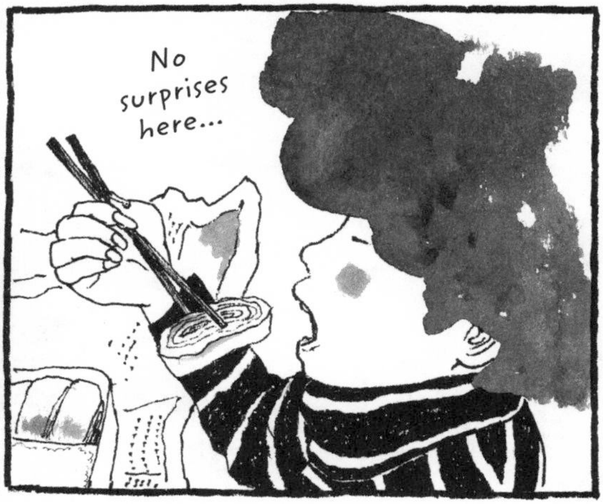
No surprises here...

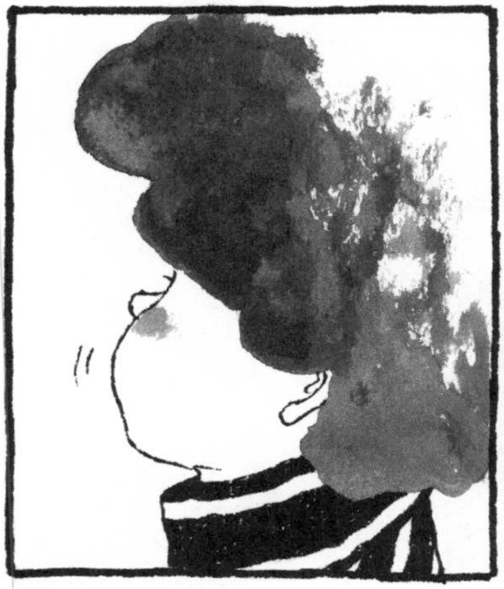

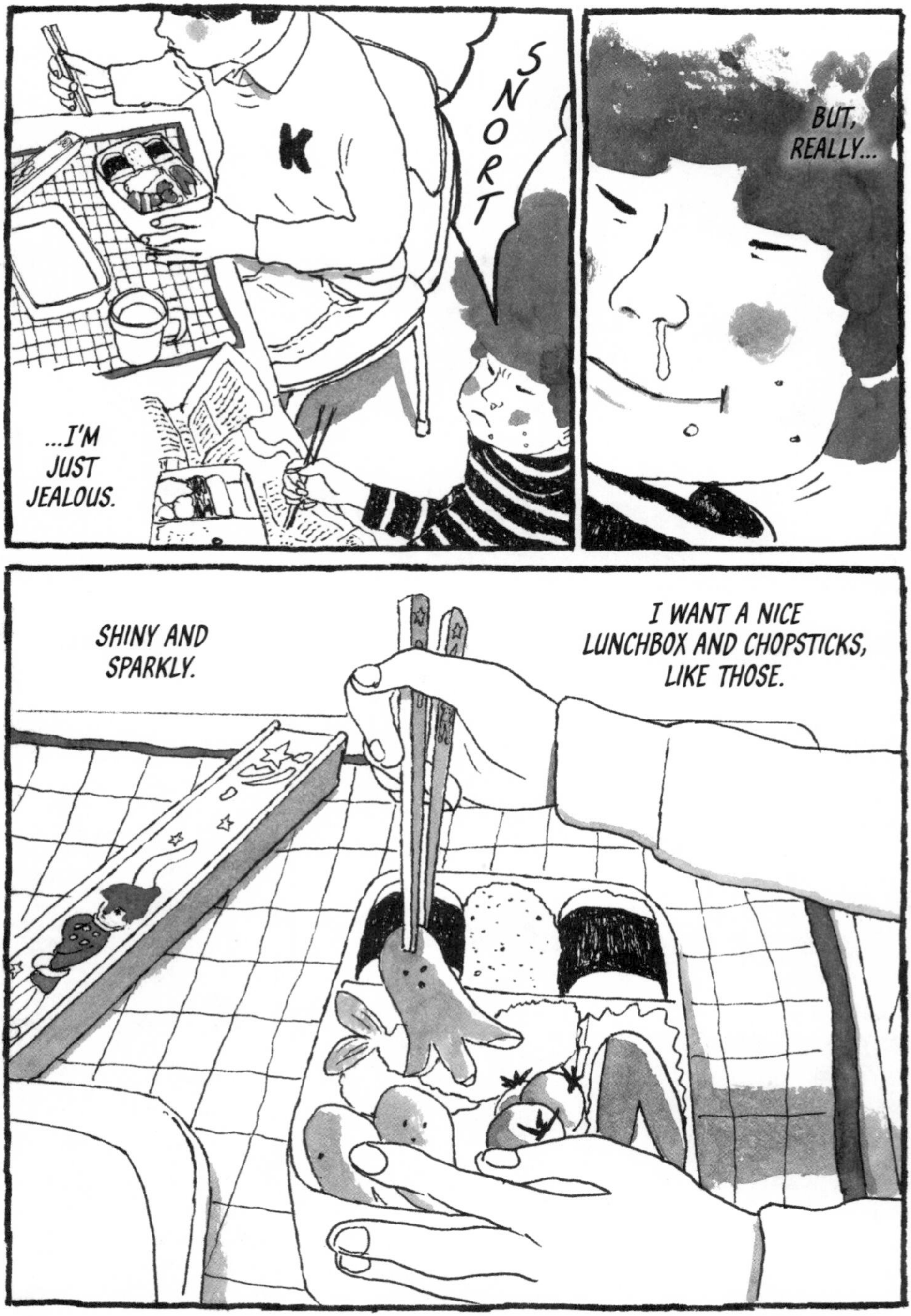
BUT, REALLY...
SNORT
...I'M JUST JEALOUS.
I WANT A NICE LUNCHBOX AND CHOPSTICKS, LIKE THOSE.
SHINY AND SPARKLY.

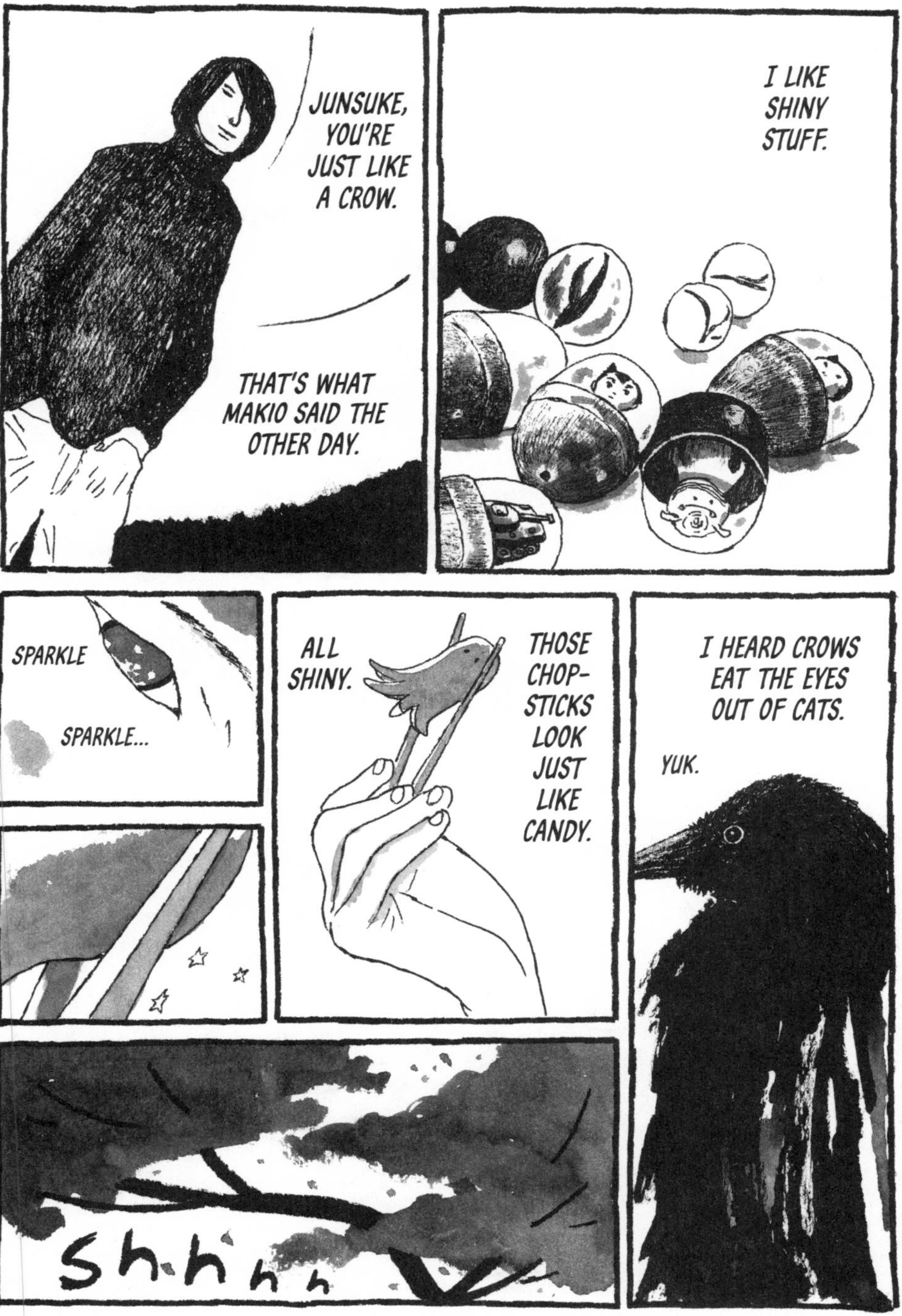
JUNSUKE, YOU'RE JUST LIKE A CROW.
THAT'S WHAT MAKIO SAID THE OTHER DAY.
I LIKE SHINY STUFF.
SPARKLE
SPARKLE...
ALL SHINY.
THOSE CHOP-STICKS LOOK JUST LIKE CANDY.
I HEARD CROWS EAT THE EYES OUT OF CATS.
YUK.
Shhhnn

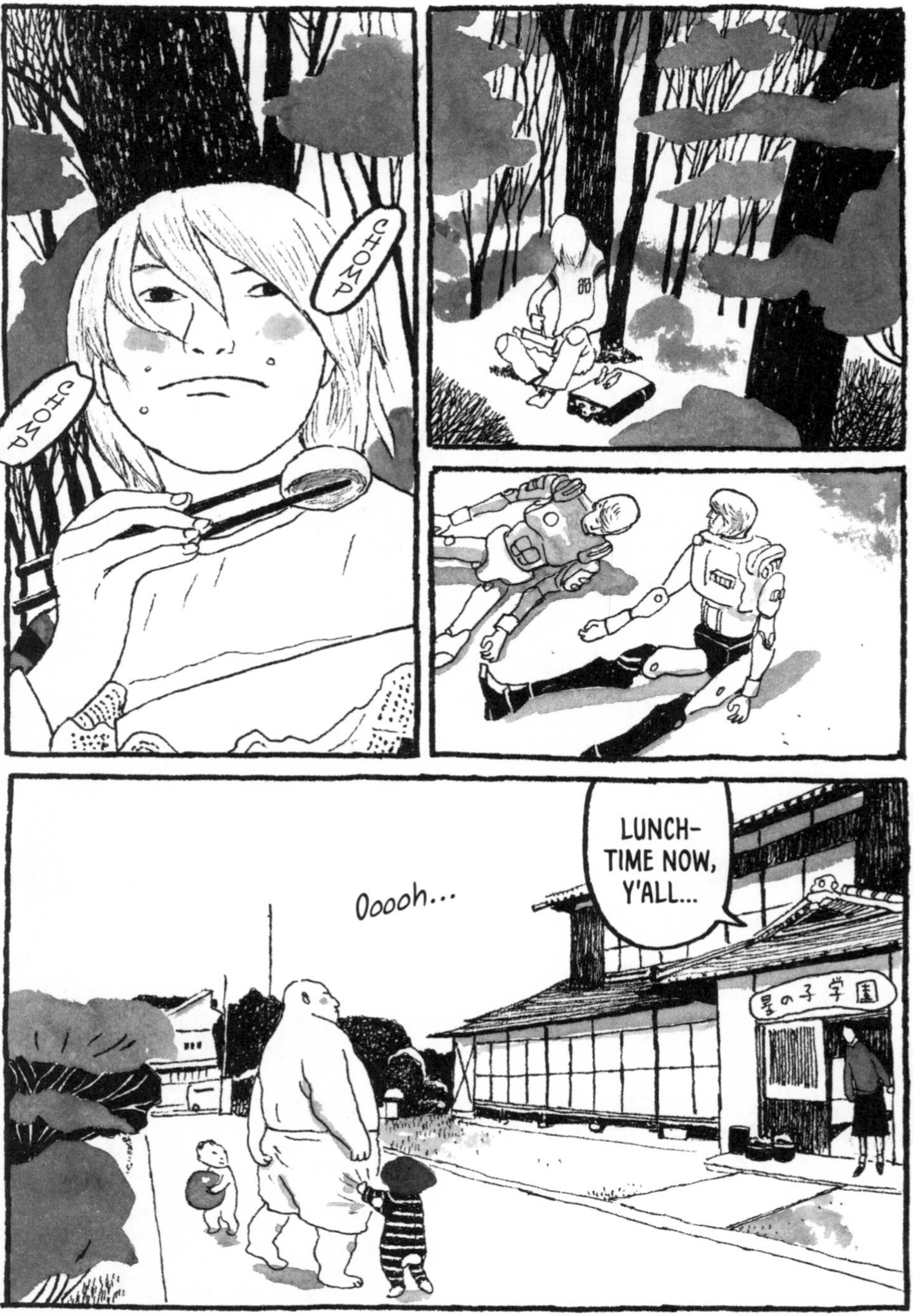
CHOMP
CHOMP
LUNCH-TIME NOW, Y'ALL...
Ooooh...
星の子学園

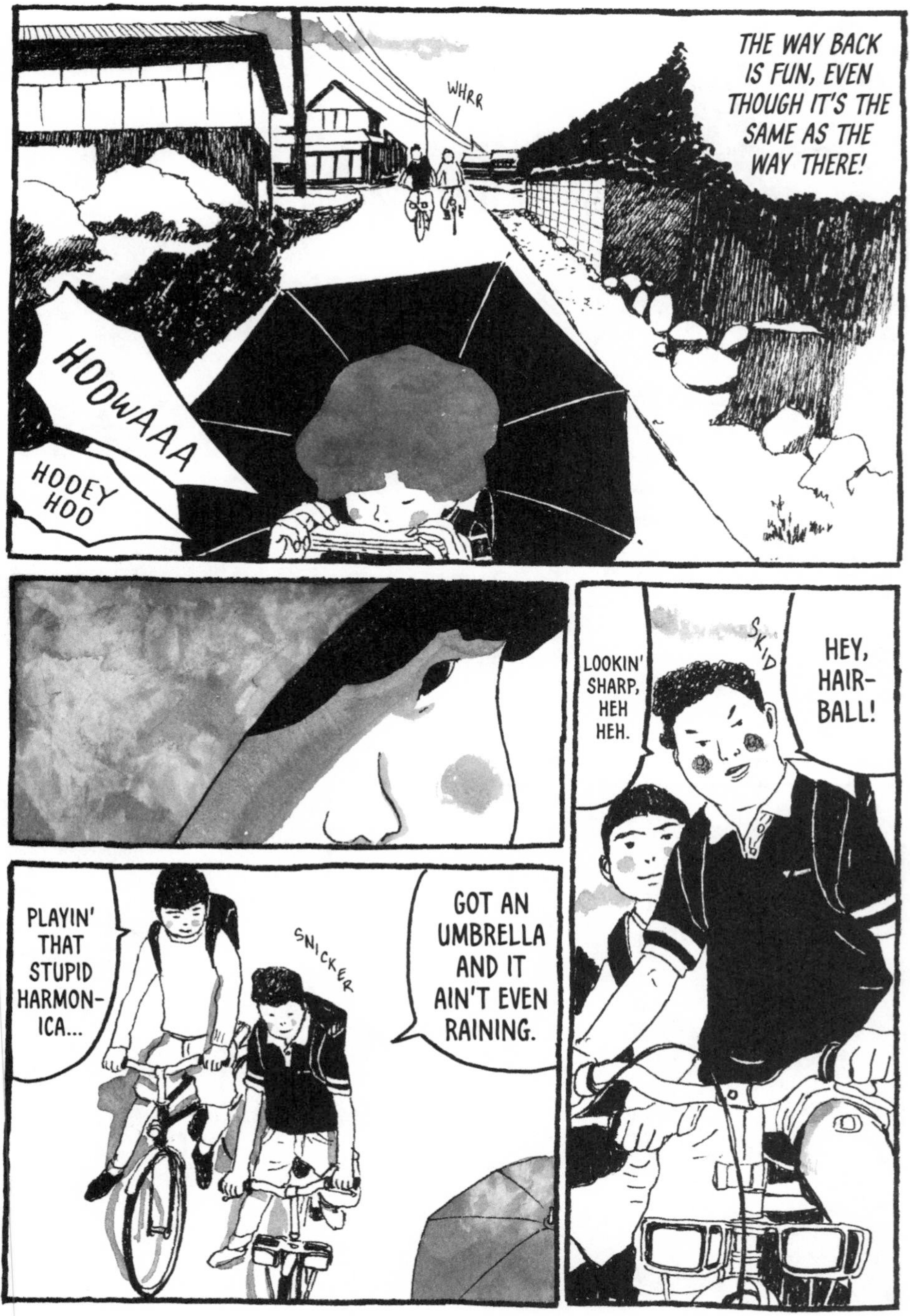
THE WAY BACK IS FUN, EVEN THOUGH IT'S THE SAME AS THE WAY THERE!
WHRR
HOOWAAA
HODEY HOO
SKID
HEY, HAIR-BALL!
LOOKIN' SHARP, HEH HEH.
GOT AN UMBRELLA AND IT AIN'T EVEN RAINING.
SNICKER
PLAYIN' THAT STUPID HARMON-ICA...

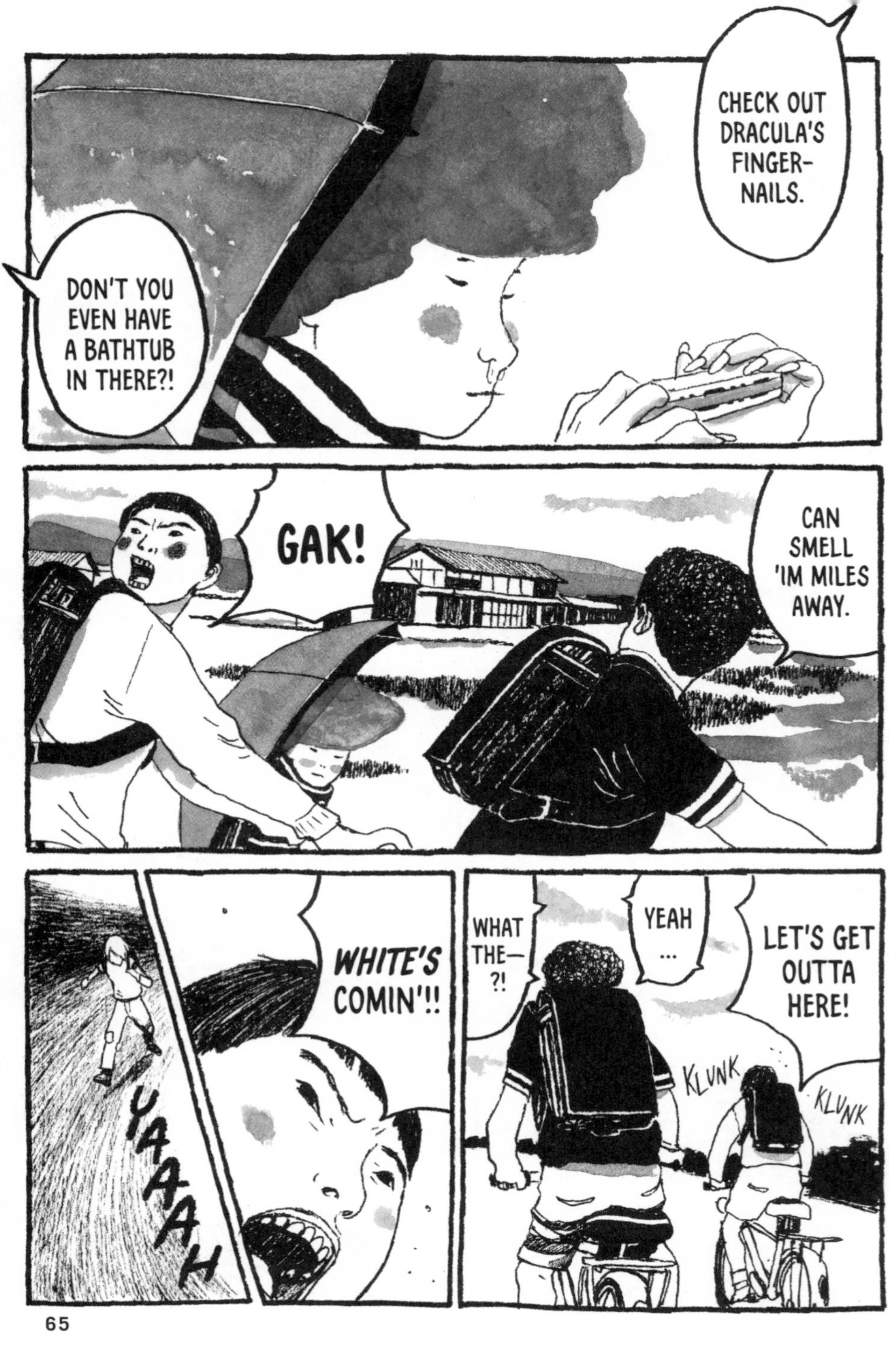
CHECK OUT DRACULA'S FINGER-NAILS.
DON'T YOU EVEN HAVE A BATHTUB IN THERE?!
CAN SMELL 'IM MILES AWAY.
GAK!
LET'S GET OUTTA HERE!
YEAH ...
WHAT THE—?!
KLUNK
KLUNK
WHITE'S COMIN'!!
YAAAAH

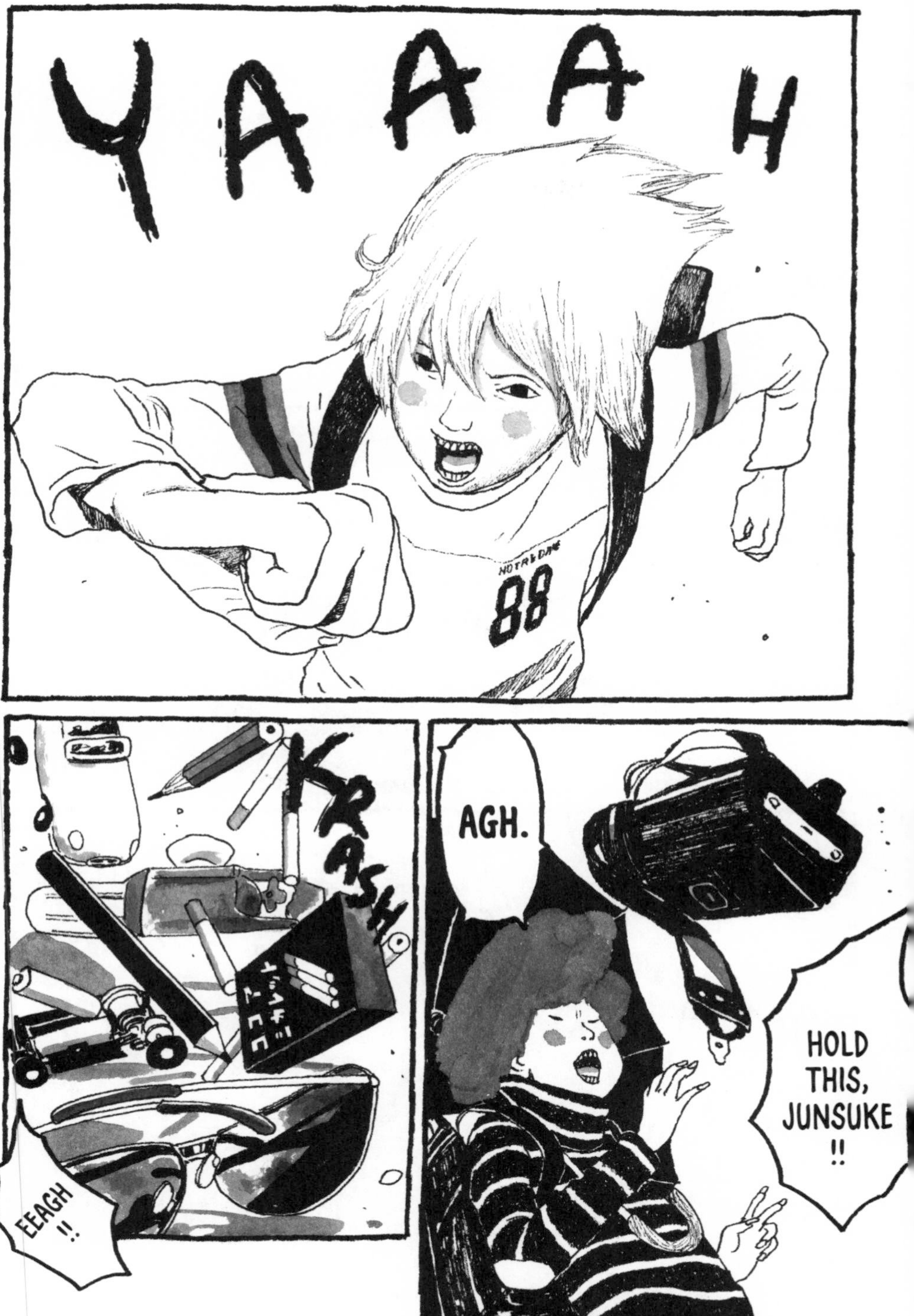
YAAAH
HOLD THIS, JUNSUKE!!
AGH.
KRASH
EEAGH!!

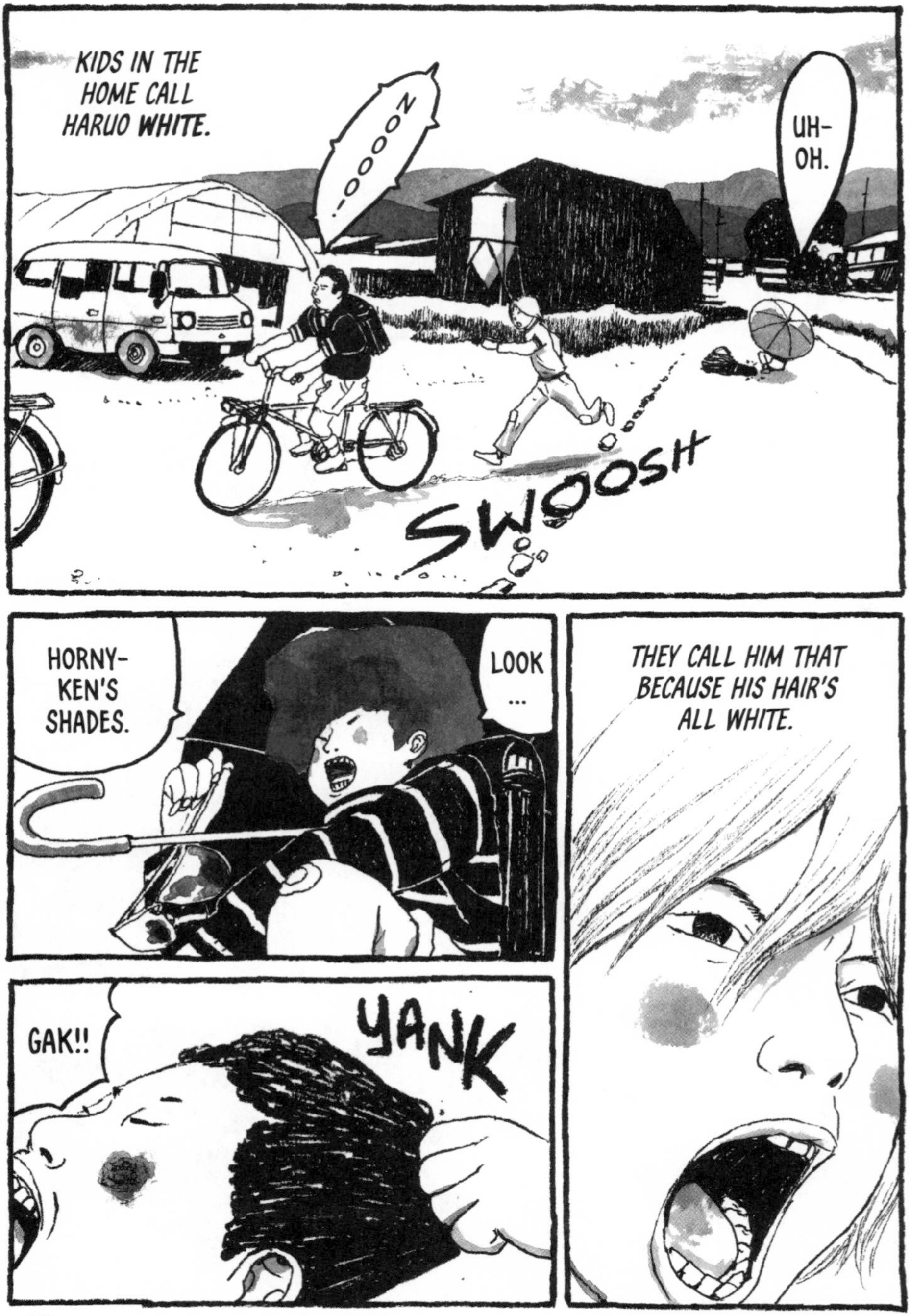
UH-OH.
KIDS IN THE HOME CALL HARUO WHITE.
NOOOO-!
SWOOSH
THEY CALL HIM THAT BECAUSE HIS HAIR'S ALL WHITE.
LOOK ...
HORNY-KEN'S SHADES.
YANK
GAK!!

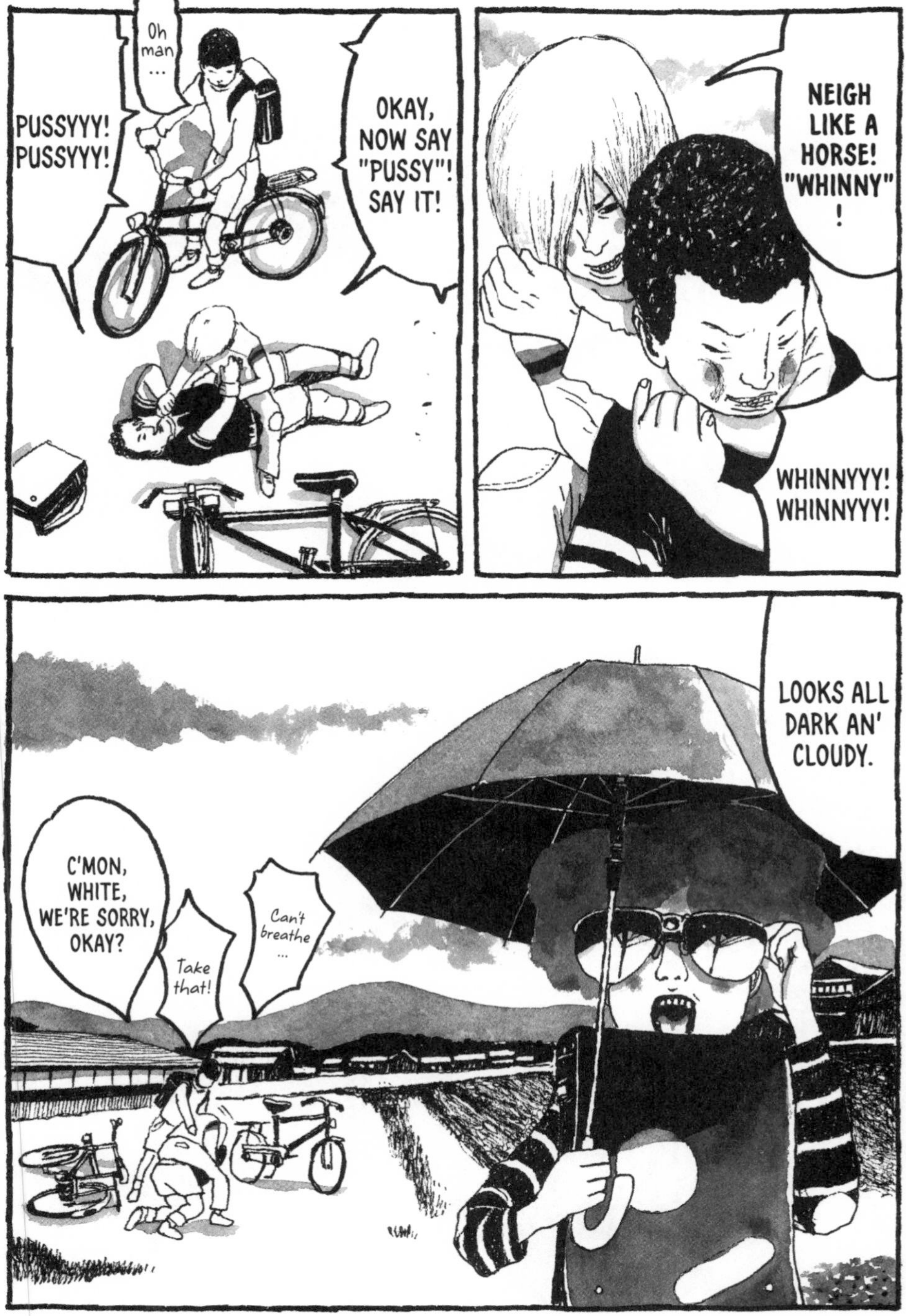
NEIGH LIKE A HORSE! "WHINNY"!
WHINNYYY! WHINNYYY!
OKAY, NOW SAY "PUSSY"! SAY IT!
Oh man...
PUSSYYY! PUSSYYY!
LOOKS ALL DARK AN' CLOUDY.
Can't breathe...
Take that!
C'MON, WHITE, WE'RE SORRY, OKAY?

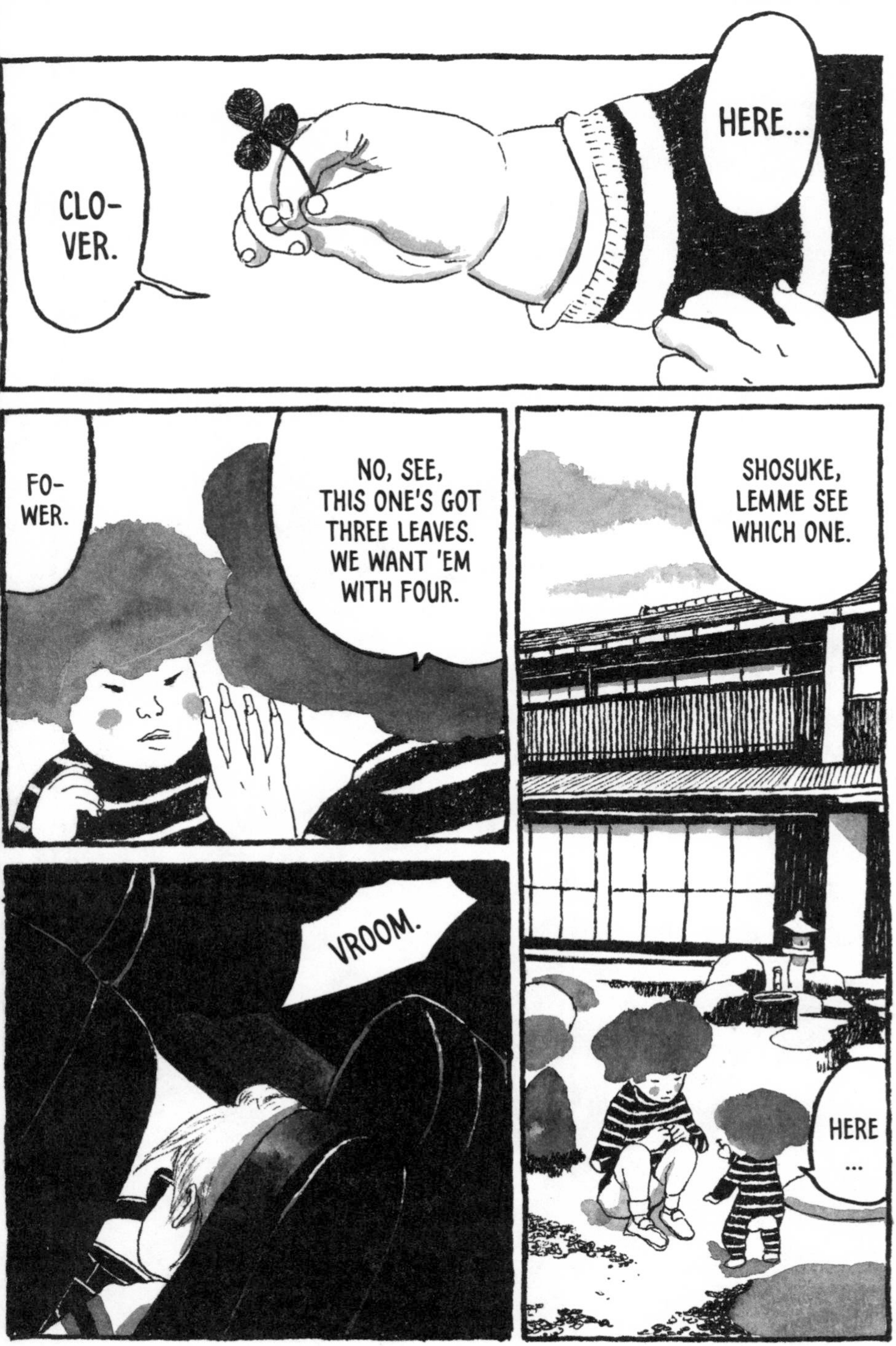
HERE...
CLO-VER.
SHOSUKE, LEMME SEE WHICH ONE.
HERE ...
NO, SEE, THIS ONE'S GOT THREE LEAVES. WE WANT 'EM WITH FOUR.
FO-WER.
VROOM.

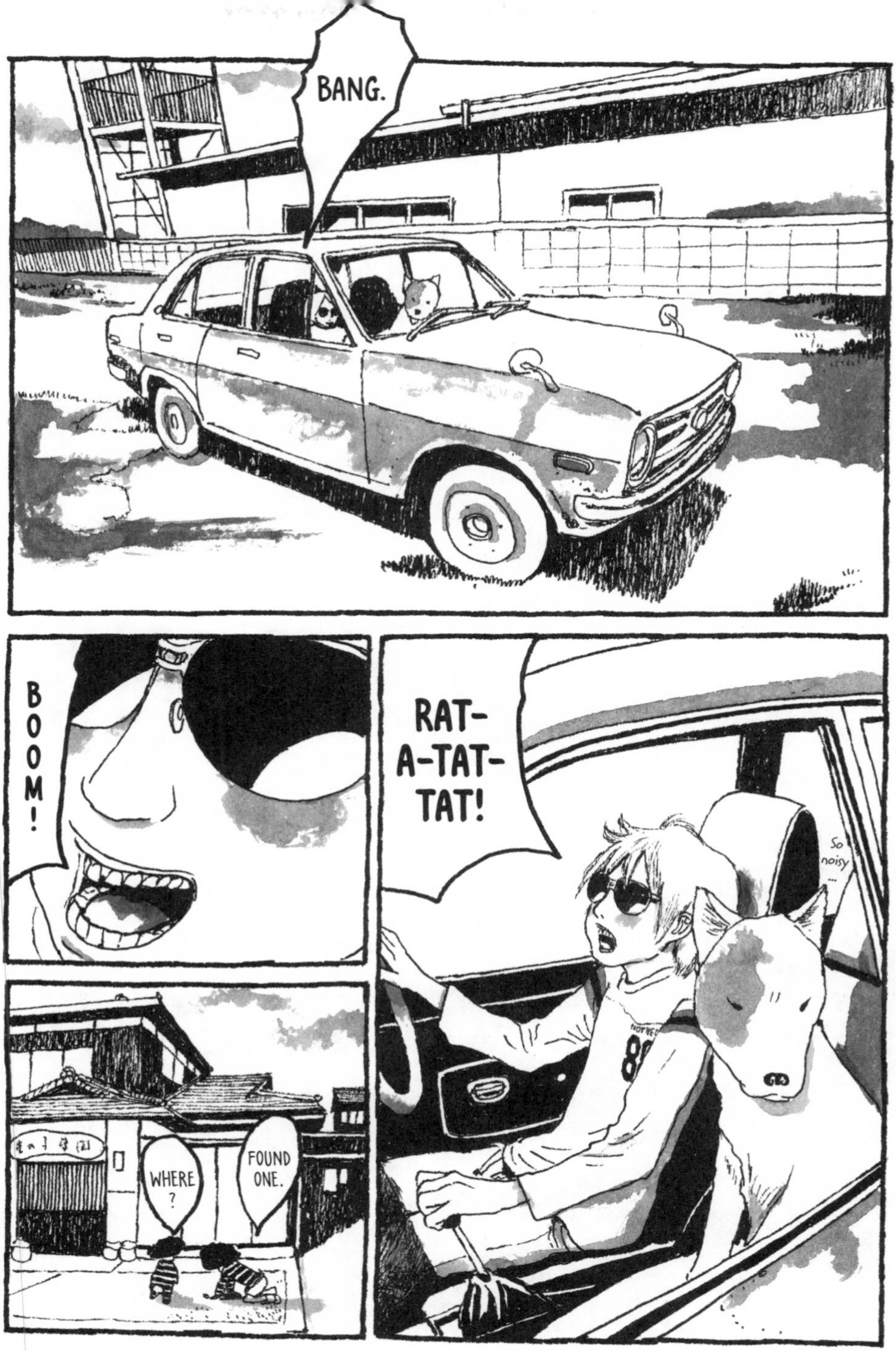
BANG.
RAT-A-TAT-TAT!
So noisy...
BOOOM!
FOUND ONE.
WHERE?

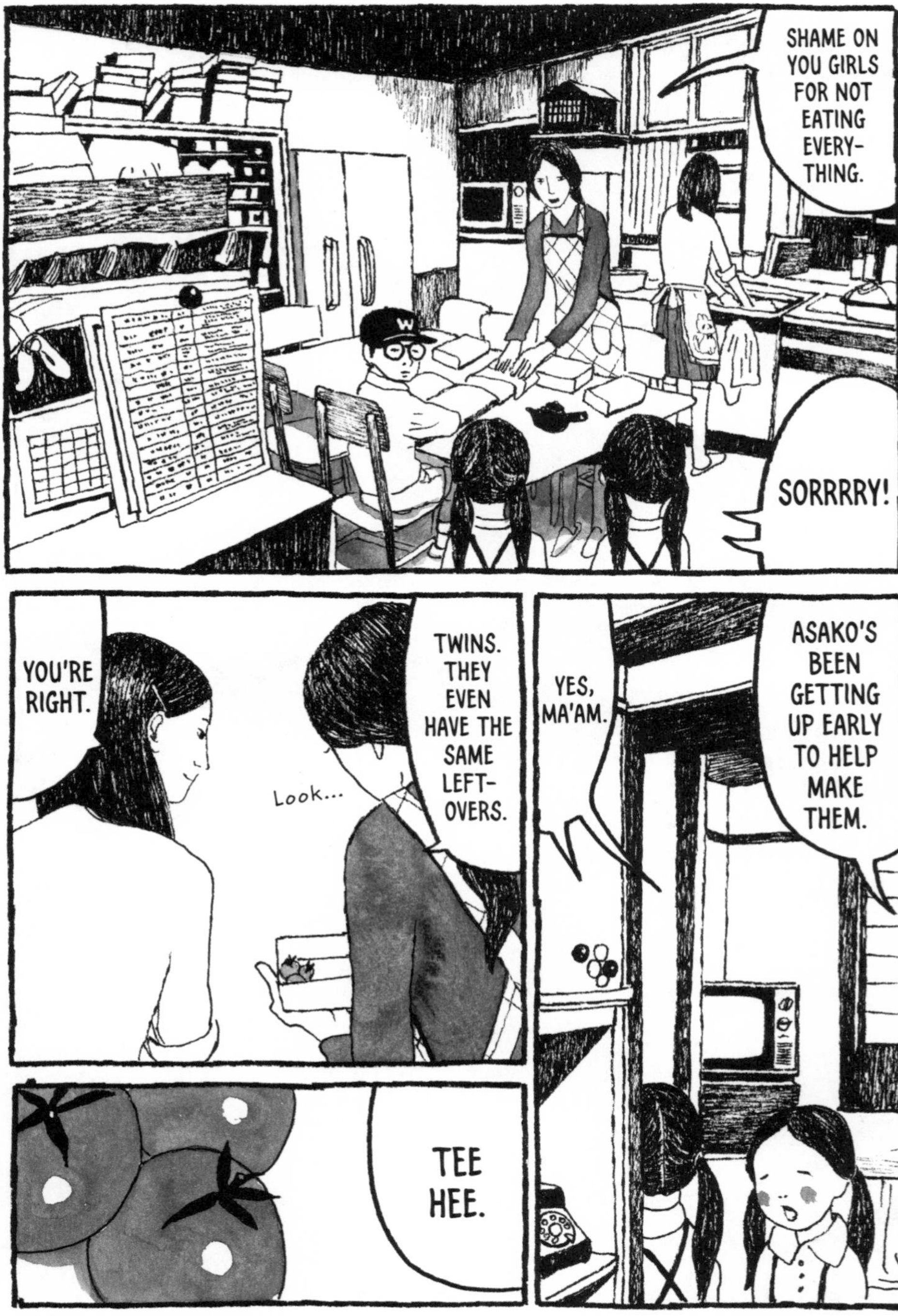
SHAME ON YOU GIRLS FOR NOT EATING EVERY-THING.
SORRRRY!
ASAKO'S BEEN GETTING UP EARLY TO HELP MAKE THEM.
YES, MA'AM.
TWINS. THEY EVEN HAVE THE SAME LEFT-OVERS.
Look...
YOU'RE RIGHT.
TEE HEE.

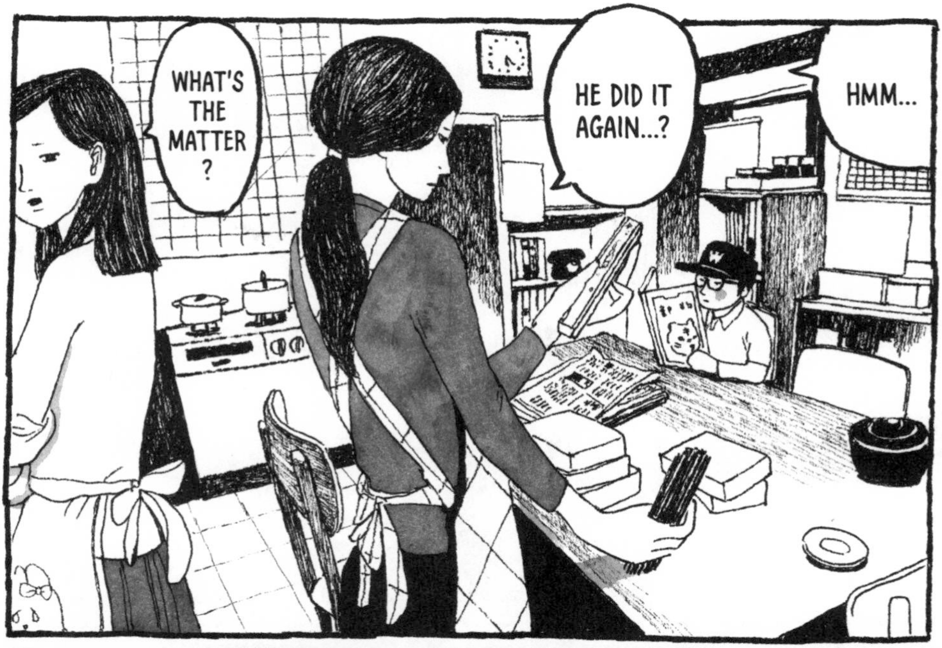
HMM...
HE DID IT AGAIN...?
WHAT'S THE MATTER?

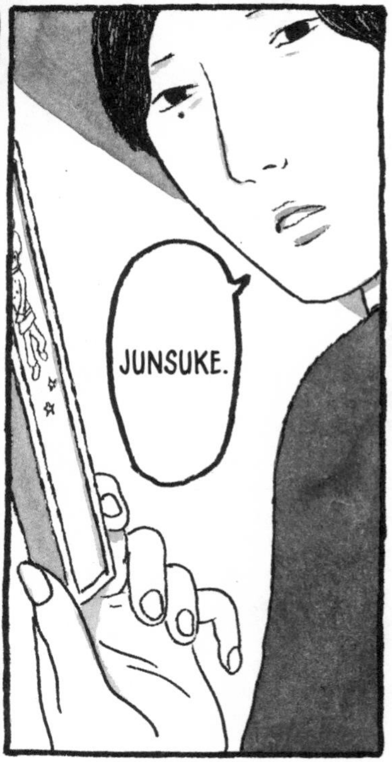
JUNSUKE.

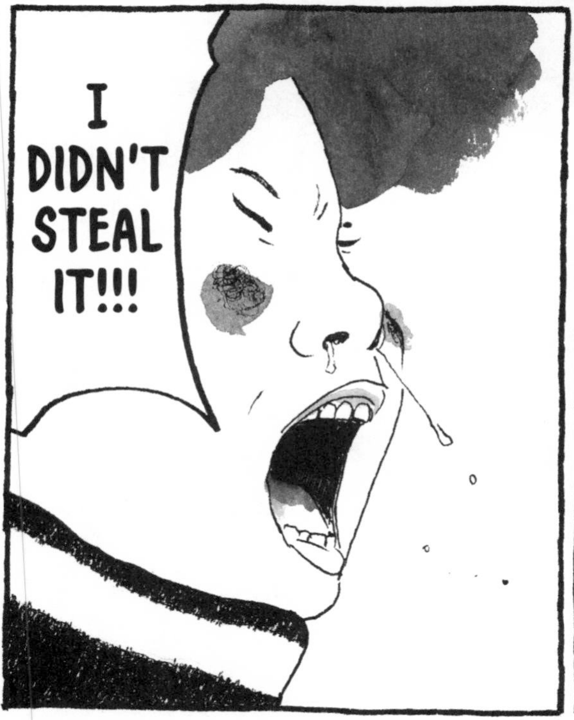
I DIDN'T STEAL IT!!!

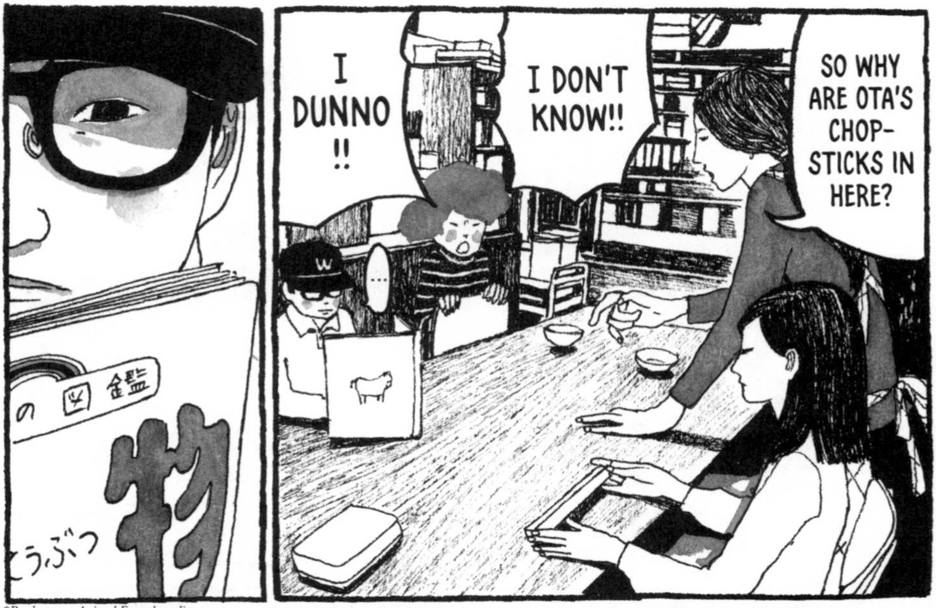
SO WHY ARE OTA'S CHOPSTICKS IN HERE?
I DON'T KNOW!!
I DUNNO !!
...

*Book cover: Animal Encyclopedia

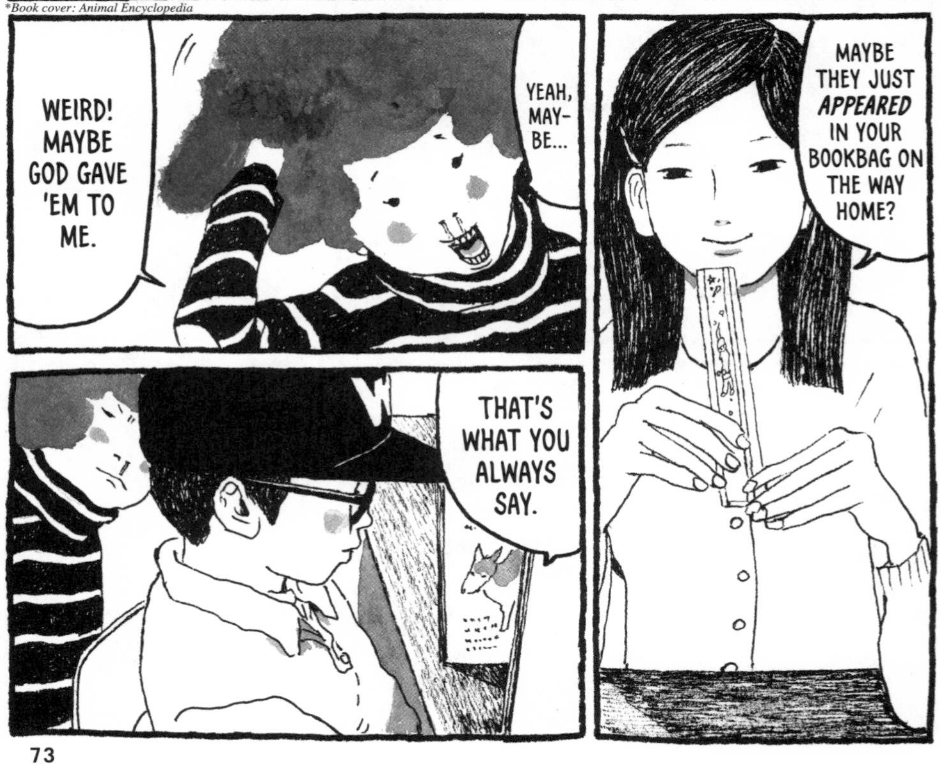
MAYBE THEY JUST *APPEARED* IN YOUR BOOKBAG ON THE WAY HOME?
YEAH, MAY-BE...
WEIRD! MAYBE GOD GAVE 'EM TO ME.
THAT'S WHAT YOU ALWAYS SAY.

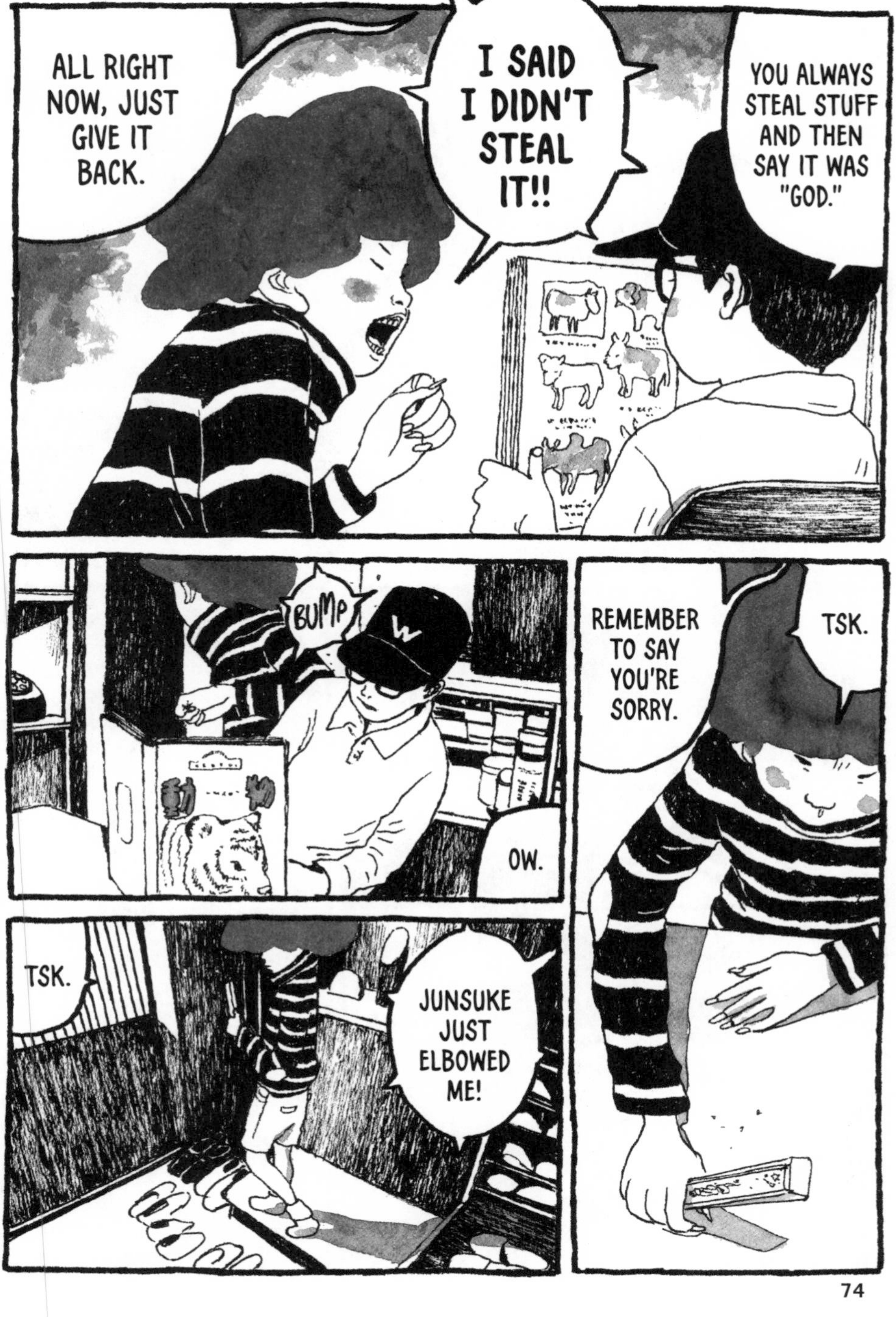
ALL RIGHT NOW, JUST GIVE IT BACK.
I SAID I DIDN'T STEAL IT!!
YOU ALWAYS STEAL STUFF AND THEN SAY IT WAS "GOD."
BUMP
OW.
TSK.
JUNSUKE JUST ELBOWED ME!
REMEMBER TO SAY YOU'RE SORRY.
TSK.

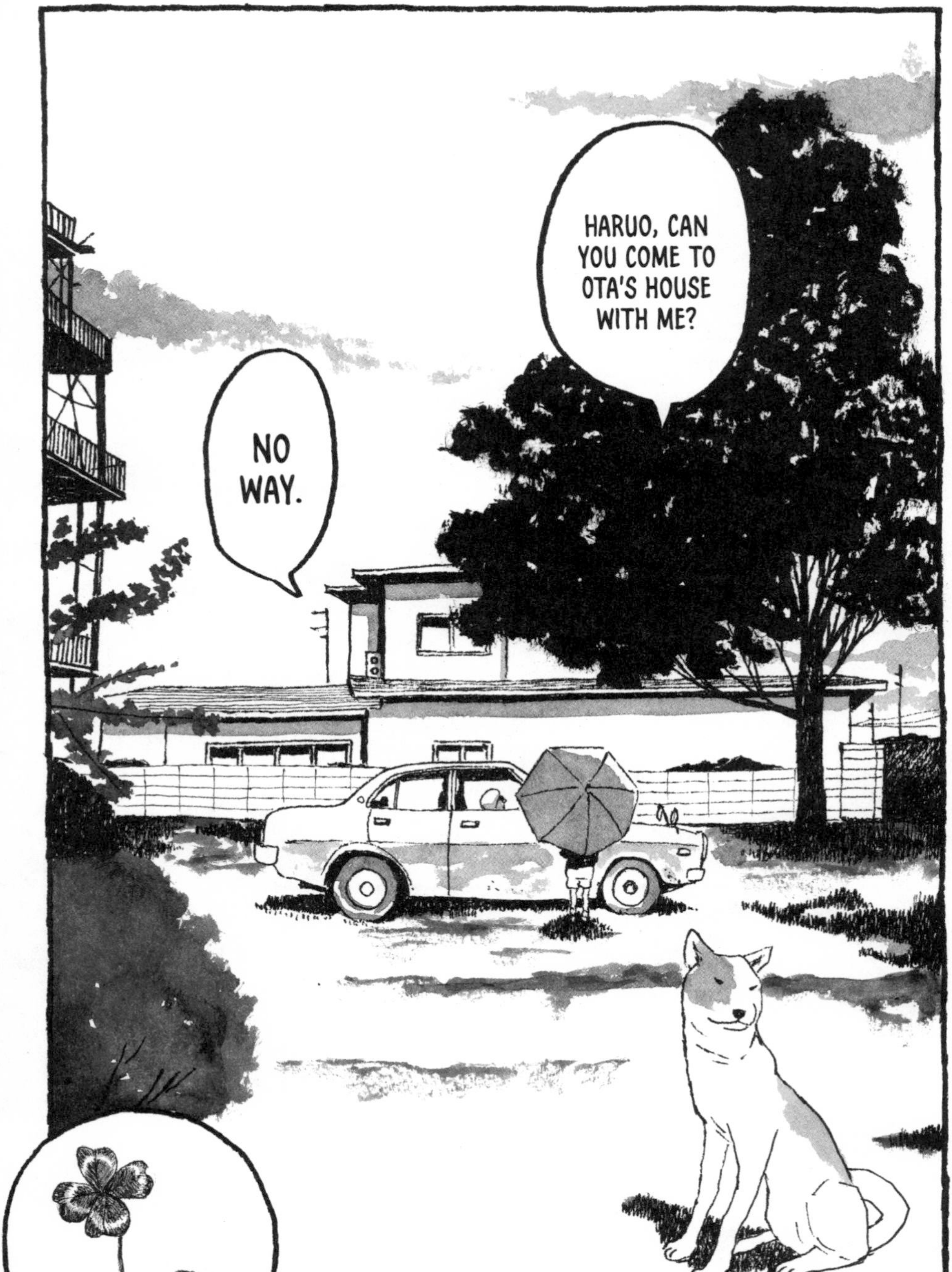
HARUO, CAN YOU COME TO OTA'S HOUSE WITH ME?
NO WAY.

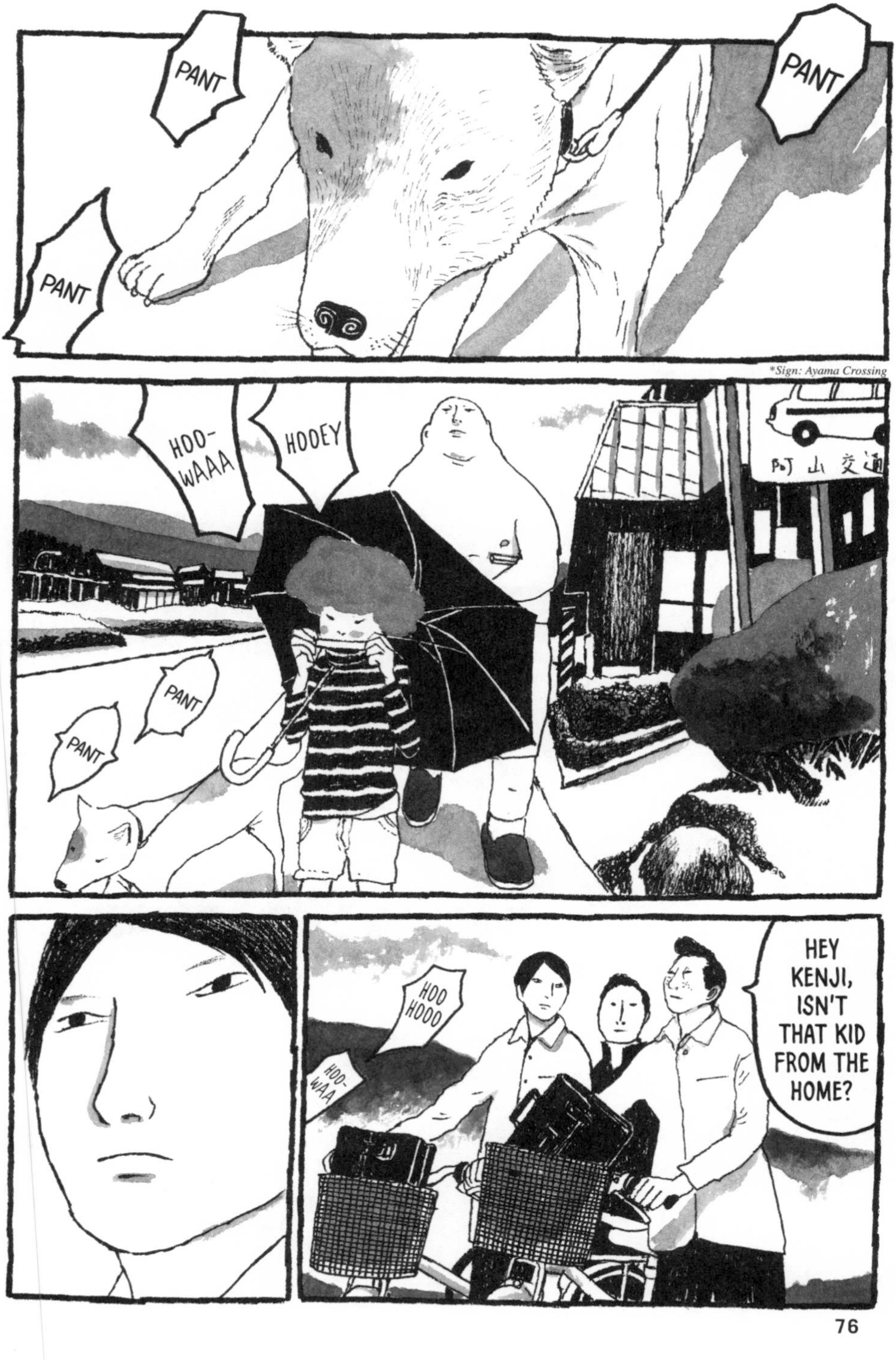
PANT
PANT
PANT
*Sign: Ayama Crossing
阿山交通
HOOEY
HOO-WAAA
PANT
PANT
HEY KENJI, ISN'T THAT KID FROM THE HOME?
HOO HOOO
HOO-WAA

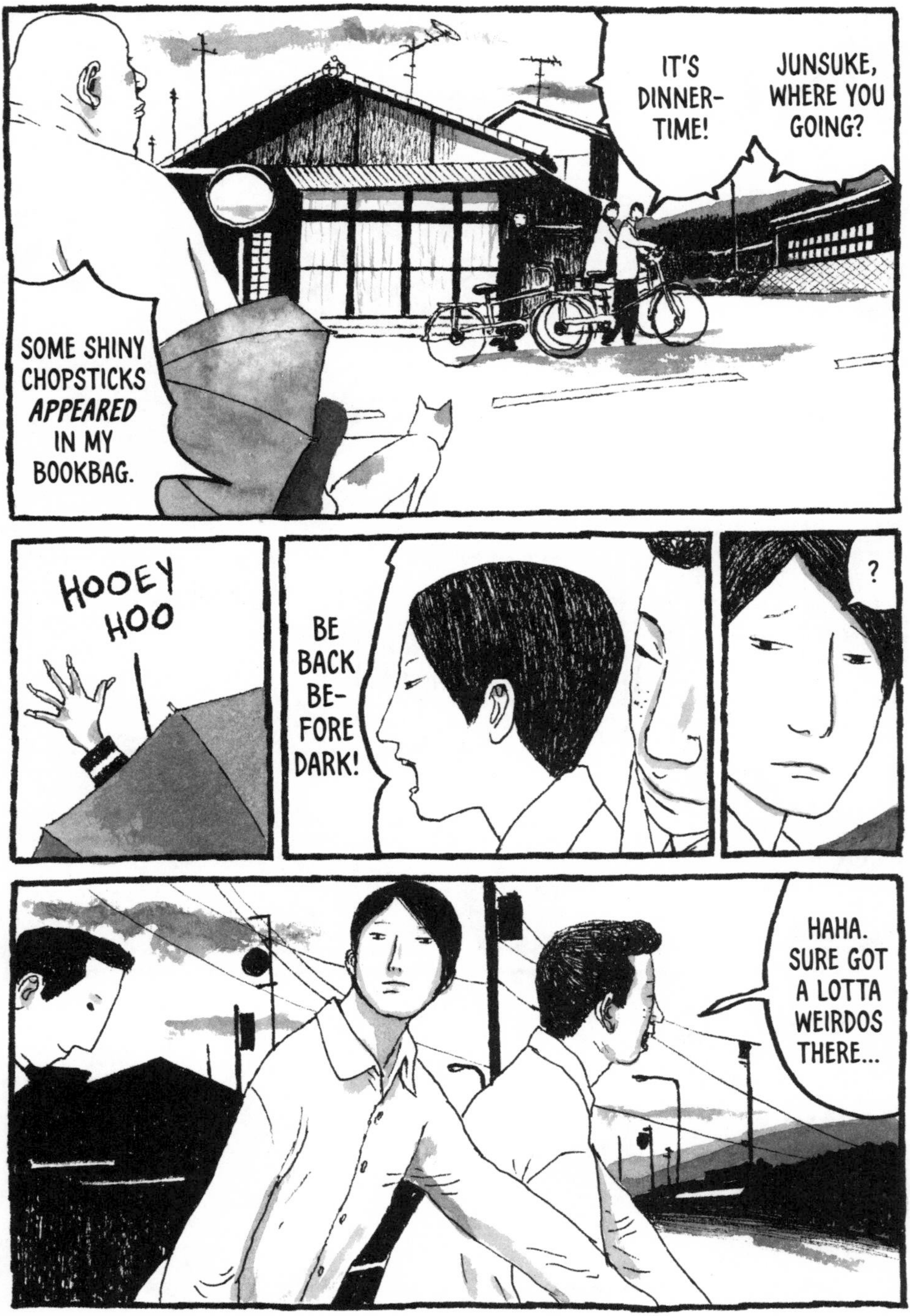
JUNSUKE, WHERE YOU GOING?
IT'S DINNER-TIME!
SOME SHINY CHOPSTICKS *APPEARED* IN MY BOOKBAG.
?
BE BACK BE-FORE DARK!
HOOEY HOO
HAHA. SURE GOT A LOTTA WEIRDOS THERE...

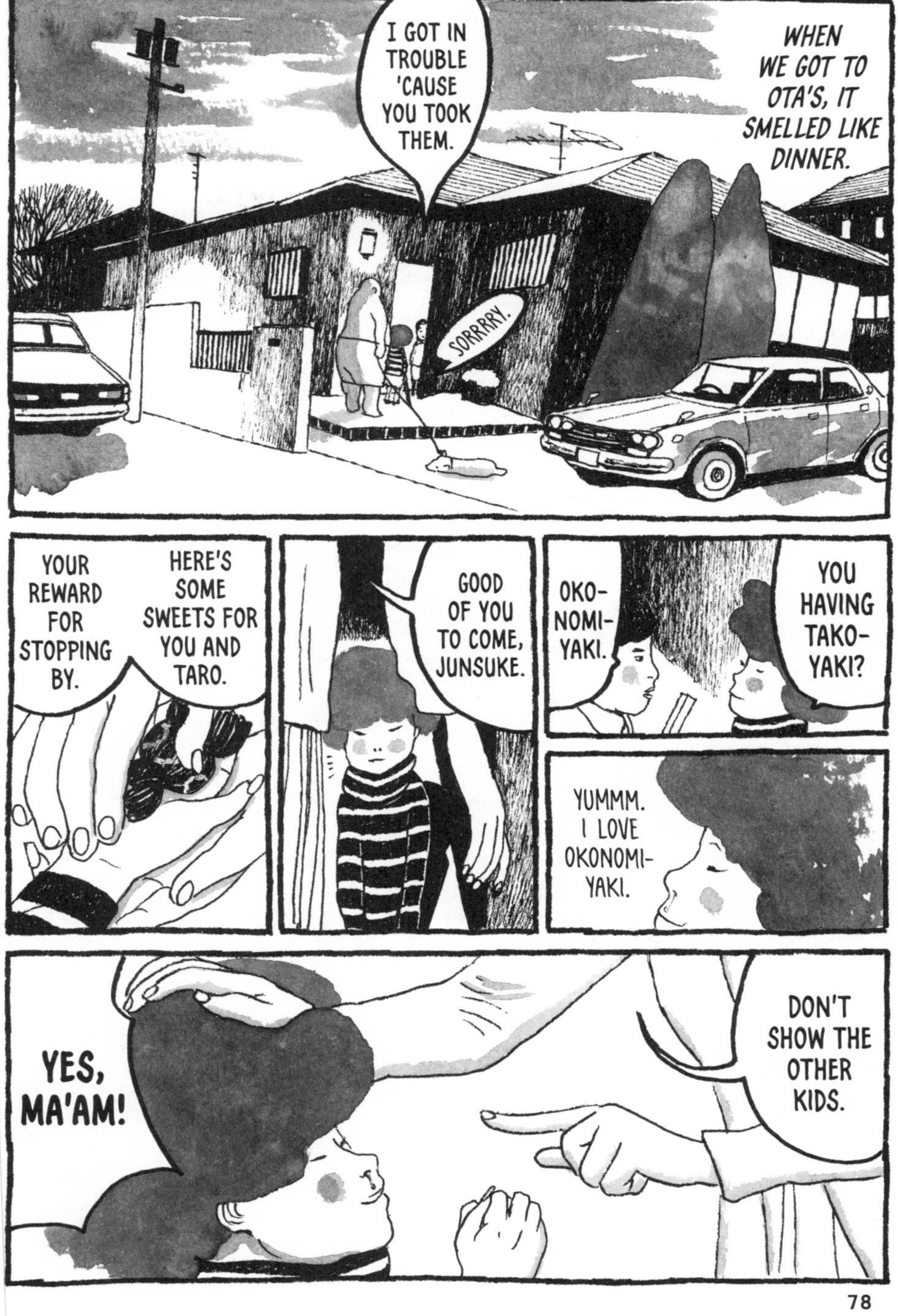
WHEN WE GOT TO OTA'S, IT SMELLED LIKE DINNER.
I GOT IN TROUBLE 'CAUSE YOU TOOK THEM.
SORRRRY.
YOU HAVING TAKO-YAKI?
OKO-NOMI-YAKI.
YUMMM. I LOVE OKONOMI-YAKI.
GOOD OF YOU TO COME, JUNSUKE.
HERE'S SOME SWEETS FOR YOU AND TARO.
YOUR REWARD FOR STOPPING BY.
DON'T SHOW THE OTHER KIDS.
YES, MA'AM!

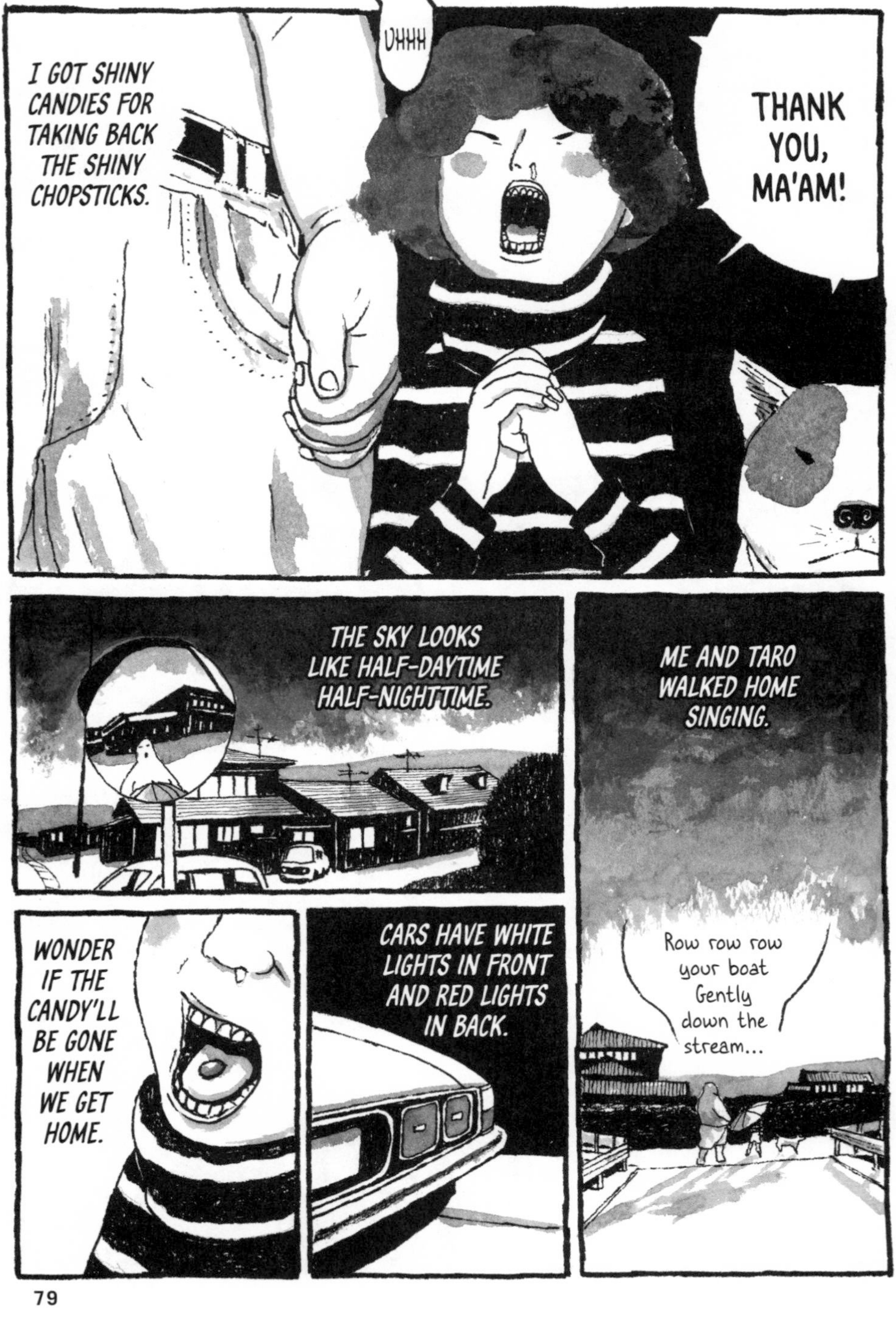
THANK YOU, MA'AM!
UHHH
I GOT SHINY CANDIES FOR TAKING BACK THE SHINY CHOPSTICKS.
ME AND TARO WALKED HOME SINGING.
Row row row your boat Gently down the stream...
THE SKY LOOKS LIKE HALF-DAYTIME HALF-NIGHTTIME.
CARS HAVE WHITE LIGHTS IN FRONT AND RED LIGHTS IN BACK.
WONDER IF THE CANDY'LL BE GONE WHEN WE GET HOME.

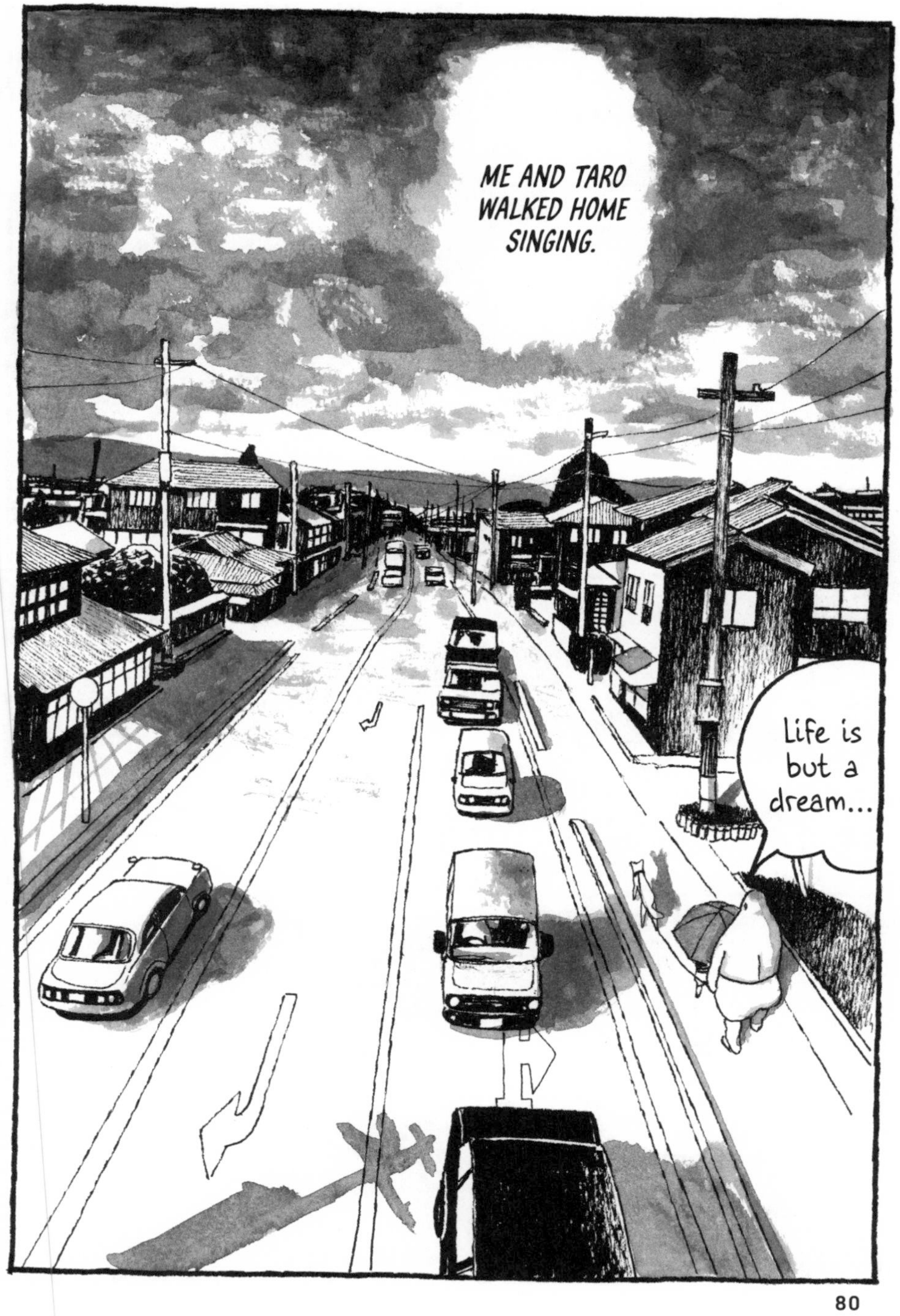
ME AND TARO WALKED HOME SINGING.
Life is but a dream...

CHAPTER 3

"Why do girls
always cry?"

"'Cause
almost nothin'
can beat a
girl's tears."

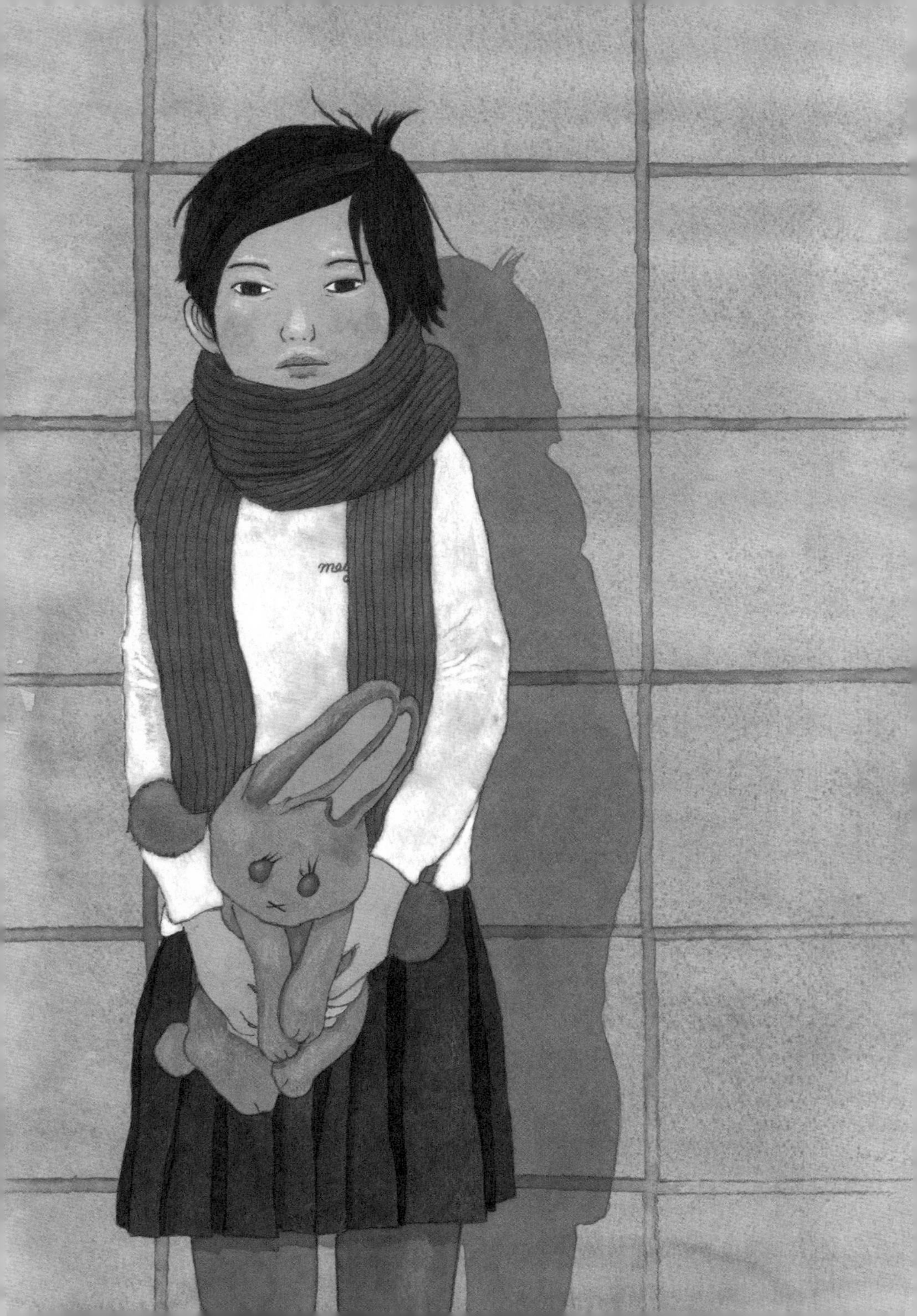

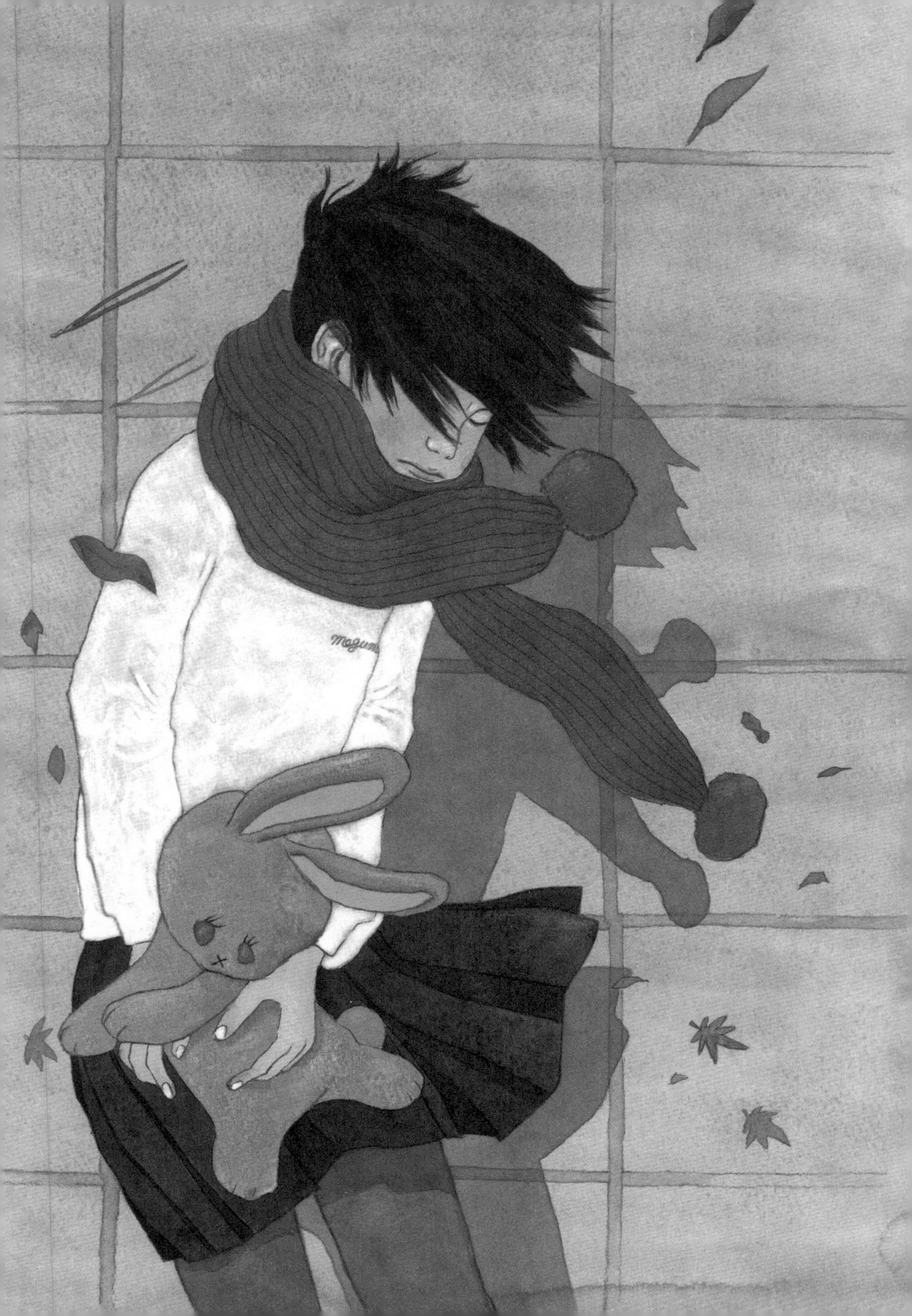

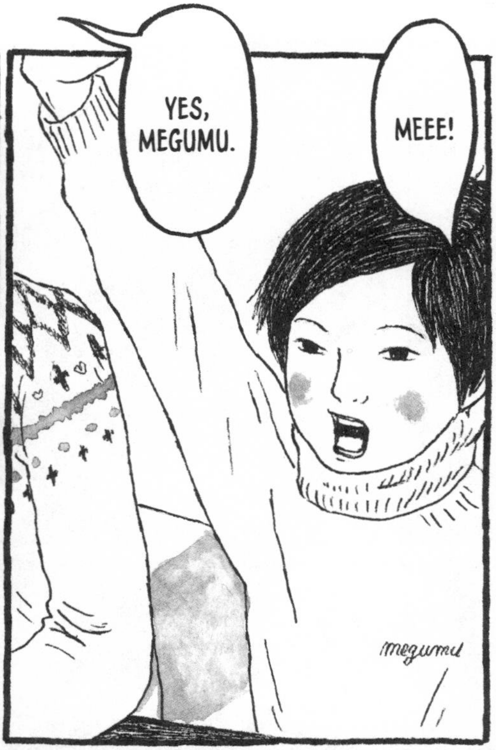
MEEE!
YES, MEGUMU.
megumu
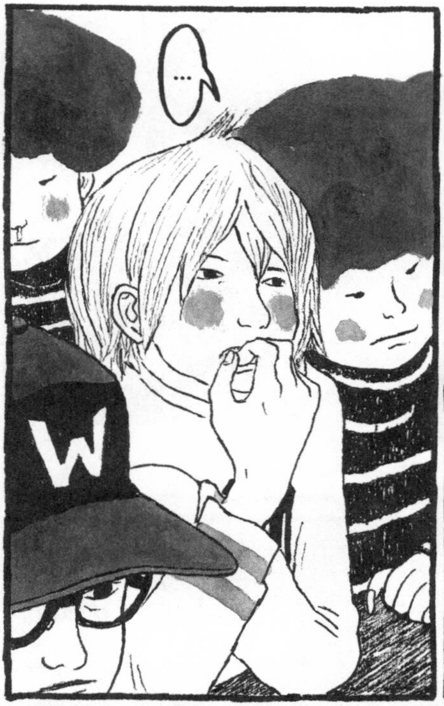
...
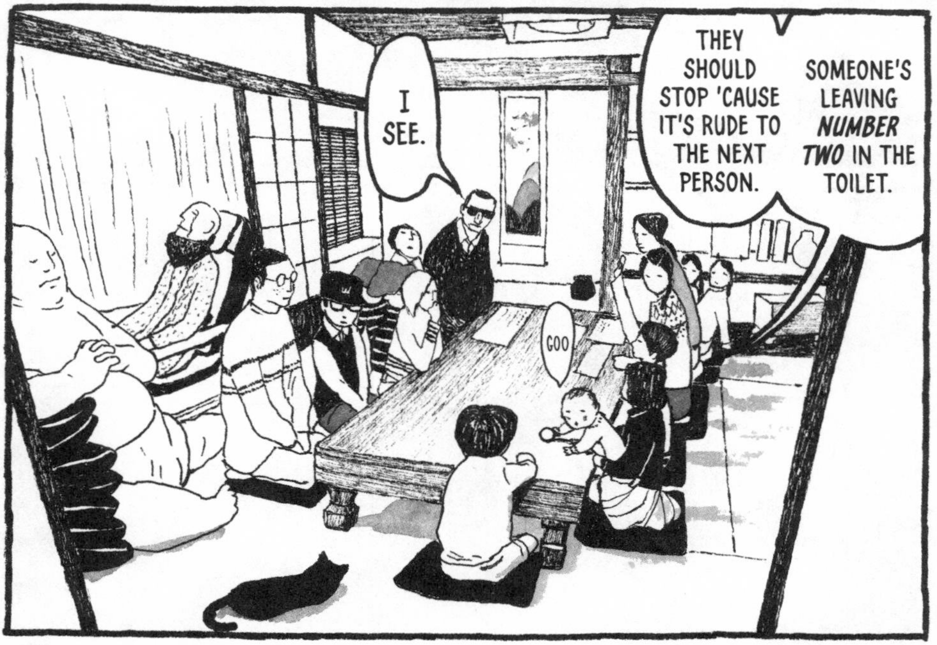
SOMEONE'S LEAVING NUMBER TWO IN THE TOILET.
THEY SHOULD STOP 'CAUSE IT'S RUDE TO THE NEXT PERSON.
I SEE.
GOO

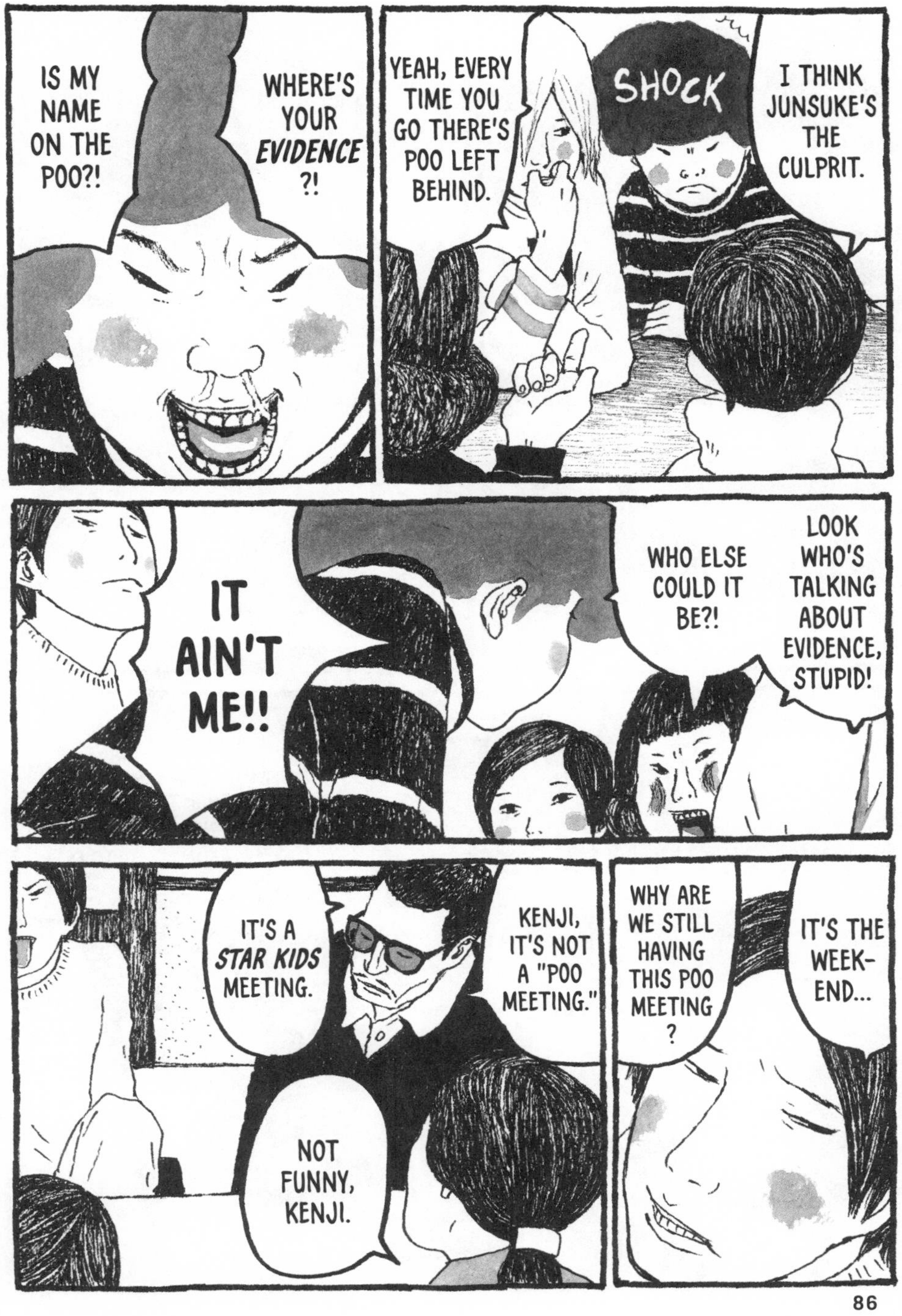
I THINK JUNSUKE'S THE CULPRIT.
SHOCK
YEAH, EVERY TIME YOU GO THERE'S POO LEFT BEHIND.
WHERE'S YOUR *EVIDENCE*?!
IS MY NAME ON THE POO?!
LOOK WHO'S TALKING ABOUT EVIDENCE, STUPID!
WHO ELSE COULD IT BE?!
IT AIN'T ME!!
IT'S THE WEEK-END...
WHY ARE WE STILL HAVING THIS POO MEETING?
KENJI, IT'S NOT A "POO MEETING."
IT'S A *STAR KIDS* MEETING.
NOT FUNNY, KENJI.

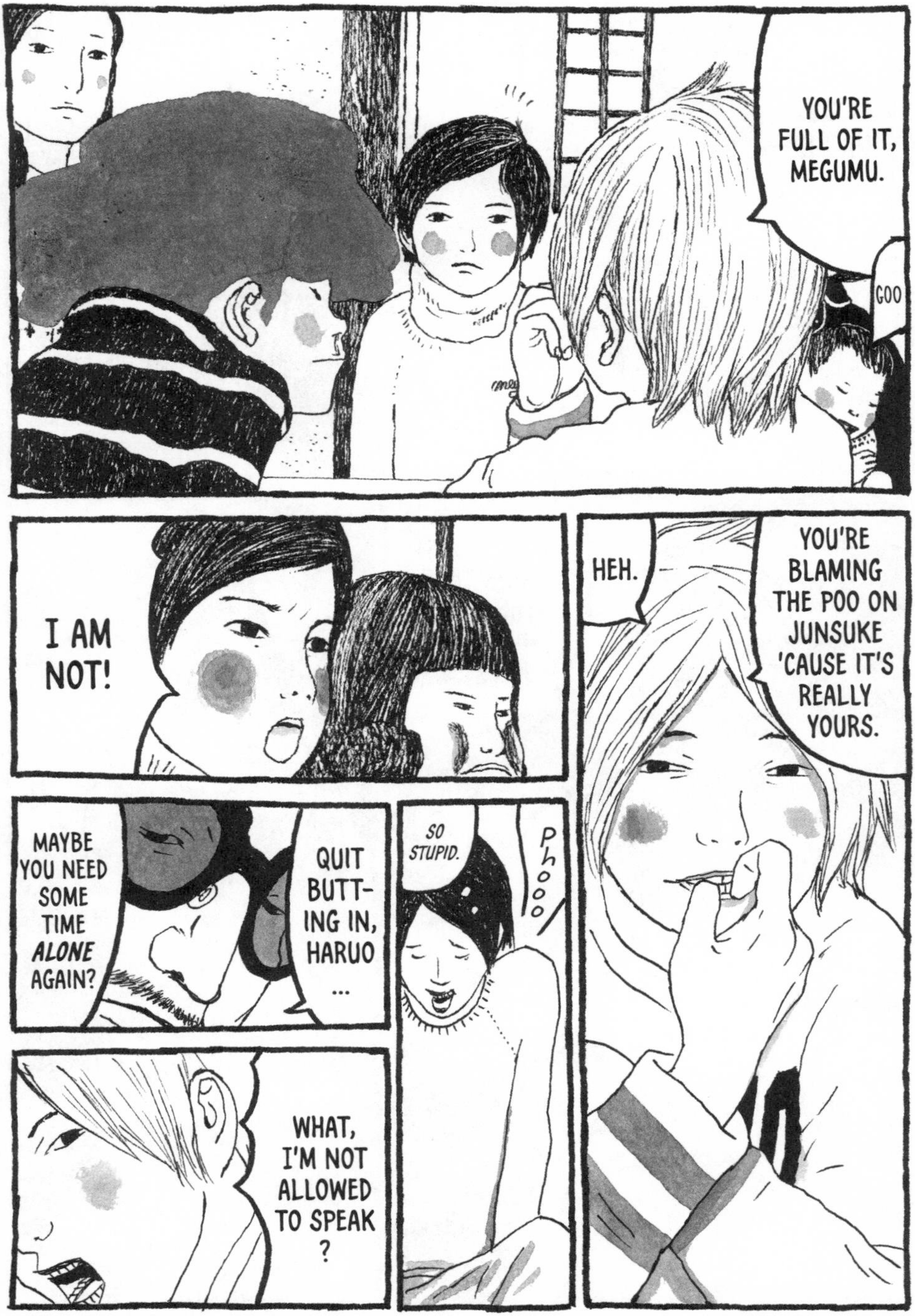
YOU'RE FULL OF IT, MEGUMU.
GOO
HEH.
YOU'RE BLAMING THE POO ON JUNSUKE 'CAUSE IT'S REALLY YOURS.
I AM NOT!
Phoooo
SO STUPID.
QUIT BUTT-ING IN, HARUO ...
MAYBE YOU NEED SOME TIME *ALONE* AGAIN?
WHAT, I'M NOT ALLOWED TO SPEAK ?

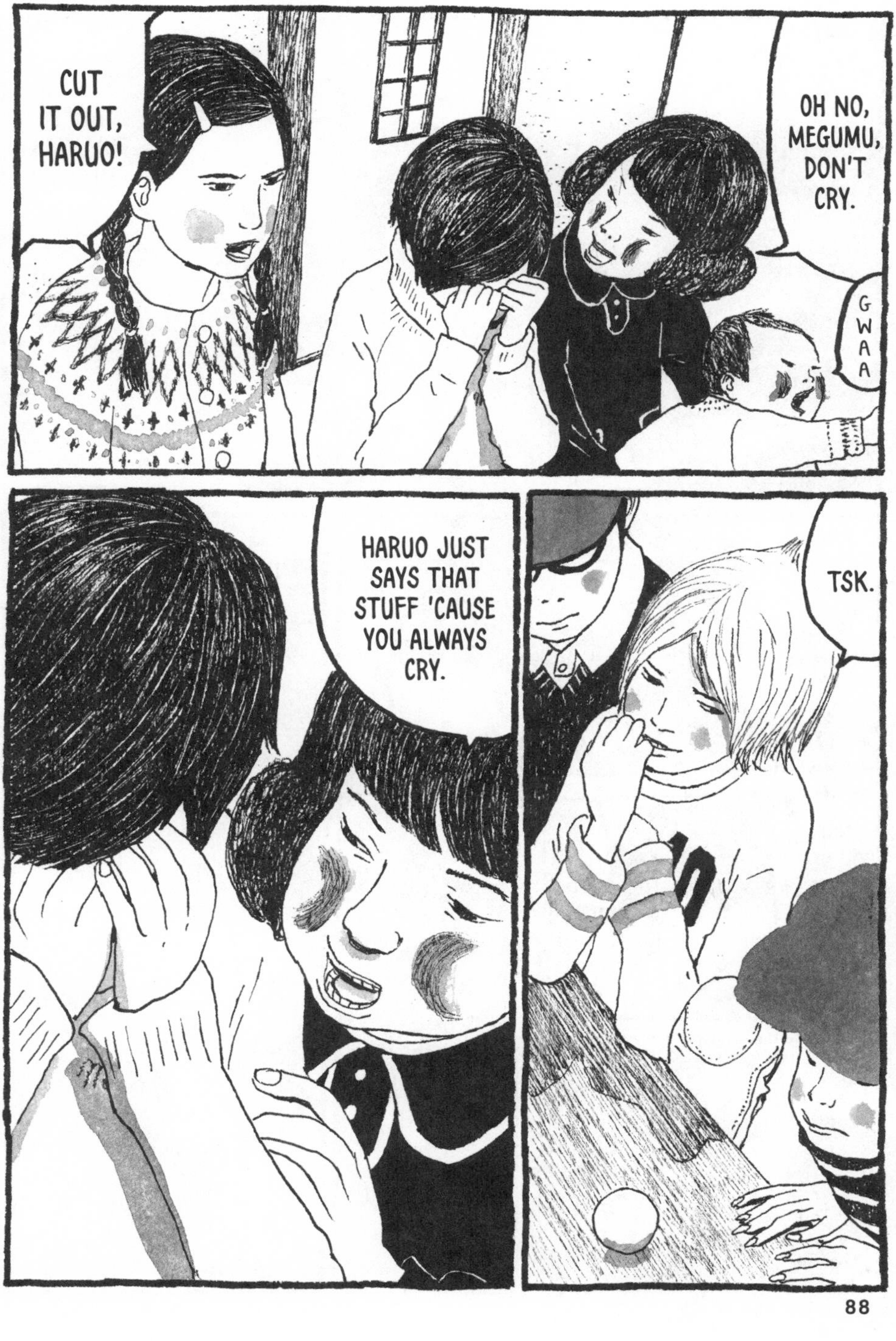
OH NO, MEGUMU, DON'T CRY.
GWAA
CUT IT OUT, HARUO!
TSK.
HARUO JUST SAYS THAT STUFF 'CAUSE YOU ALWAYS CRY.

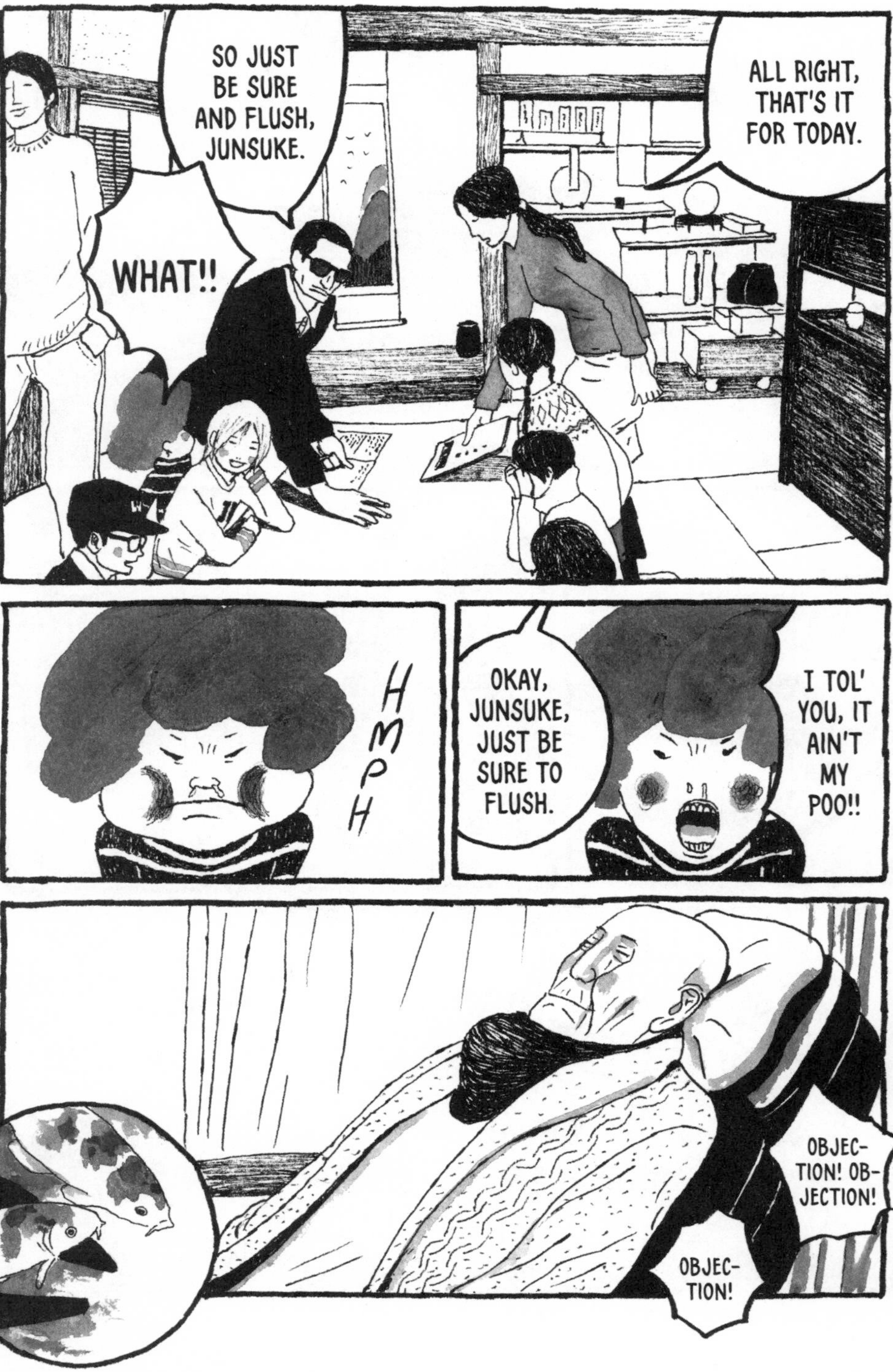
ALL RIGHT, THAT'S IT FOR TODAY.
SO JUST BE SURE AND FLUSH, JUNSUKE.
WHAT!!
OKAY, JUNSUKE, JUST BE SURE TO FLUSH.
I TOL' YOU, IT AIN'T MY POO!!
HMPH
OBJECTION! OBJECTION!
OBJECTION!

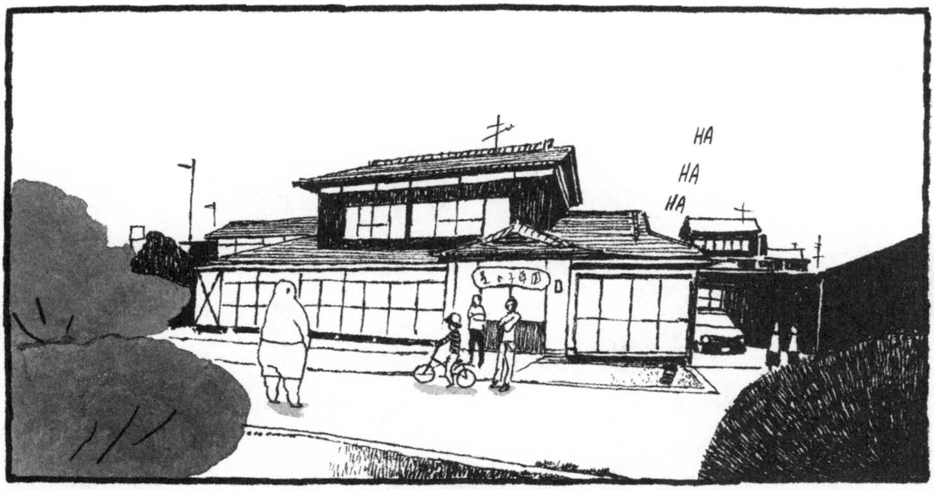
HA
HA
HA

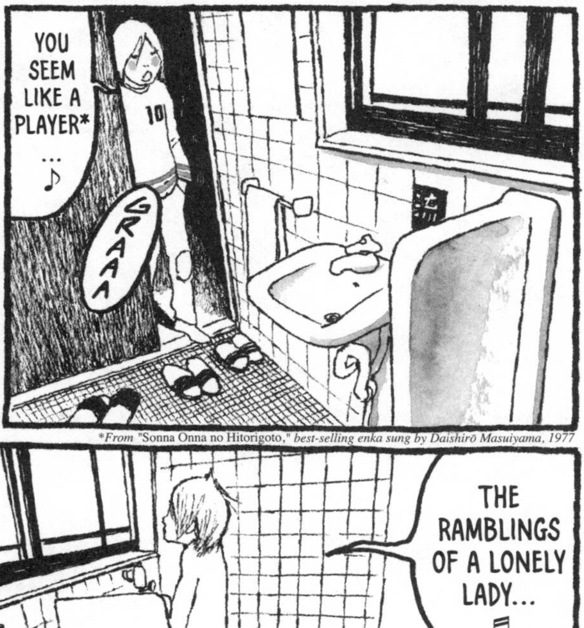
YOU SEEM LIKE A PLAYER* ... ♪
GRAAA

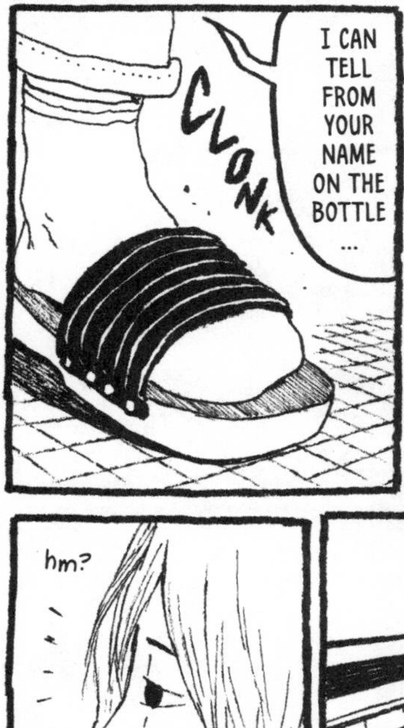
I CAN TELL FROM YOUR NAME ON THE BOTTLE ...
CLONK

*From "Sonna Onna no Hitorigoto," best-selling enka sung by Daishirō Masuiyama, 1977

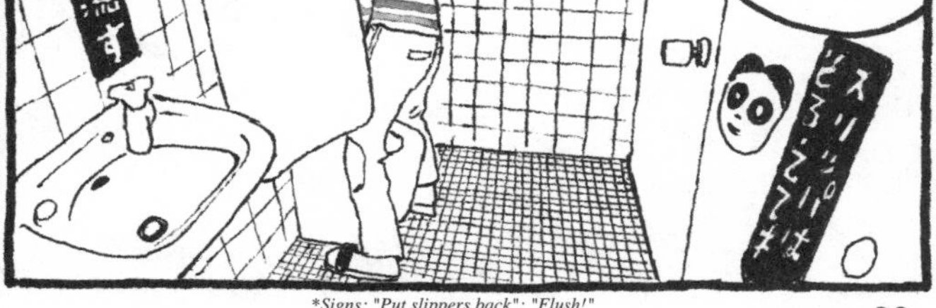
THE RAMBLINGS OF A LONELY LADY... ♬
流す

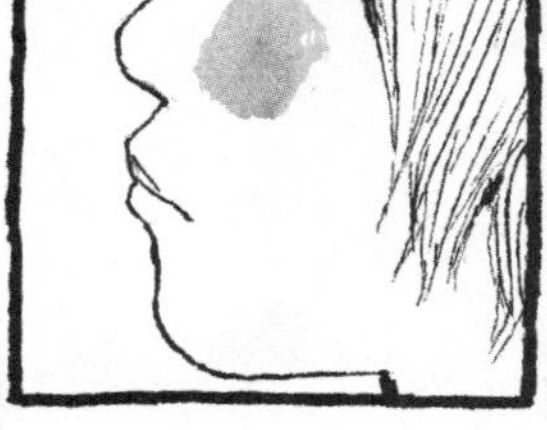
hm?

*Signs: "Put slippers back"; "Flush!"

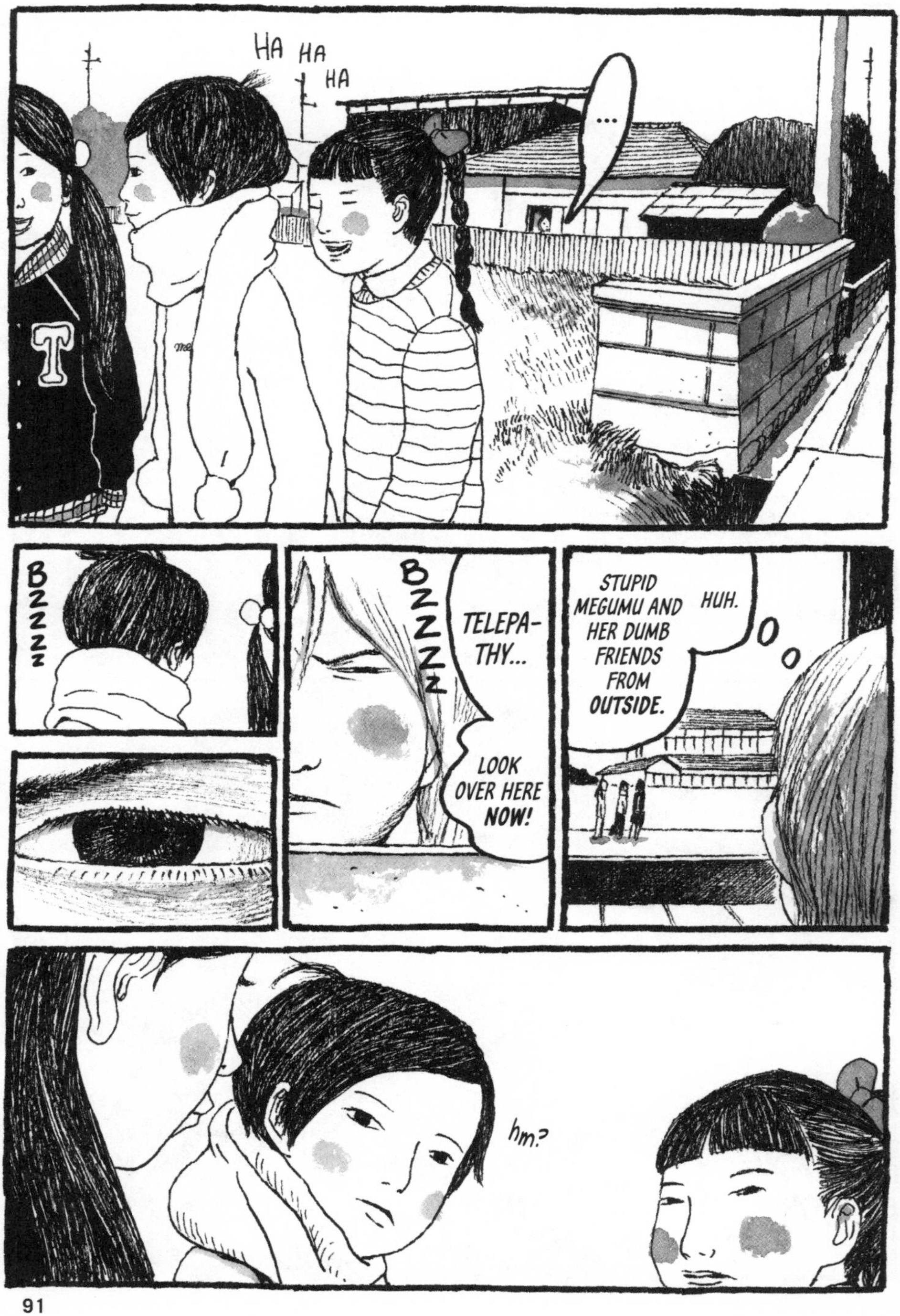
HA HA HA
...
HUH.
STUPID MEGUMU AND HER DUMB FRIENDS FROM OUTSIDE.
BZZZZZ
TELEPA-THY...
LOOK OVER HERE NOW!
BZZZZZ
hm?

WHAT-SA-MAT-TER?
CREEPY ...
THOUGHT SOMEONE WAS WATCHING US.
HEH HEH HEH.
TELE-PATHY RULES!
I SAID, DON'T LET GO!!
QUIT LETTING GO!!

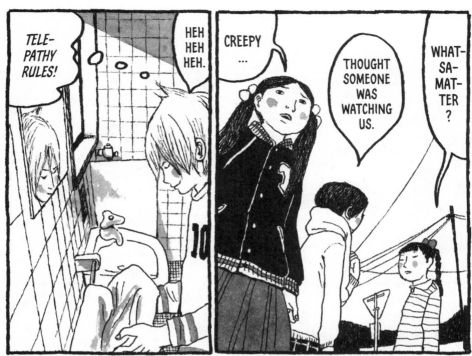

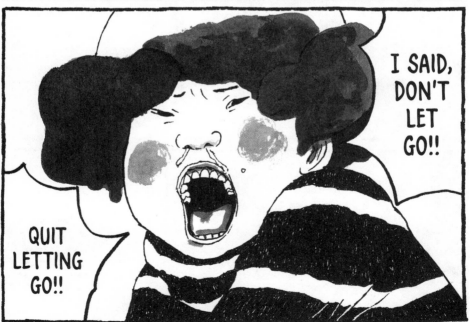

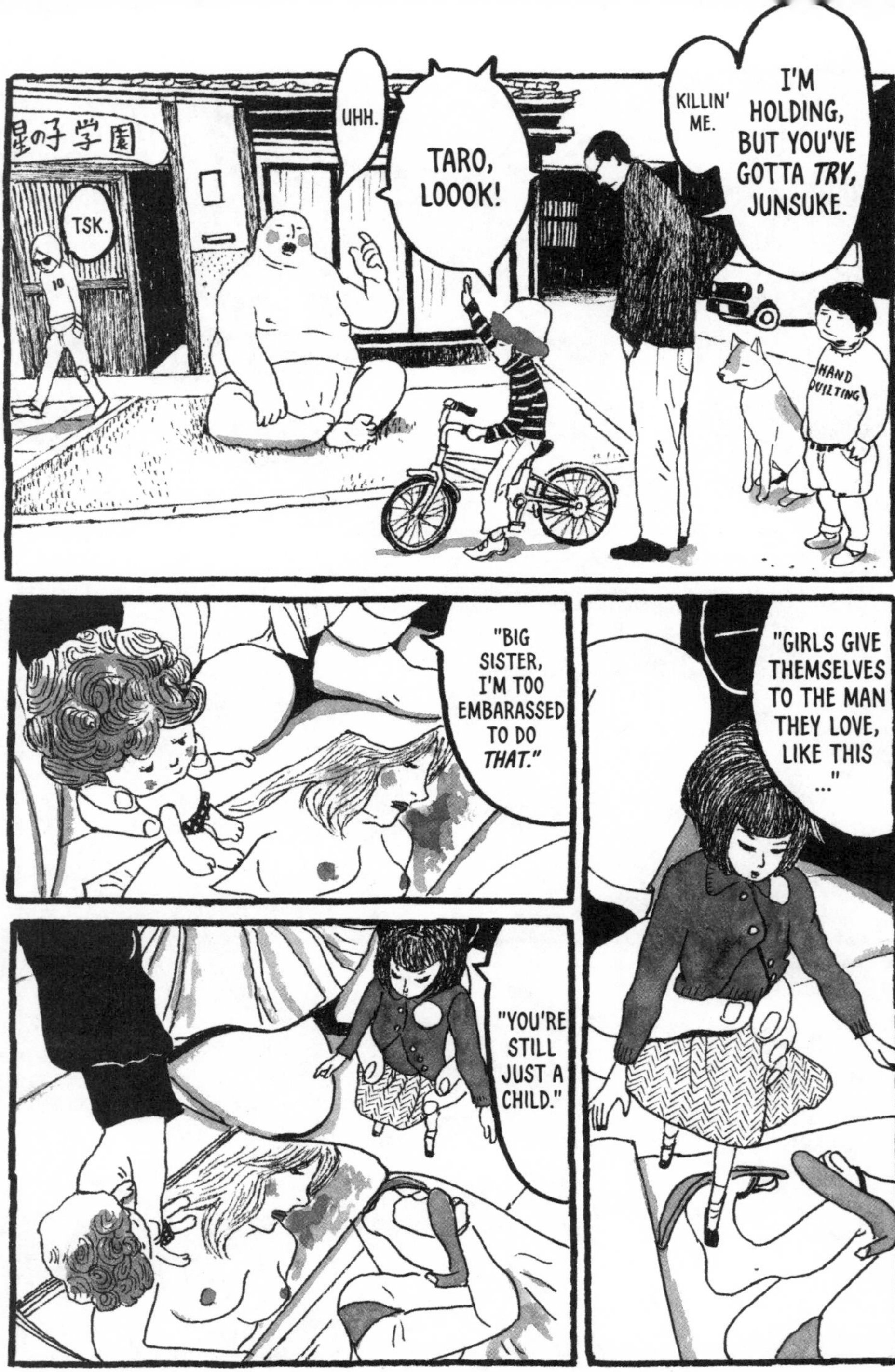
I'M HOLDING, BUT YOU'VE GOTTA *TRY*, JUNSUKE.
KILLIN' ME.
TARO, LOOOK!
UHH.
星の子学園
TSK.
"GIRLS GIVE THEMSELVES TO THE MAN THEY LOVE, LIKE THIS ..."
"BIG SISTER, I'M TOO EMBARASSED TO DO *THAT*."
"YOU'RE STILL JUST A CHILD."

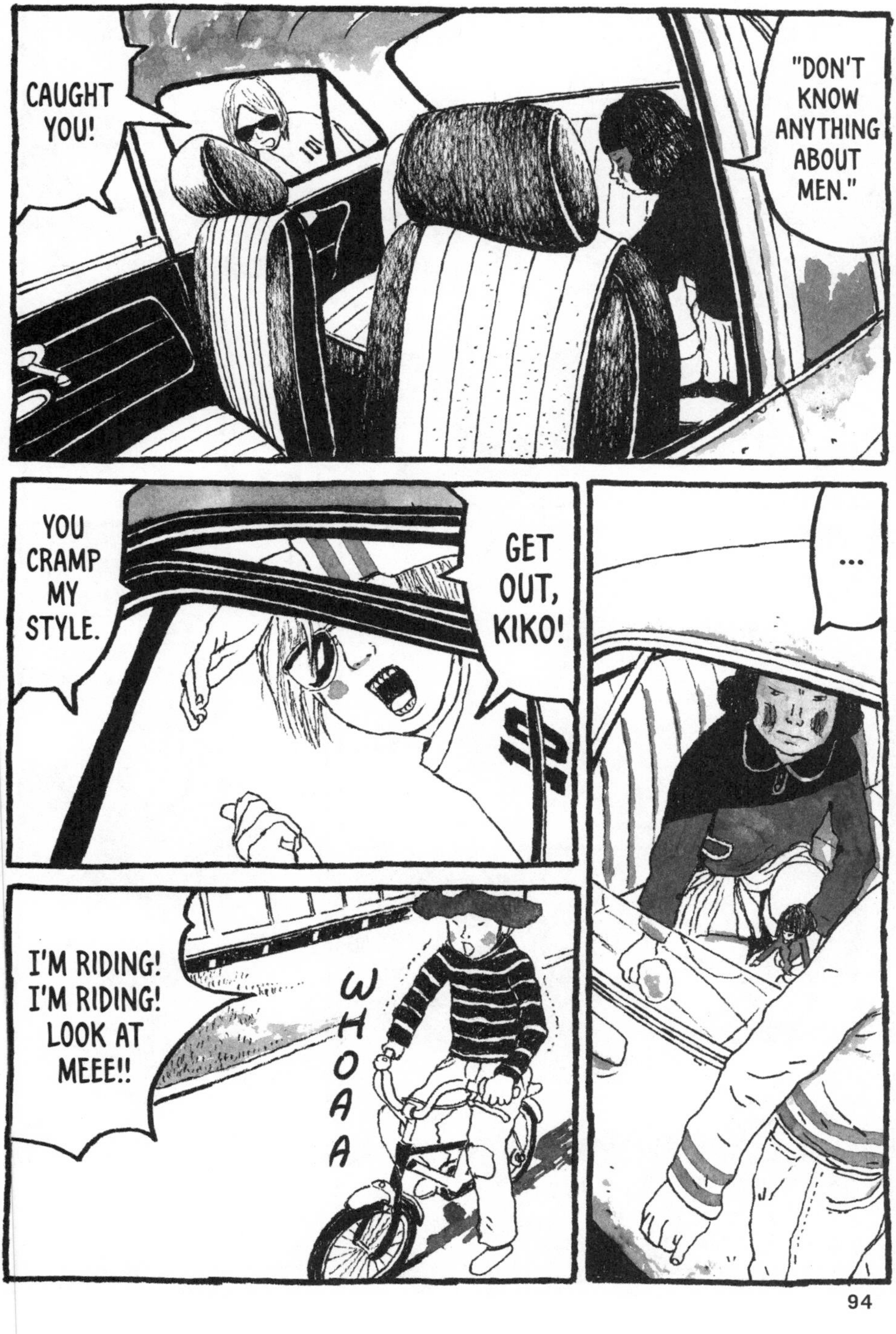
"DON'T KNOW ANYTHING ABOUT MEN."
CAUGHT YOU!
...
GET OUT, KIKO!
YOU CRAMP MY STYLE.
WHOAAA
I'M RIDING! I'M RIDING! LOOK AT MEEE!!

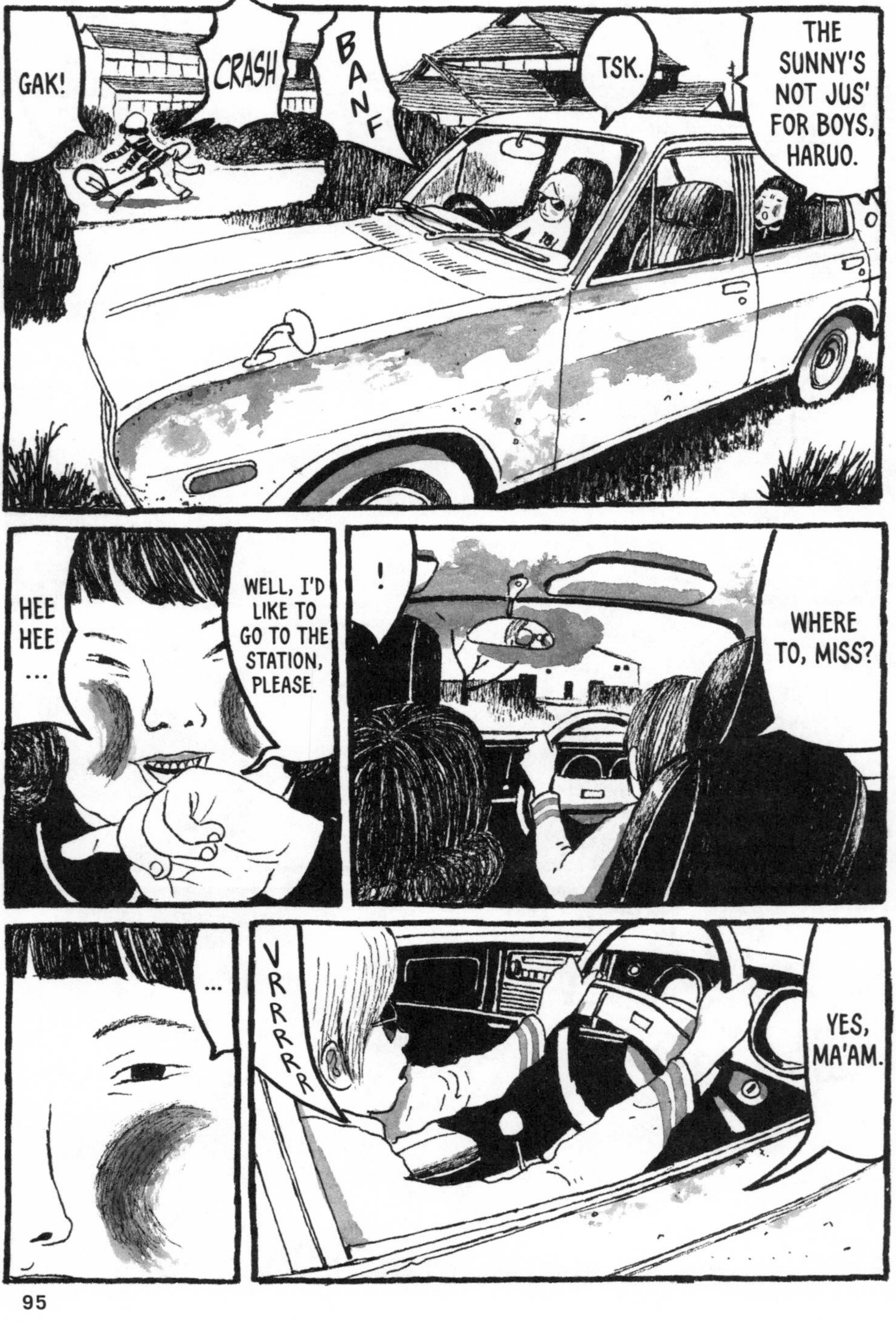
THE SUNNY'S NOT JUS' FOR BOYS, HARUO.
TSK.
BANF
CRASH
GAK!
WHERE TO, MISS?
!
WELL, I'D LIKE TO GO TO THE STATION, PLEASE.
HEE HEE ...
YES, MA'AM.
VRRRRR
...

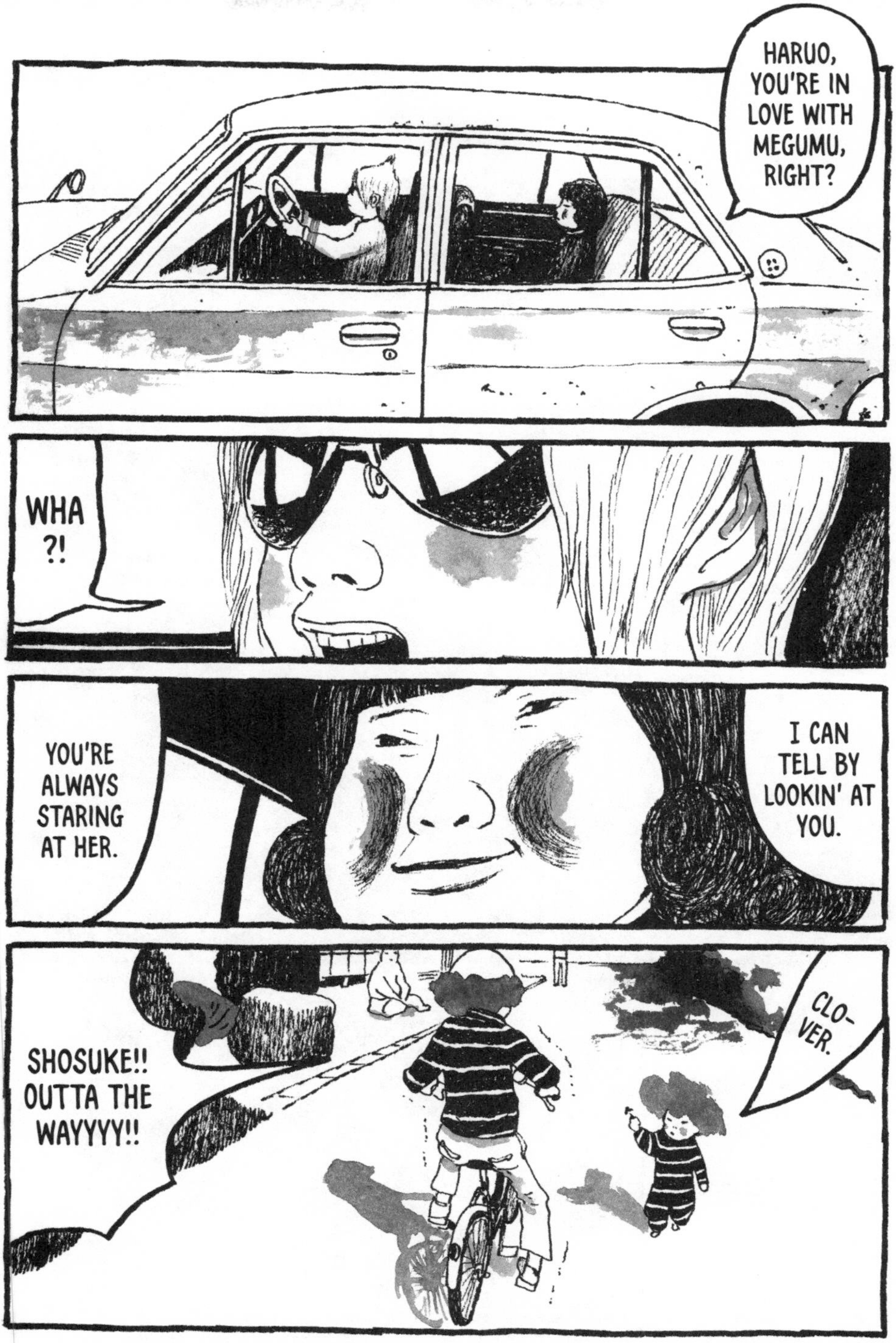
HARUO, YOU'RE IN LOVE WITH MEGUMU, RIGHT?
WHA ?!
I CAN TELL BY LOOKIN' AT YOU.
YOU'RE ALWAYS STARING AT HER.
CLO-VER.
SHOSUKE!! OUTTA THE WAYYYY!!

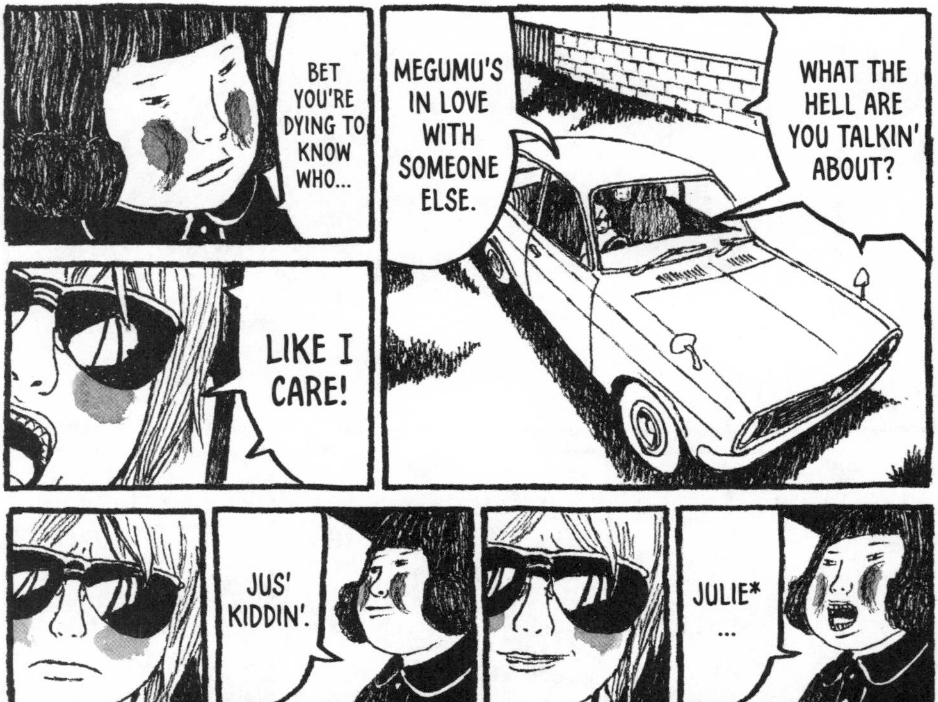
BET YOU'RE DYING TO KNOW WHO...
MEGUMU'S IN LOVE WITH SOMEONE ELSE.
WHAT THE HELL ARE YOU TALKIN' ABOUT?
LIKE I CARE!
...
JUS' KIDDIN'.
TSK.
JULIE* ...

*Nickname of entertainer and former teen idol Kenji Sawada

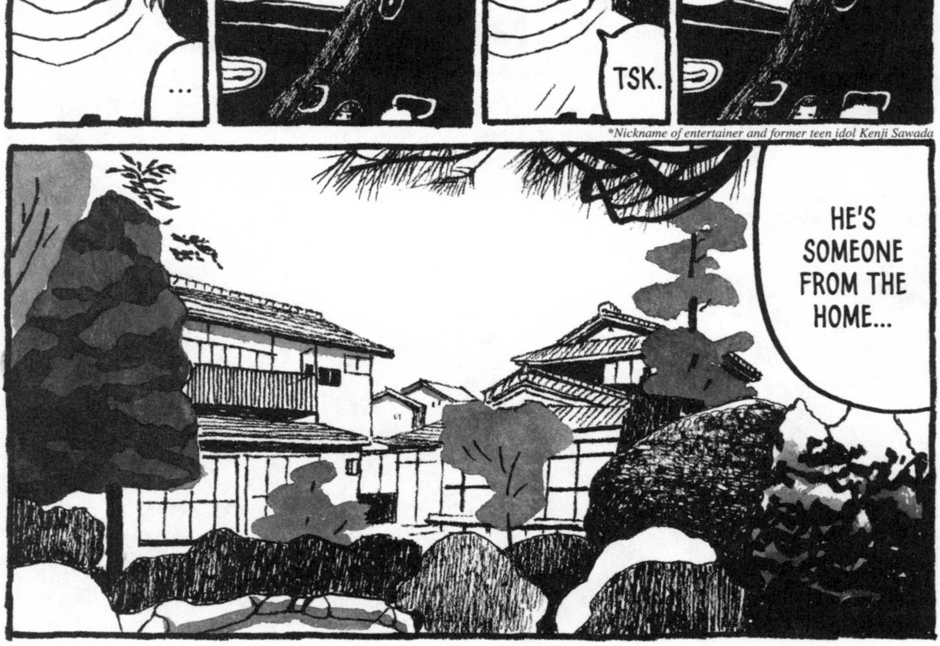
HE'S SOMEONE FROM THE HOME...

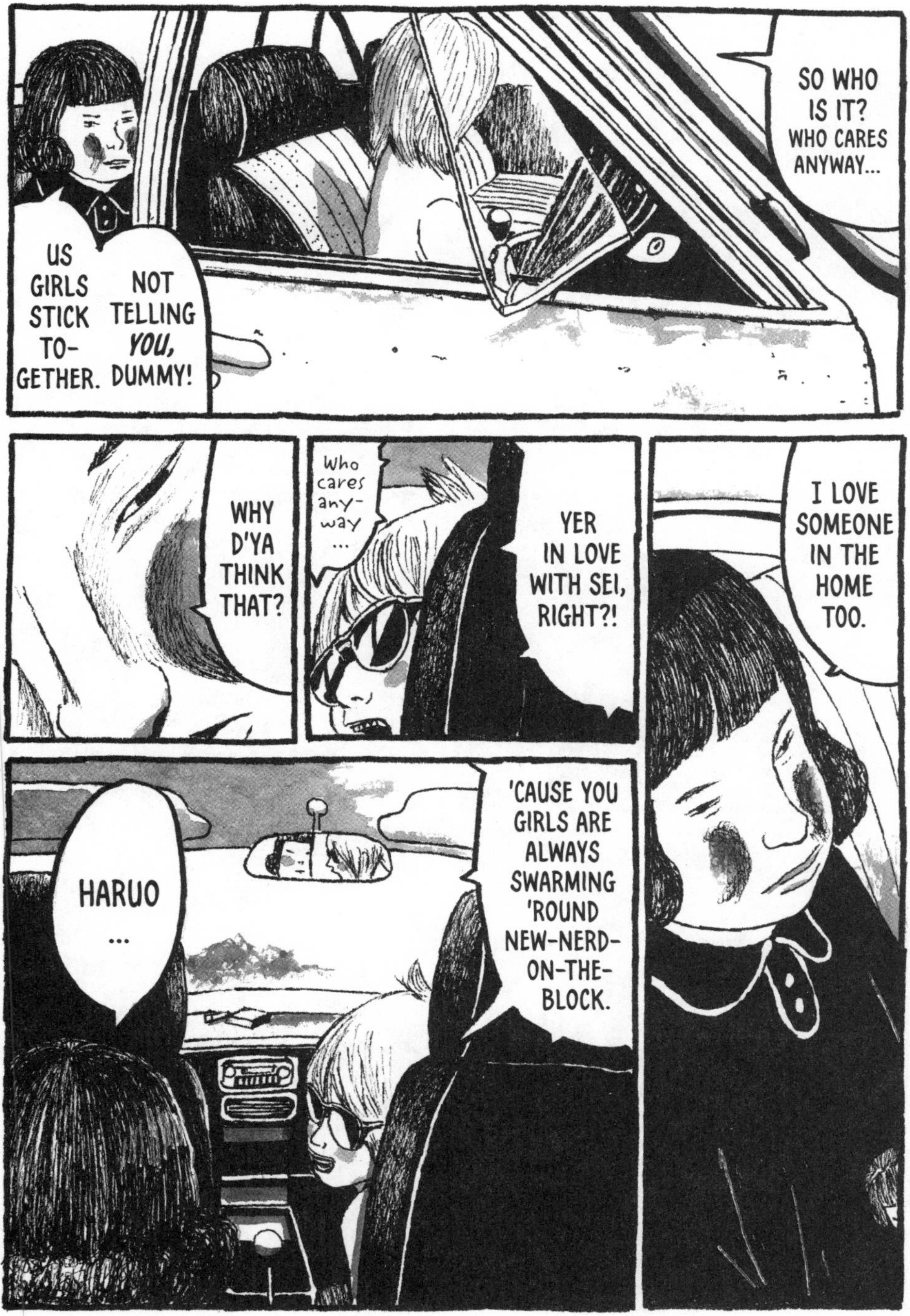
SO WHO IS IT? WHO CARES ANYWAY...
NOT TELLING *YOU*, DUMMY!
US GIRLS STICK TO-GETHER.
I LOVE SOMEONE IN THE HOME TOO.
YER IN LOVE WITH SEI, RIGHT?!
Who cares any-way ...
WHY D'YA THINK THAT?
'CAUSE YOU GIRLS ARE ALWAYS SWARMING 'ROUND NEW-NERD-ON-THE-BLOCK.
HARUO ...

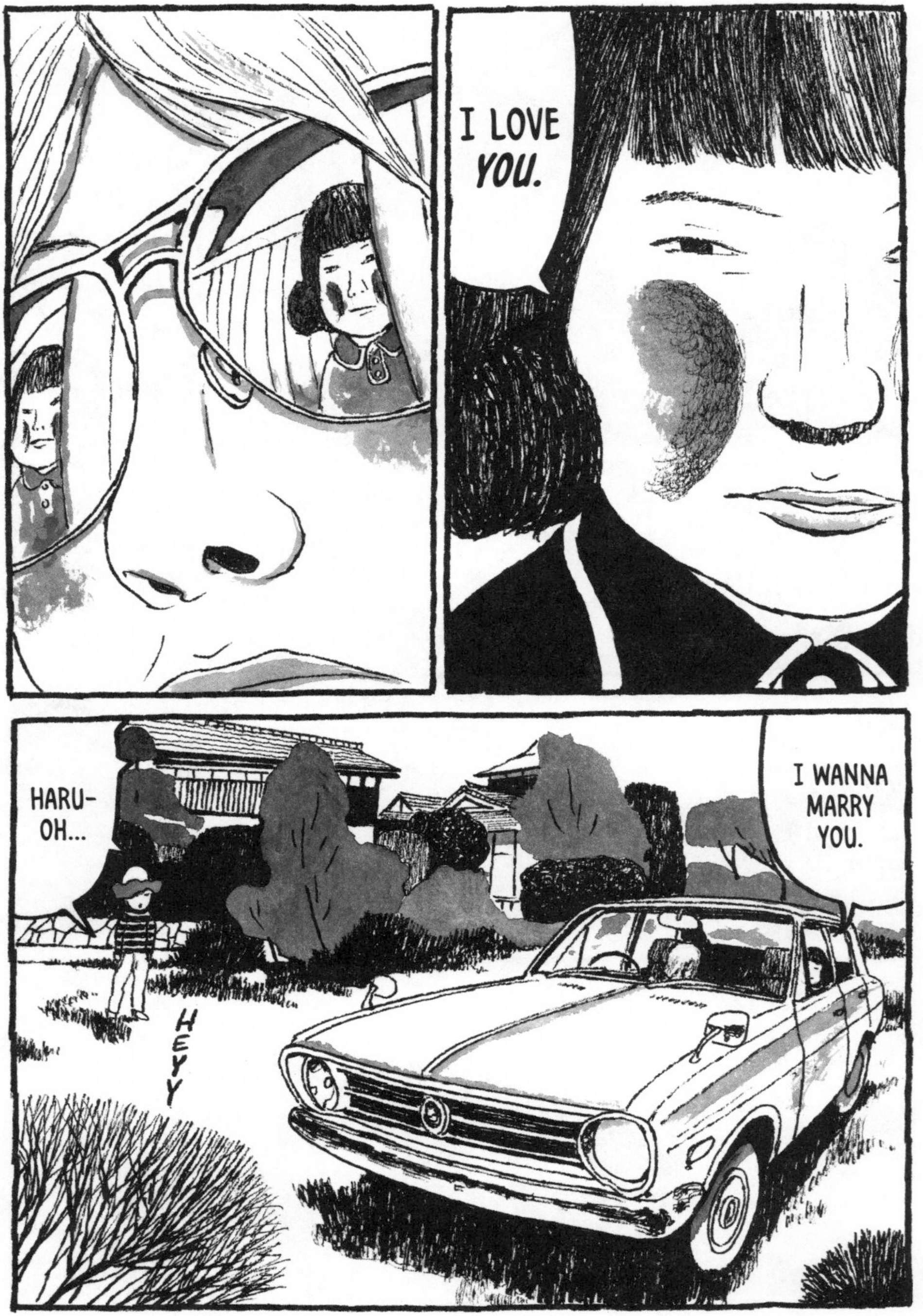
I LOVE *YOU.*
I WANNA MARRY YOU.
HARU-OH...
HEYY

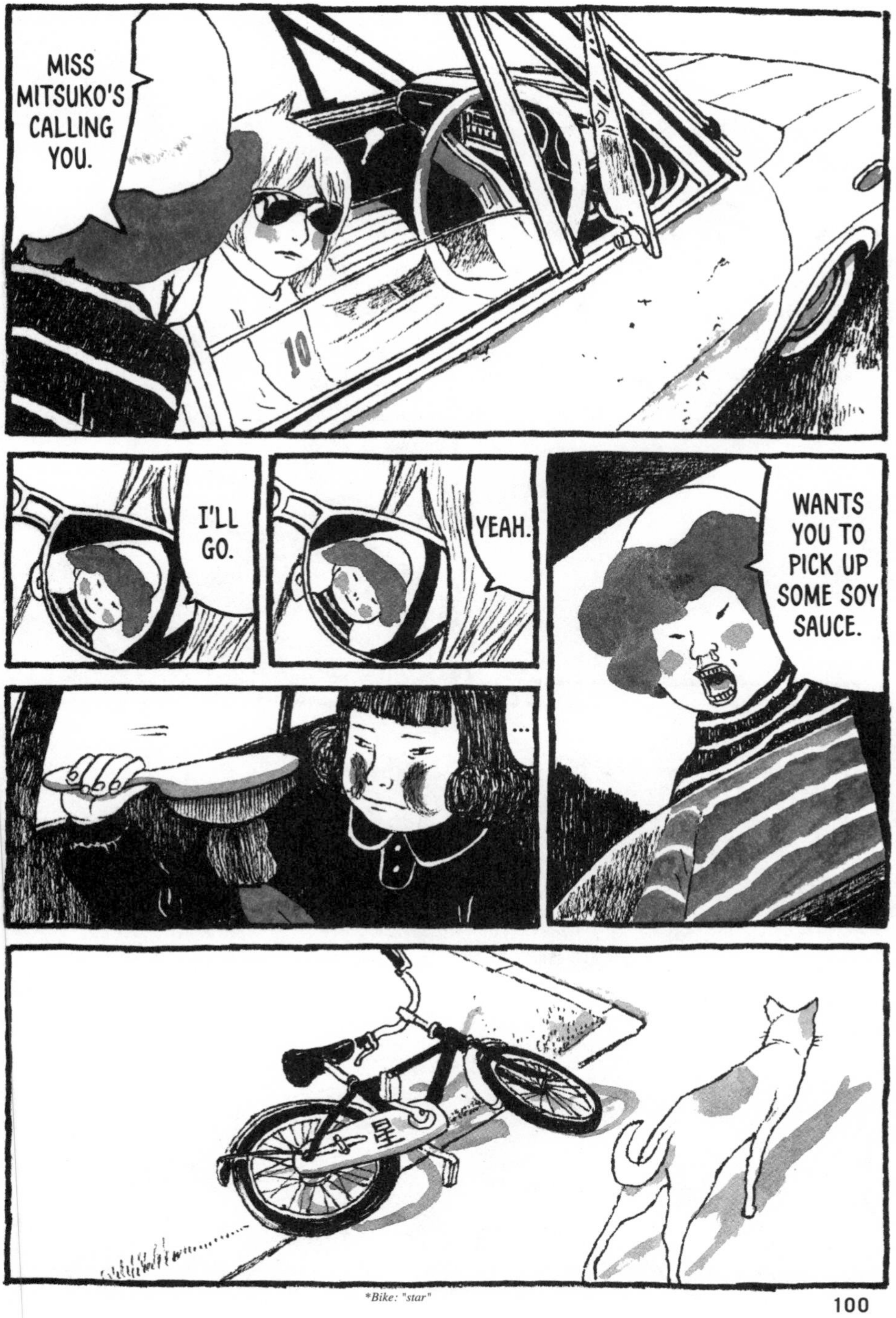
MISS MITSUKO'S CALLING YOU.
WANTS YOU TO PICK UP SOME SOY SAUCE.
YEAH.
I'LL GO.
...
星

*Bike: "star"

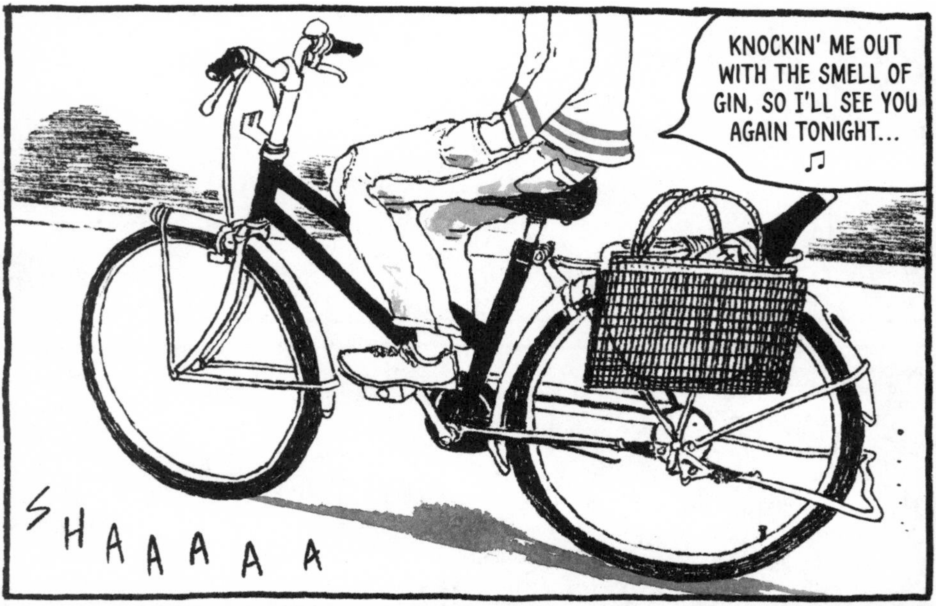
KNOCKIN' ME OUT WITH THE SMELL OF GIN, SO I'LL SEE YOU AGAIN TONIGHT... ♫
SHAAAAA
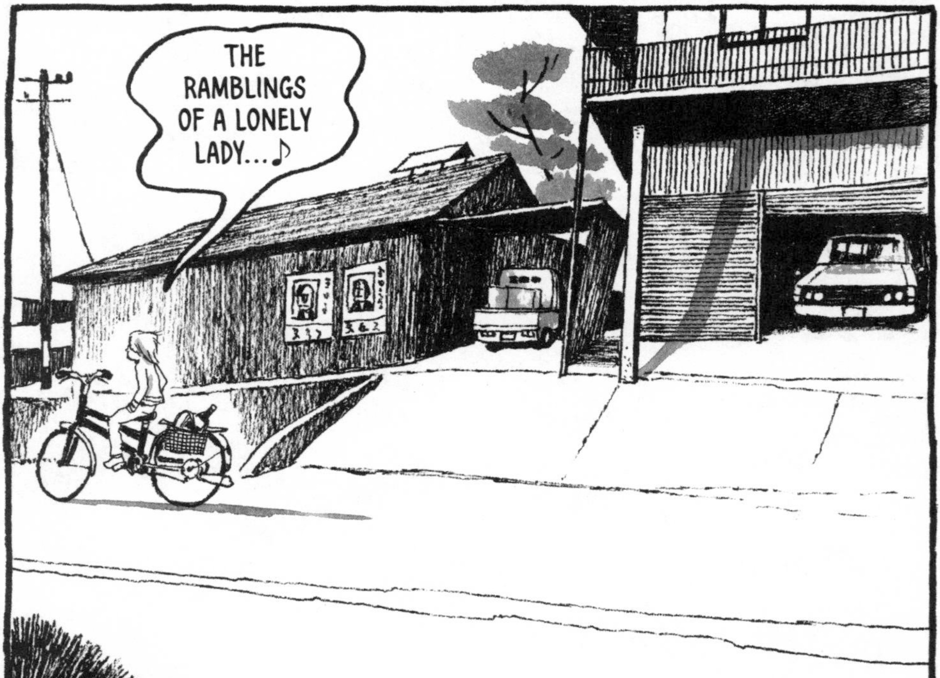
THE RAMBLINGS OF A LONELY LADY...♪

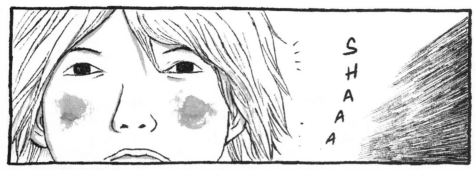

SHAAA

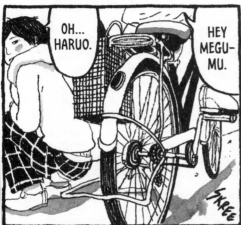

OH... HARUO.

HEY MEGU-MU.

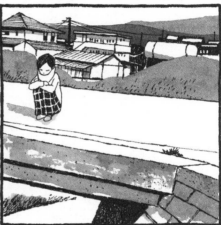

SKREE

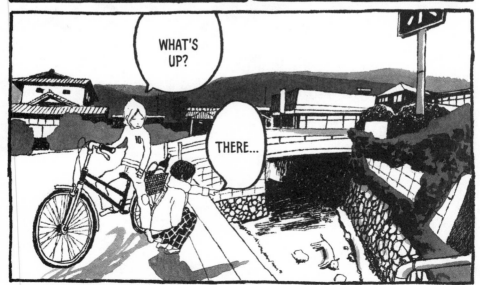

WHAT'S UP?

THERE...

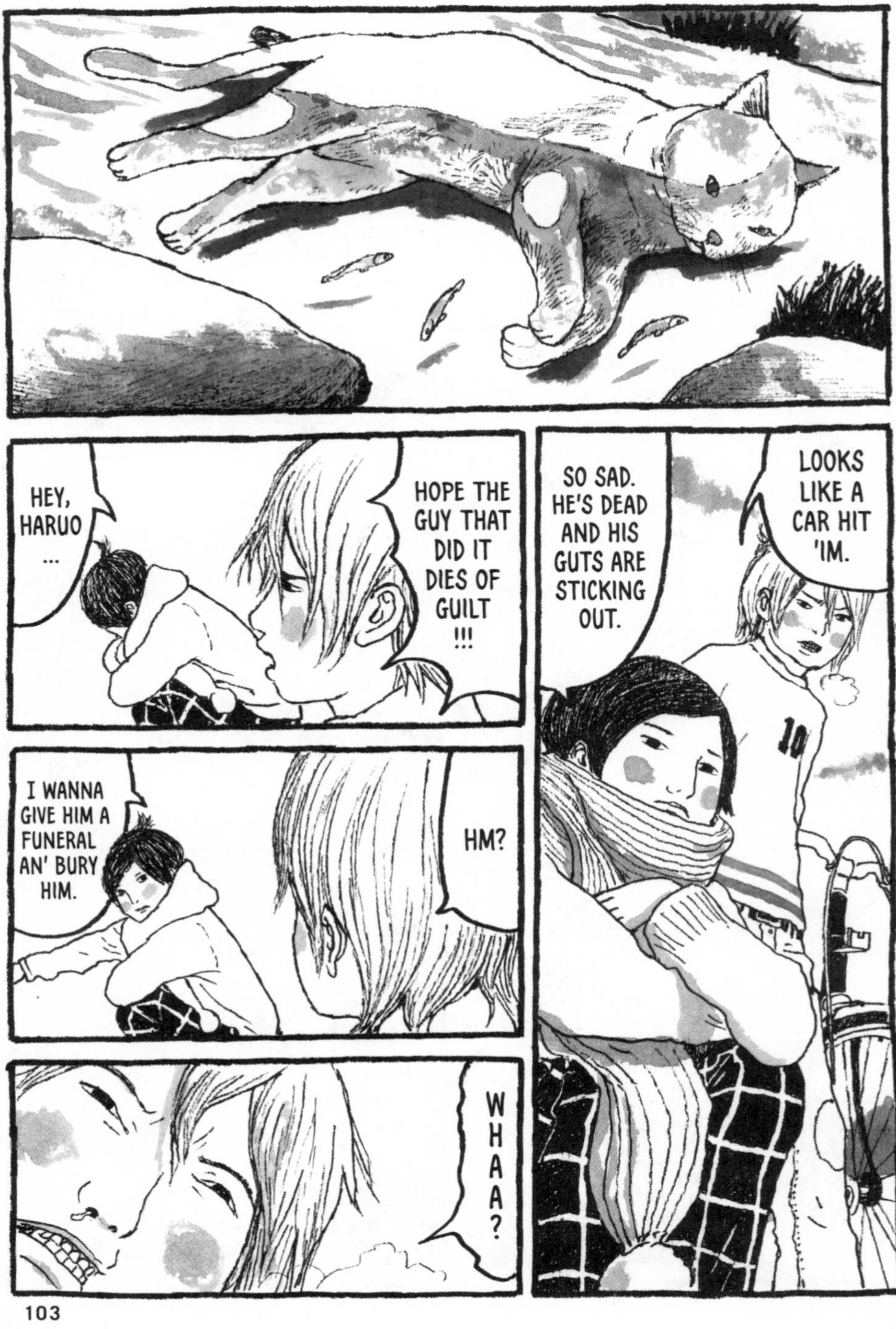
LOOKS LIKE A CAR HIT 'IM.
SO SAD. HE'S DEAD AND HIS GUTS ARE STICKING OUT.
HOPE THE GUY THAT DID IT DIES OF GUILT !!!
HEY, HARUO ...
HM?
I WANNA GIVE HIM A FUNERAL AN' BURY HIM.
WHAAA?

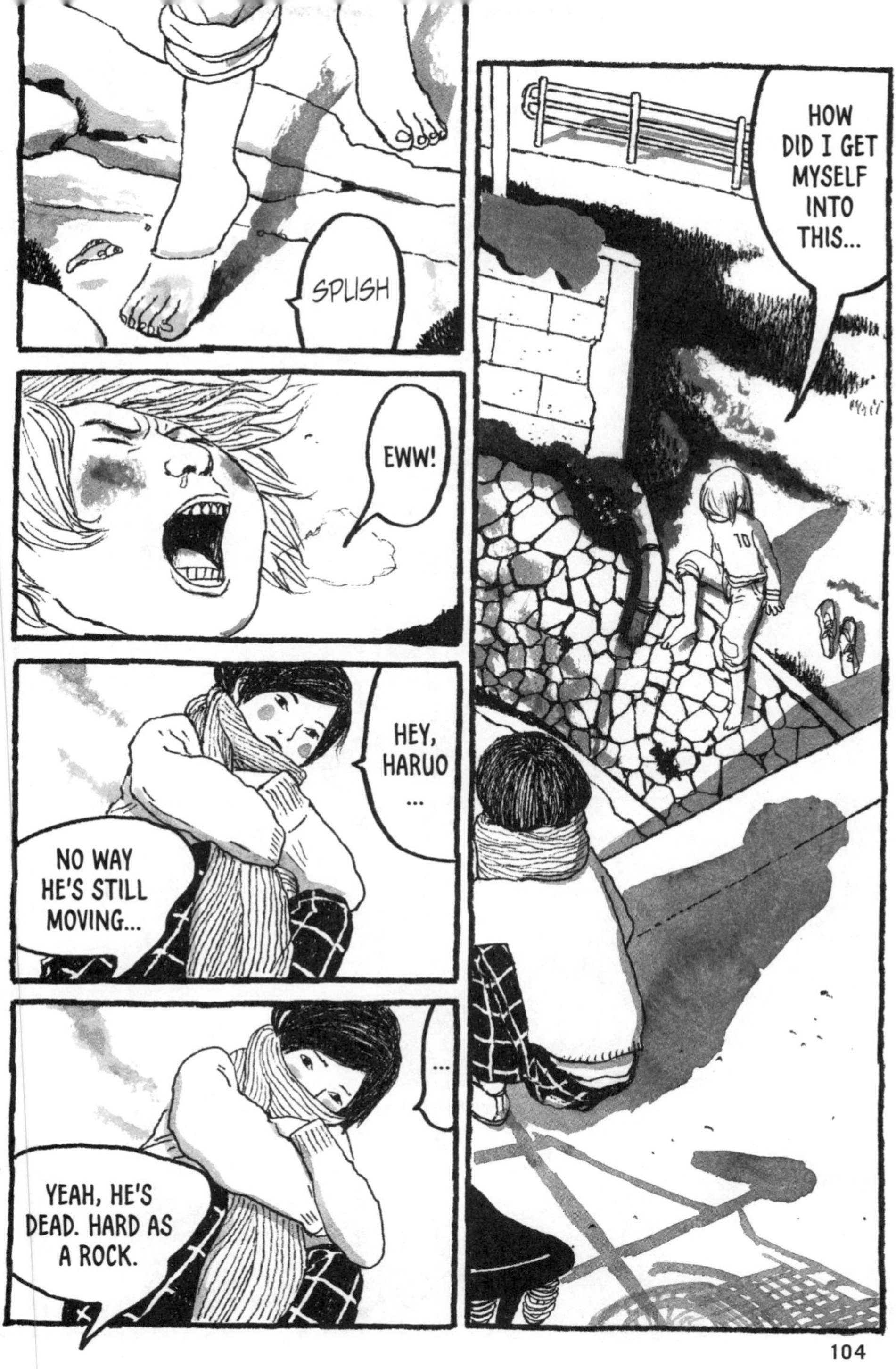
HOW DID I GET MYSELF INTO THIS...
SPLISH
EWW!
HEY, HARUO ...
NO WAY HE'S STILL MOVING...
...
YEAH, HE'S DEAD. HARD AS A ROCK.

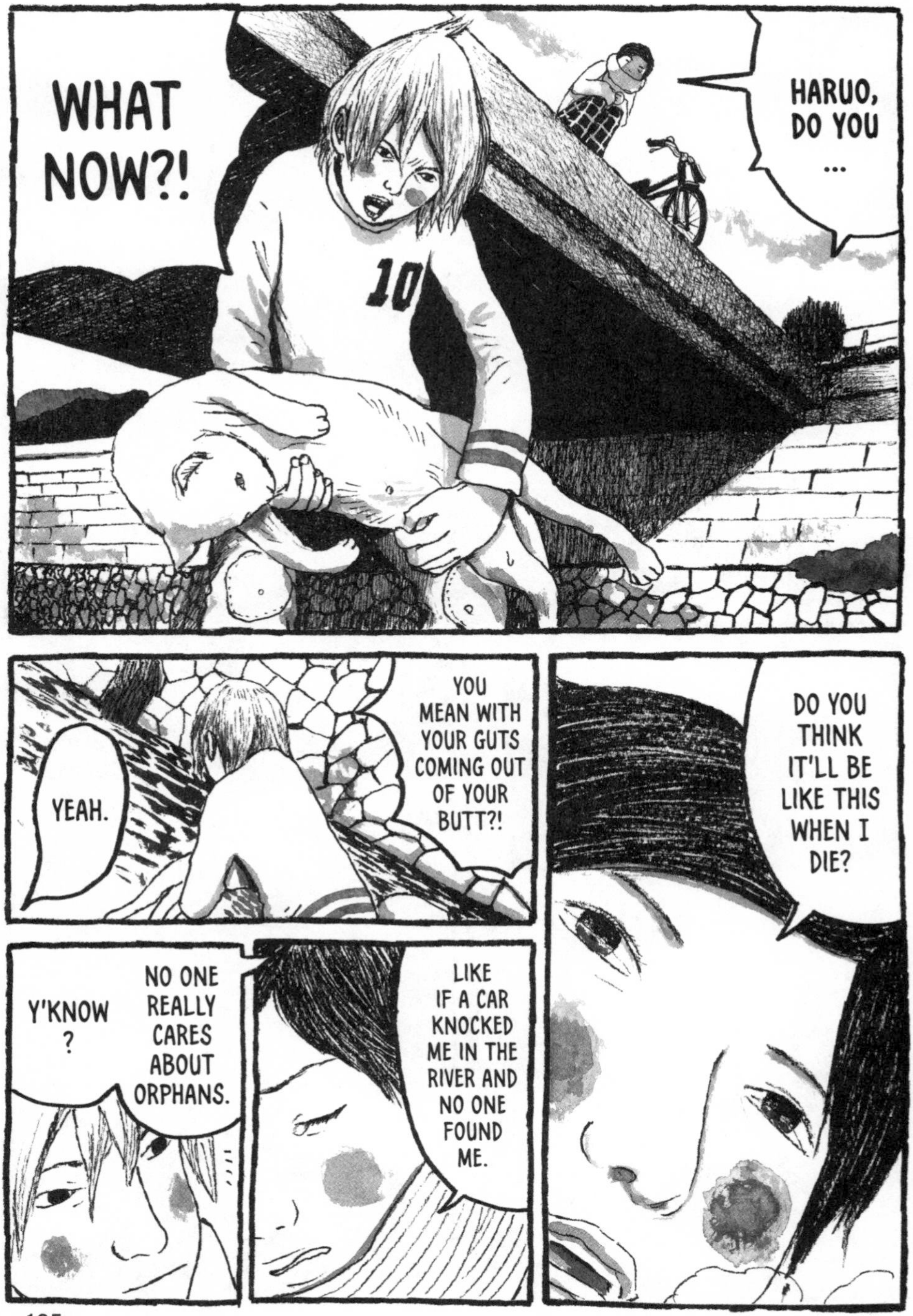
HARUO, DO YOU ...
WHAT NOW?!
DO YOU THINK IT'LL BE LIKE THIS WHEN I DIE?
YOU MEAN WITH YOUR GUTS COMING OUT OF YOUR BUTT?!
YEAH.
LIKE IF A CAR KNOCKED ME IN THE RIVER AND NO ONE FOUND ME.
NO ONE REALLY CARES ABOUT ORPHANS.
Y'KNOW ?

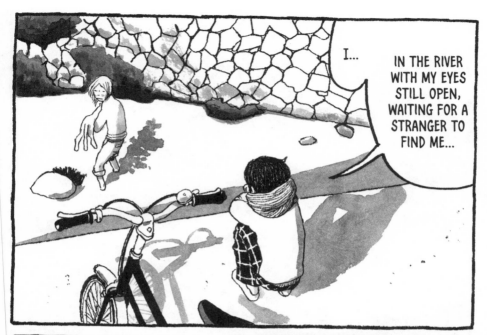

I...

IN THE RIVER WITH MY EYES STILL OPEN, WAITING FOR A STRANGER TO FIND ME...

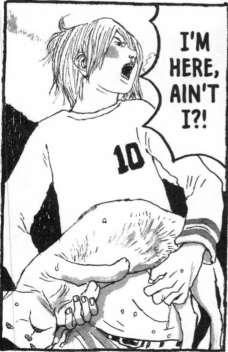

I'M HERE, AIN'T I?!

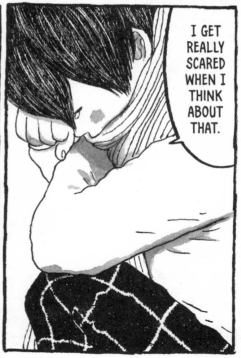

I GET REALLY SCARED WHEN I THINK ABOUT THAT.

106

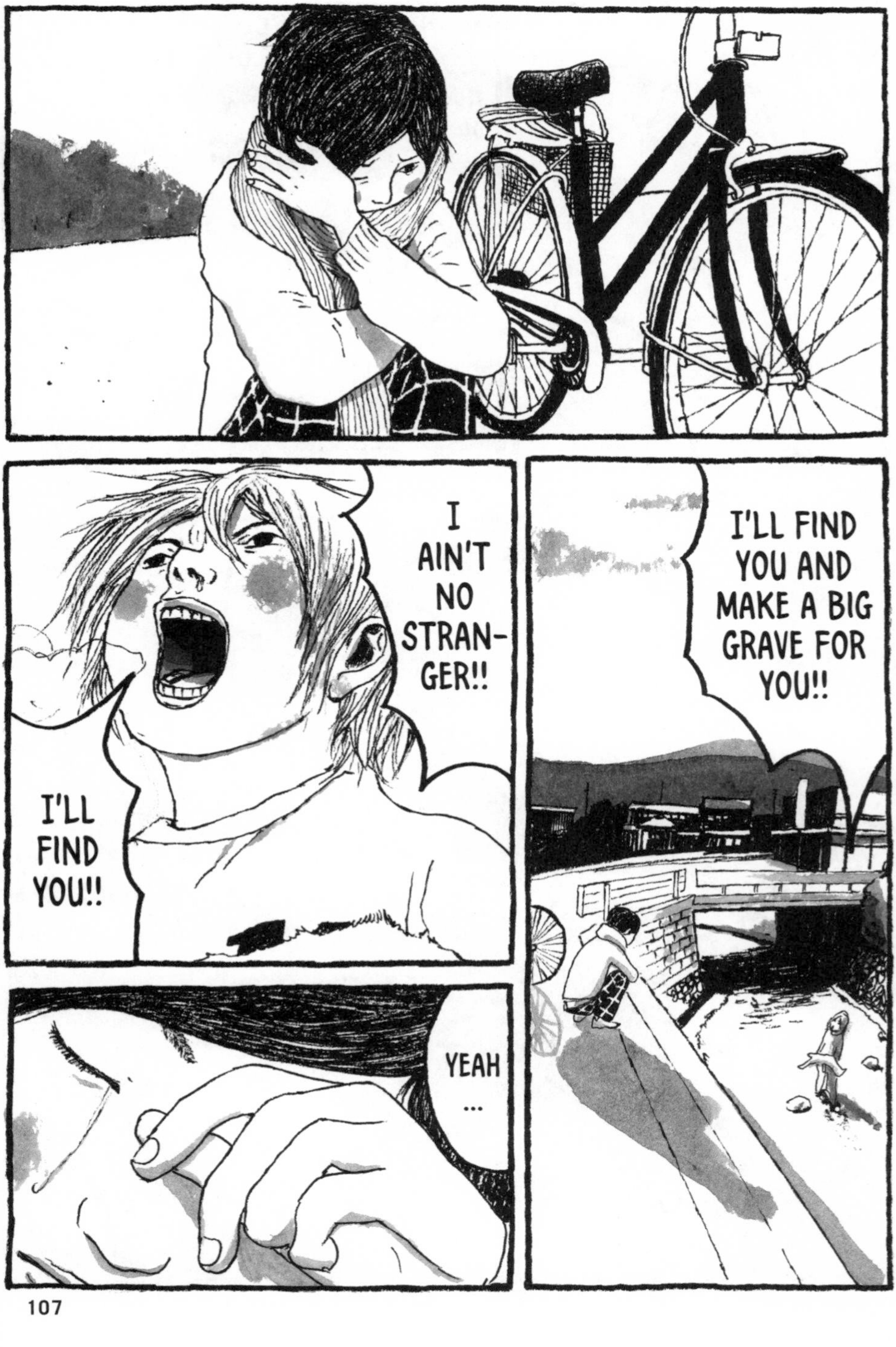
I'LL FIND YOU AND MAKE A BIG GRAVE FOR YOU!!
I AIN'T NO STRANGER!!
I'LL FIND YOU!!
YEAH ...

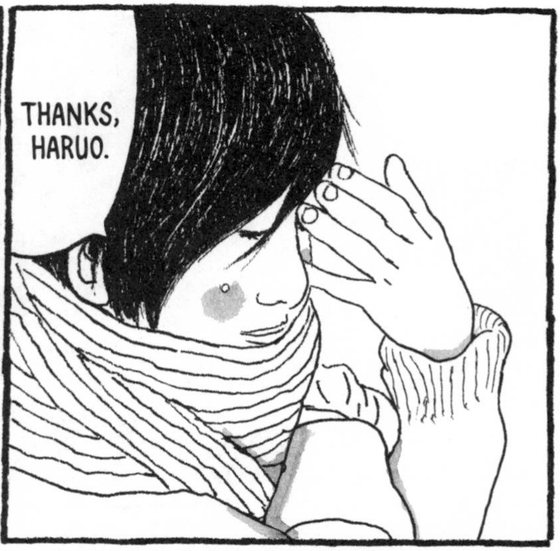
THANKS, HARUO.
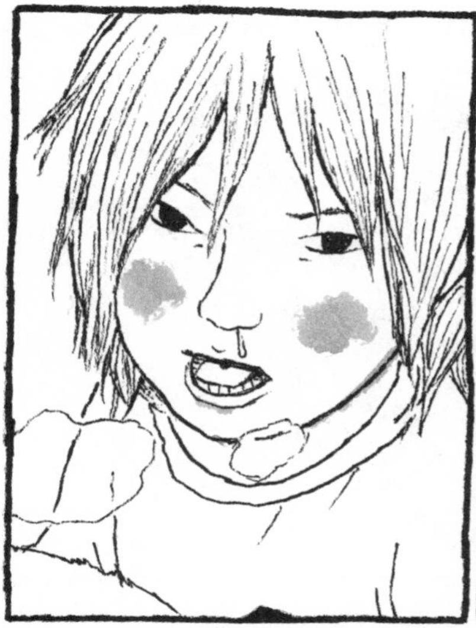
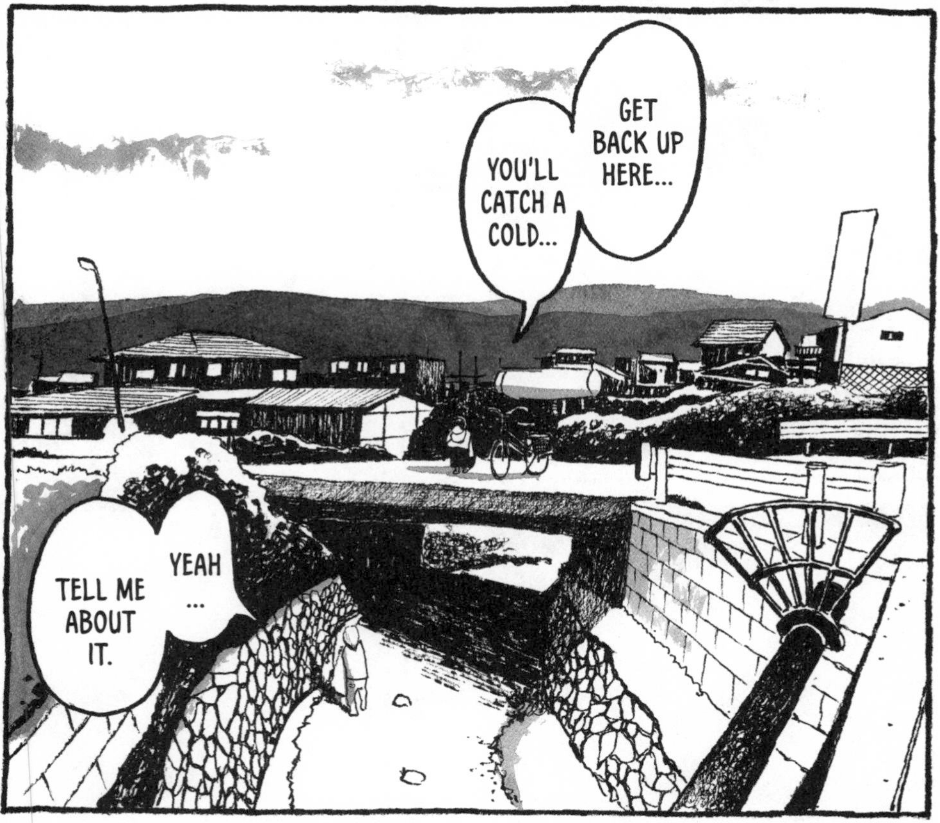
GET BACK UP HERE...
YOU'LL CATCH A COLD...
YEAH ...
TELL ME ABOUT IT.

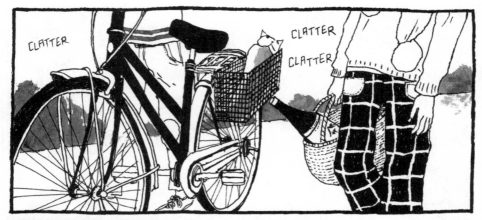

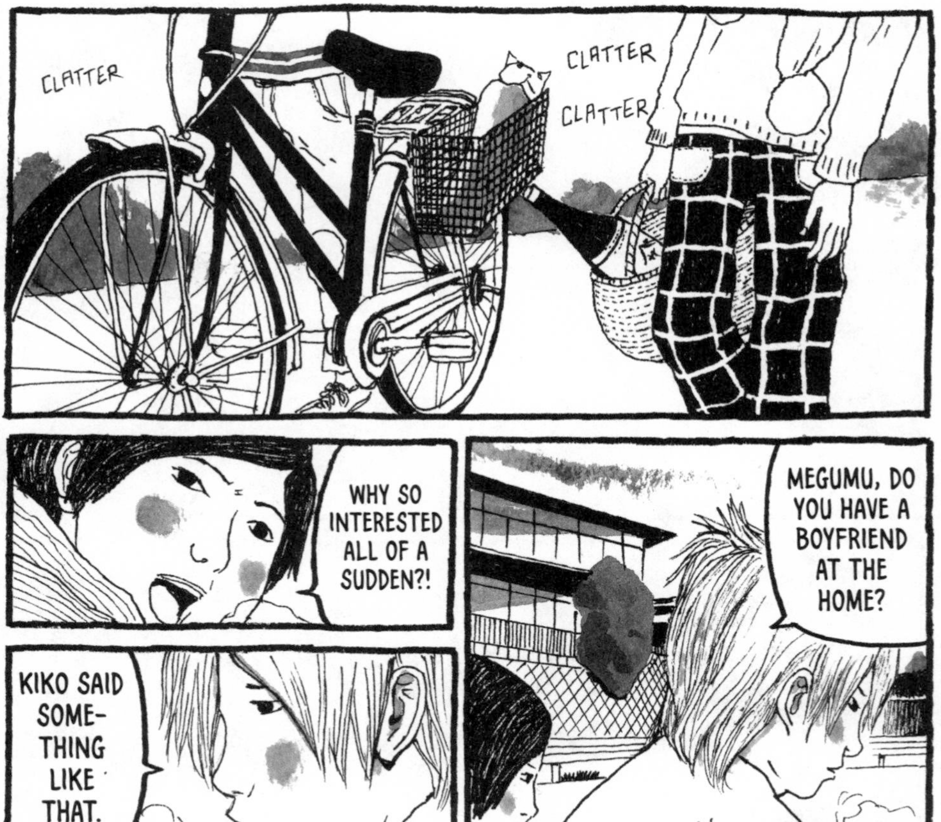

CLATTER
CLATTER
CLATTER
MEGUMU, DO YOU HAVE A BOYFRIEND AT THE HOME?
WHY SO INTERESTED ALL OF A SUDDEN?!
KIKO SAID SOMETHING LIKE THAT.
KIKO SAID *THAT?*
SHE'S A REAL BIG-MOUTH.
WELL, DO YOU?

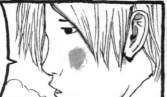

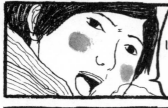

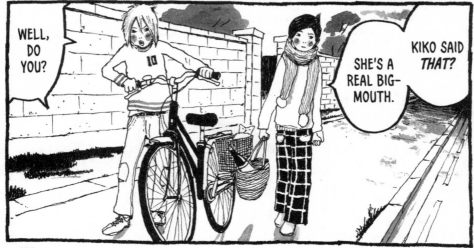

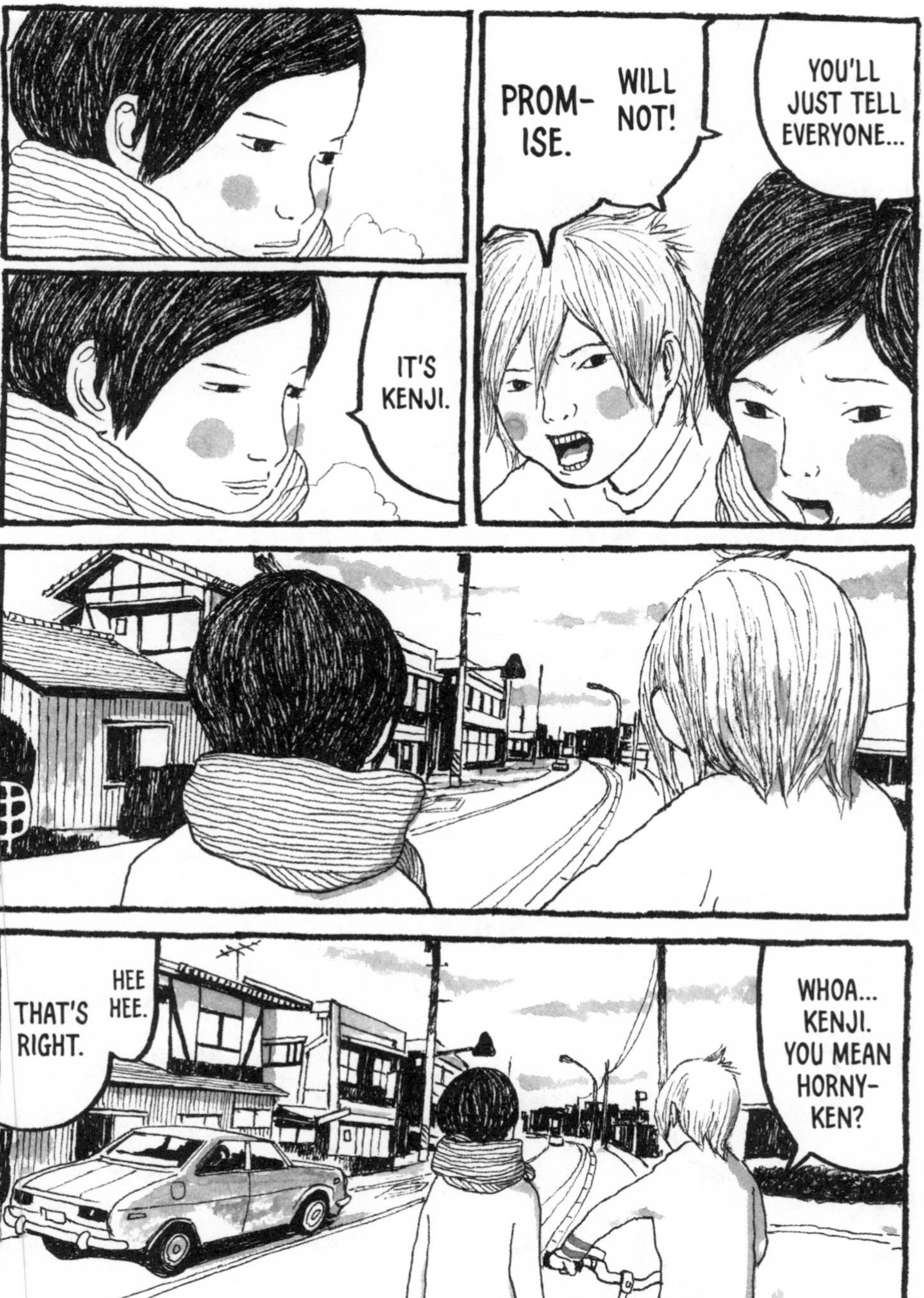
YOU'LL JUST TELL EVERYONE...
WILL NOT!
PROM-ISE.
IT'S KENJI.
WHOA... KENJI. YOU MEAN HORNY-KEN?
HEE HEE.
THAT'S RIGHT.

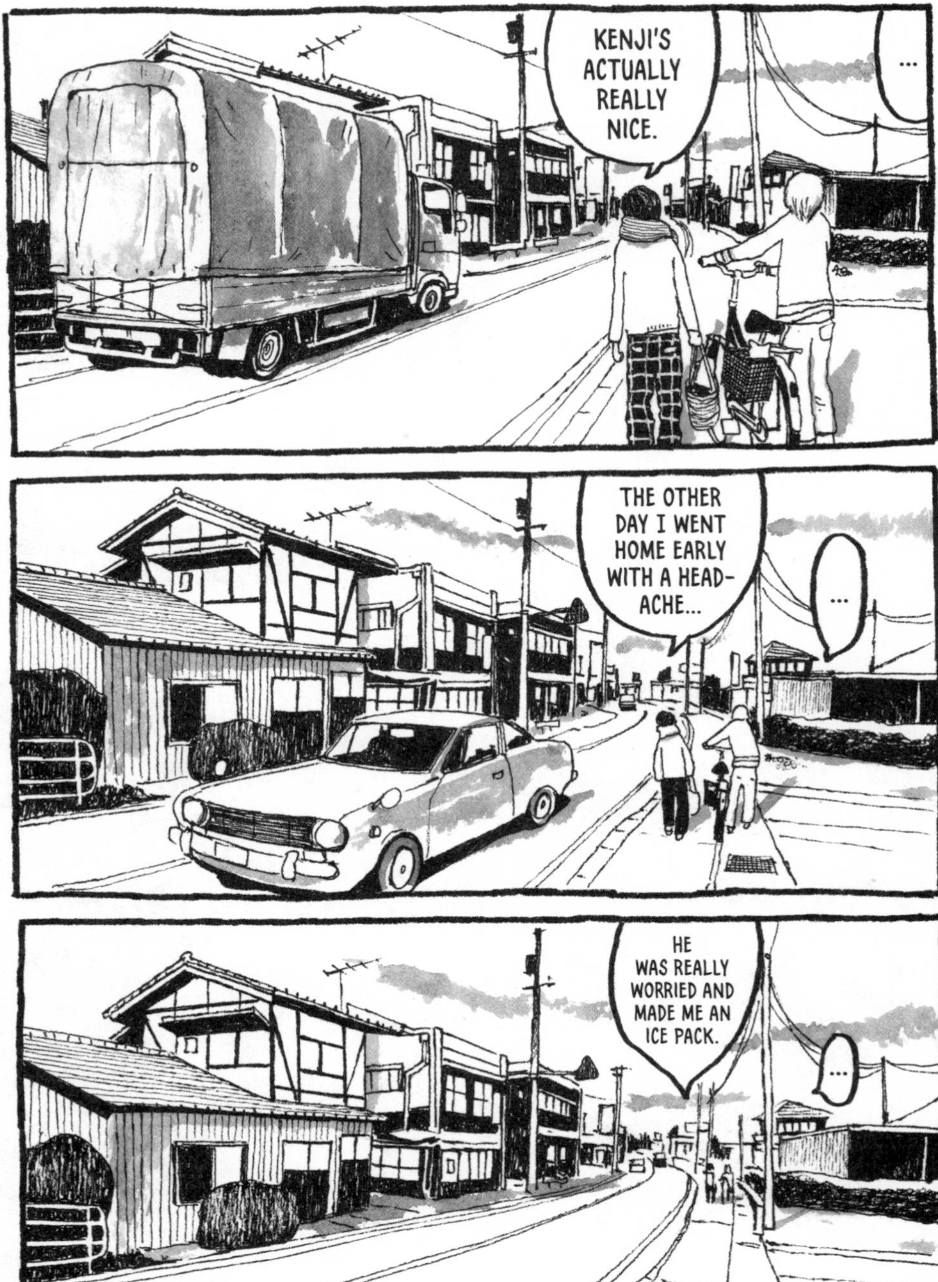
...
KENJI'S ACTUALLY REALLY NICE.
...
THE OTHER DAY I WENT HOME EARLY WITH A HEAD-ACHE...
...
HE WAS REALLY WORRIED AND MADE ME AN ICE PACK.

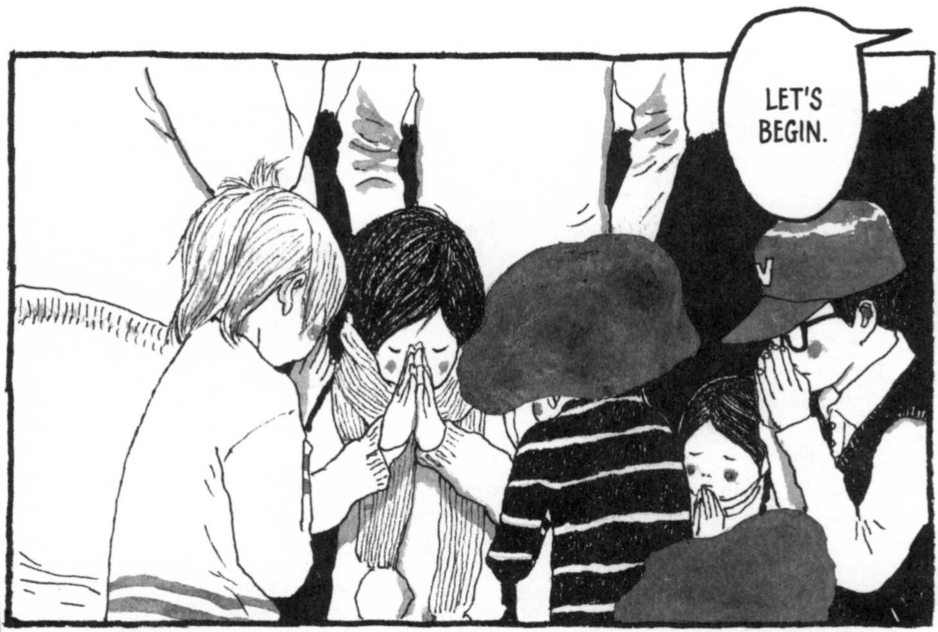
LET'S BEGIN.

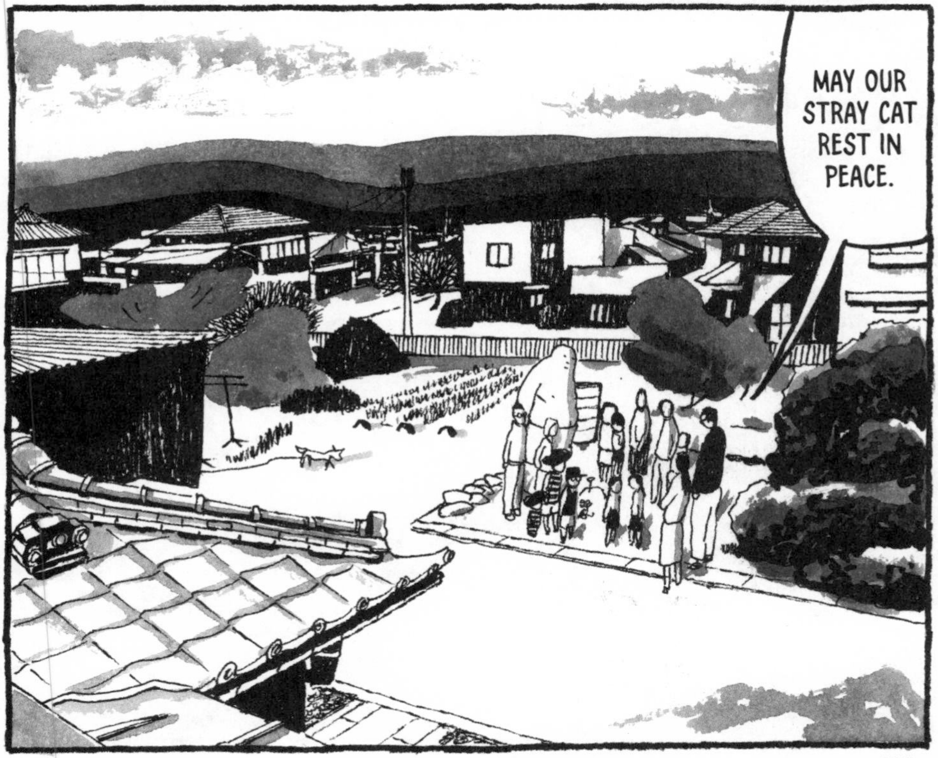
MAY OUR STRAY CAT REST IN PEACE.

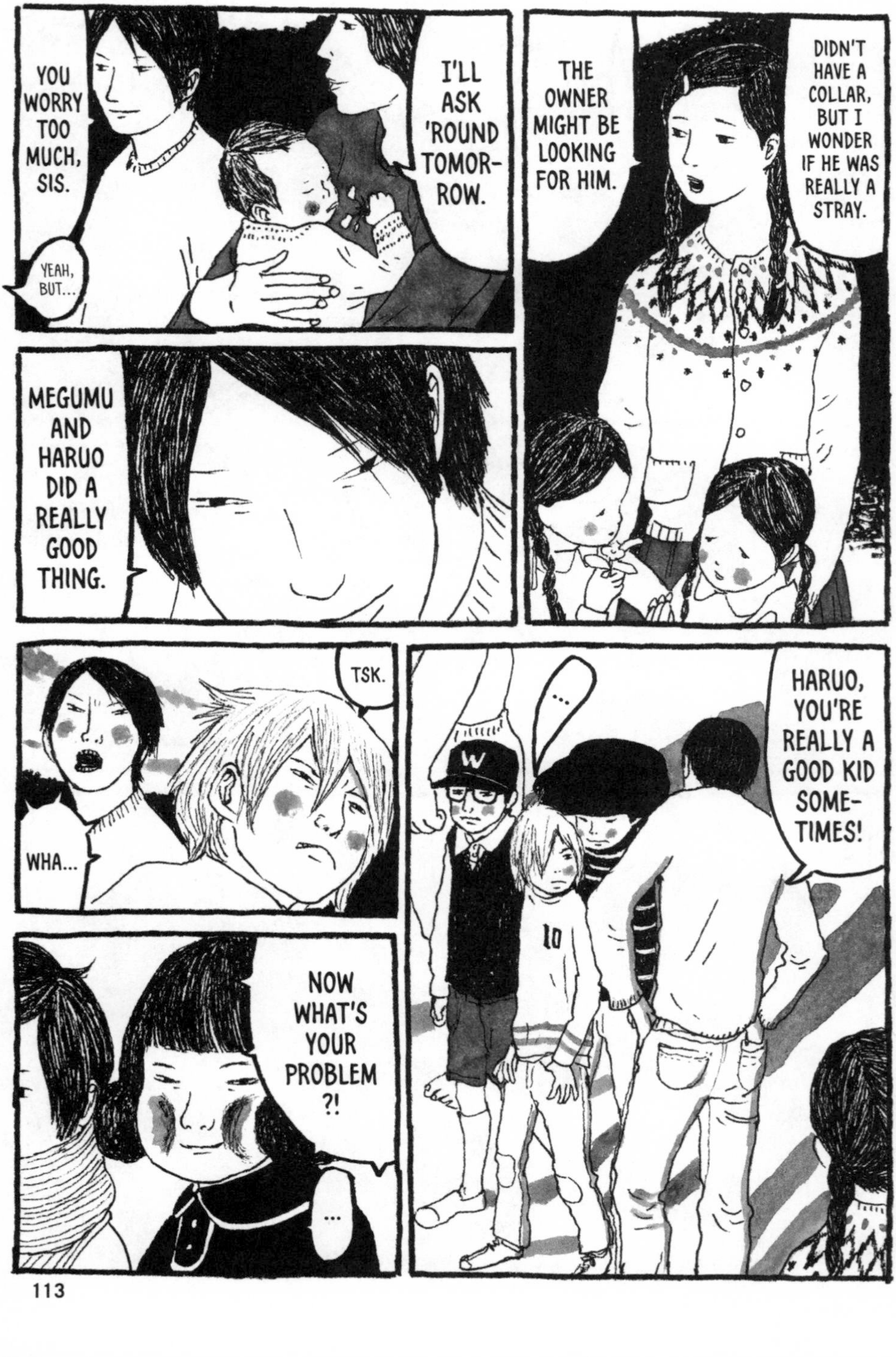
DIDN'T HAVE A COLLAR, BUT I WONDER IF HE WAS REALLY A STRAY.
THE OWNER MIGHT BE LOOKING FOR HIM.
I'LL ASK 'ROUND TOMORROW.
YOU WORRY TOO MUCH, SIS.
YEAH, BUT...
MEGUMU AND HARUO DID A REALLY GOOD THING.
HARUO, YOU'RE REALLY A GOOD KID SOMETIMES!
...
TSK.
WHA...
NOW WHAT'S YOUR PROBLEM?!
...

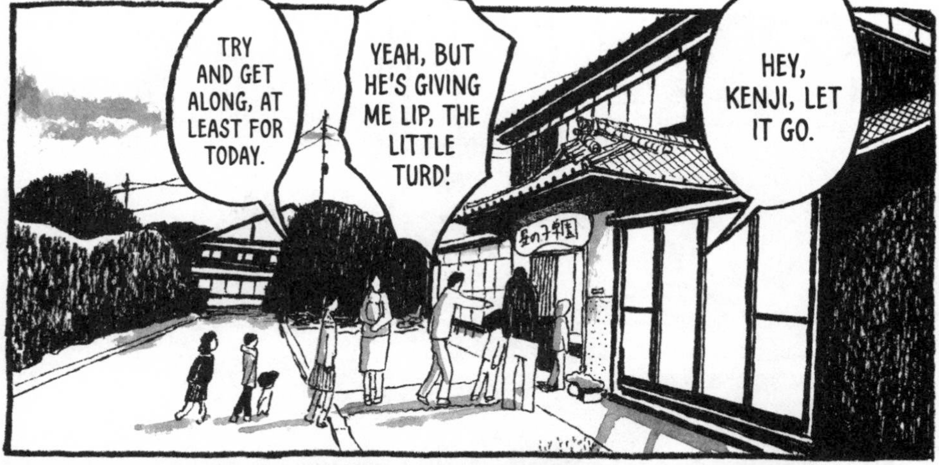
HEY, KENJI, LET IT GO.
YEAH, BUT HE'S GIVING ME LIP, THE LITTLE TURD!
TRY AND GET ALONG, AT LEAST FOR TODAY.
星の子学園

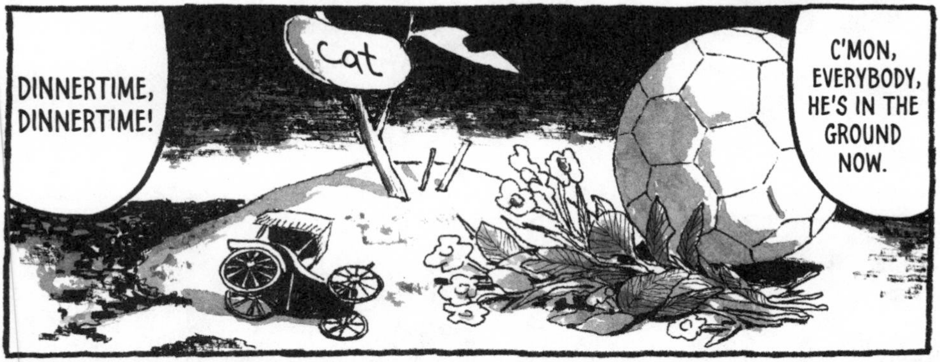
C'MON, EVERYBODY, HE'S IN THE GROUND NOW.
cat
DINNERTIME, DINNERTIME!

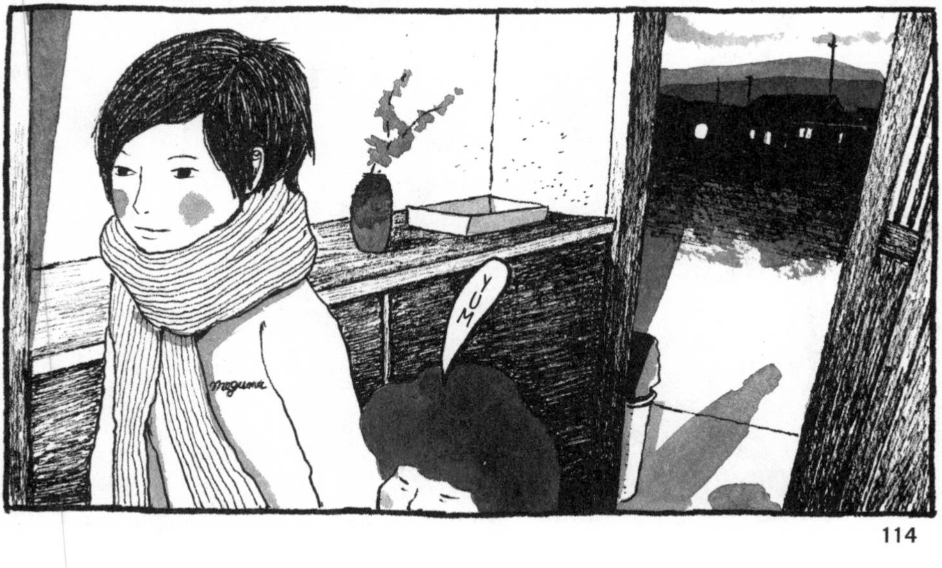
YUM

CHAPTER 4

"Whaddya wanna be when you grow up?"

"A spy and a racecar driver and a boxing champion."

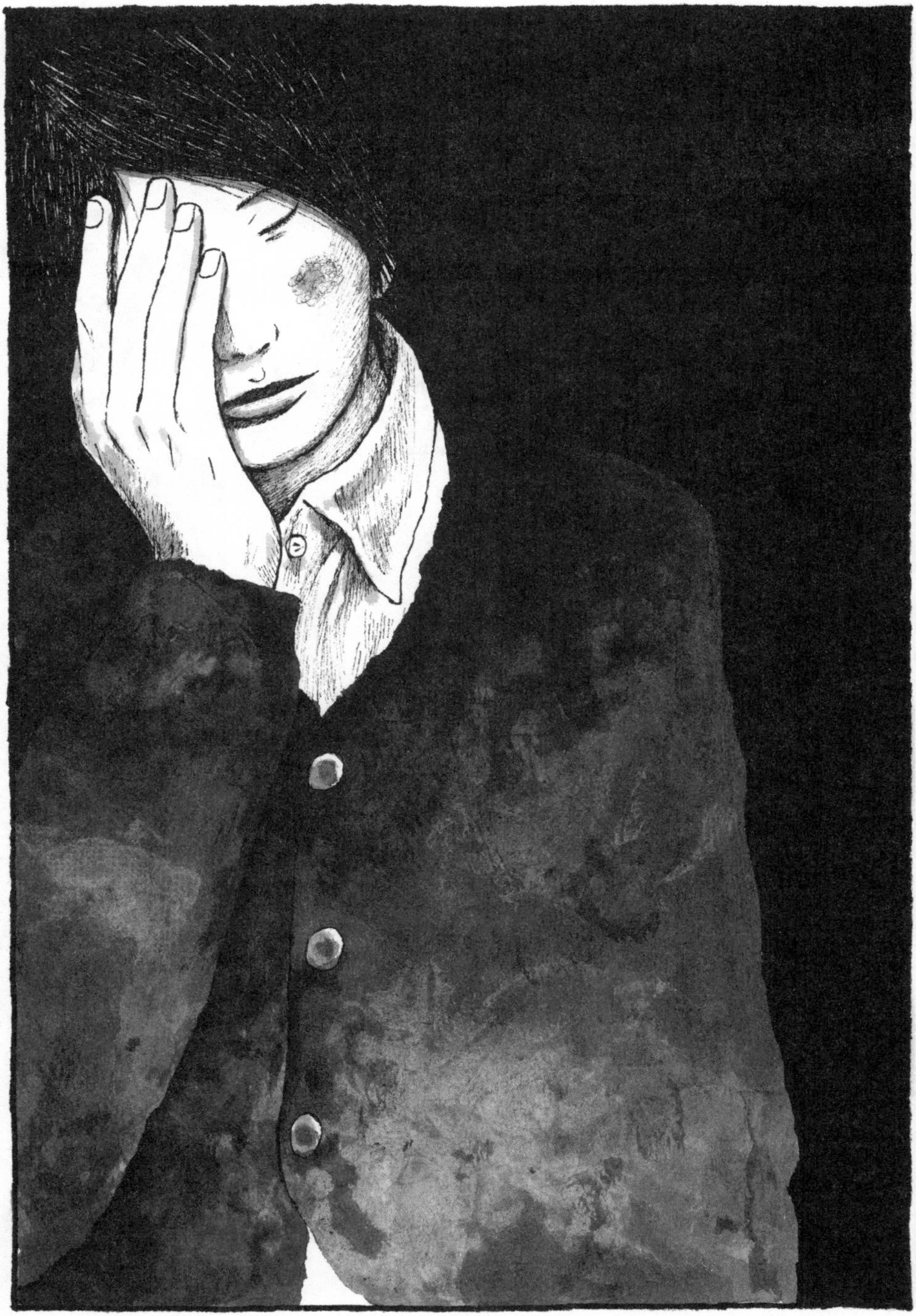

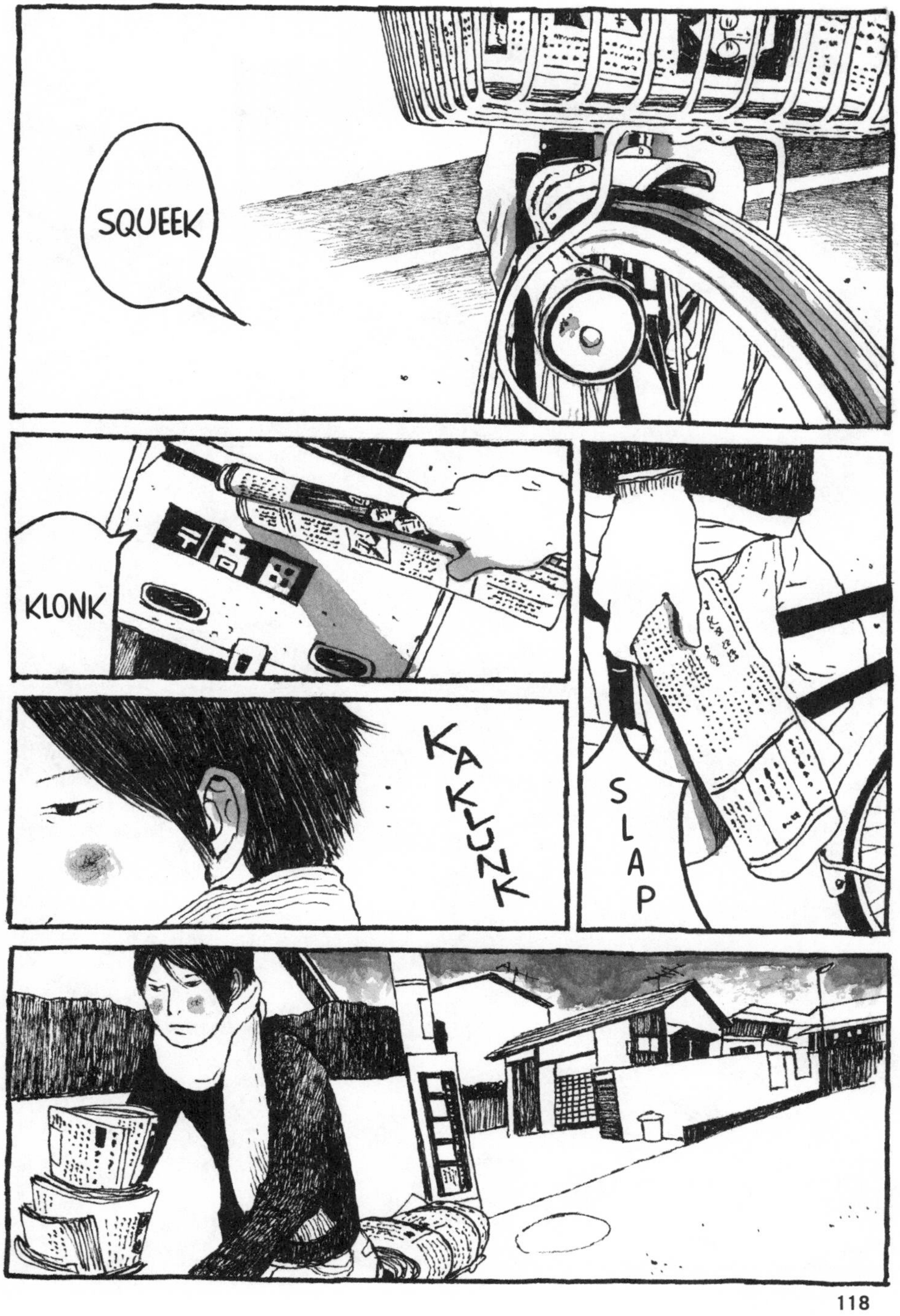
SQUEEK
SLAP
KLONK
KAKLUNK

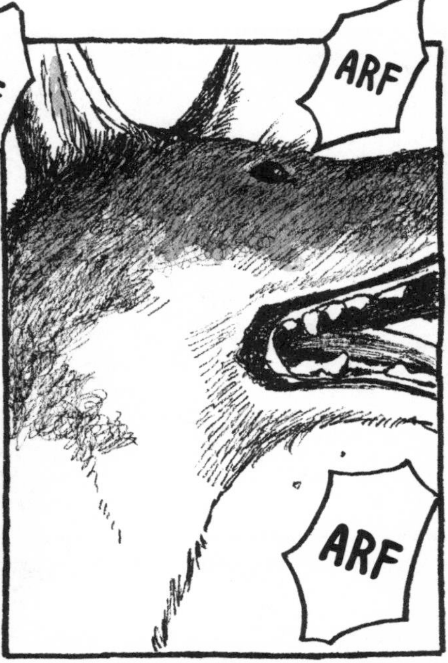
ARF
ARF
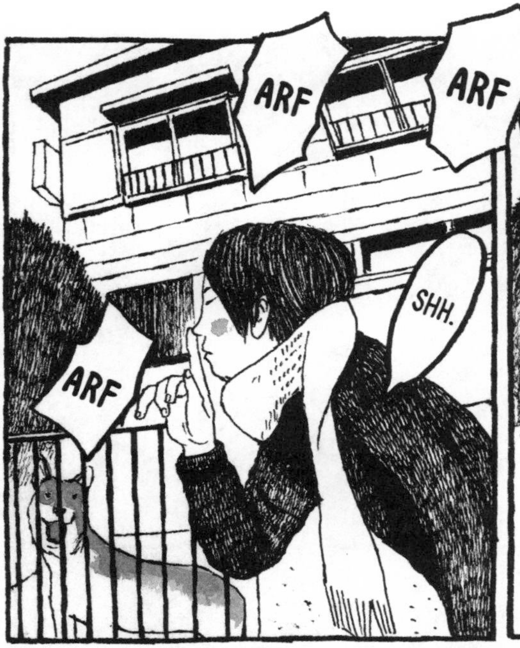
ARF
ARF
SHH.
ARF
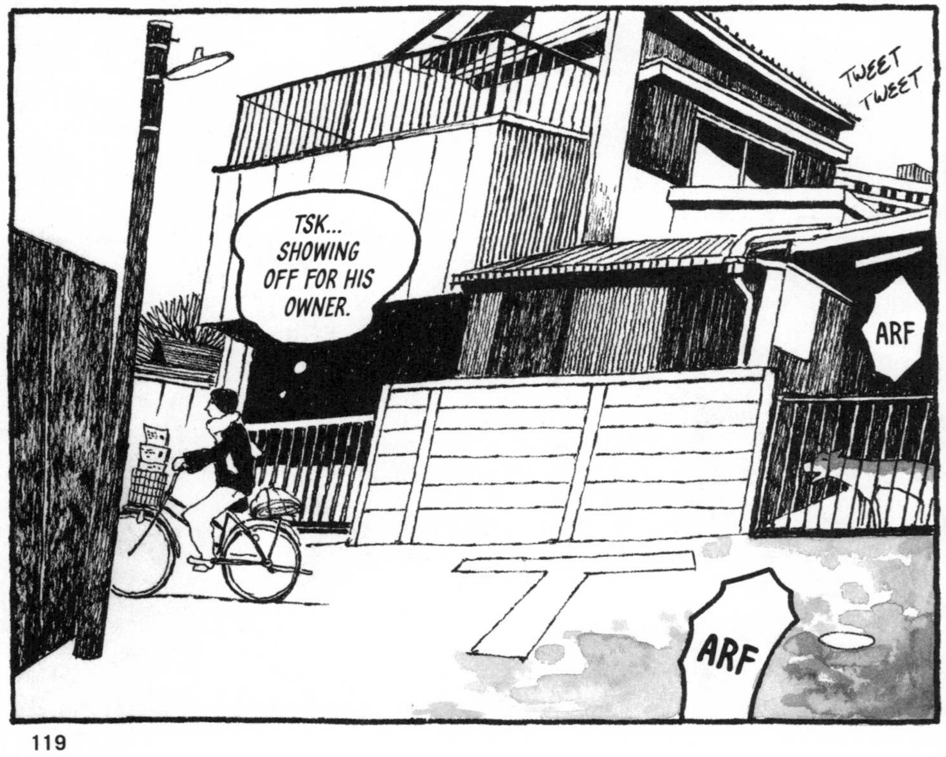
TWEET TWEET
ARF
TSK... SHOWING OFF FOR HIS OWNER.
ARF

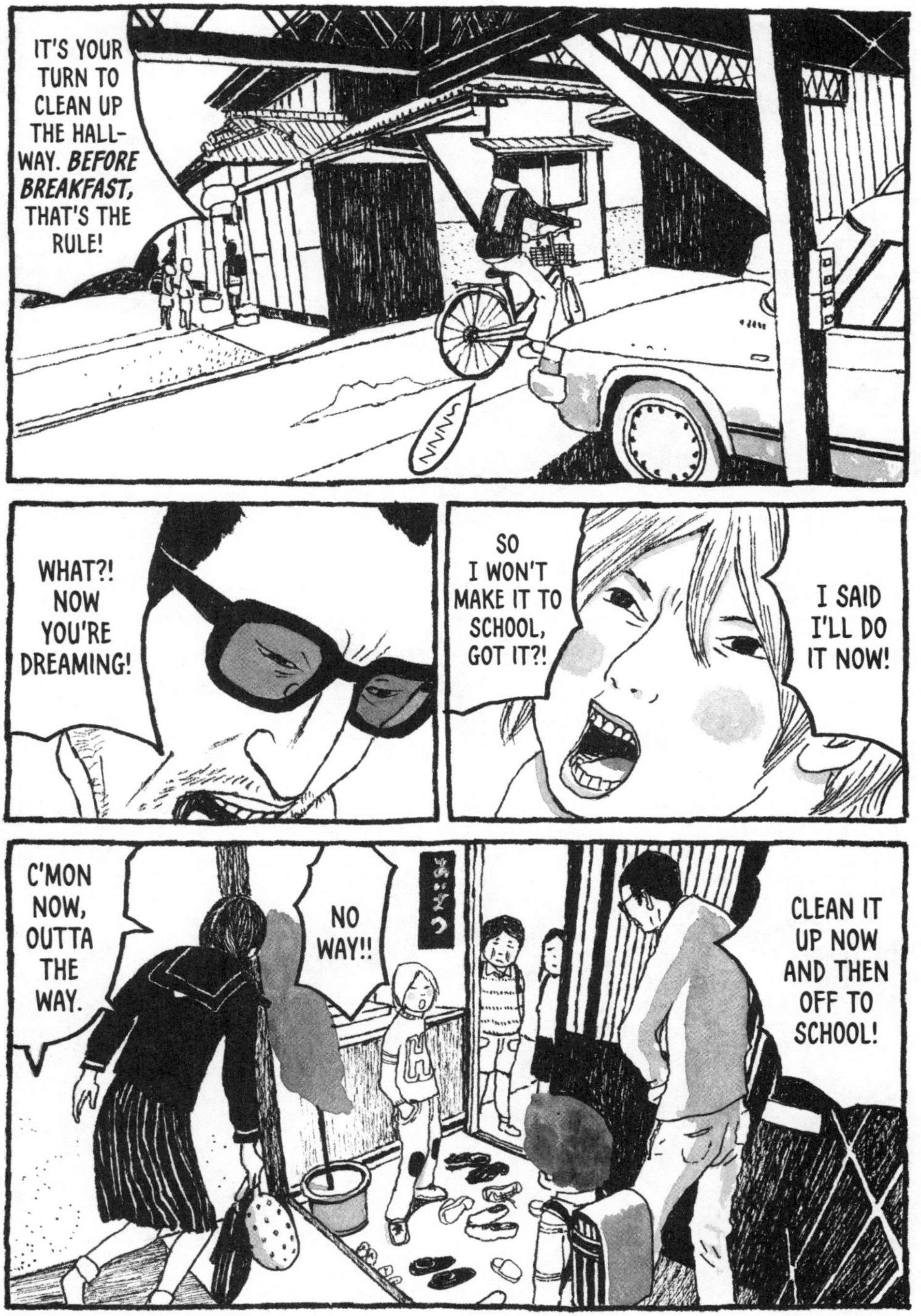
IT'S YOUR TURN TO CLEAN UP THE HALL-WAY. *BEFORE BREAKFAST,* THAT'S THE RULE!
NNNN
I SAID I'LL DO IT NOW!
SO I WON'T MAKE IT TO SCHOOL, GOT IT?!
WHAT?! NOW YOU'RE DREAMING!
CLEAN IT UP NOW AND THEN OFF TO SCHOOL!
NO WAY!!
C'MON NOW, OUTTA THE WAY.

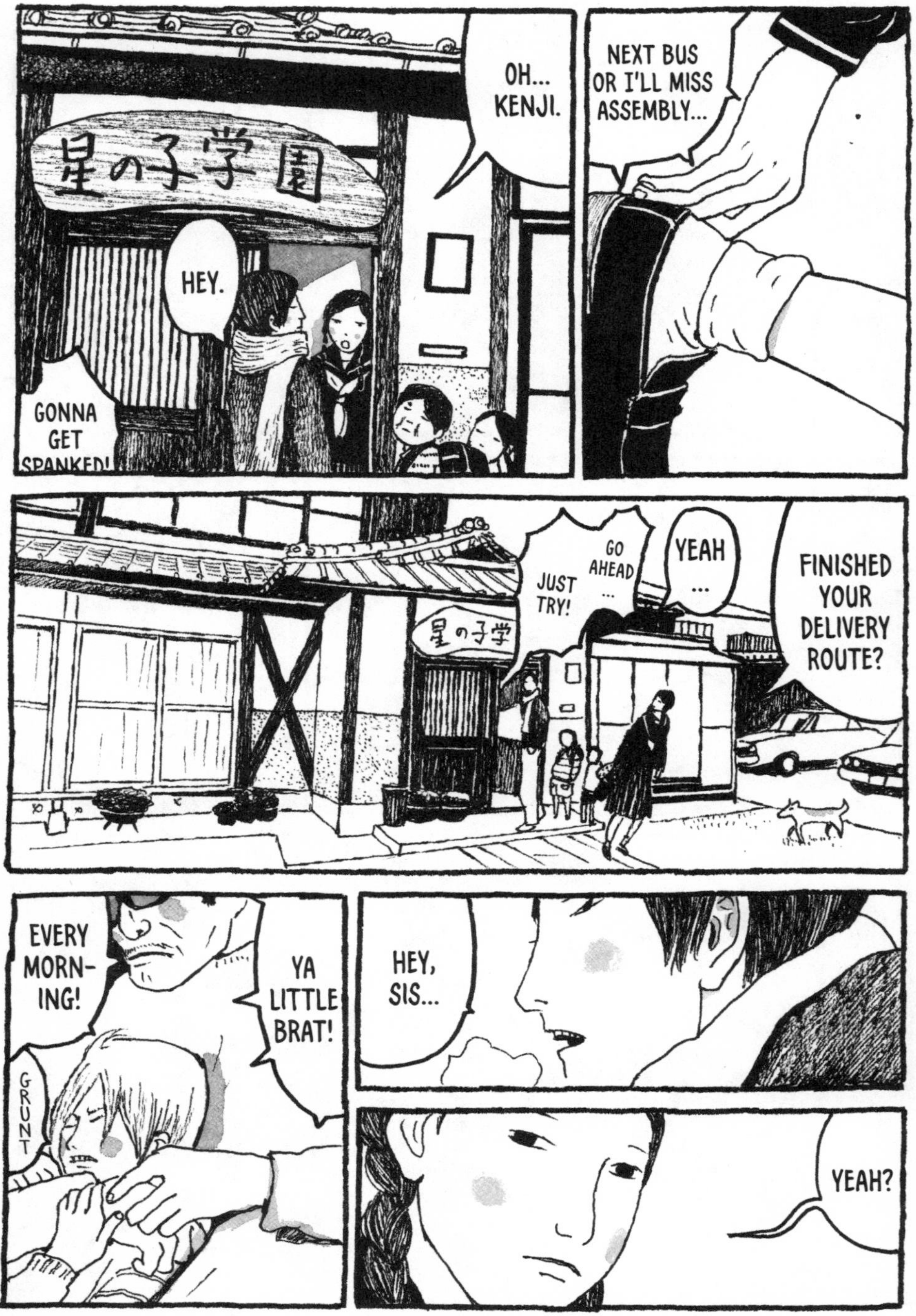
NEXT BUS OR I'LL MISS ASSEMBLY...
OH... KENJI.
HEY.
GONNA GET SPANKED!
FINISHED YOUR DELIVERY ROUTE?
YEAH ...
GO AHEAD ...
JUST TRY!
HEY, SIS...
YEAH?
YA LITTLE BRAT!
EVERY MORN-ING!
GRUNT
星の子学園

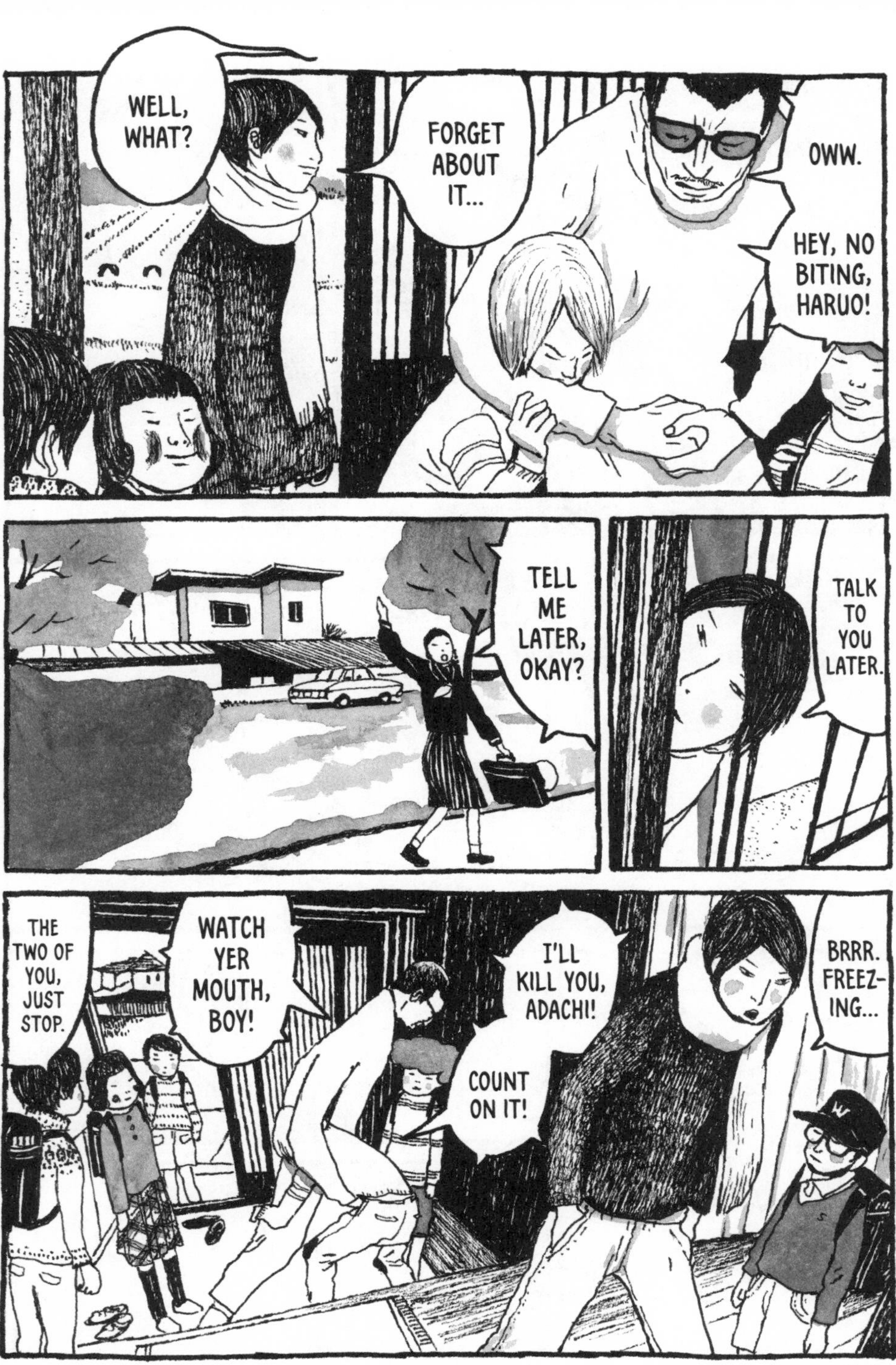
OWW.
HEY, NO BITING, HARUO!
WELL, WHAT?
FORGET ABOUT IT...
TALK TO YOU LATER.
TELL ME LATER, OKAY?
BRRR. FREEZ- ING...
I'LL KILL YOU, ADACHI!
COUNT ON IT!
WATCH YER MOUTH, BOY!
THE TWO OF YOU, JUST STOP.

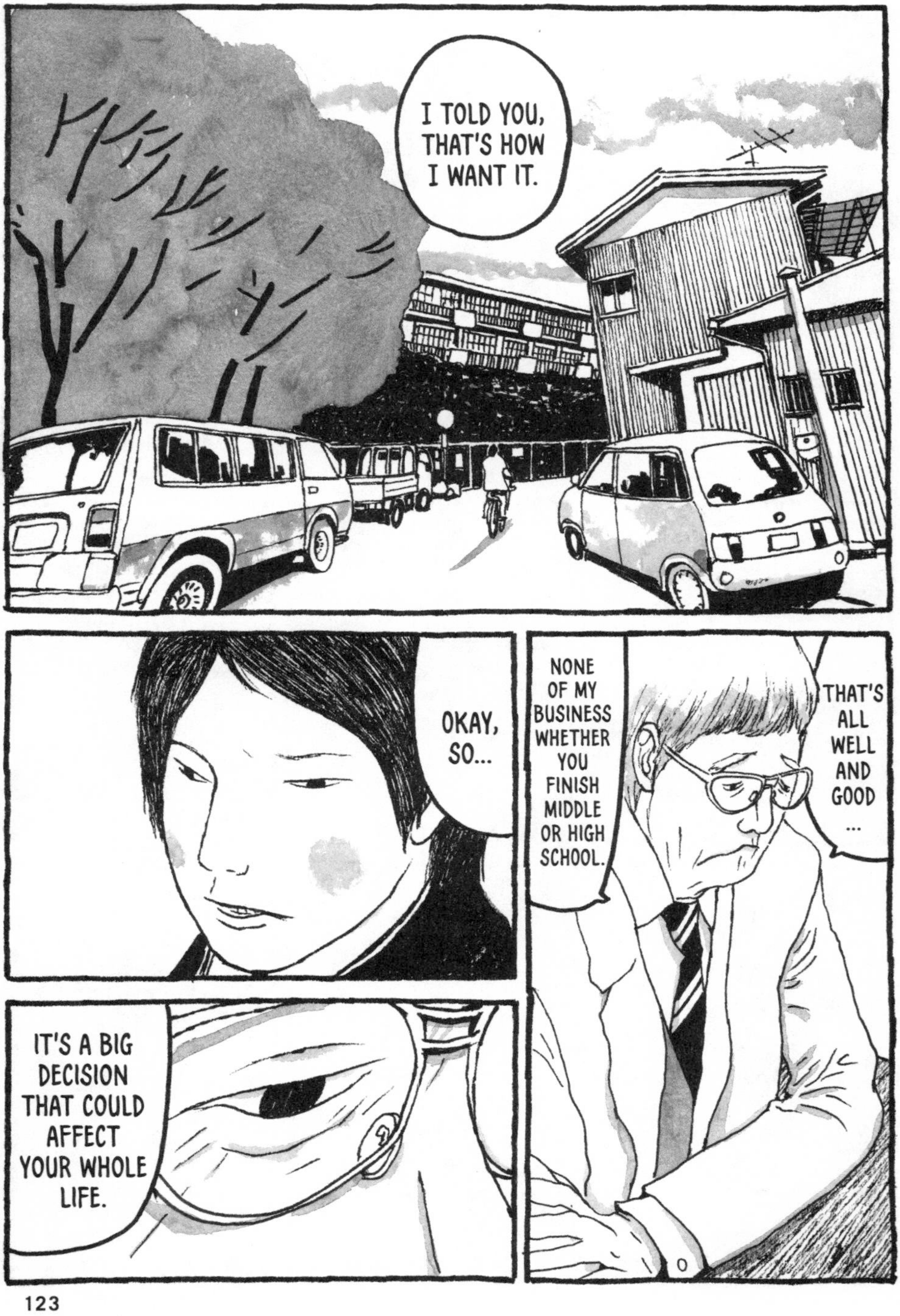
I TOLD YOU, THAT'S HOW I WANT IT.
THAT'S ALL WELL AND GOOD ...
NONE OF MY BUSINESS WHETHER YOU FINISH MIDDLE OR HIGH SCHOOL.
OKAY, SO...
IT'S A BIG DECISION THAT COULD AFFECT YOUR WHOLE LIFE.

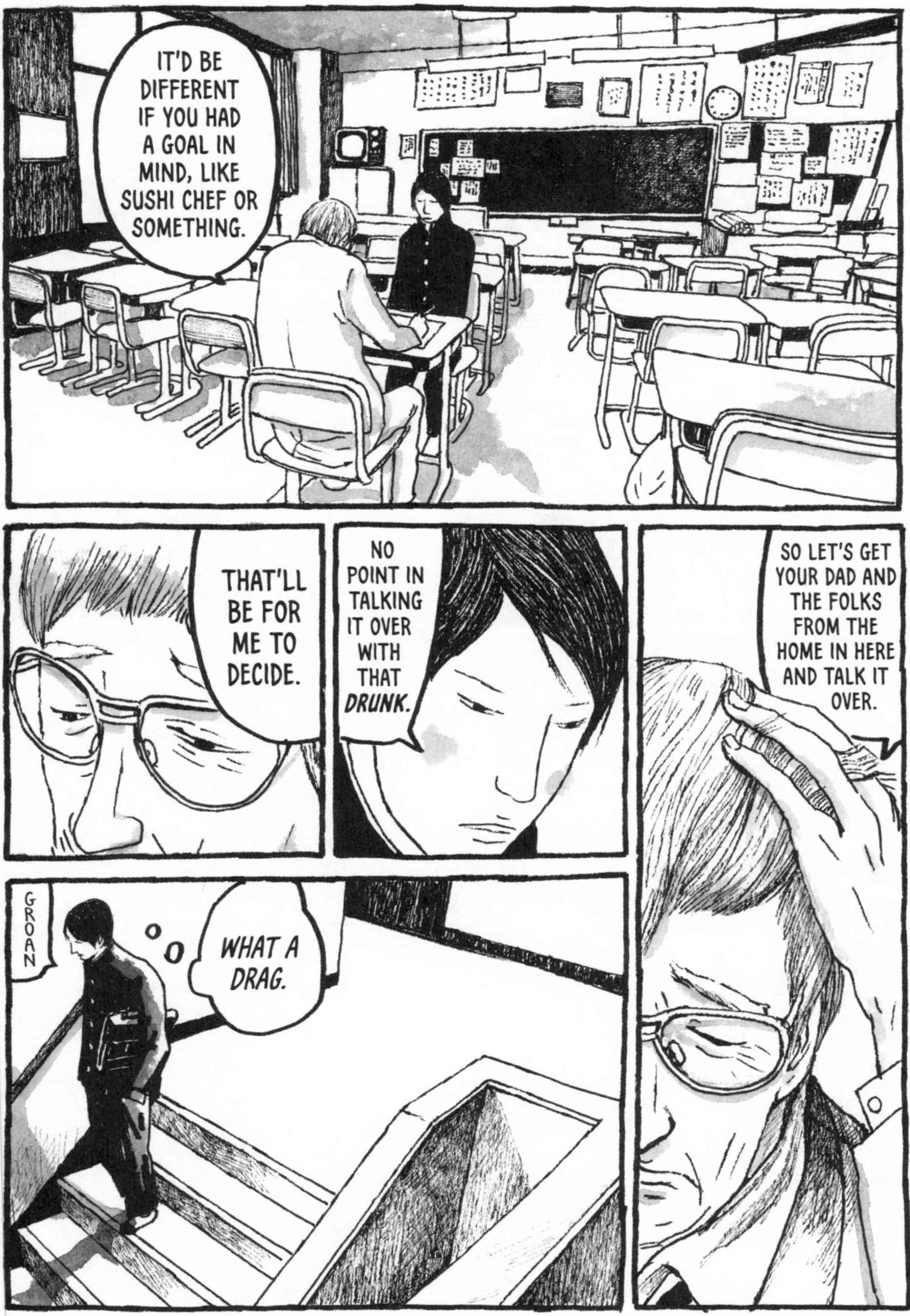
IT'D BE DIFFERENT IF YOU HAD A GOAL IN MIND, LIKE SUSHI CHEF OR SOMETHING.
SO LET'S GET YOUR DAD AND THE FOLKS FROM THE HOME IN HERE AND TALK IT OVER.
NO POINT IN TALKING IT OVER WITH THAT *DRUNK.*
THAT'LL BE FOR ME TO DECIDE.
WHAT A DRAG.
GROAN

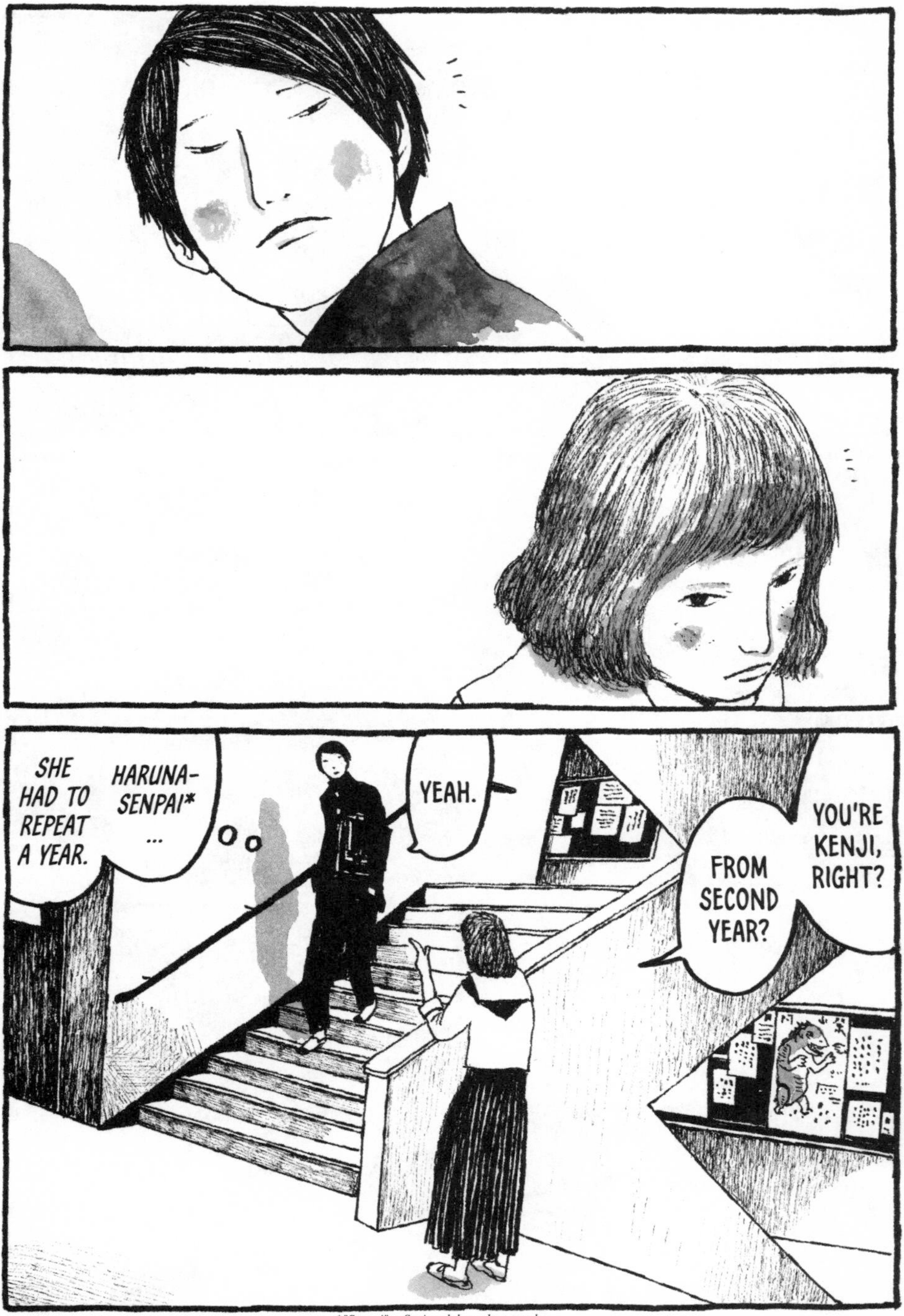
YOU'RE KENJI, RIGHT?
FROM SECOND YEAR?
YEAH.
HARUNA-SENPAI* ...
SHE HAD TO REPEAT A YEAR.

*"Senpai" = Senior club or class member

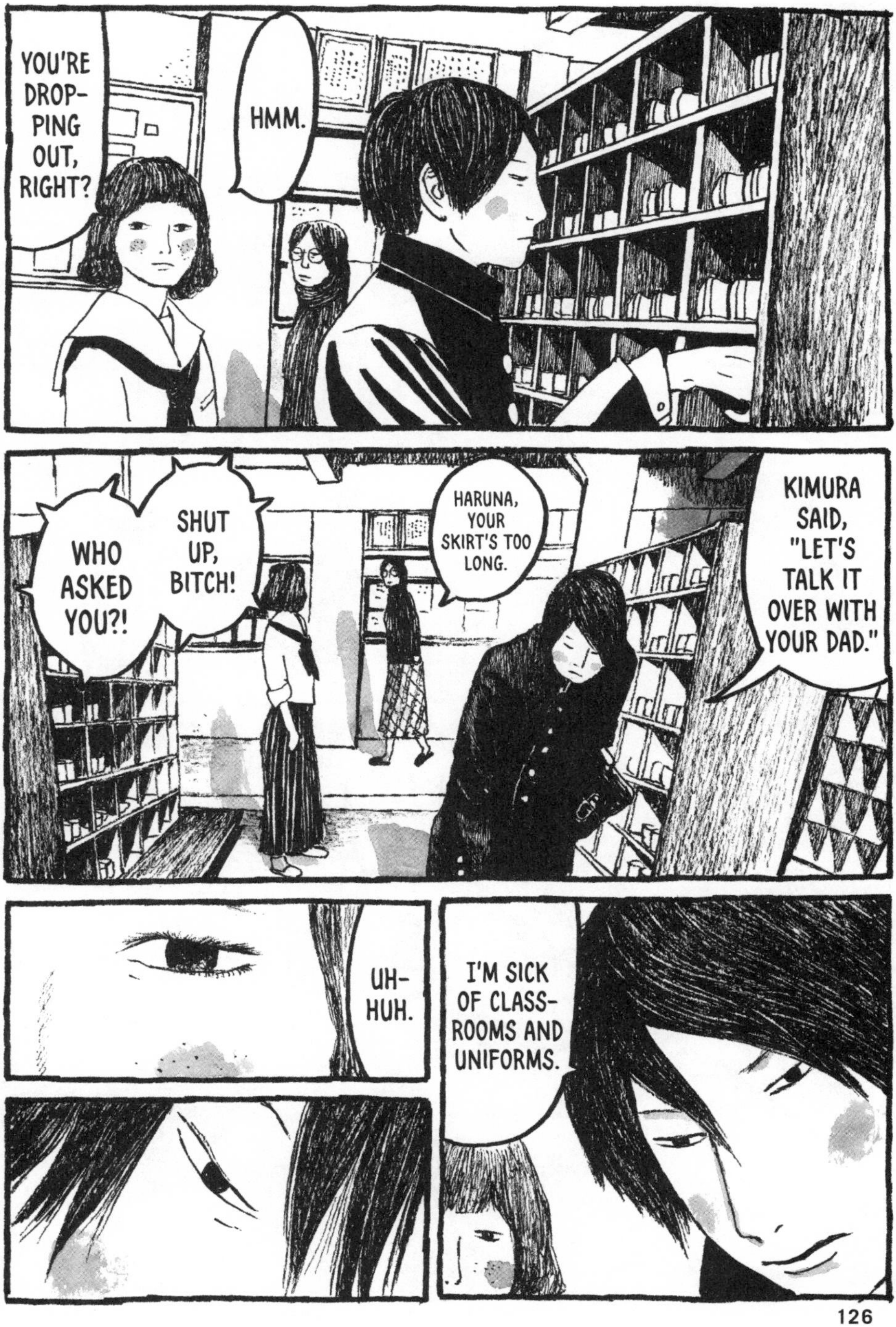
HMM.
YOU'RE DROPPING OUT, RIGHT?
KIMURA SAID, "LET'S TALK IT OVER WITH YOUR DAD."
HARUNA, YOUR SKIRT'S TOO LONG.
SHUT UP, BITCH!
WHO ASKED YOU?!
I'M SICK OF CLASSROOMS AND UNIFORMS.
UH-HUH.

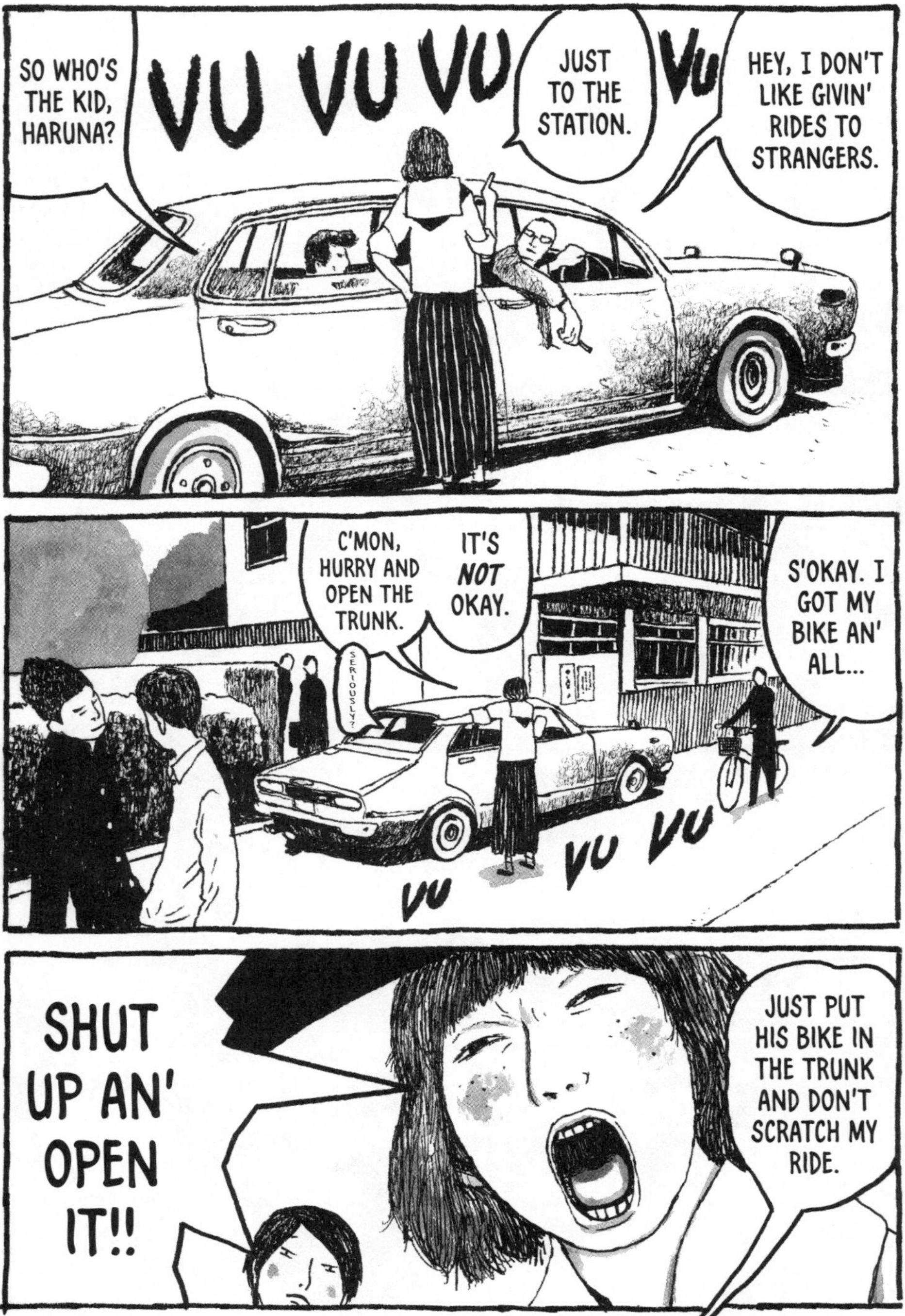

HEY, I DON'T LIKE GIVIN' RIDES TO STRANGERS.
VU
JUST TO THE STATION.
VU VU VU VU
SO WHO'S THE KID, HARUNA?
S'OKAY. I GOT MY BIKE AN' ALL...
IT'S *NOT* OKAY.
C'MON, HURRY AND OPEN THE TRUNK.
SERIOUSLY?
VU VU VU
JUST PUT HIS BIKE IN THE TRUNK AND DON'T SCRATCH MY RIDE.
SHUT UP AN' OPEN IT!!

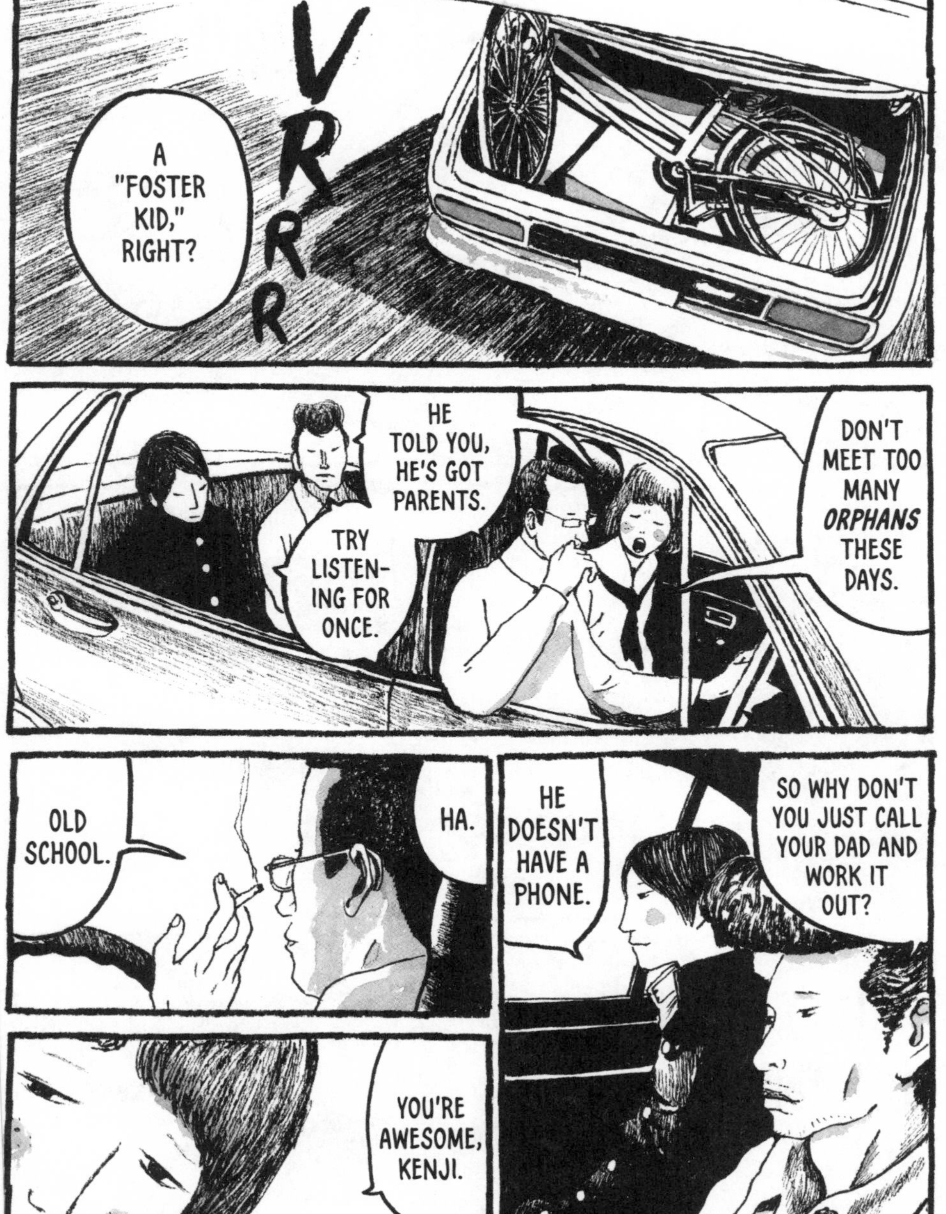
A "FOSTER KID," RIGHT?
VRRR
DON'T MEET TOO MANY *ORPHANS* THESE DAYS.
HE TOLD YOU, HE'S GOT PARENTS.
TRY LISTEN-ING FOR ONCE.
SO WHY DON'T YOU JUST CALL YOUR DAD AND WORK IT OUT?
HE DOESN'T HAVE A PHONE.
HA.
OLD SCHOOL.
YOU'RE AWESOME, KENJI.

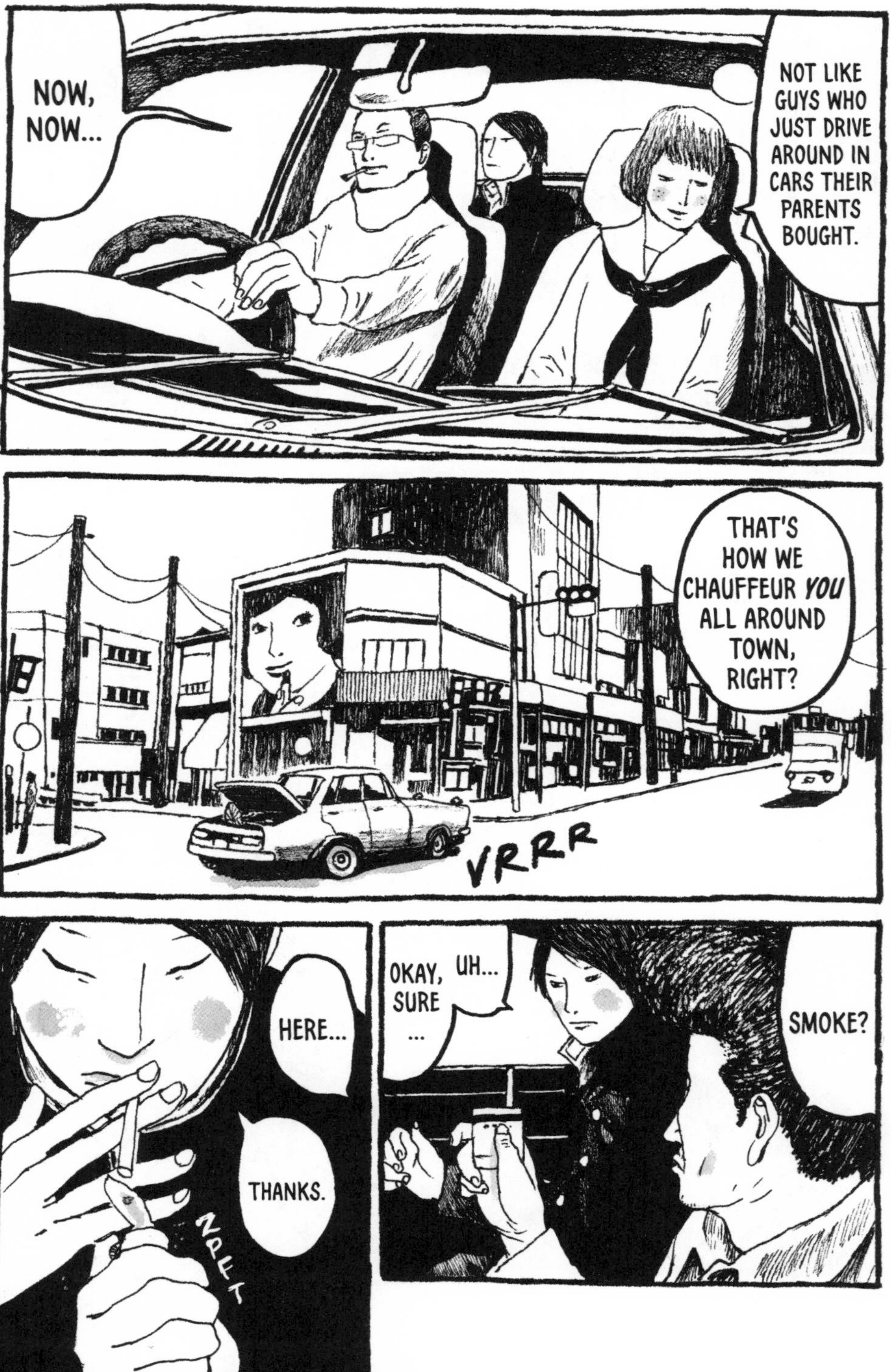
NOT LIKE GUYS WHO JUST DRIVE AROUND IN CARS THEIR PARENTS BOUGHT.
NOW, NOW...
THAT'S HOW WE CHAUFFEUR *YOU* ALL AROUND TOWN, RIGHT?
VRRR
SMOKE?
UH...
OKAY, SURE ...
HERE...
THANKS.
ZPFT

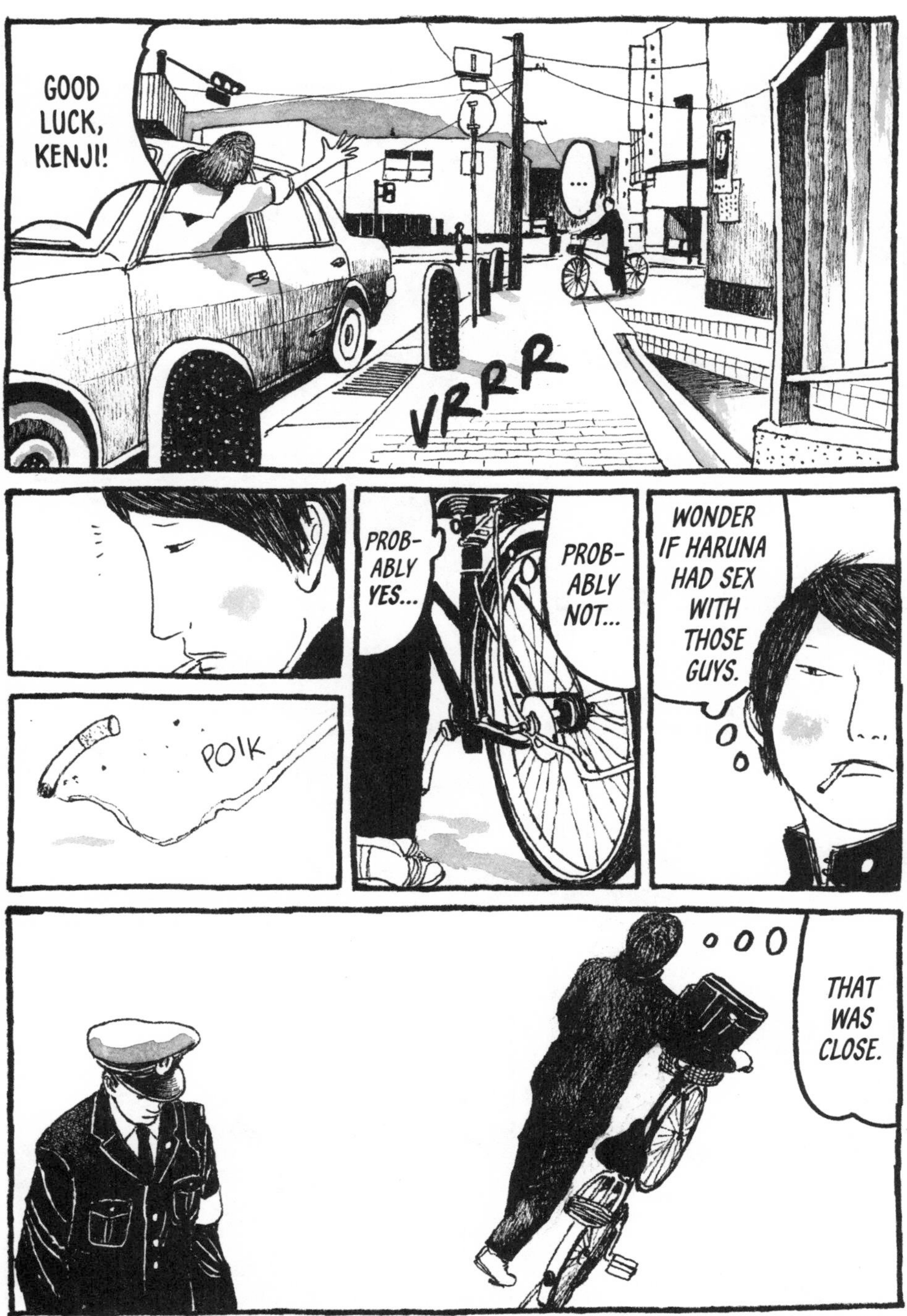
GOOD LUCK, KENJI!
...
VRRR
WONDER IF HARUNA HAD SEX WITH THOSE GUYS.
PROBABLY NOT...
PROBABLY YES...
POIK
THAT WAS CLOSE.

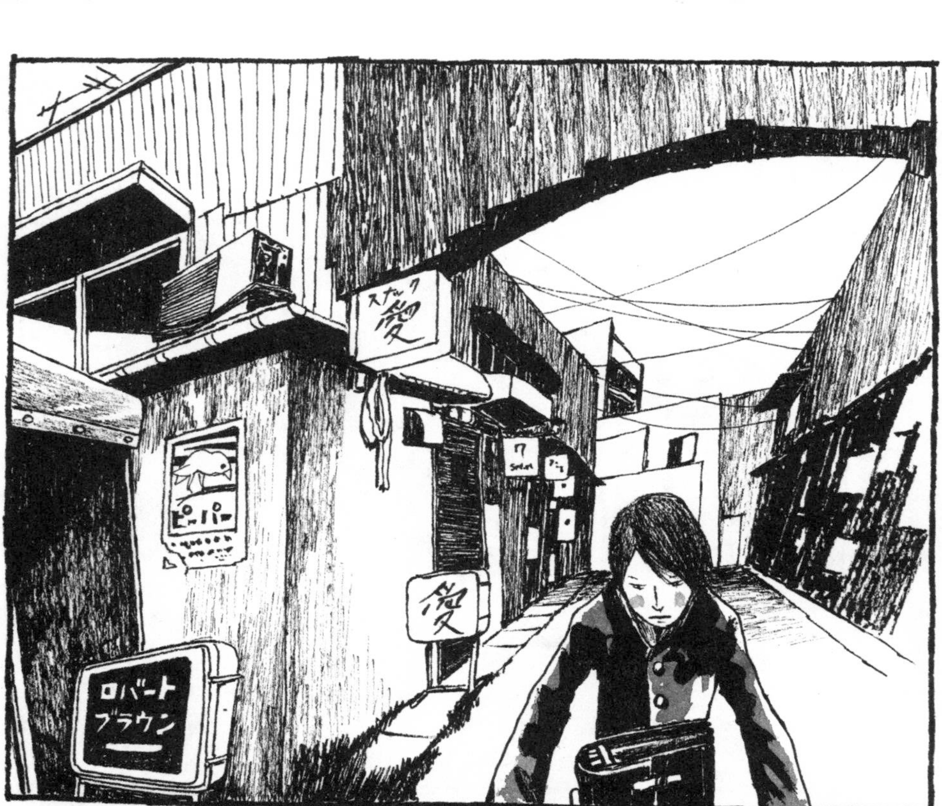
スナック
愛
愛
ピーパー
ロバート
ブラウン
*Signs: Love Bar, Peeper

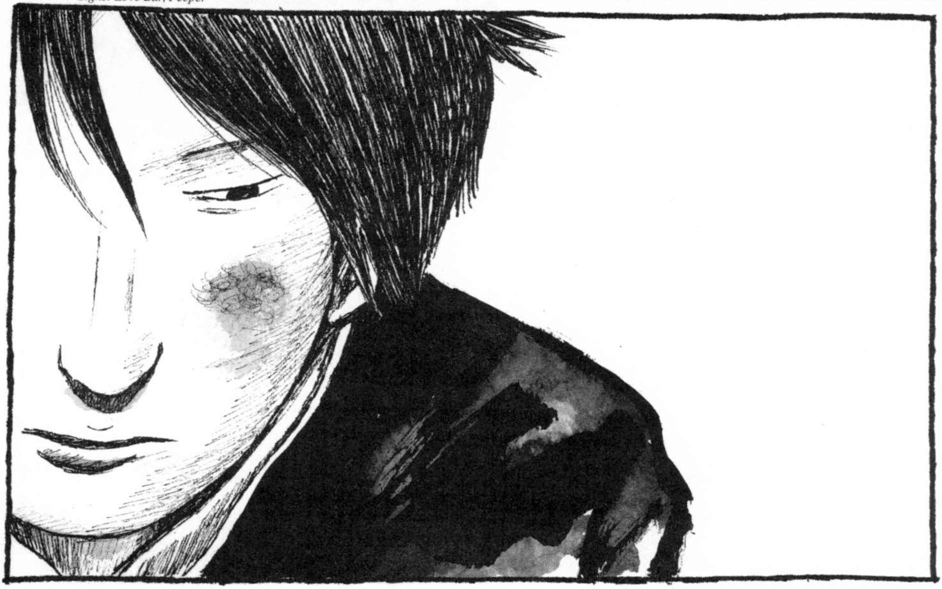

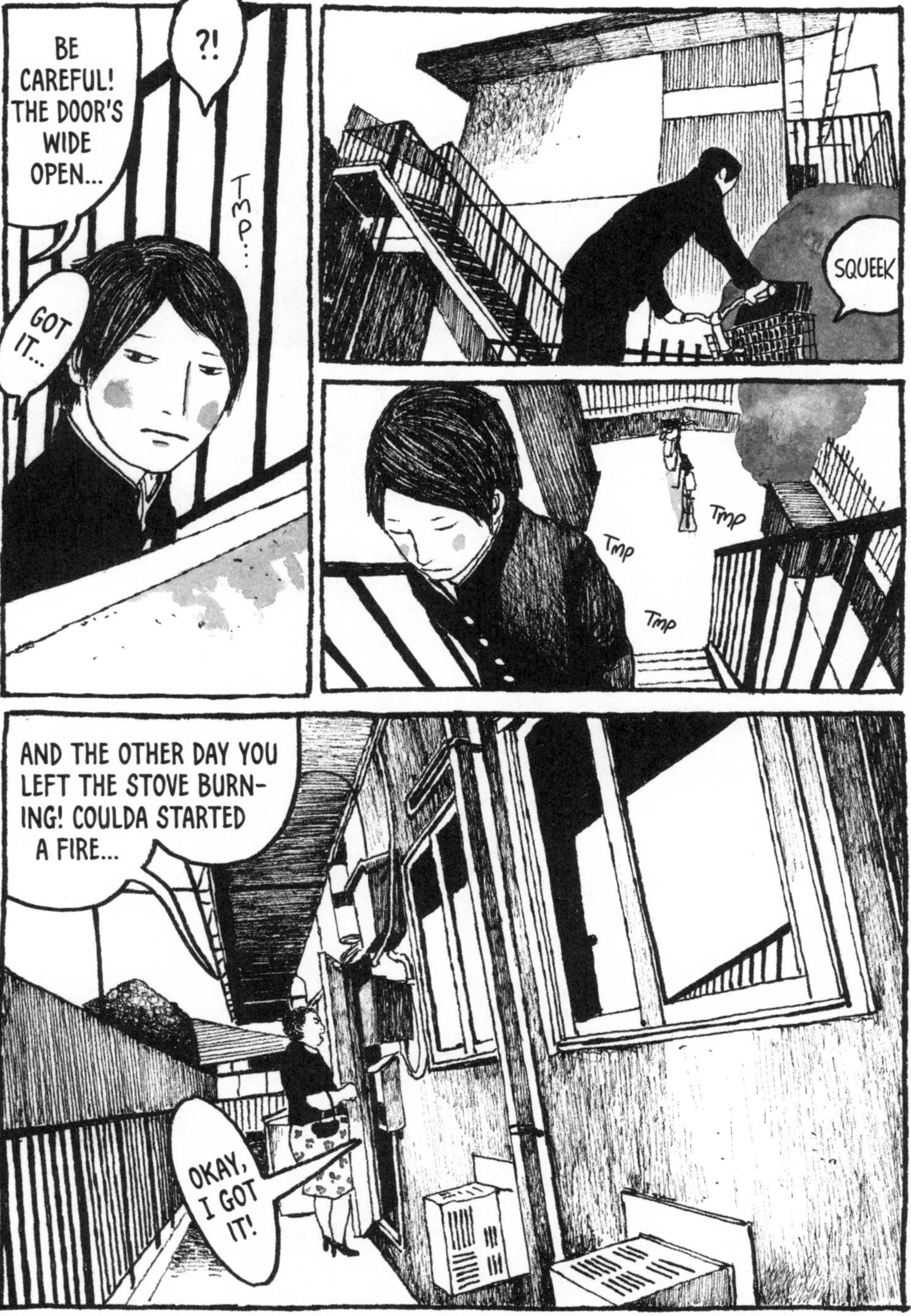
SQUEEK
Tmp
Tmp
Tmp
?!
BE CAREFUL! THE DOOR'S WIDE OPEN...
TMP...
GOT IT...
AND THE OTHER DAY YOU LEFT THE STOVE BURN-ING! COULDA STARTED A FIRE...
OKAY, I GOT IT!

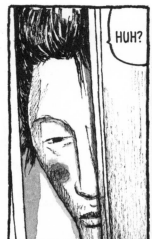

HUH?

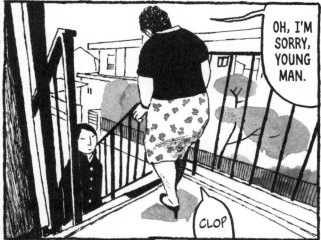

OH, I'M SORRY, YOUNG MAN.

CLOP

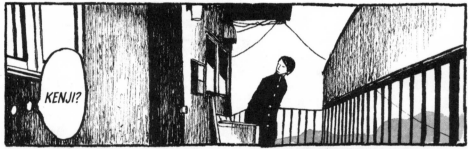

KENJI?

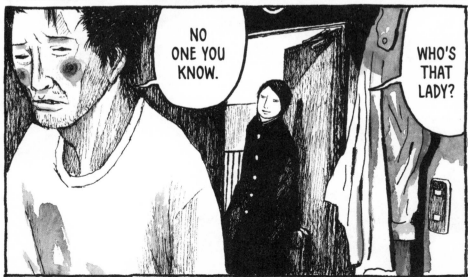

NO ONE YOU KNOW.

WHO'S THAT LADY?

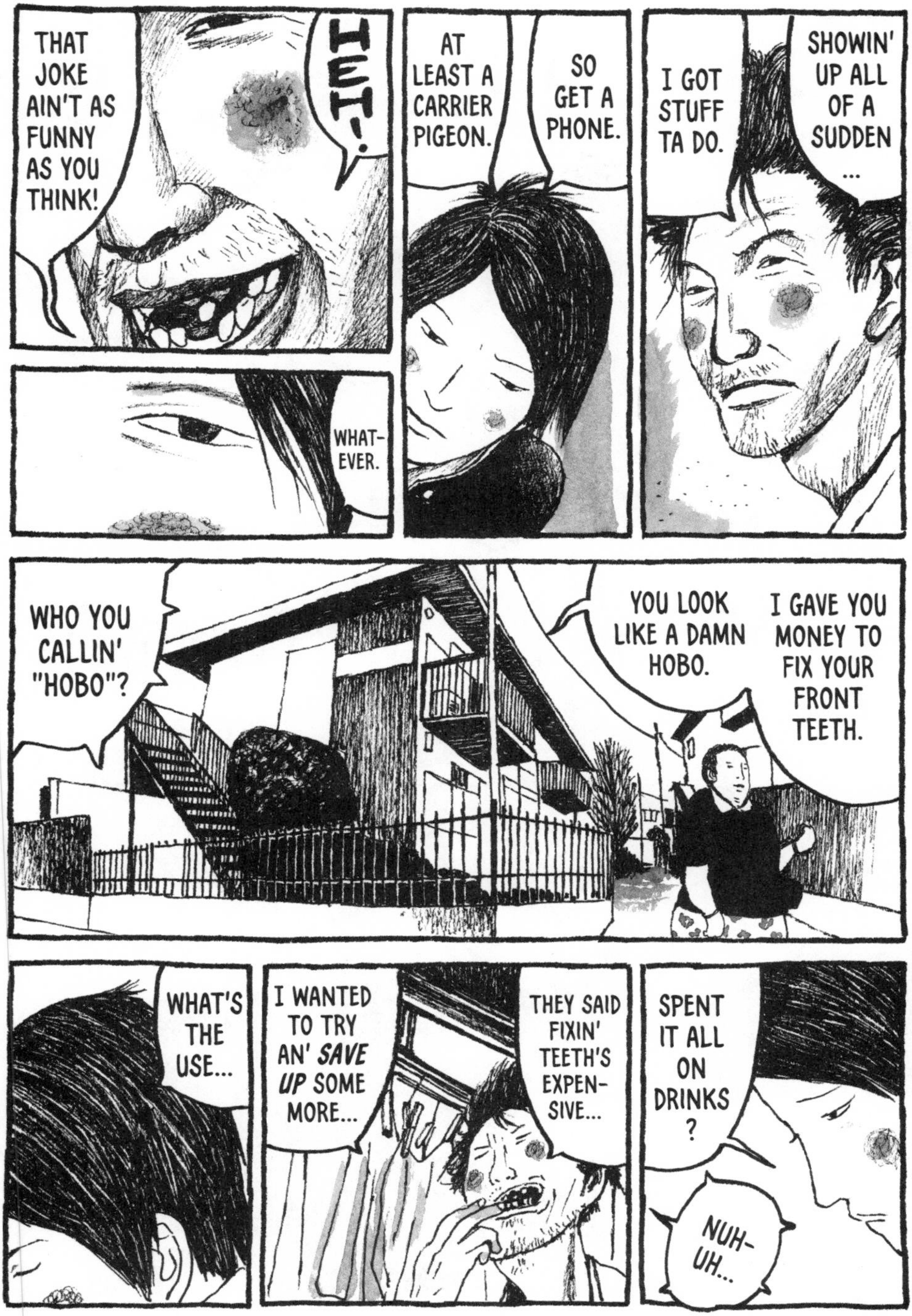
SHOWIN' UP ALL OF A SUDDEN ...
I GOT STUFF TA DO.
SO GET A PHONE.
AT LEAST A CARRIER PIGEON.
HEH!
THAT JOKE AIN'T AS FUNNY AS YOU THINK!
WHAT-EVER.
I GAVE YOU MONEY TO FIX YOUR FRONT TEETH.
YOU LOOK LIKE A DAMN HOBO.
WHO YOU CALLIN' "HOBO"?
SPENT IT ALL ON DRINKS ?
NUH-UH...
THEY SAID FIXIN' TEETH'S EXPEN-SIVE...
I WANTED TO TRY AN' *SAVE UP* SOME MORE...
WHAT'S THE USE...

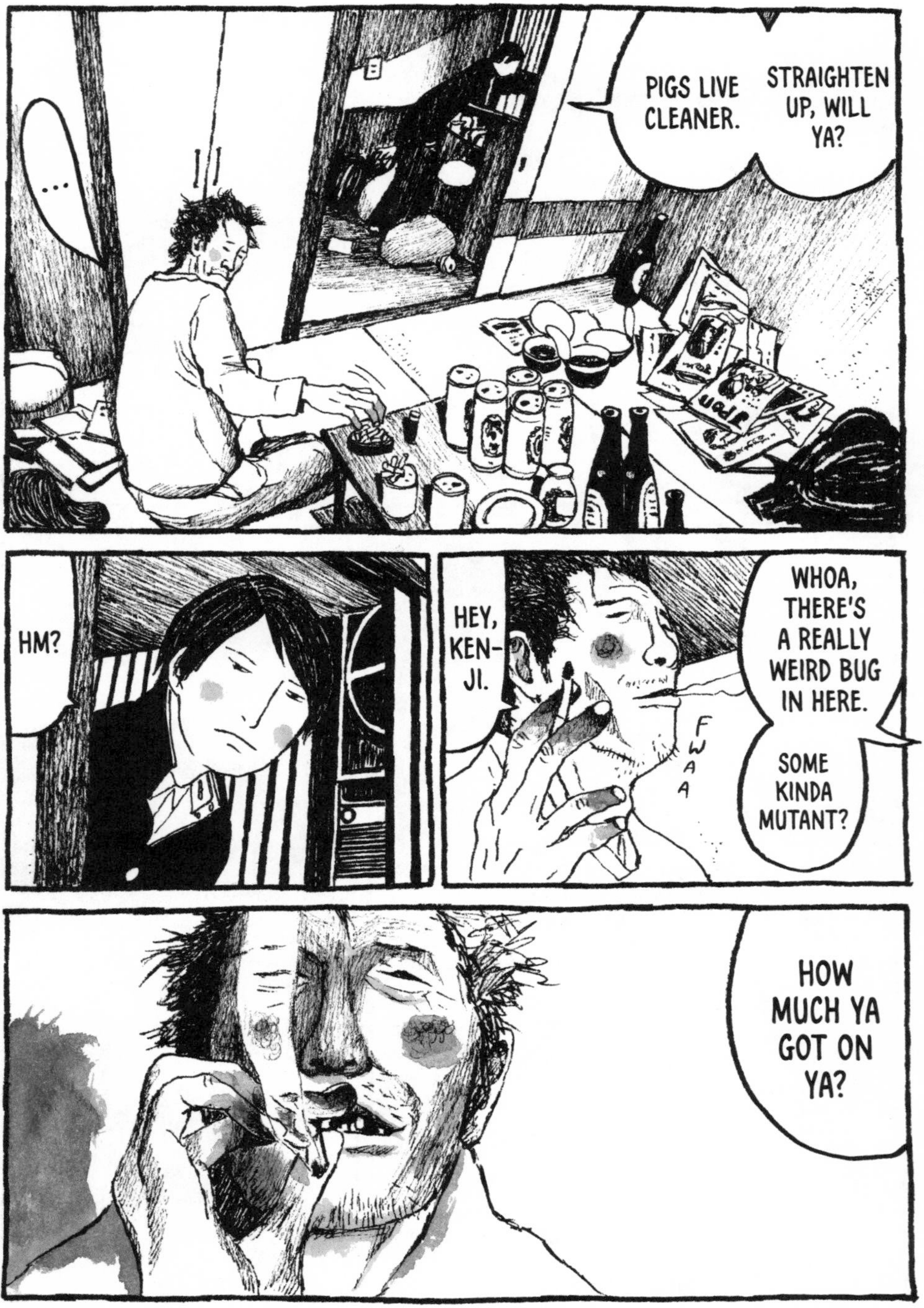
STRAIGHTEN UP, WILL YA?
PIGS LIVE CLEANER.
...
HEY, KEN-JI.
WHOA, THERE'S A REALLY WEIRD BUG IN HERE.
SOME KINDA MUTANT?
FWAA
HM?
HOW MUCH YA GOT ON YA?

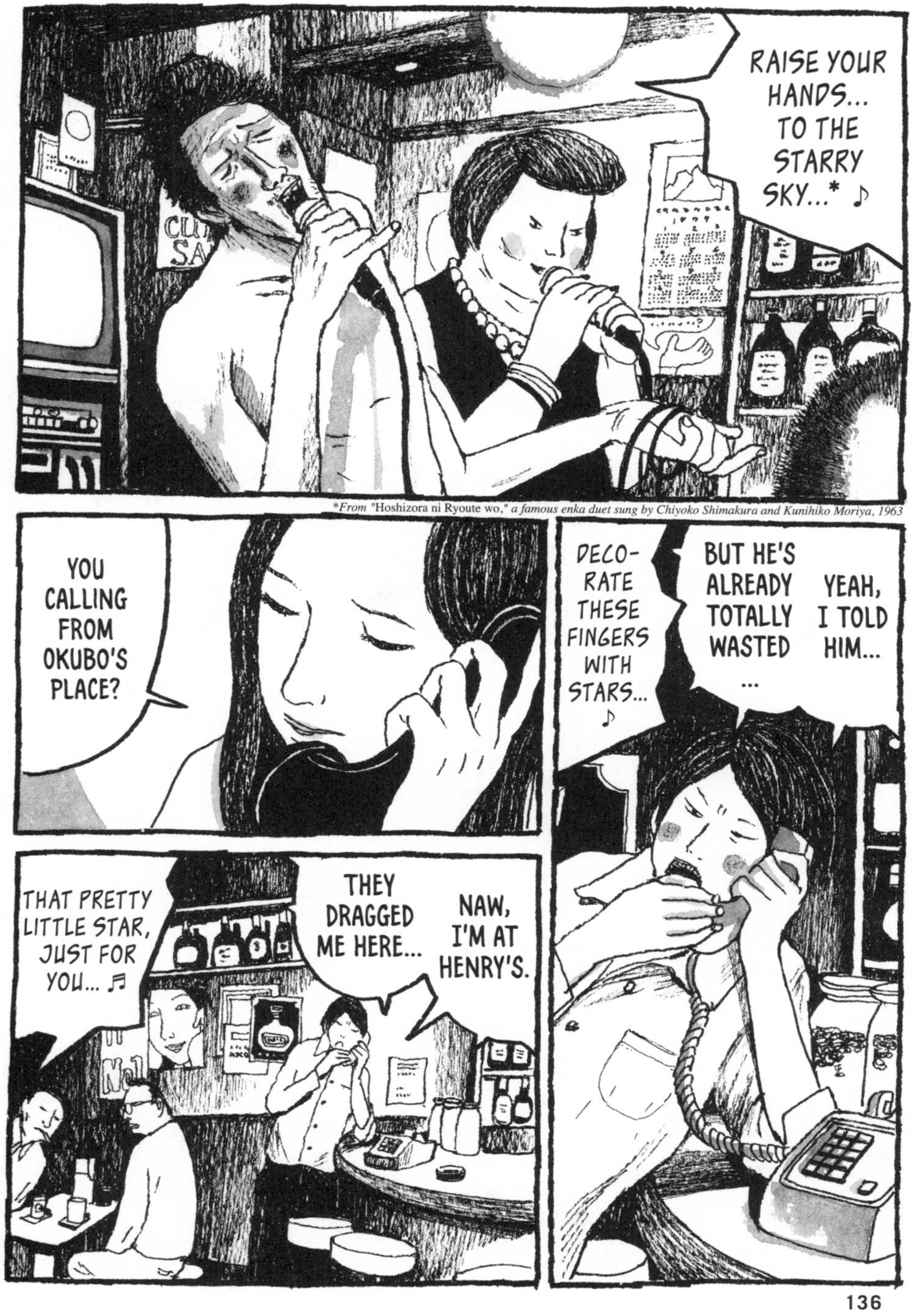
RAISE YOUR HANDS... TO THE STARRY SKY...* ♪
YEAH, I TOLD HIM...
BUT HE'S ALREADY TOTALLY WASTED ...
DECO-RATE THESE FINGERS WITH STARS... ♪
YOU CALLING FROM OKUBO'S PLACE?
NAW, I'M AT HENRY'S.
THEY DRAGGED ME HERE...
THAT PRETTY LITTLE STAR, JUST FOR YOU... ♬

**From* "Hoshizora ni Ryoute wo," *a famous enka duet sung by* Chiyoko Shimakura *and* Kunihiko Moriya, 1963

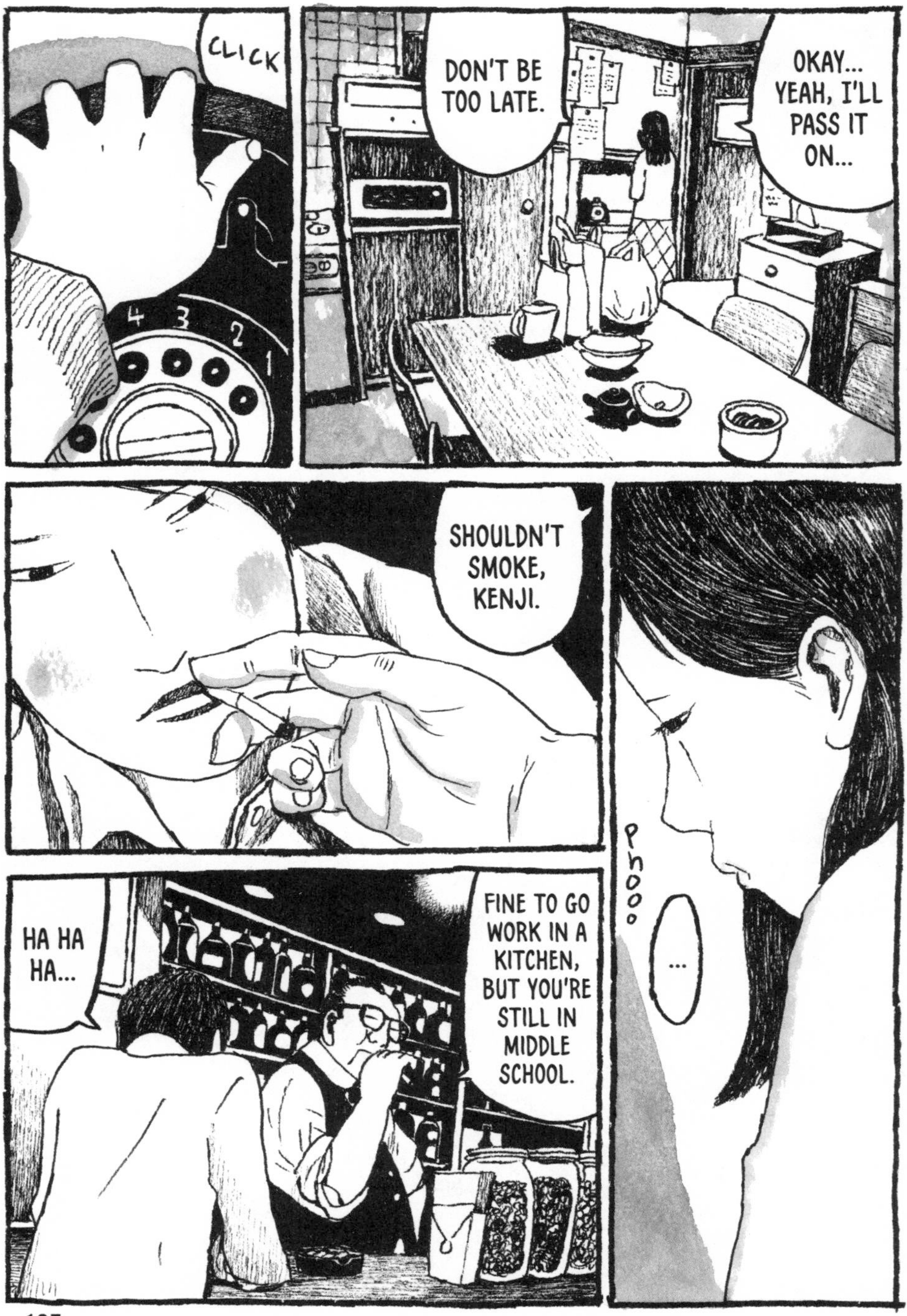
OKAY... YEAH, I'LL PASS IT ON...
DON'T BE TOO LATE.
CLICK
PHOOO
...
SHOULDN'T SMOKE, KENJI.
FINE TO GO WORK IN A KITCHEN, BUT YOU'RE STILL IN MIDDLE SCHOOL.
HA HA HA...

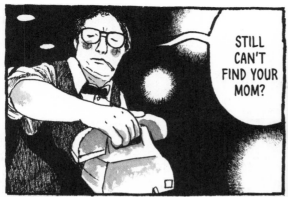

STILL CAN'T FIND YOUR MOM?
THE FOLKS AT THE HOME SAID SHE'S LIVING WITH A NEW GUY IN NAGOYA ...
DECORATE THESE FINGERS WITH STARS... ♪
NO POINT IN TALKING TO *HIM*.
YOU TRY LISTENING TO THEM WHILE JUST DRINKING COLA.

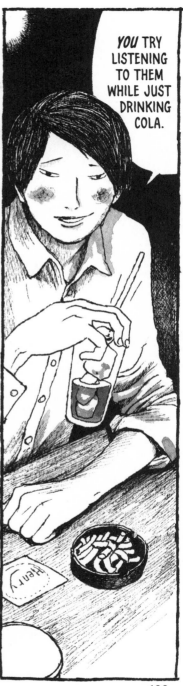

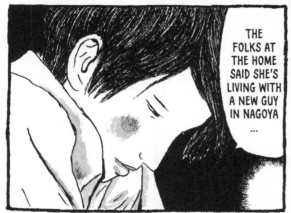

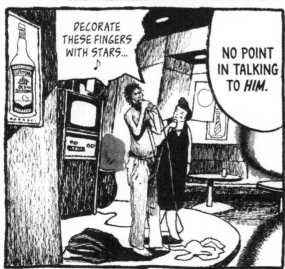

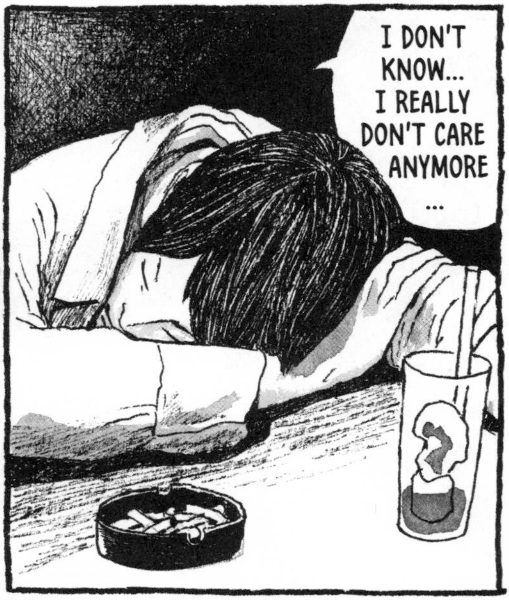
I DON'T KNOW... I REALLY DON'T CARE ANYMORE ...
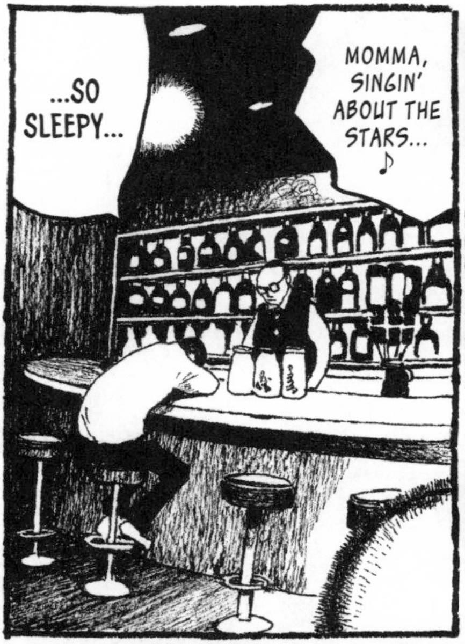
MOMMA, SINGIN' ABOUT THE STARS... ♪
...SO SLEEPY...
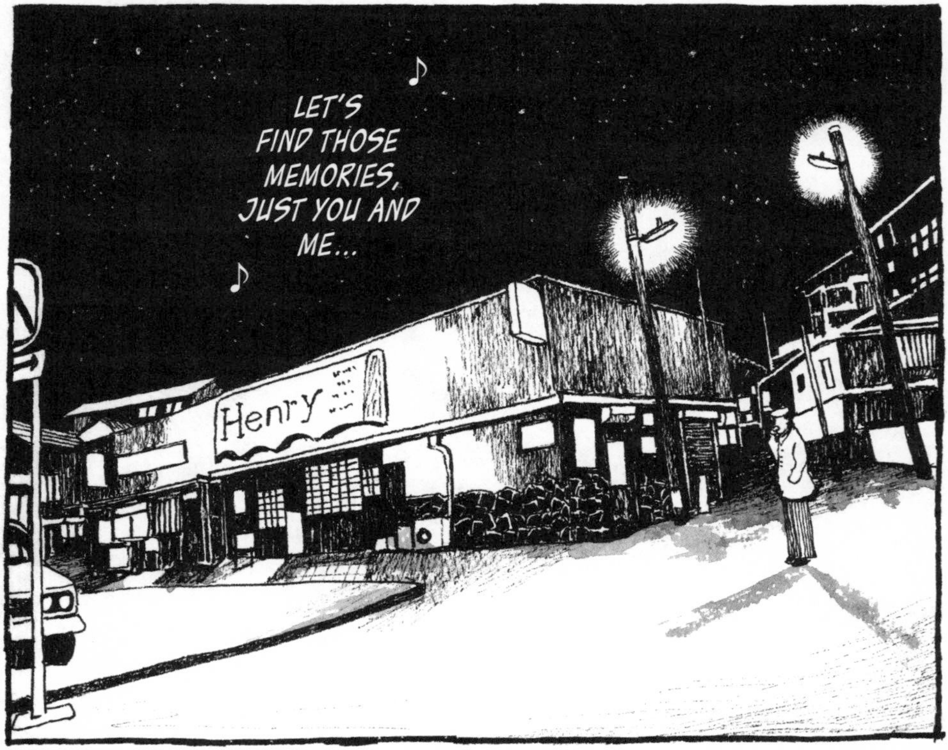
♪
LET'S FIND THOSE MEMORIES, JUST YOU AND ME...
♪
Henry

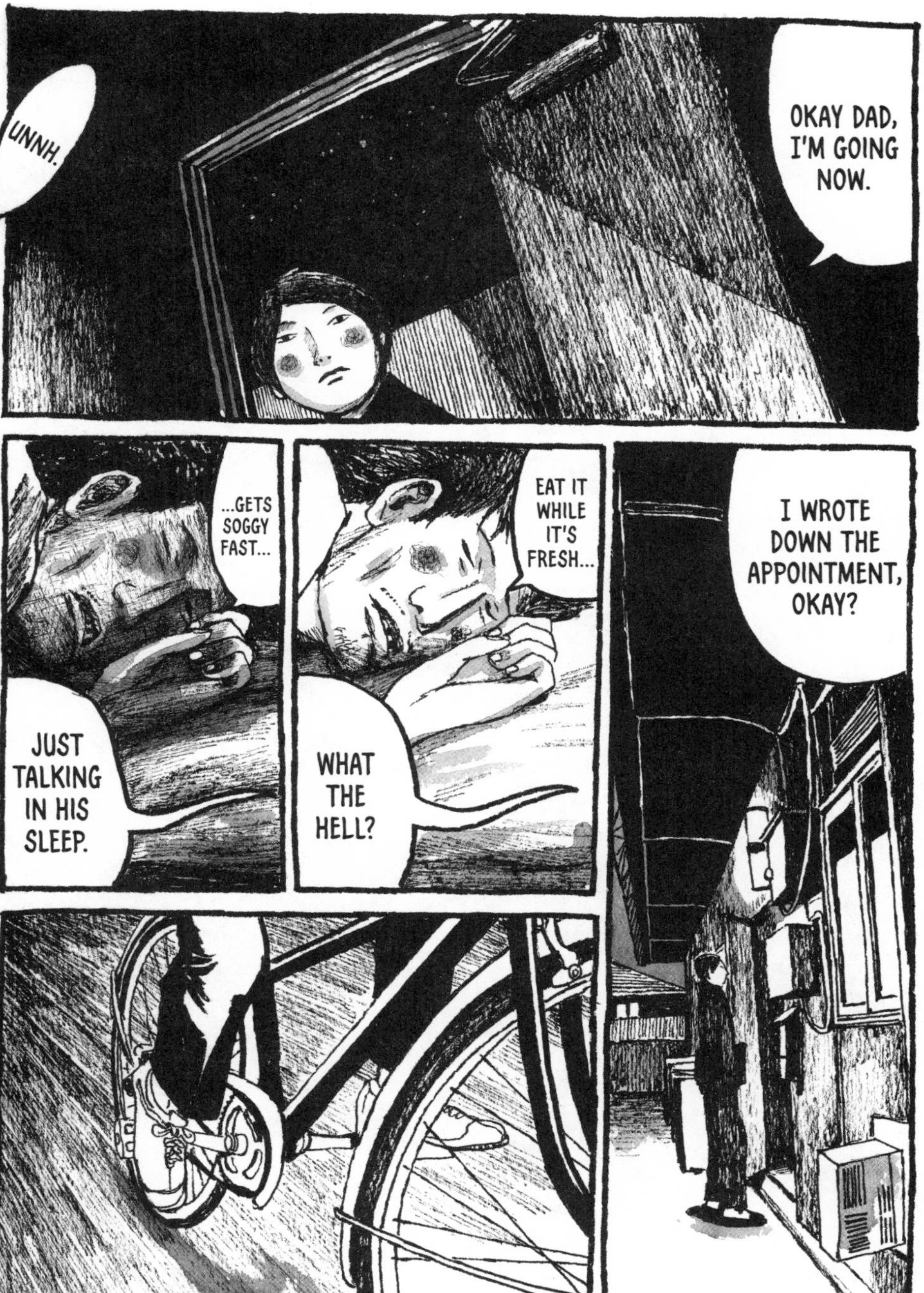
OKAY DAD, I'M GOING NOW.
UNNH.
I WROTE DOWN THE APPOINTMENT, OKAY?
EAT IT WHILE IT'S FRESH...
WHAT THE HELL?
...GETS SOGGY FAST...
JUST TALKING IN HIS SLEEP.

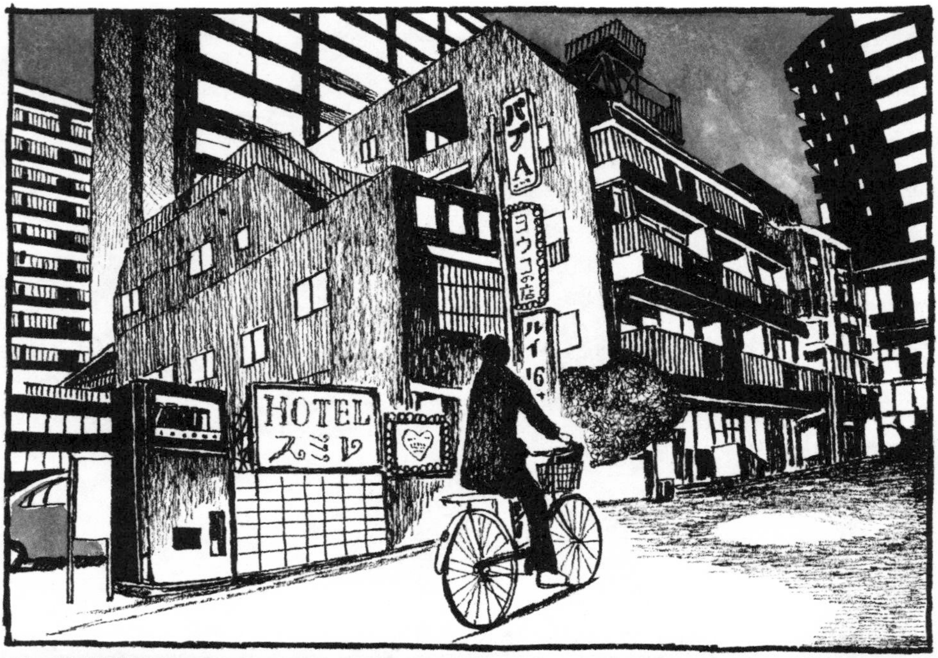
パブA
ヨウコの店
ルイ16
HOTEL
スミレ
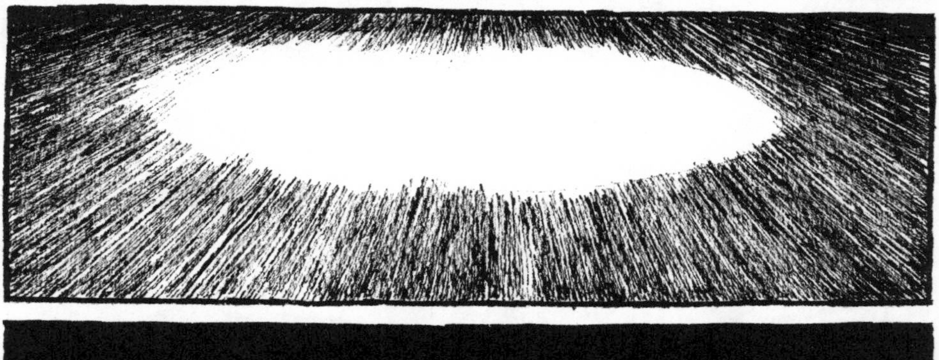
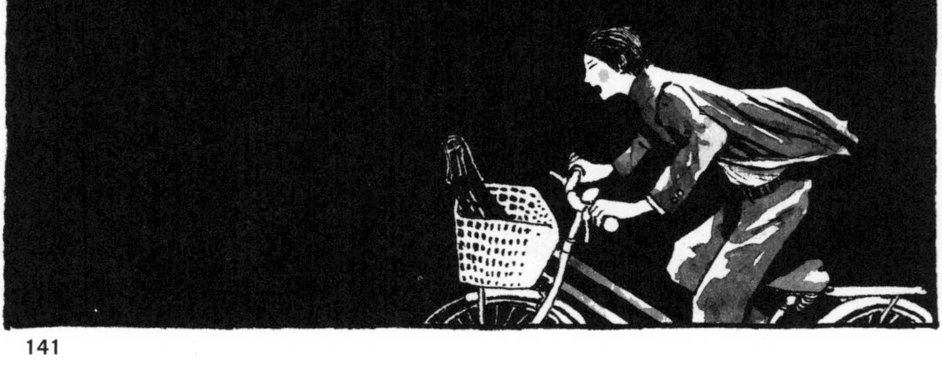

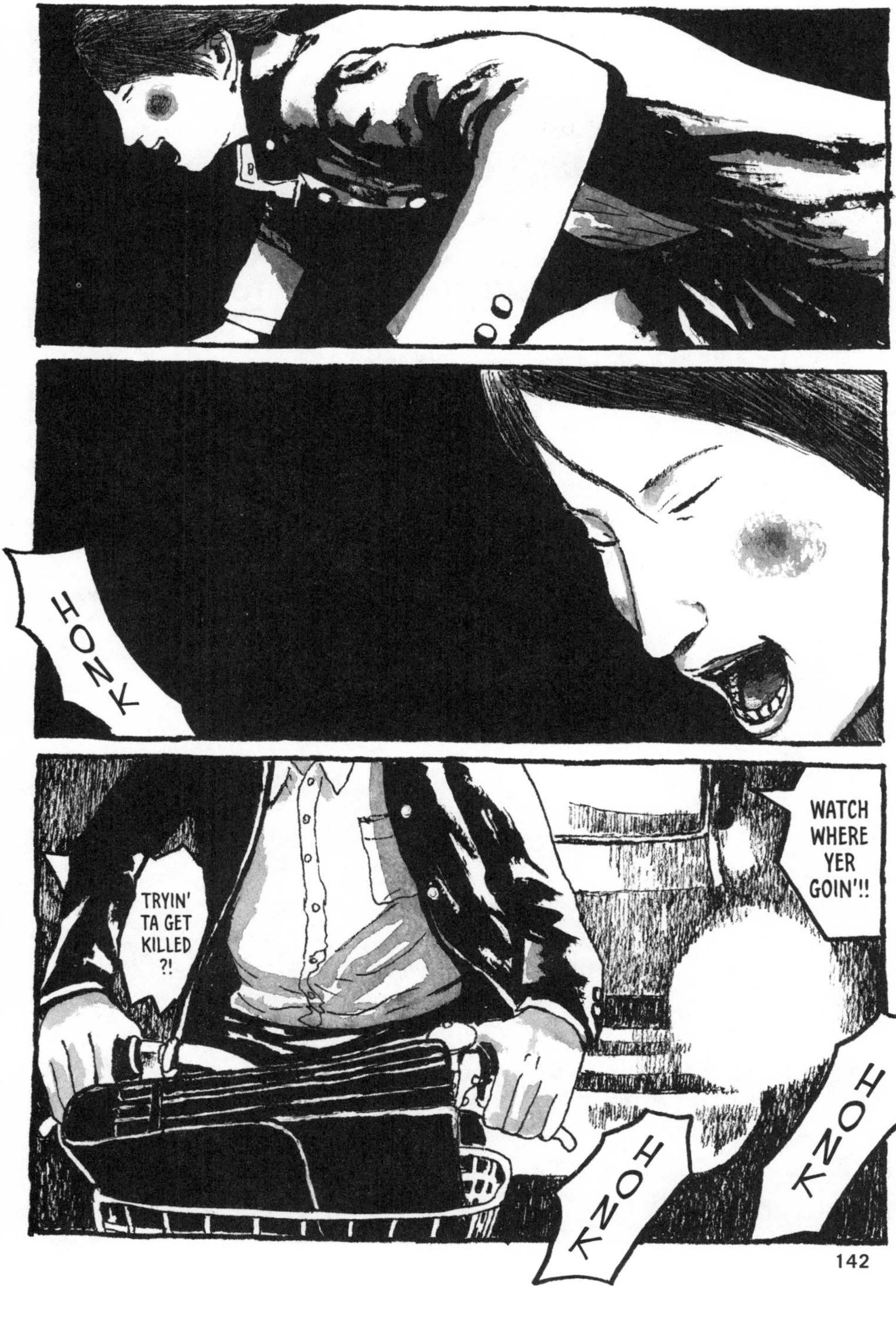
HONK
WATCH WHERE YER GOIN'!!
TRYIN' TA GET KILLED?!
HONK
HONK

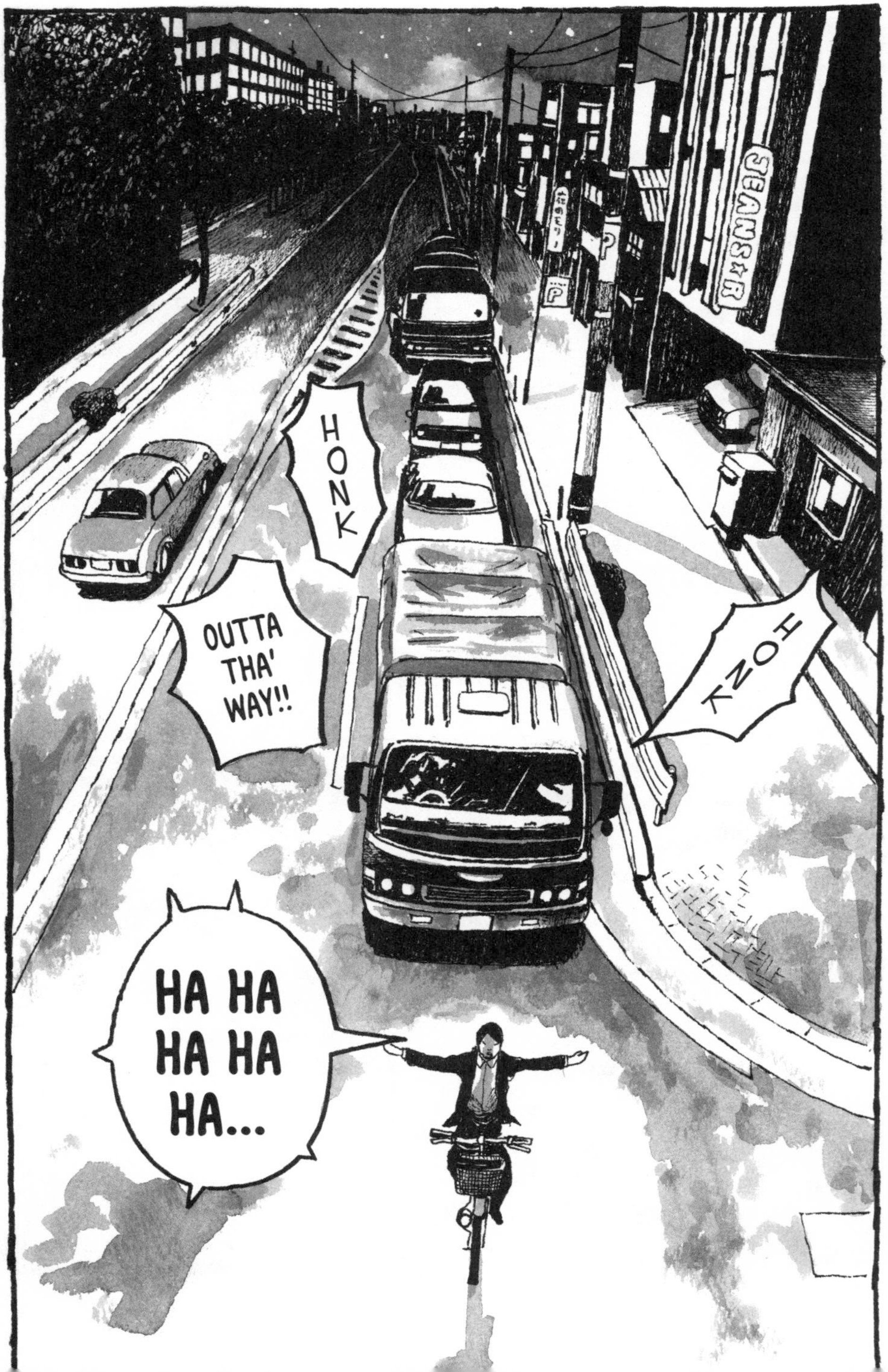
JEANS☆R
HONK
HONK
OUTTA THA' WAY!!
HA HA HA HA HA...

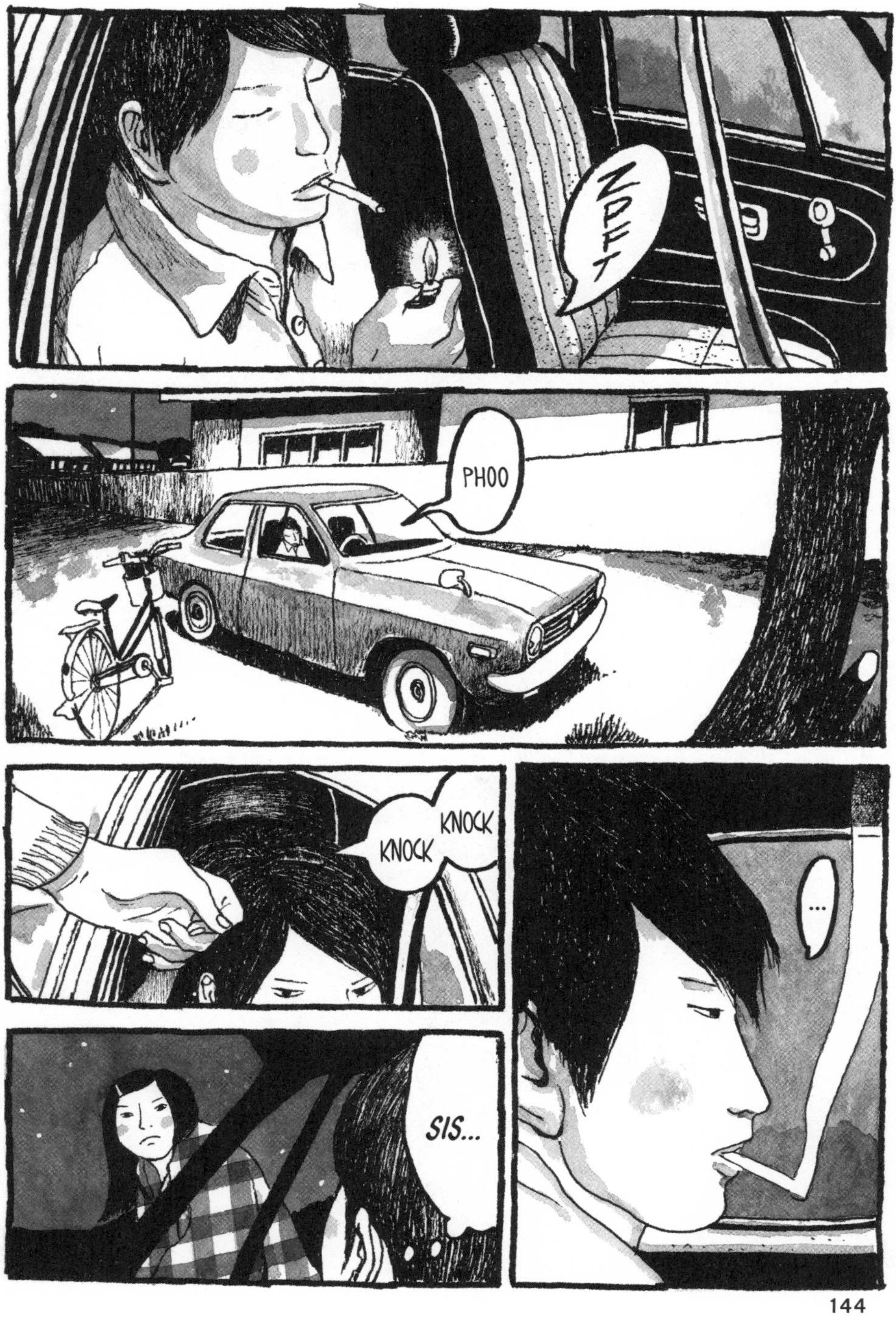
NPFT
PHOO
...
KNOCK
KNOCK
SIS...

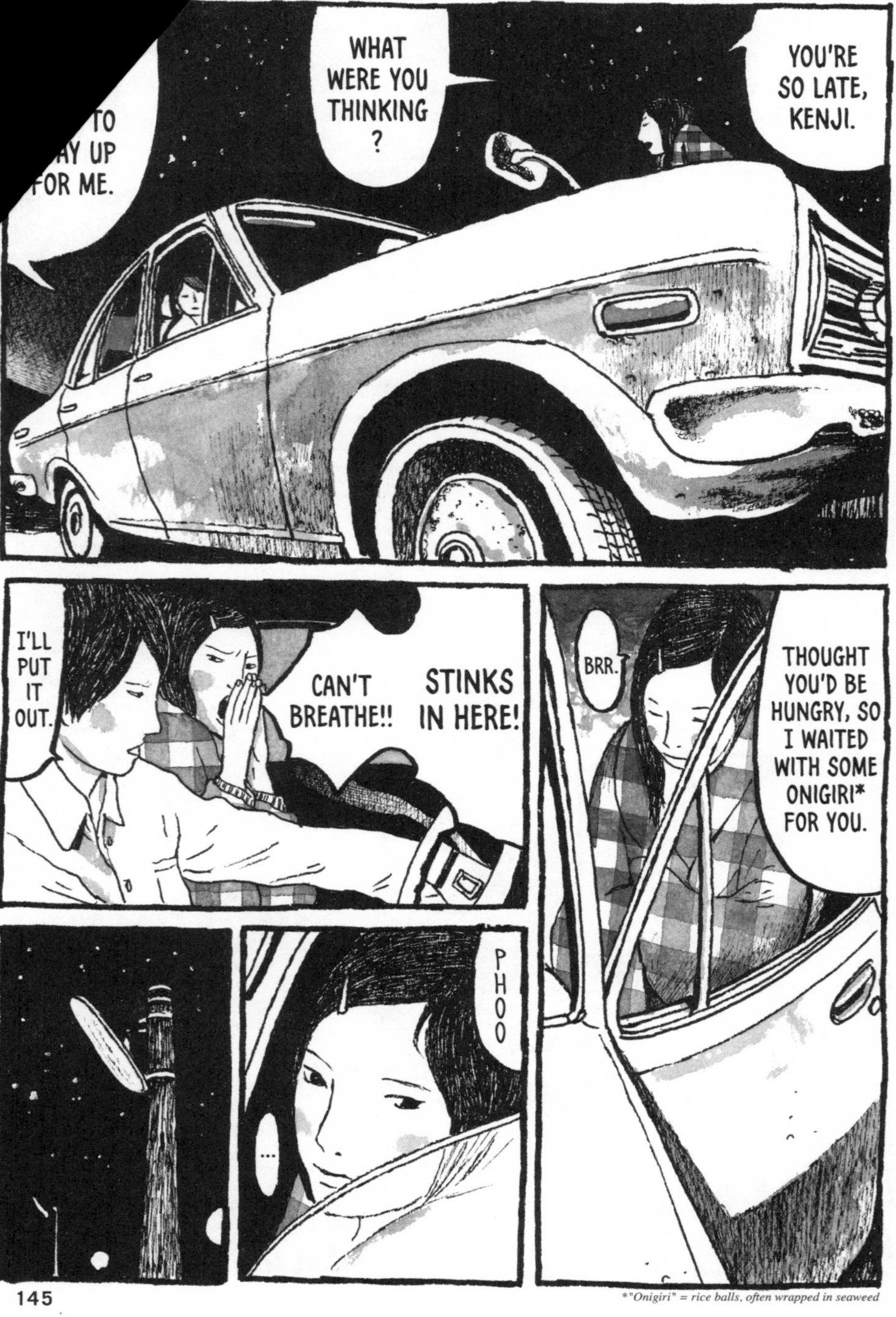
YOU'RE SO LATE, KENJI.
WHAT WERE YOU THINKING?
TO AY UP FOR ME.
THOUGHT YOU'D BE HUNGRY, SO I WAITED WITH SOME ONIGIRI* FOR YOU.
BRR.
STINKS IN HERE!
CAN'T BREATHE!!
I'LL PUT IT OUT.
PHOO
...

*"*Onigiri*" = *rice balls, often wrapped in seaweed*

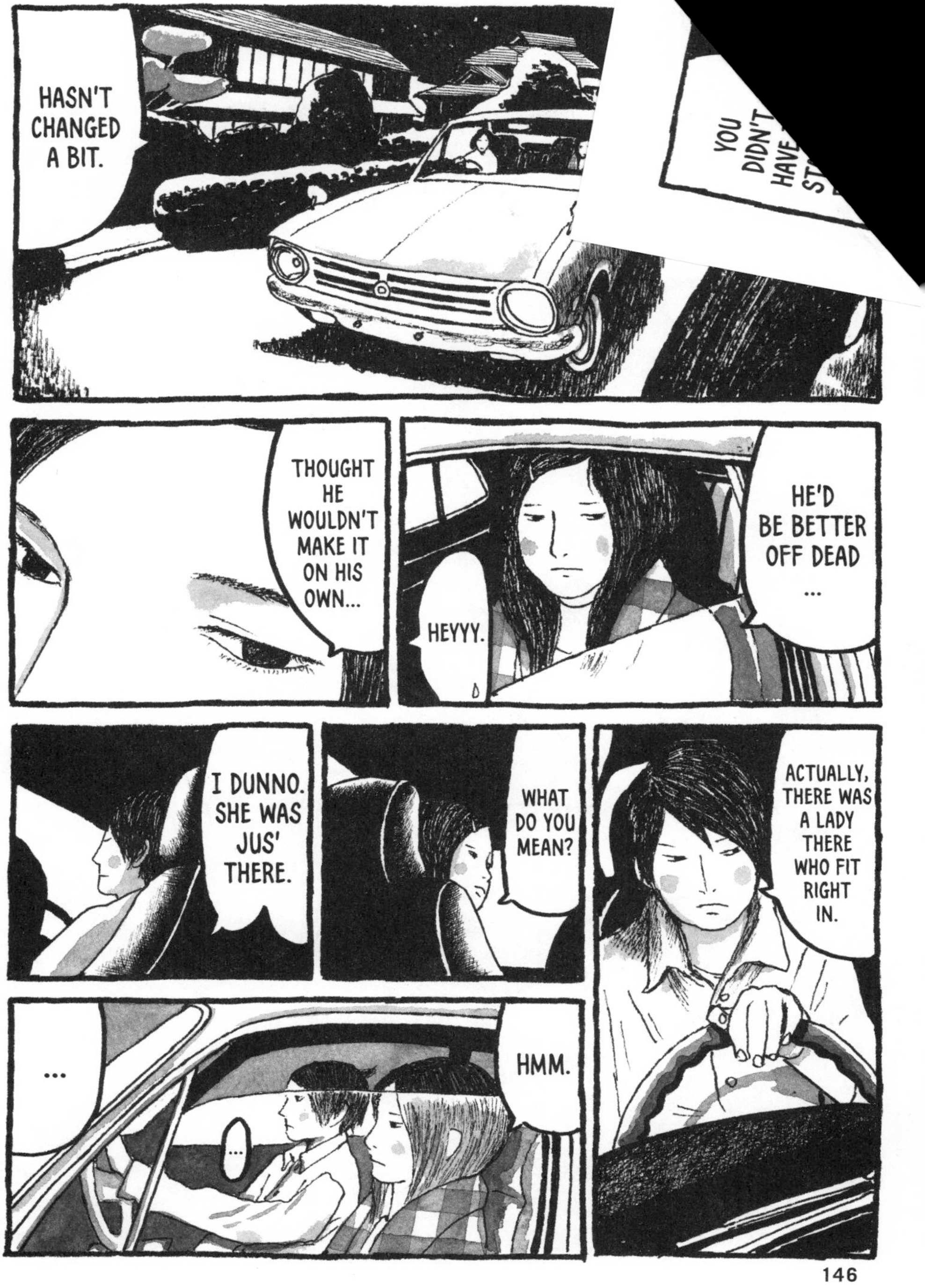
HASN'T CHANGED A BIT.
HE'D BE BETTER OFF DEAD ...
HEYYY.
THOUGHT HE WOULDN'T MAKE IT ON HIS OWN...
ACTUALLY, THERE WAS A LADY THERE WHO FIT RIGHT IN.
WHAT DO YOU MEAN?
I DUNNO. SHE WAS JUS' THERE.
HMM.
...
...

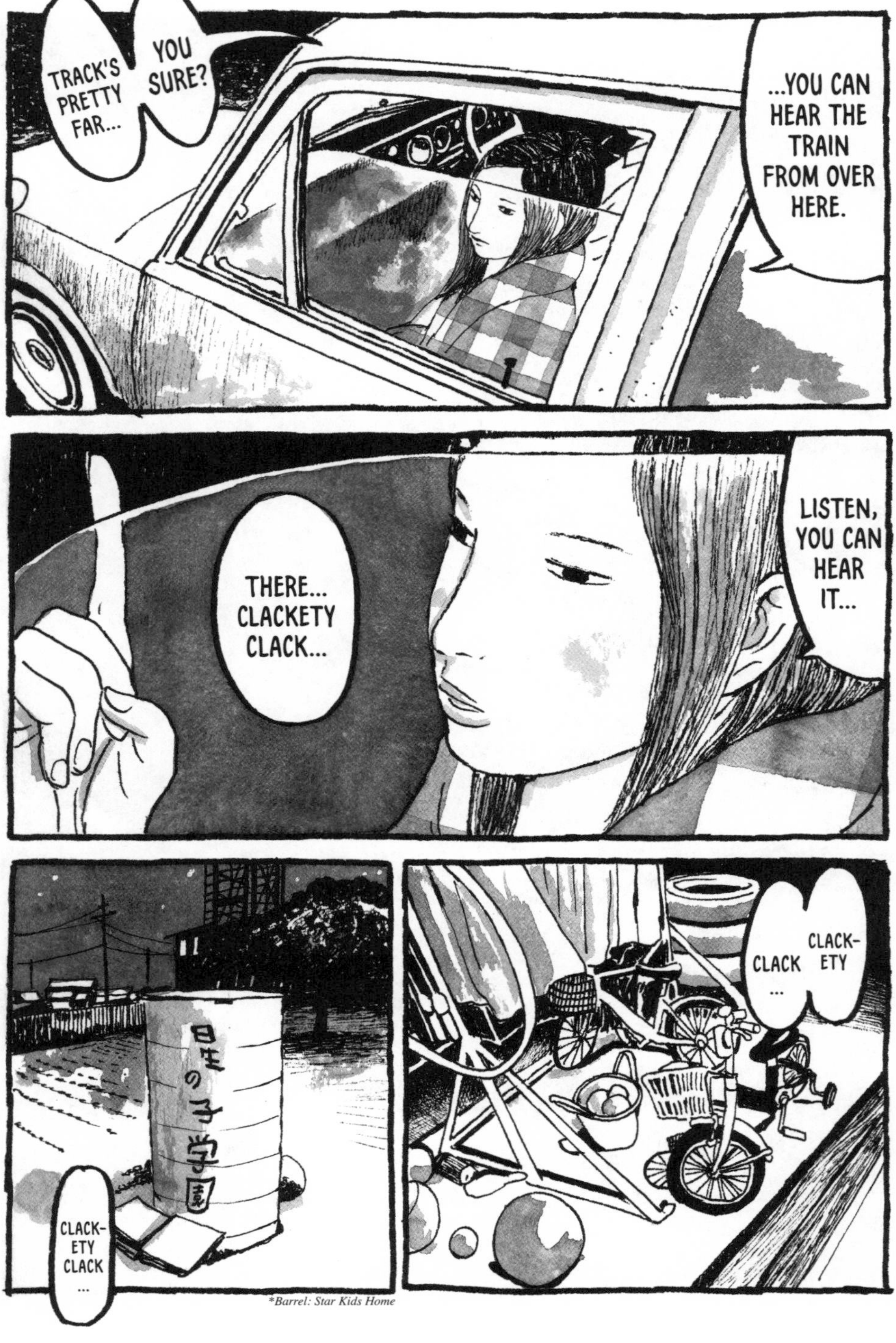
...YOU CAN HEAR THE TRAIN FROM OVER HERE.
YOU SURE?
TRACK'S PRETTY FAR...
LISTEN, YOU CAN HEAR IT...
THERE... CLACKETY CLACK...
CLACK-ETY
CLACK ...
星の子学園
CLACK-ETY CLACK ...

*Barrel: Star Kids Home

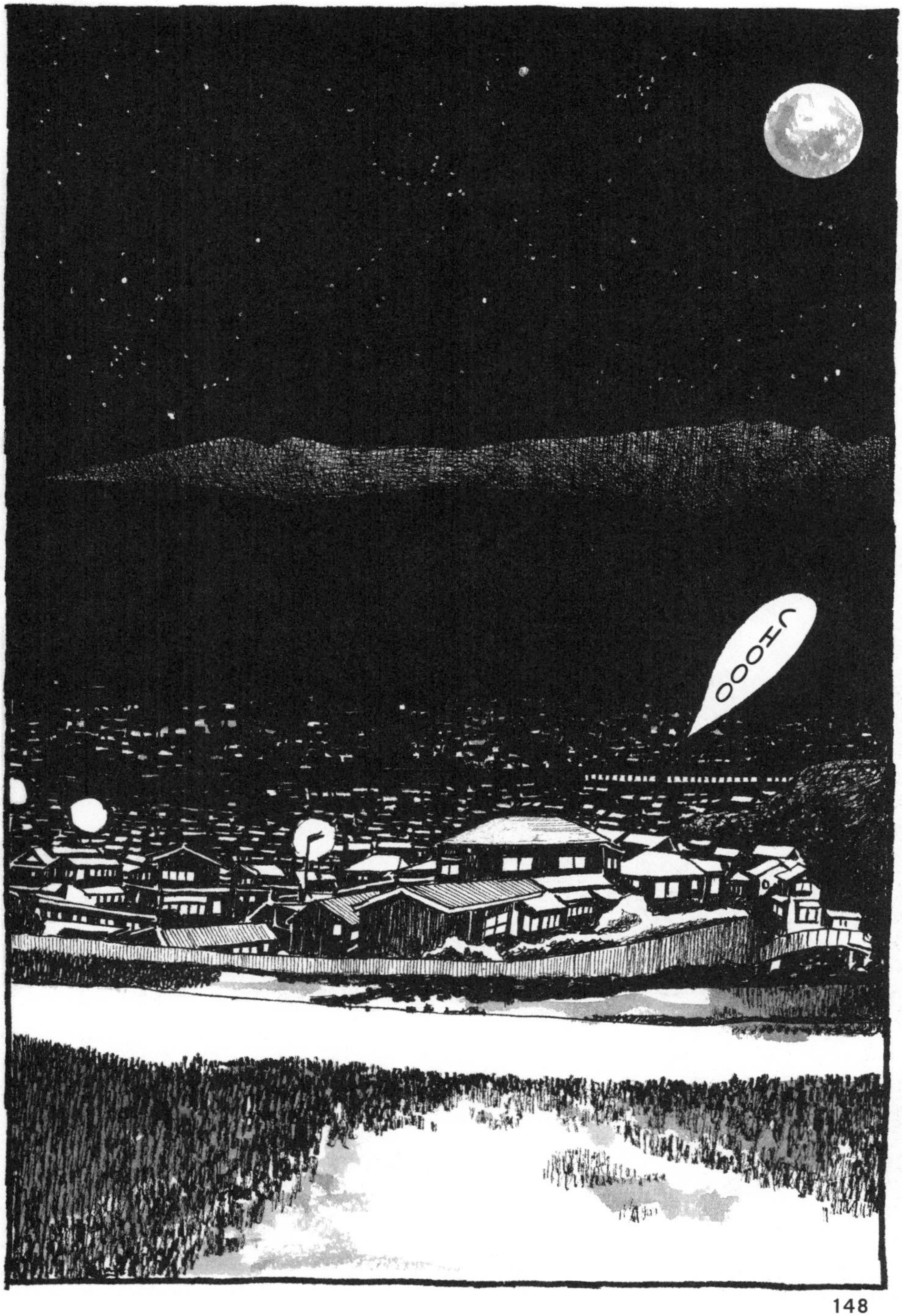
CHOOO

CHAPTER 5

"Whaddya
do when
you feel like
cryin' at
night?"

"Me, I sing."

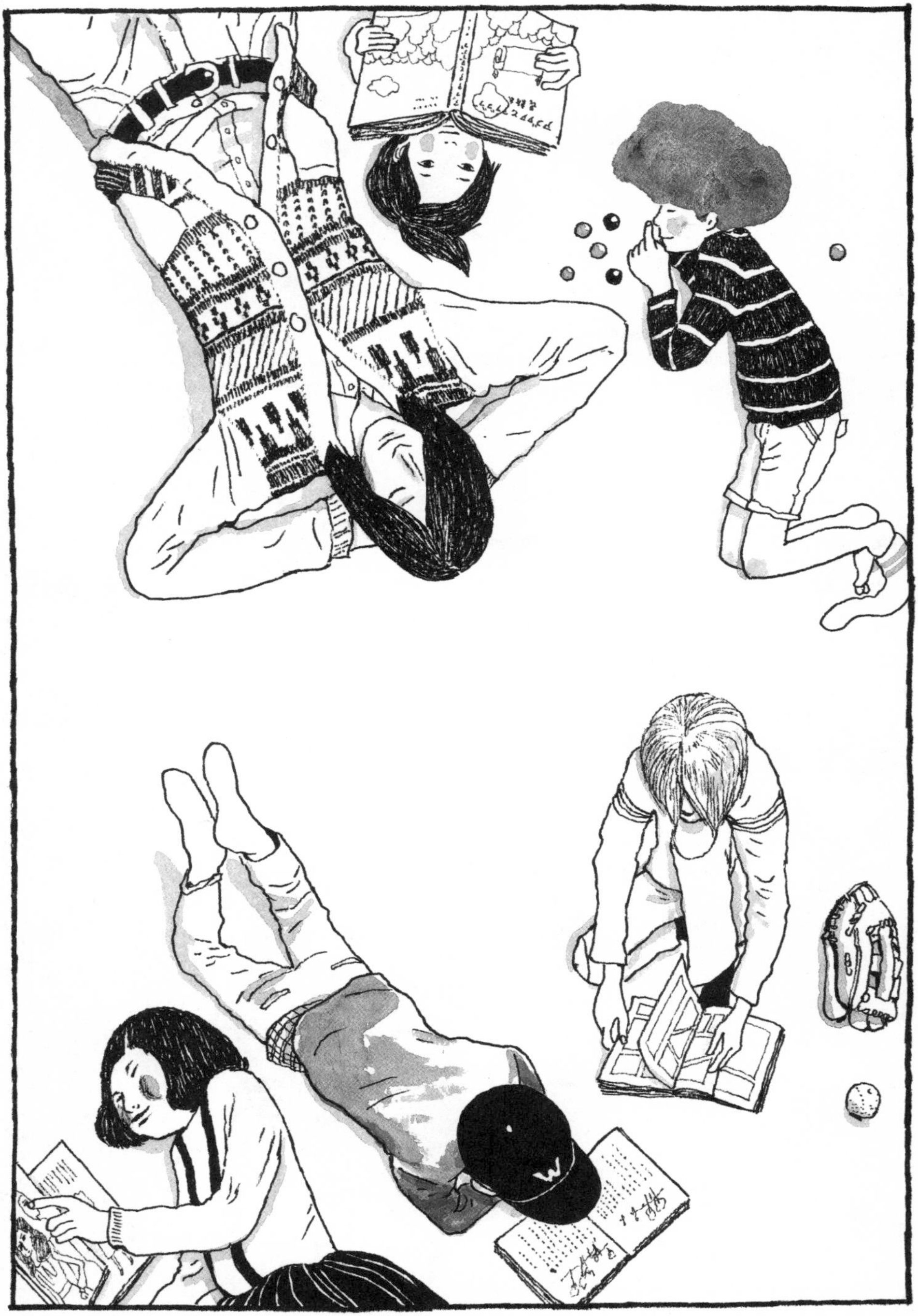

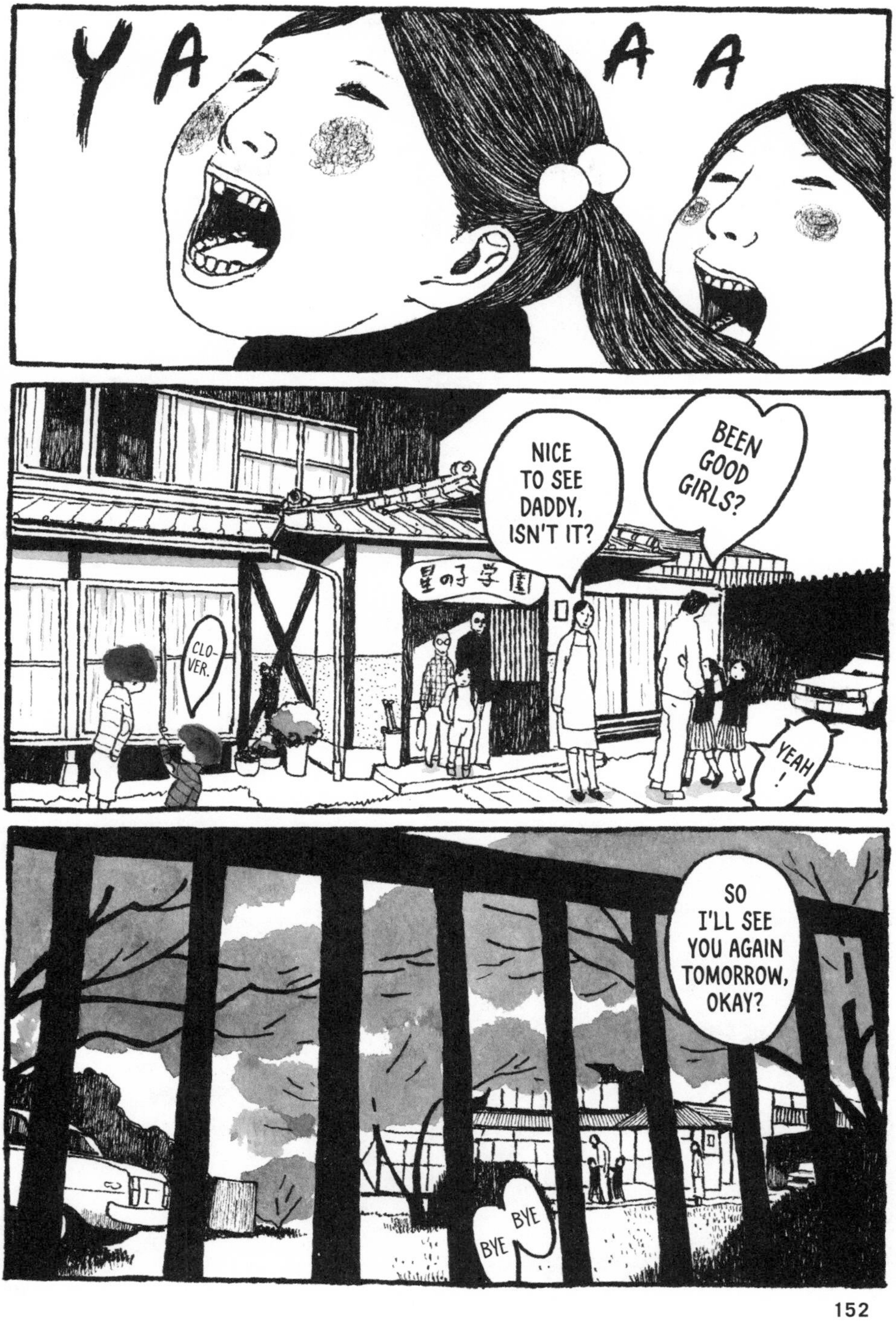
YAAA
BEEN GOOD GIRLS?
YEAH!
星の子学園
NICE TO SEE DADDY, ISN'T IT?
CLO-VER.
SO I'LL SEE YOU AGAIN TOMORROW, OKAY?
BYE BYE

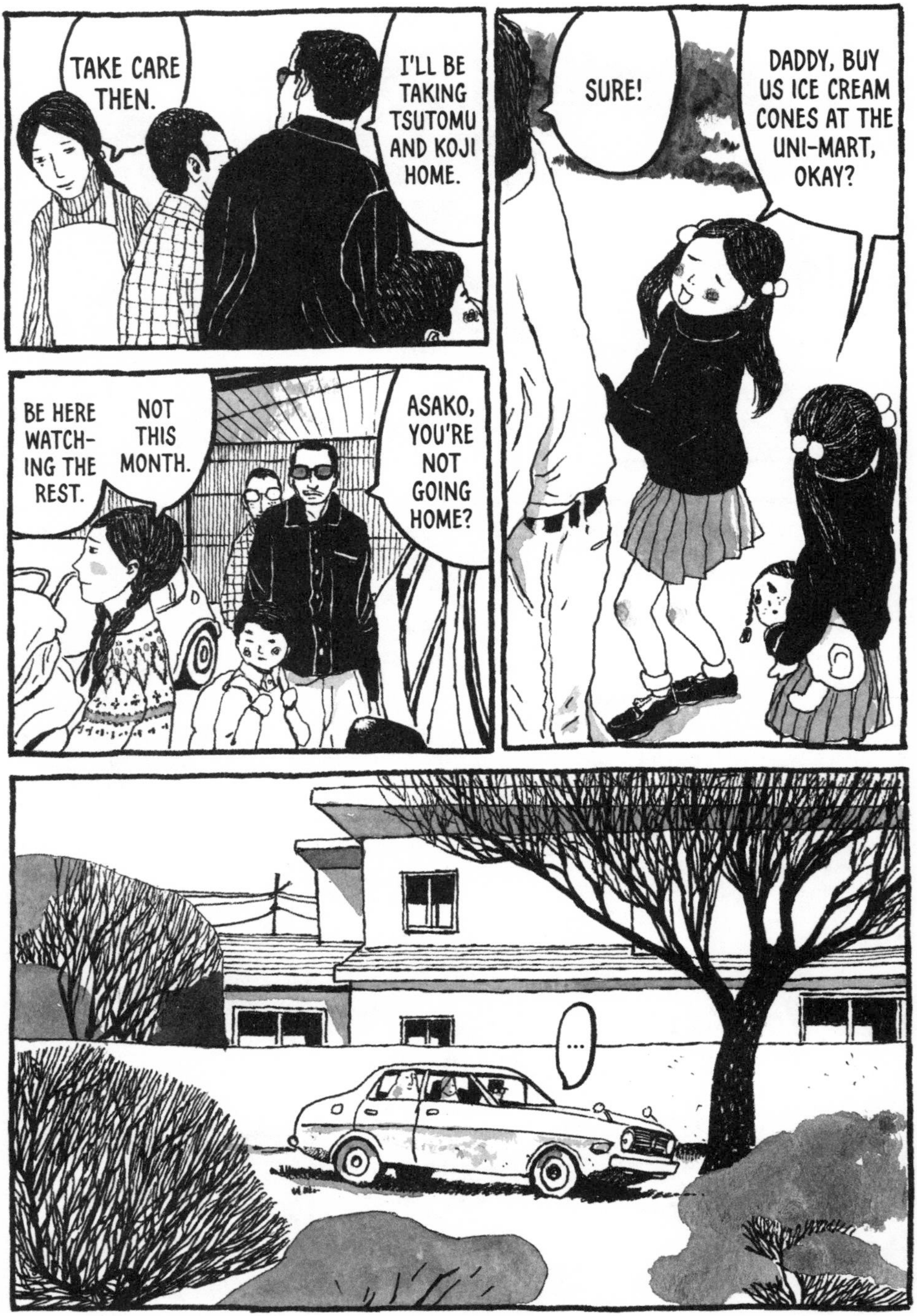
DADDY, BUY US ICE CREAM CONES AT THE UNI-MART, OKAY?
SURE!
I'LL BE TAKING TSUTOMU AND KOJI HOME.
TAKE CARE THEN.
ASAKO, YOU'RE NOT GOING HOME?
NOT THIS MONTH.
BE HERE WATCHING THE REST.
...

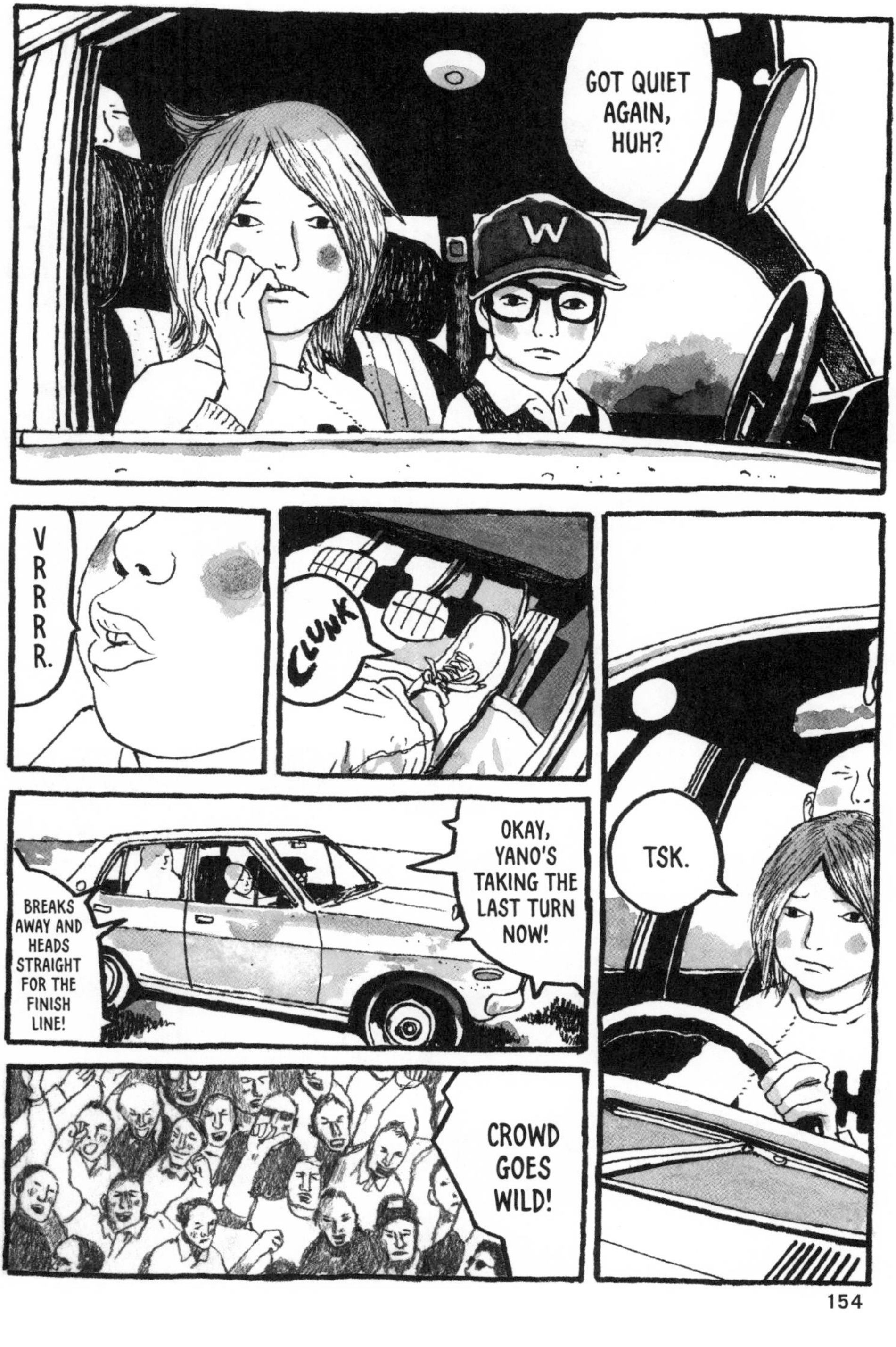
GOT QUIET AGAIN, HUH?
TSK.
CLUNK
VRRRRR.
OKAY, YANO'S TAKING THE LAST TURN NOW!
BREAKS AWAY AND HEADS STRAIGHT FOR THE FINISH LINE!
CROWD GOES WILD!

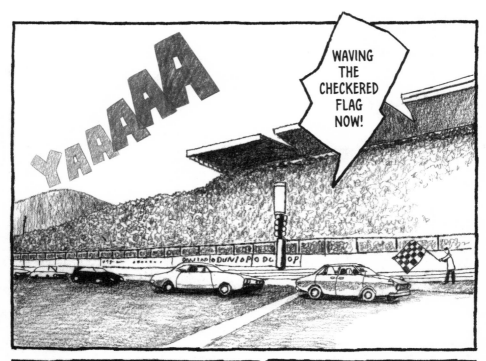

YAAAAA

WAVING THE CHECKERED FLAG NOW!

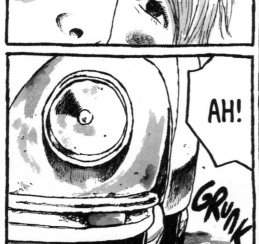

WHA

AH!

GRUNK

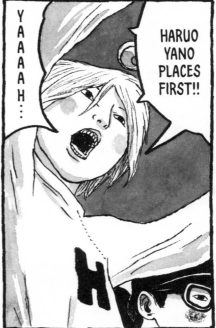

YAAAAH...

HARUO YANO PLACES FIRST!!

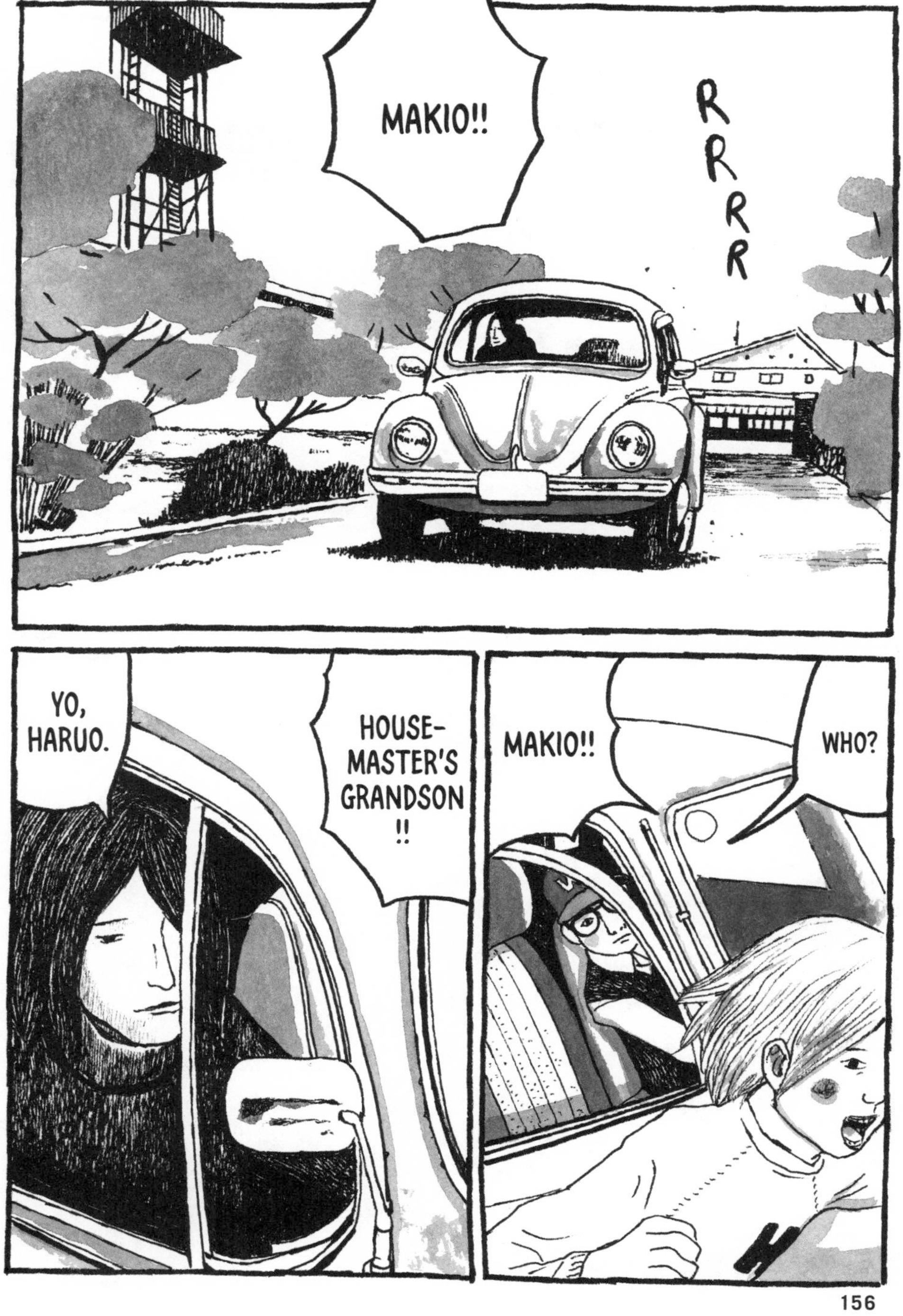
MAKIO!!
RRRR
WHO?
MAKIO!!
HOUSE-MASTER'S GRANDSON !!
YO, HARUO.

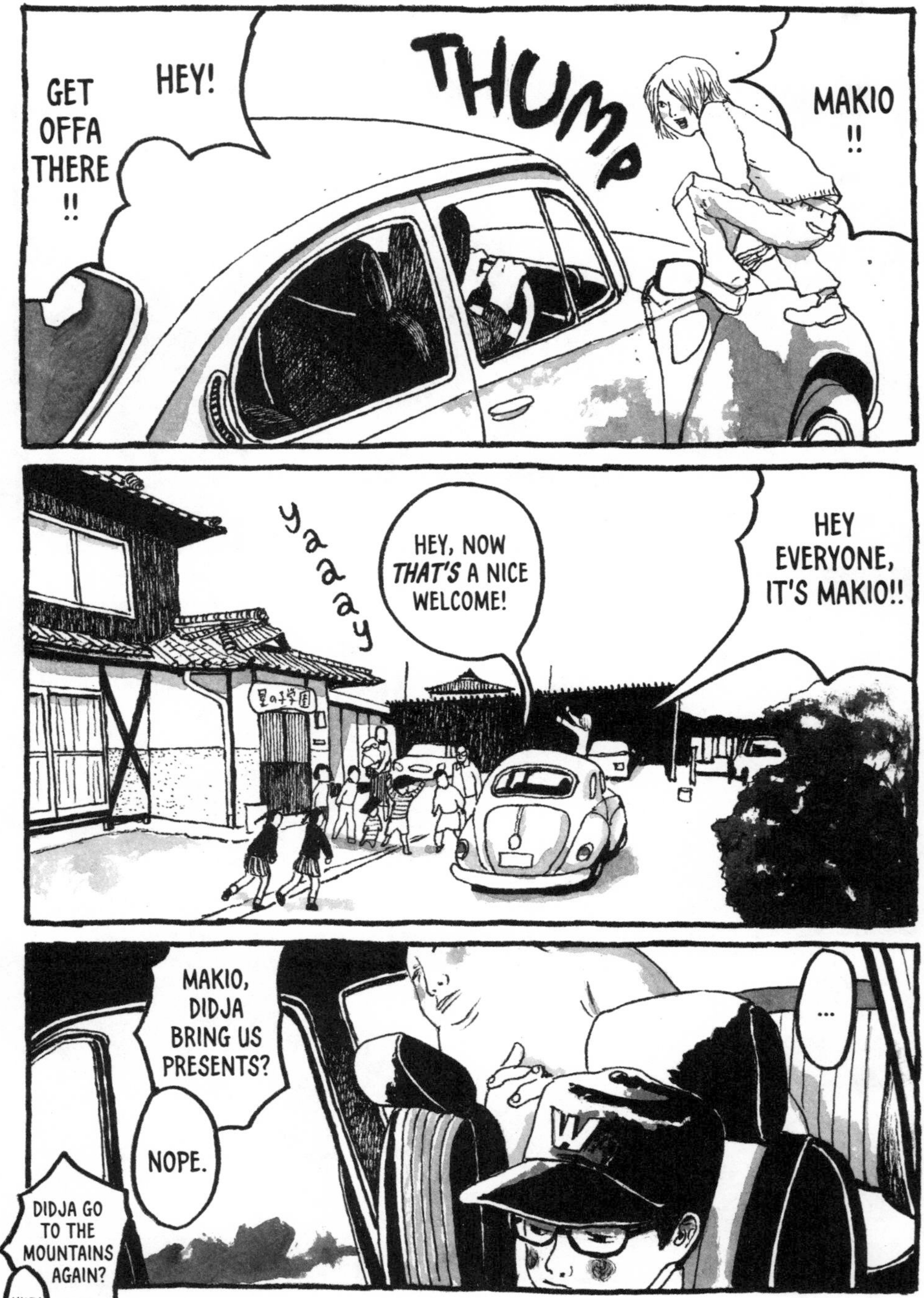
MAKIO !!
THUMP
HEY!
GET OFFA THERE !!
HEY EVERYONE, IT'S MAKIO!!
HEY, NOW *THAT'S* A NICE WELCOME!
yaaaay
星の子学園
...
MAKIO, DIDJA BRING US PRESENTS?
NOPE.
DIDJA GO TO THE MOUNTAINS AGAIN?
YUP!

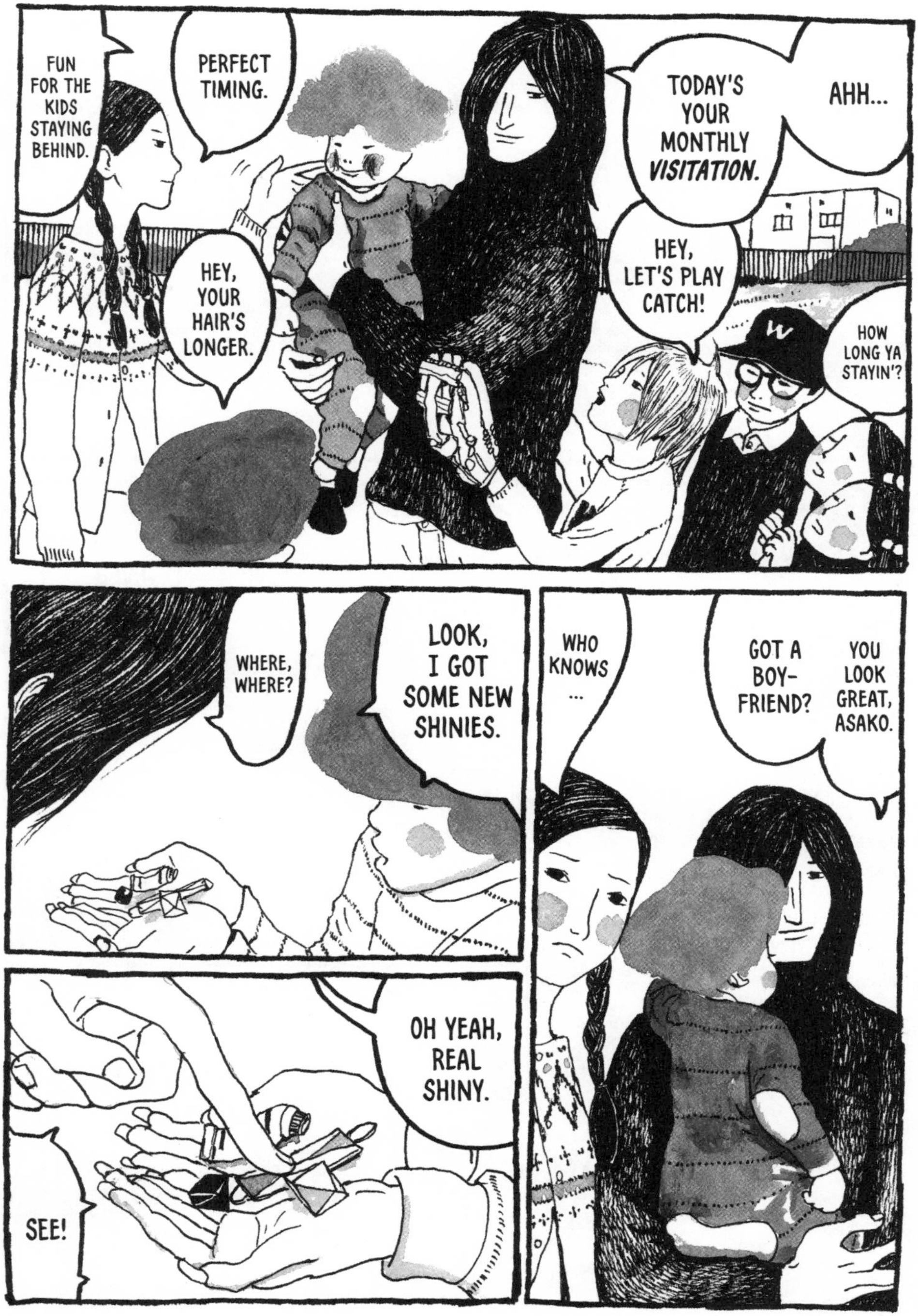
AHH...
TODAY'S YOUR MONTHLY *VISITATION.*
PERFECT TIMING.
FUN FOR THE KIDS STAYING BEHIND.
HOW LONG YA STAYIN'?
HEY, LET'S PLAY CATCH!
HEY, YOUR HAIR'S LONGER.
YOU LOOK GREAT, ASAKO.
GOT A BOY-FRIEND?
WHO KNOWS ...
LOOK, I GOT SOME NEW SHINIES.
WHERE, WHERE?
OH YEAH, REAL SHINY.
SEE!

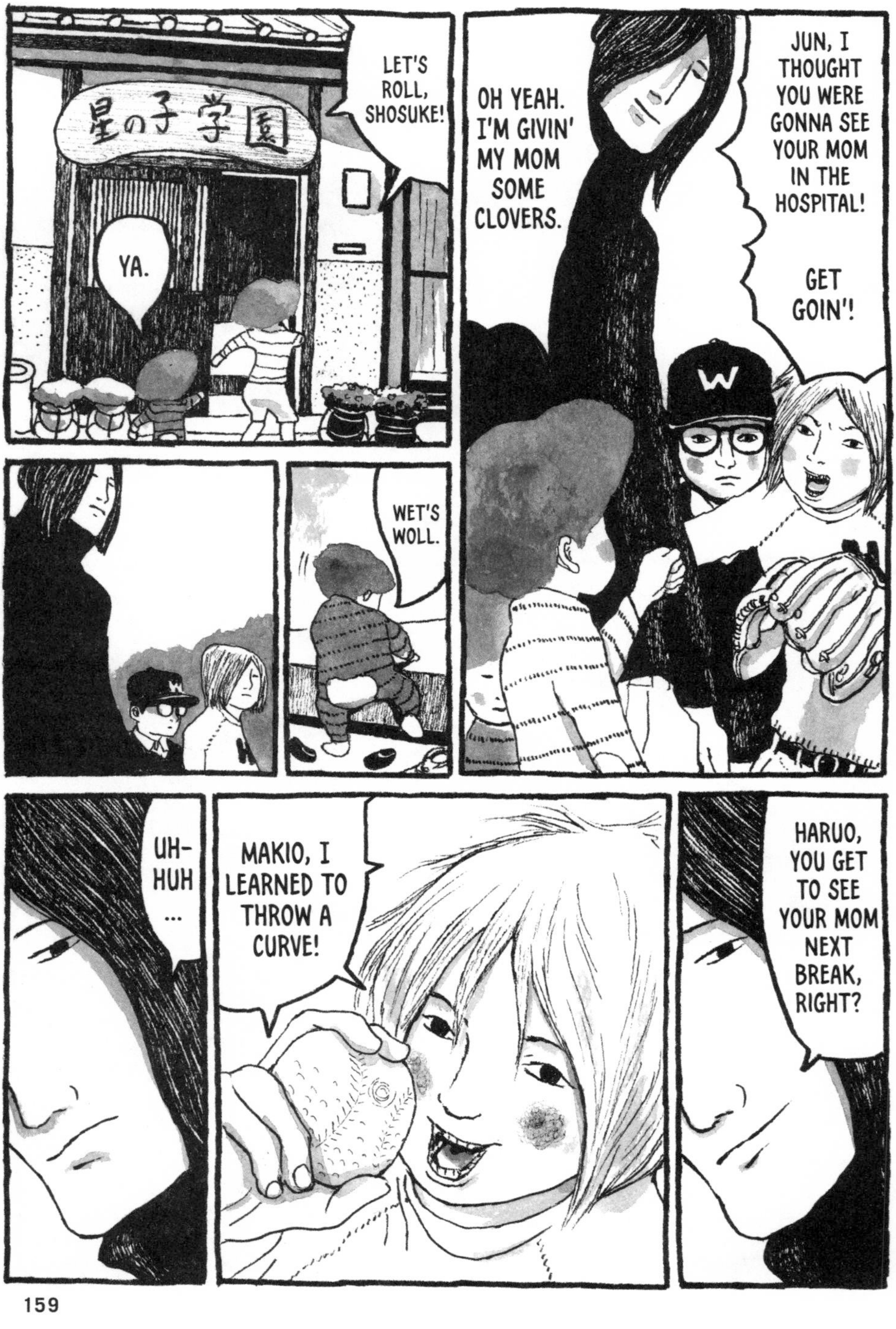
JUN, I THOUGHT YOU WERE GONNA SEE YOUR MOM IN THE HOSPITAL!
GET GOIN'!
OH YEAH. I'M GIVIN' MY MOM SOME CLOVERS.
LET'S ROLL, SHOSUKE!
星の子学園
YA.
WET'S WOLL.
HARUO, YOU GET TO SEE YOUR MOM NEXT BREAK, RIGHT?
MAKIO, I LEARNED TO THROW A CURVE!
UH-HUH ...

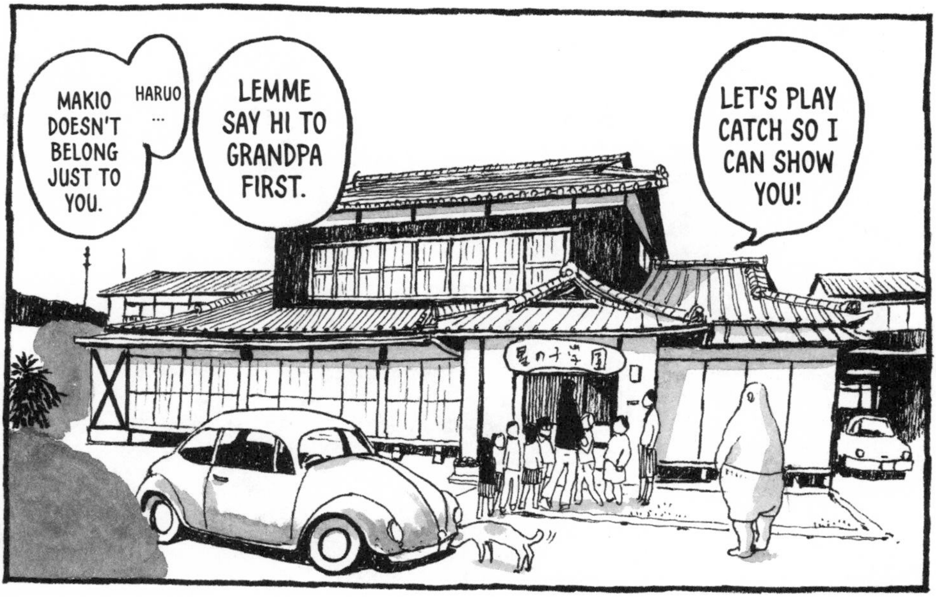
LET'S PLAY CATCH SO I CAN SHOW YOU!
LEMME SAY HI TO GRANDPA FIRST.
HARUO ...
MAKIO DOESN'T BELONG JUST TO YOU.

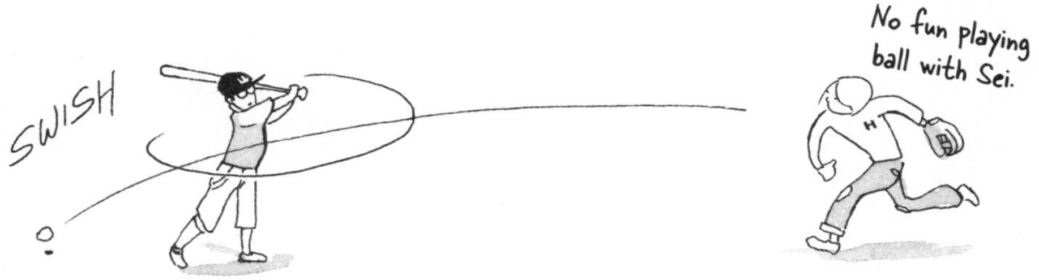
No fun playing ball with Sei.
SWISH

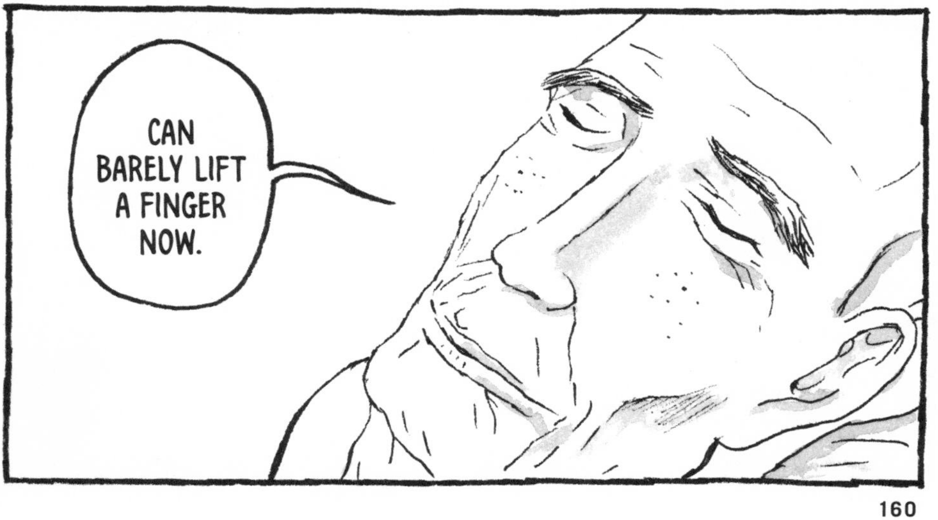
CAN BARELY LIFT A FINGER NOW.

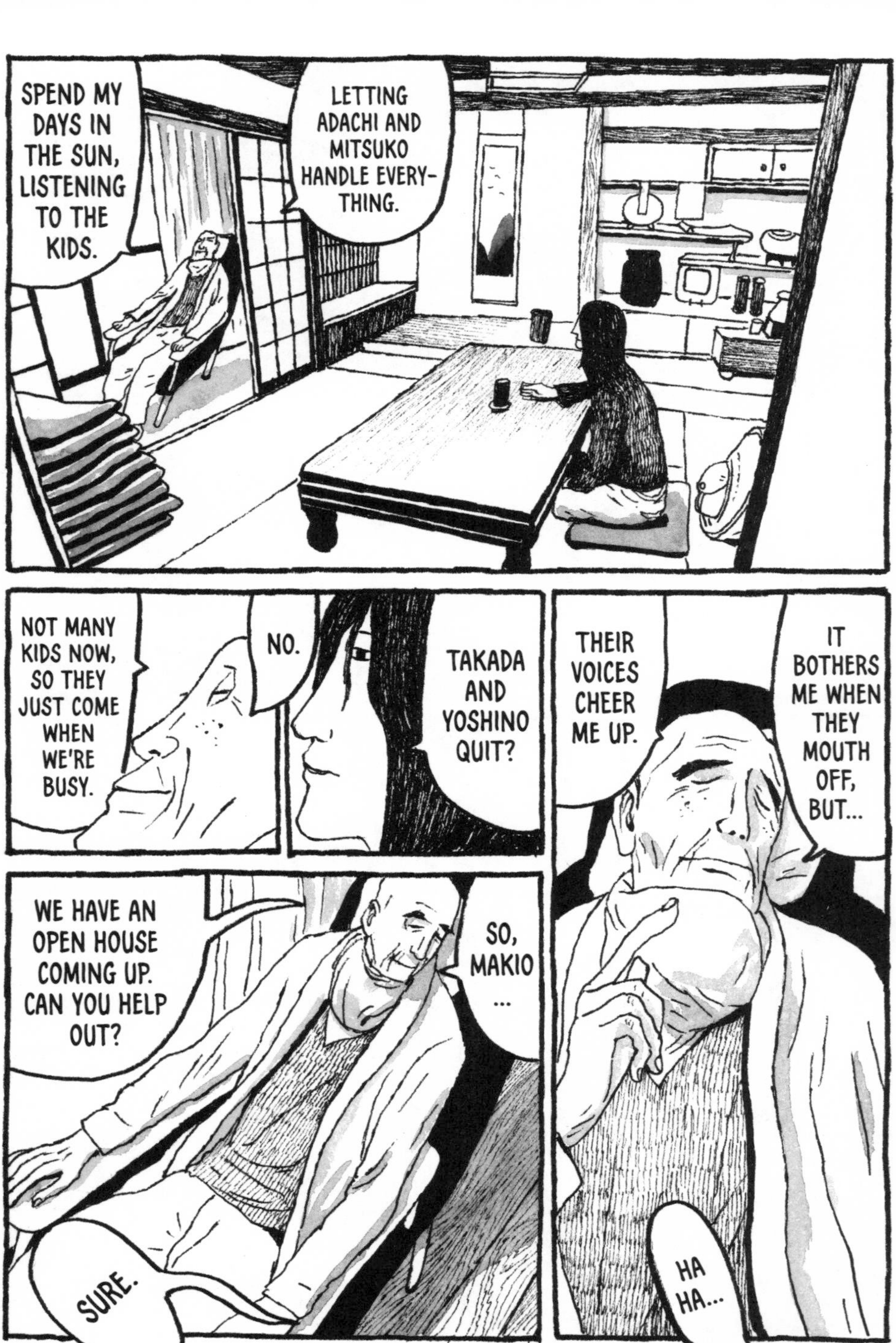
LETTING ADACHI AND MITSUKO HANDLE EVERY-THING.
SPEND MY DAYS IN THE SUN, LISTENING TO THE KIDS.
IT BOTHERS ME WHEN THEY MOUTH OFF, BUT...
THEIR VOICES CHEER ME UP.
HA HA...
TAKADA AND YOSHINO QUIT?
NO.
NOT MANY KIDS NOW, SO THEY JUST COME WHEN WE'RE BUSY.
SO, MAKIO ...
WE HAVE AN OPEN HOUSE COMING UP. CAN YOU HELP OUT?
SURE.

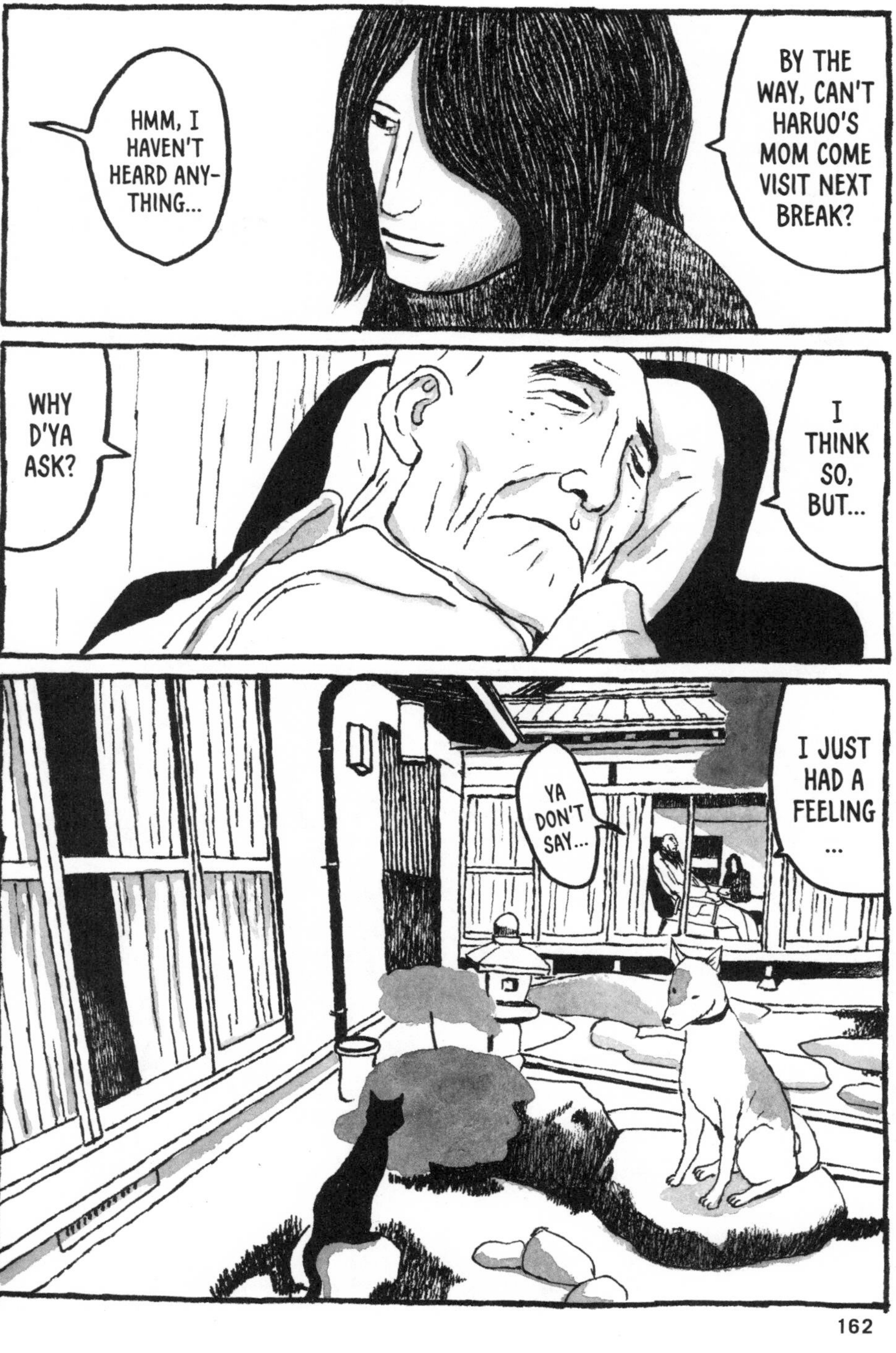
BY THE WAY, CAN'T HARUO'S MOM COME VISIT NEXT BREAK?
HMM, I HAVEN'T HEARD ANYTHING...
I THINK SO, BUT...
WHY D'YA ASK?
I JUST HAD A FEELING ...
YA DON'T SAY...

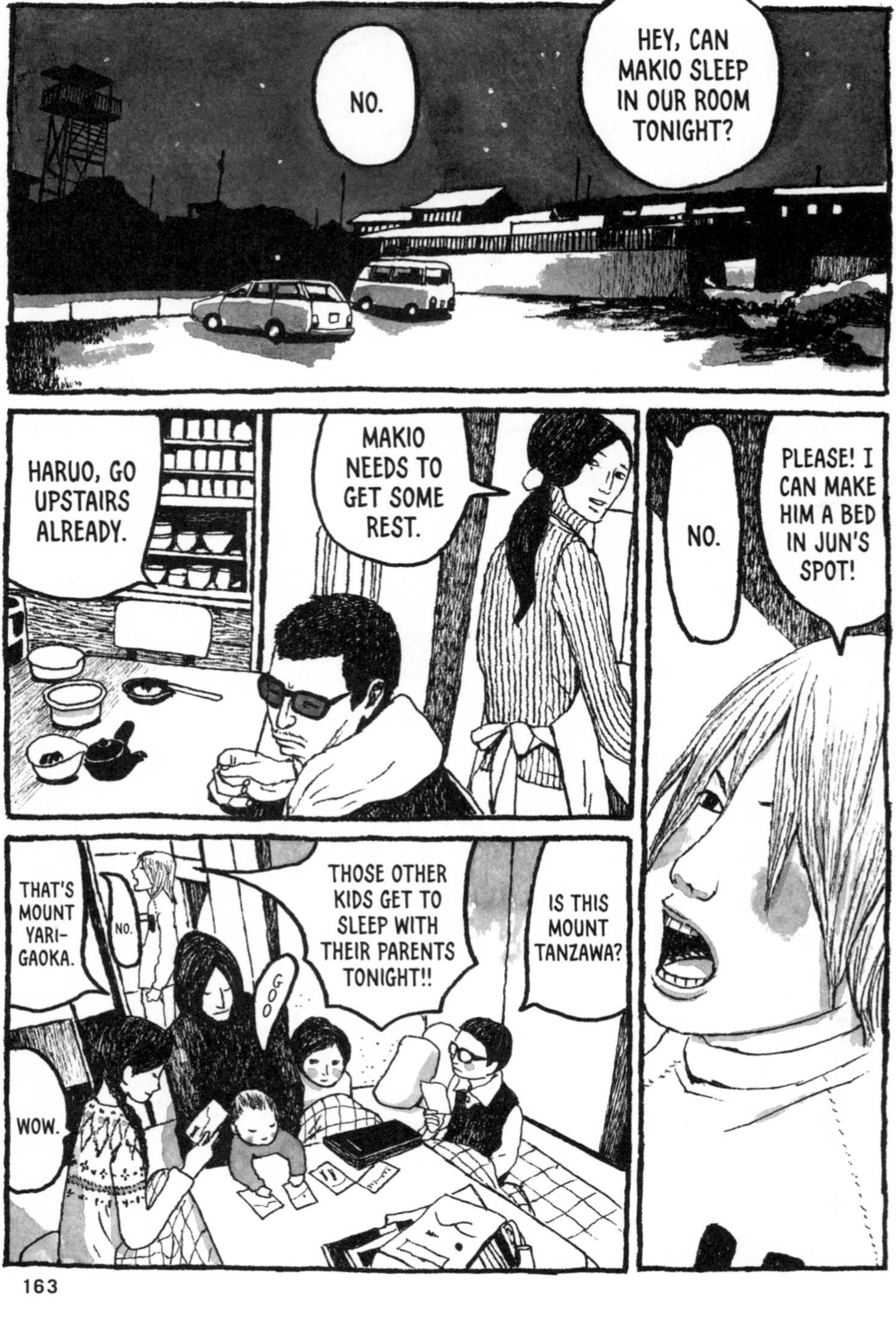
HEY, CAN MAKIO SLEEP IN OUR ROOM TONIGHT?
NO.
PLEASE! I CAN MAKE HIM A BED IN JUN'S SPOT!
NO.
MAKIO NEEDS TO GET SOME REST.
HARUO, GO UPSTAIRS ALREADY.
IS THIS MOUNT TANZAWA?
THOSE OTHER KIDS GET TO SLEEP WITH THEIR PARENTS TONIGHT!!
GOO
NO.
THAT'S MOUNT YARI-GAOKA.
WOW.

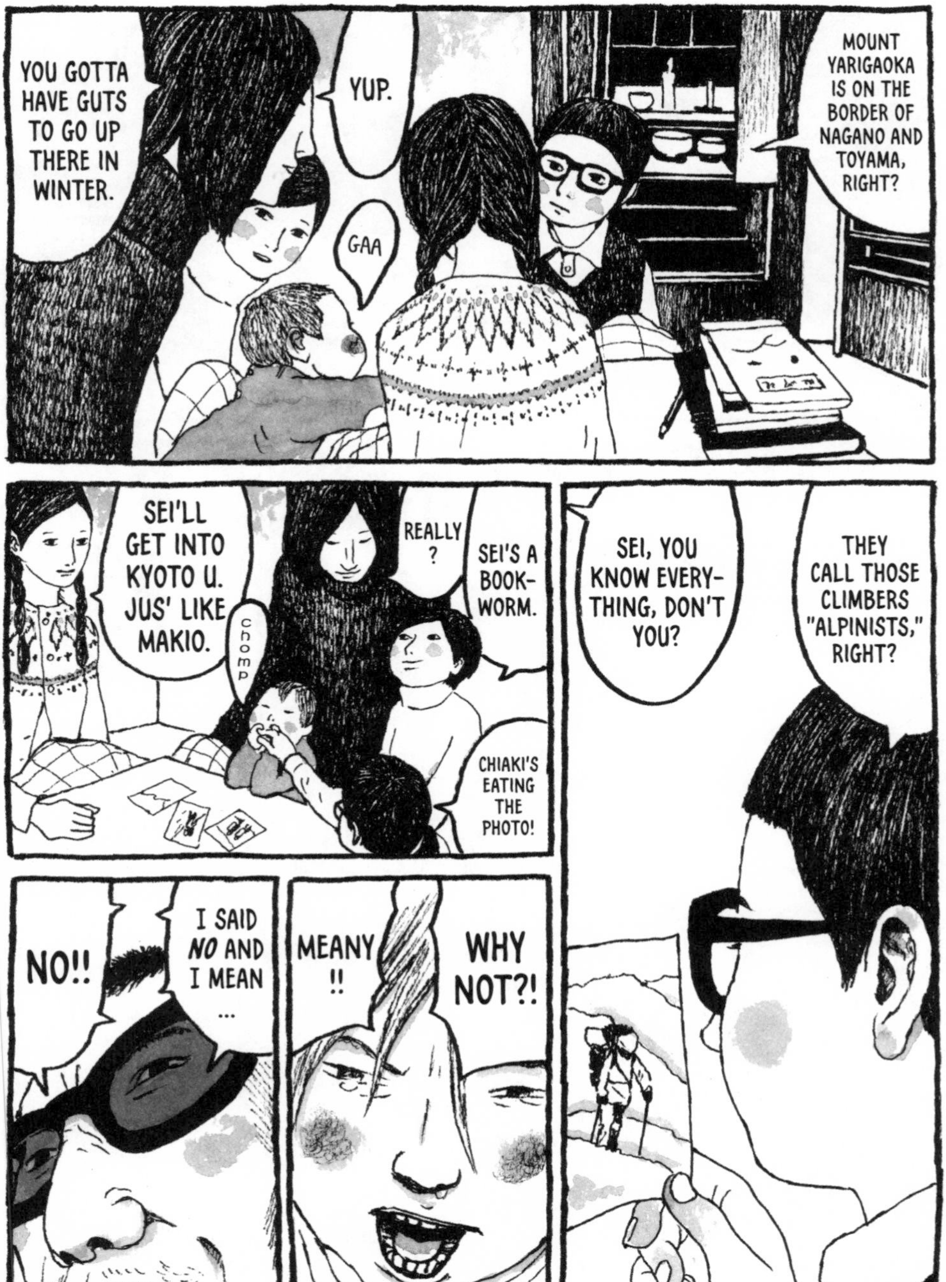
MOUNT YARIGAOKA IS ON THE BORDER OF NAGANO AND TOYAMA, RIGHT?
YUP.
YOU GOTTA HAVE GUTS TO GO UP THERE IN WINTER.
GAA
THEY CALL THOSE CLIMBERS "ALPINISTS," RIGHT?
SEI, YOU KNOW EVERY-THING, DON'T YOU?
SEI'S A BOOK-WORM.
REALLY?
SEI'LL GET INTO KYOTO U. JUS' LIKE MAKIO.
CHOMP
CHIAKI'S EATING THE PHOTO!
WHY NOT?!
MEANY!!
I SAID *NO* AND I MEAN ...
NO!!

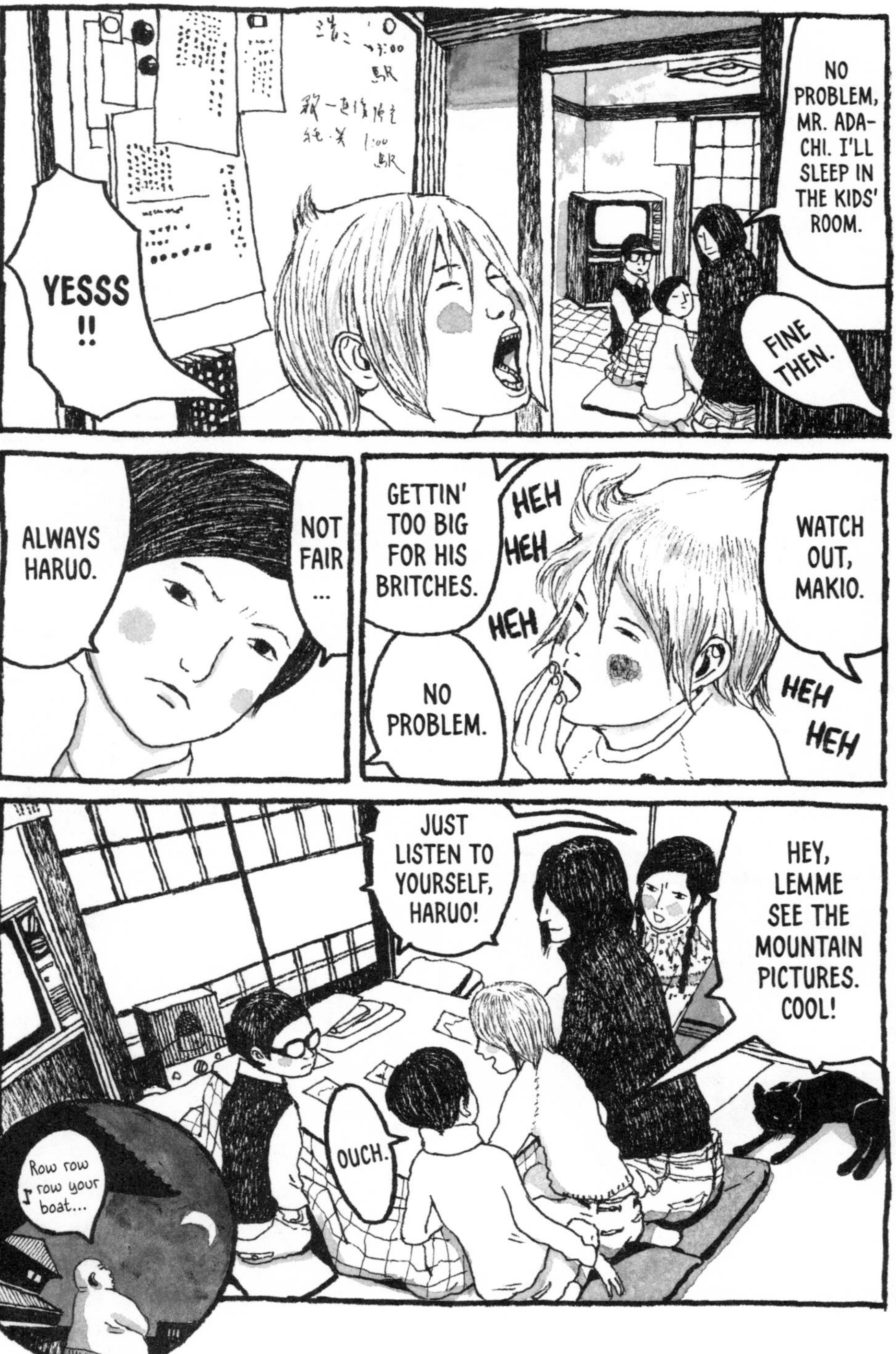
NO PROBLEM, MR. ADA-CHI. I'LL SLEEP IN THE KIDS' ROOM.
FINE THEN.
YESSS!!
WATCH OUT, MAKIO.
HEH HEH
GETTIN' TOO BIG FOR HIS BRITCHES.
HEH HEH
HEH
NO PROBLEM.
NOT FAIR...
ALWAYS HARUO.
HEY, LEMME SEE THE MOUNTAIN PICTURES. COOL!
JUST LISTEN TO YOURSELF, HARUO!
OUCH.
Row row row your boat...

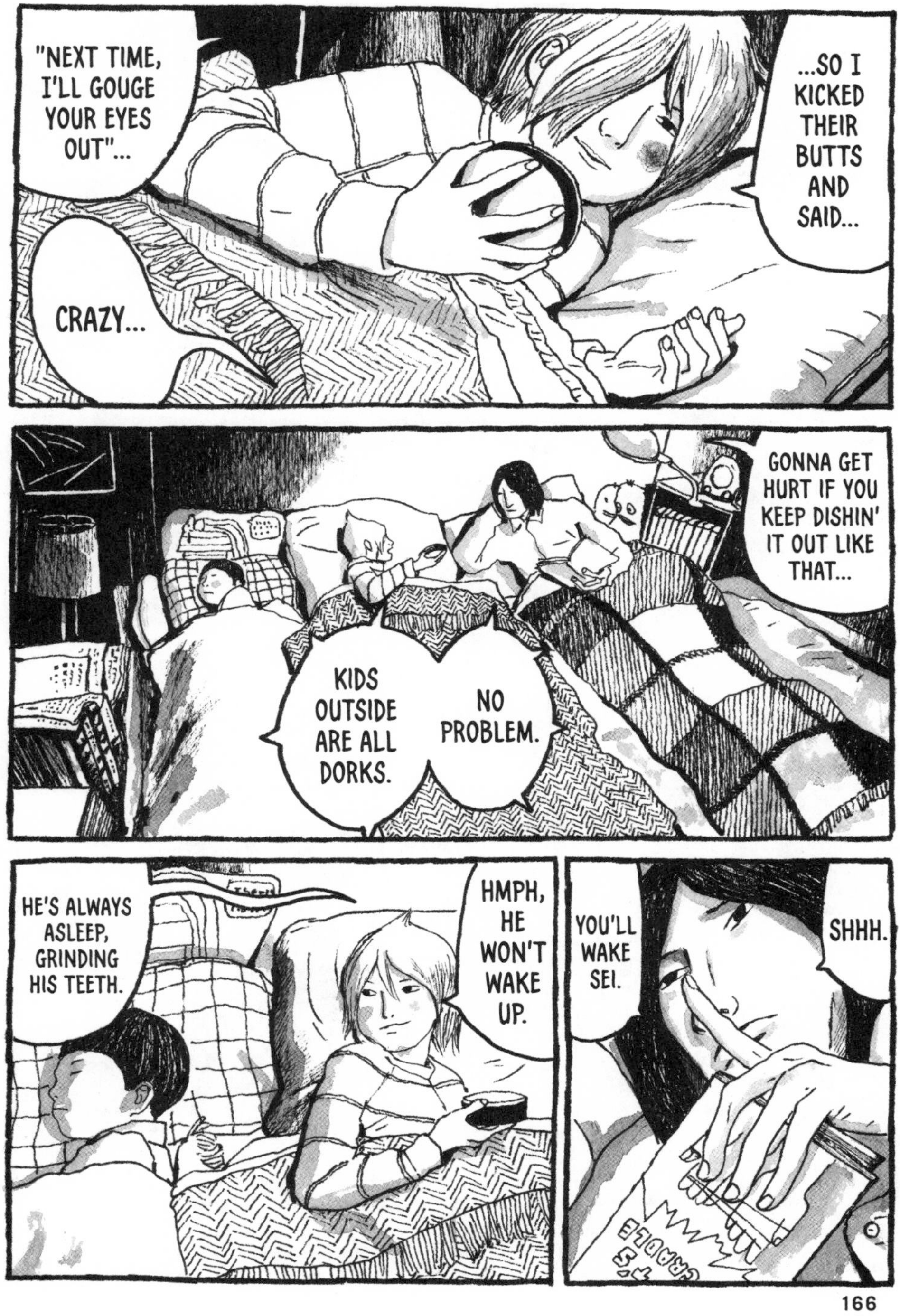
...SO I KICKED THEIR BUTTS AND SAID...
"NEXT TIME, I'LL GOUGE YOUR EYES OUT"...
CRAZY...
GONNA GET HURT IF YOU KEEP DISHIN' IT OUT LIKE THAT...
NO PROBLEM.
KIDS OUTSIDE ARE ALL DORKS.
SHHH.
YOU'LL WAKE SEI.
HMPH, HE WON'T WAKE UP.
HE'S ALWAYS ASLEEP, GRINDING HIS TEETH.

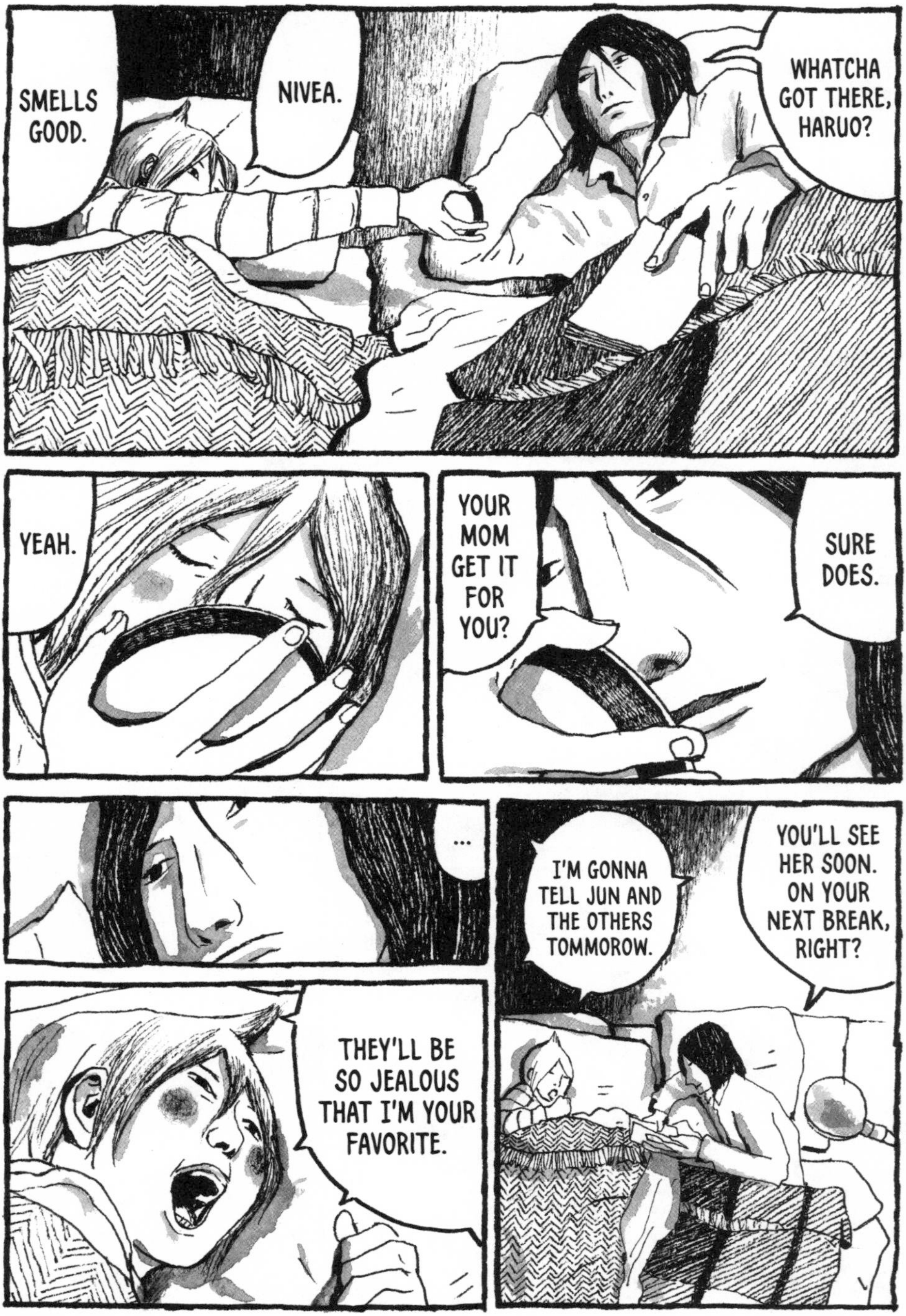
WHATCHA GOT THERE, HARUO?
NIVEA.
SMELLS GOOD.
SURE DOES.
YOUR MOM GET IT FOR YOU?
YEAH.
YOU'LL SEE HER SOON. ON YOUR NEXT BREAK, RIGHT?
I'M GONNA TELL JUN AND THE OTHERS TOMMOROW.
...
THEY'LL BE SO JEALOUS THAT I'M YOUR FAVORITE.

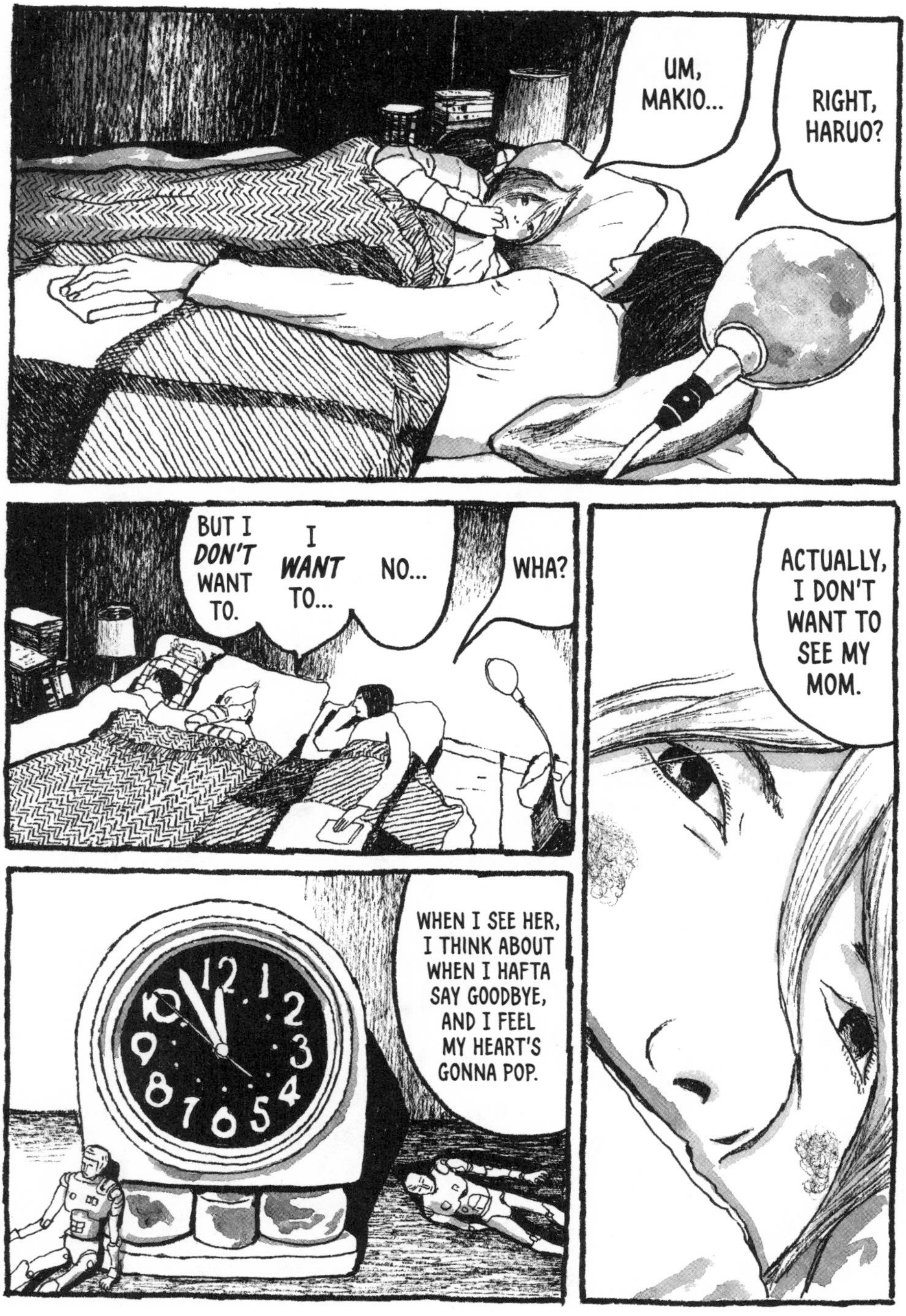
RIGHT, HARUO?
UM, MAKIO...
WHA?
NO...
I *WANT* TO...
BUT I *DON'T* WANT TO.
ACTUALLY, I DON'T WANT TO SEE MY MOM.
WHEN I SEE HER, I THINK ABOUT WHEN I HAFTA SAY GOODBYE, AND I FEEL MY HEART'S GONNA POP.

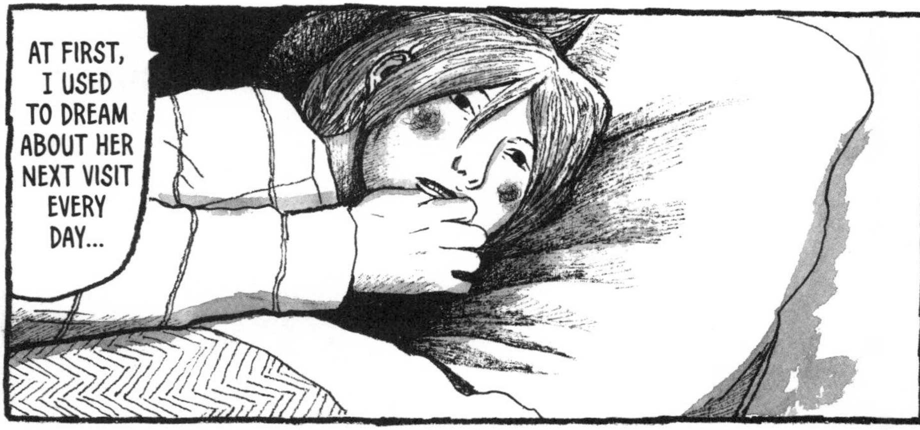
AT FIRST, I USED TO DREAM ABOUT HER NEXT VISIT EVERY DAY...
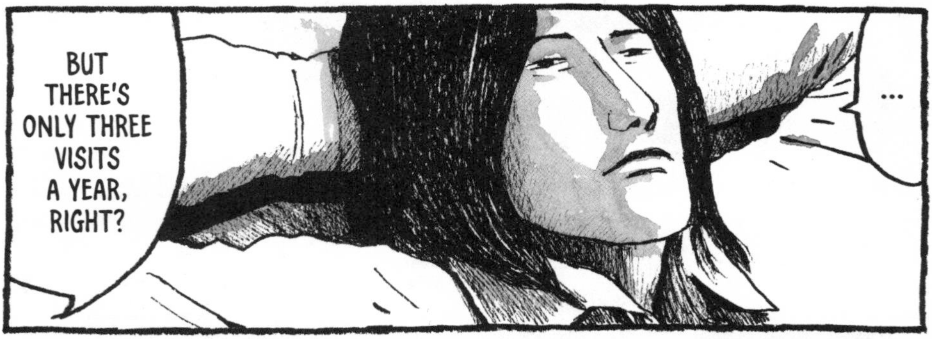
...
BUT THERE'S ONLY THREE VISITS A YEAR, RIGHT?
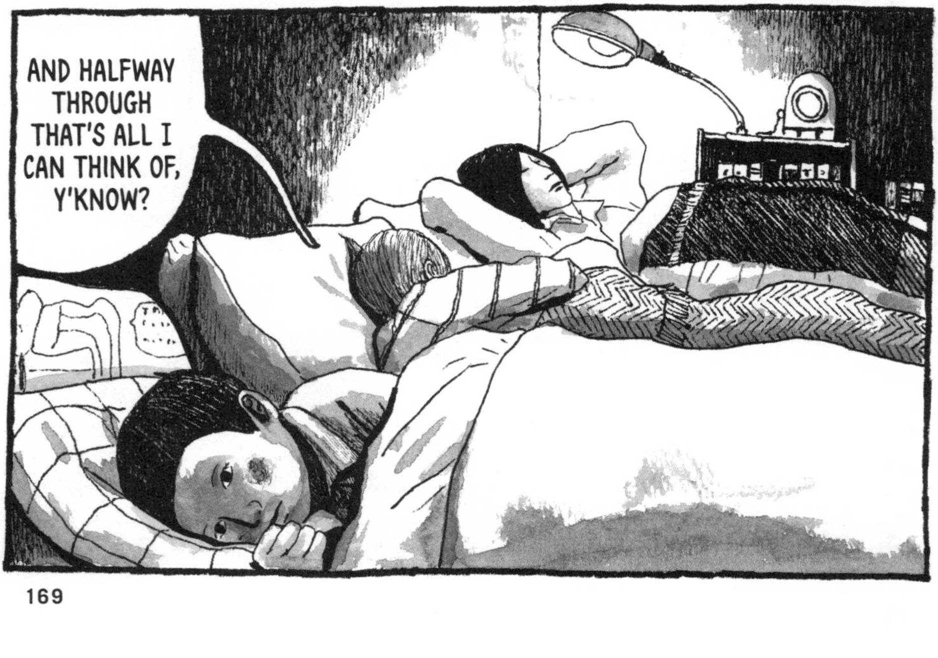
AND HALFWAY THROUGH THAT'S ALL I CAN THINK OF, Y'KNOW?

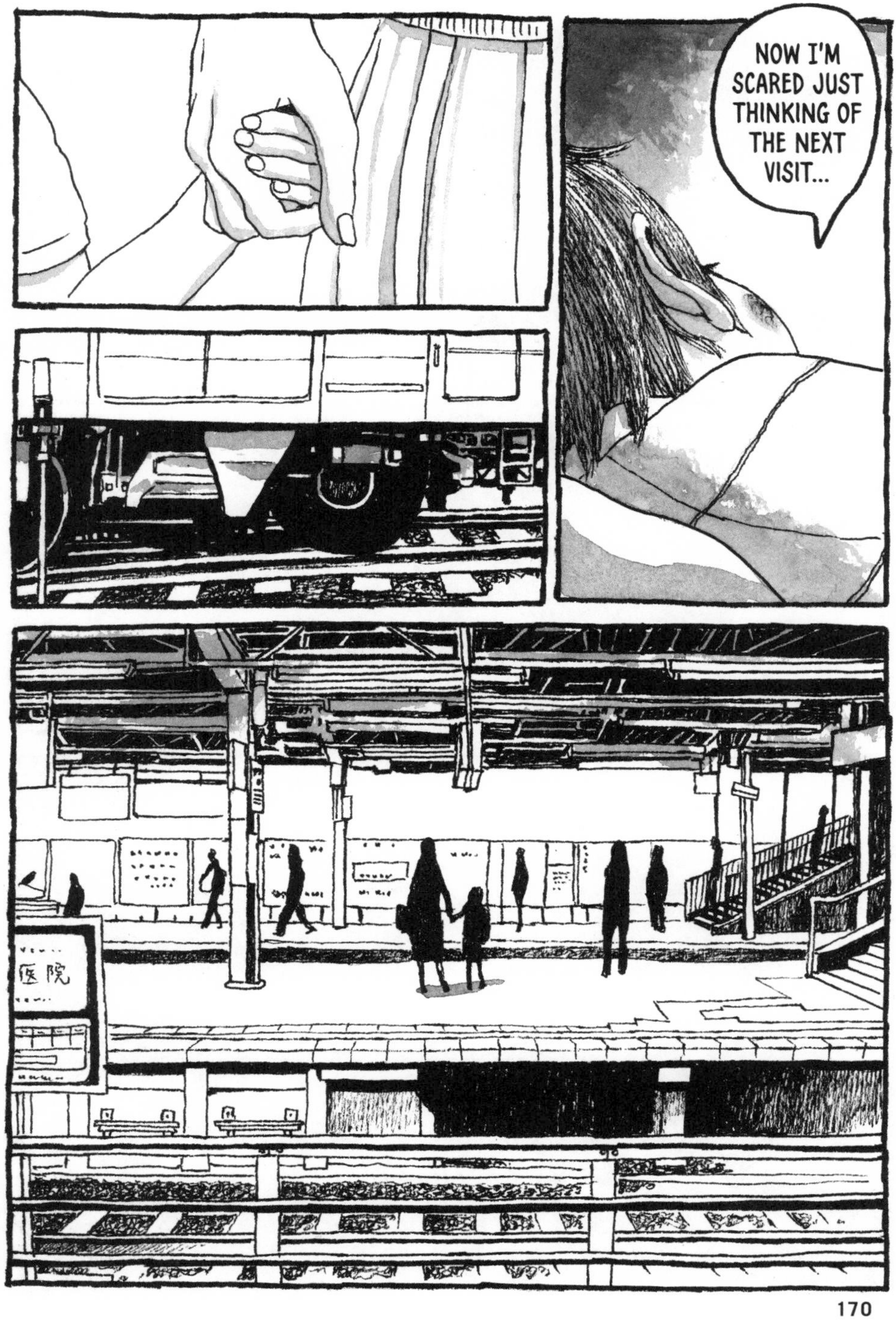
NOW I'M SCARED JUST THINKING OF THE NEXT VISIT...

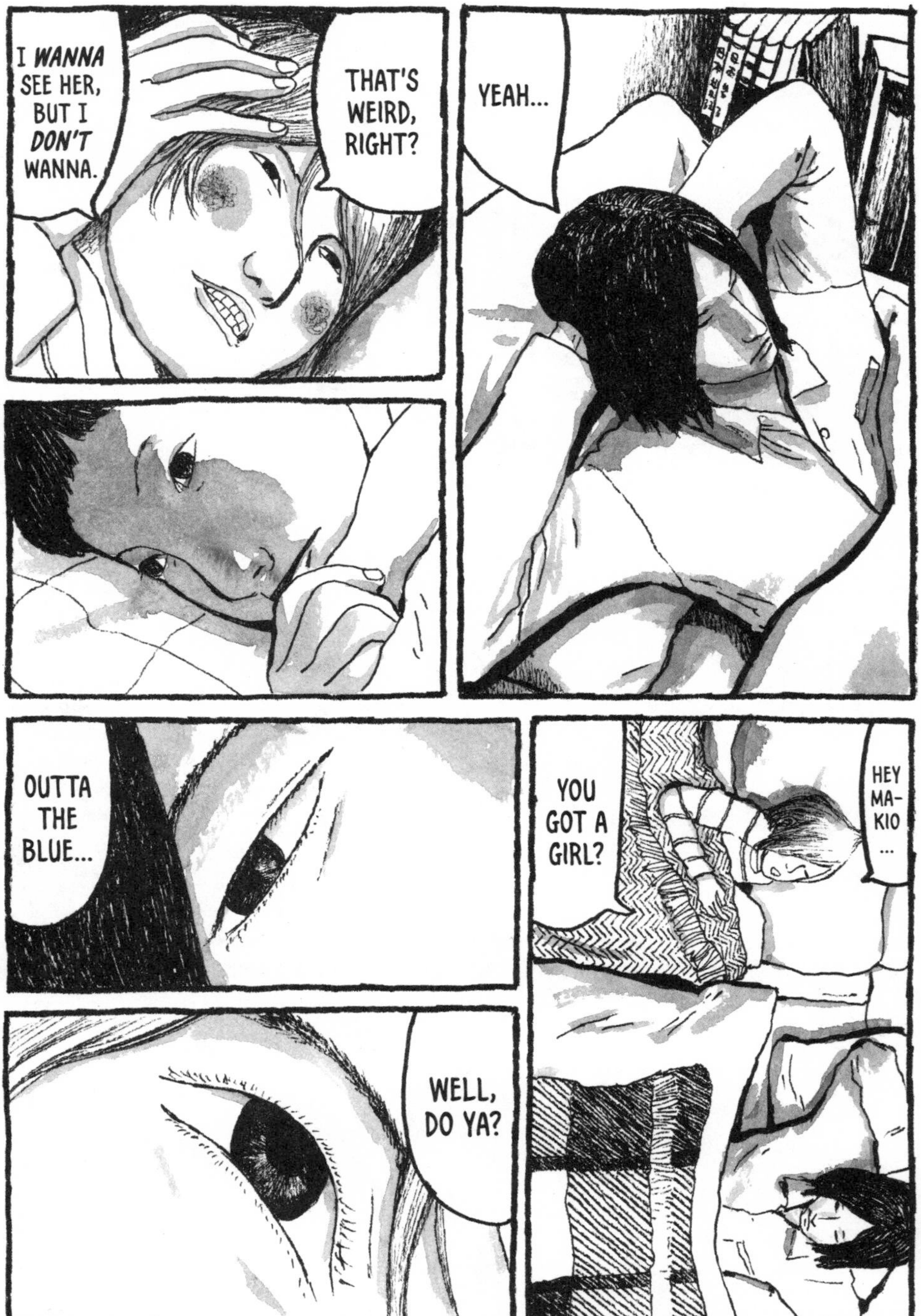
YEAH...
THAT'S WEIRD, RIGHT?
I *WANNA* SEE HER, BUT I *DON'T* WANNA.
HEY MAKIO...
YOU GOT A GIRL?
OUTTA THE BLUE...
WELL, DO YA?

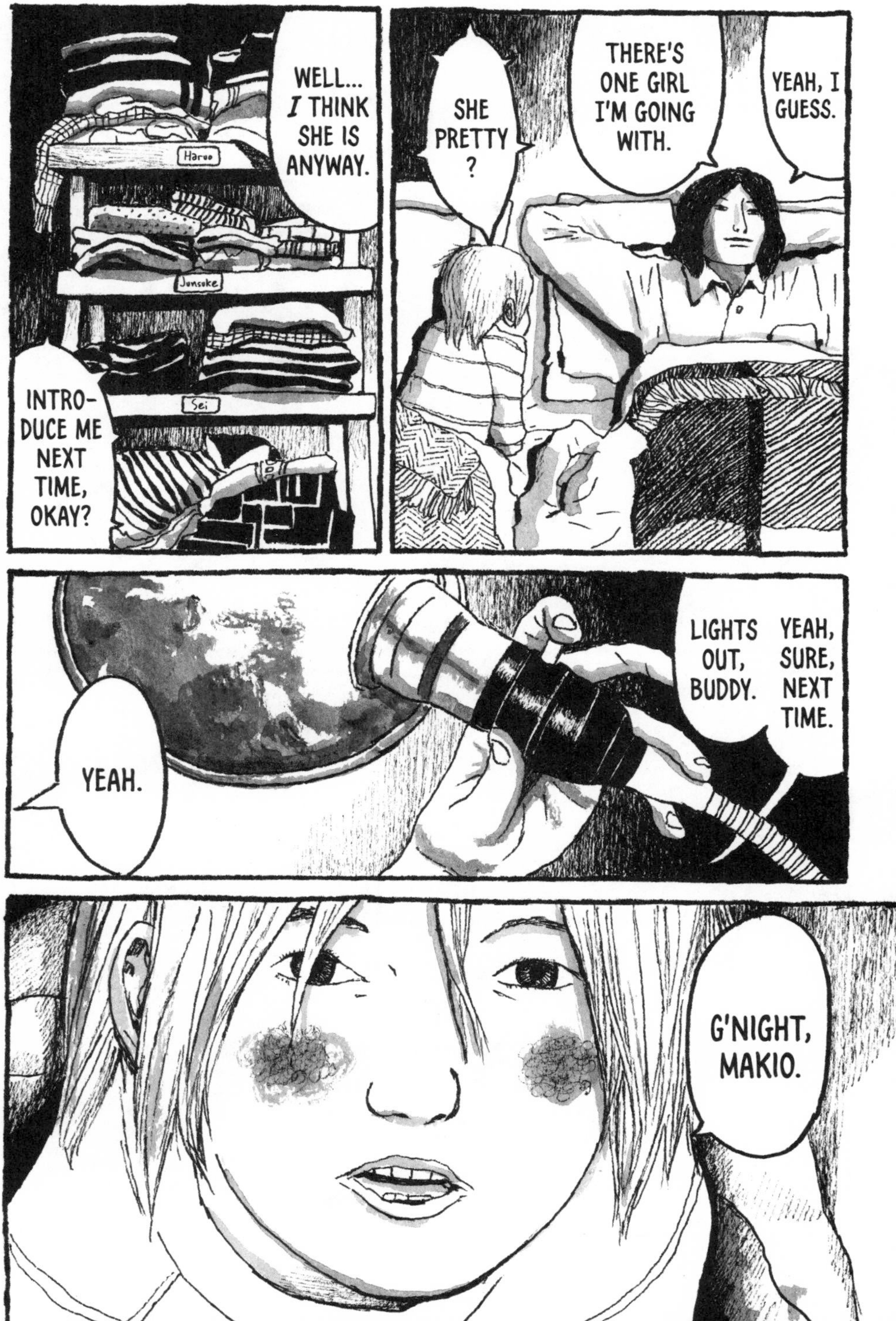
YEAH, I GUESS.
THERE'S ONE GIRL I'M GOING WITH.
SHE PRETTY?
WELL... *I* THINK SHE IS ANYWAY.
Haruo
Junsuke
Sei
INTRODUCE ME NEXT TIME, OKAY?
YEAH, SURE, NEXT TIME.
LIGHTS OUT, BUDDY.
YEAH.
G'NIGHT, MAKIO.

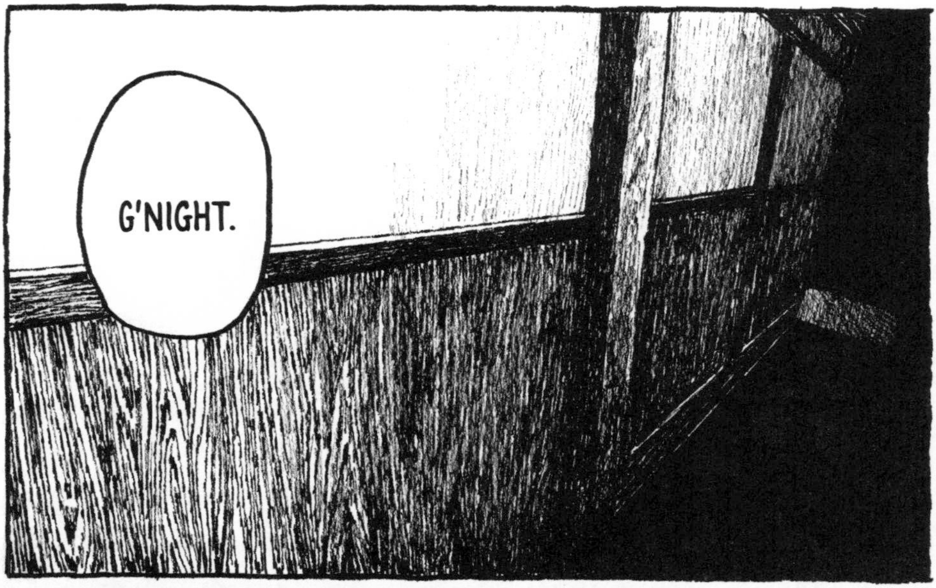
G'NIGHT.
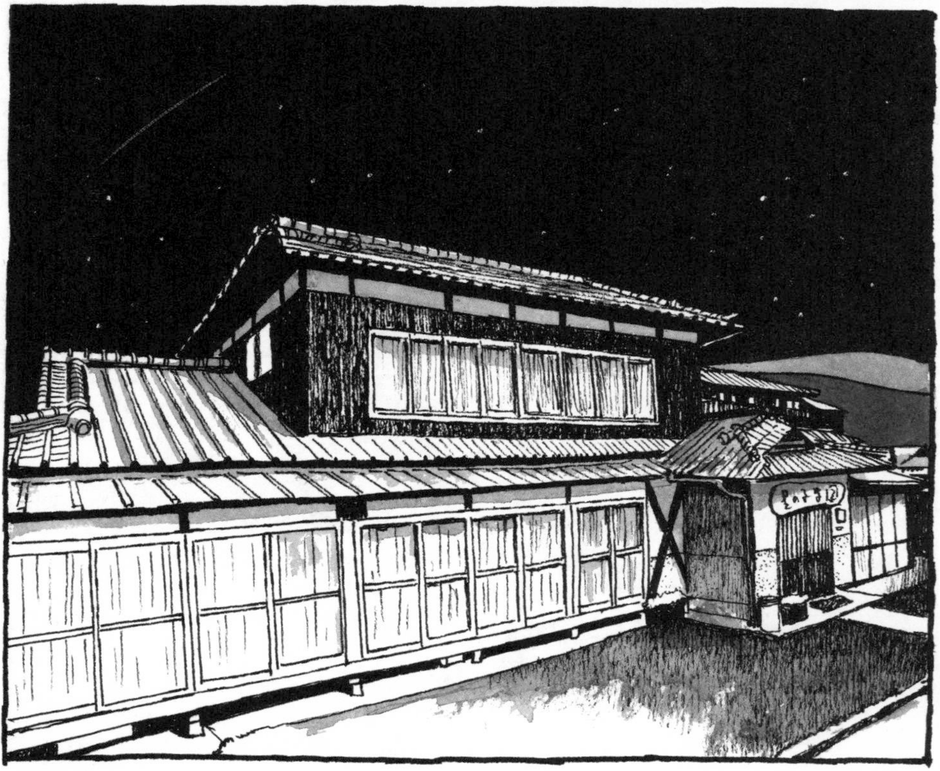

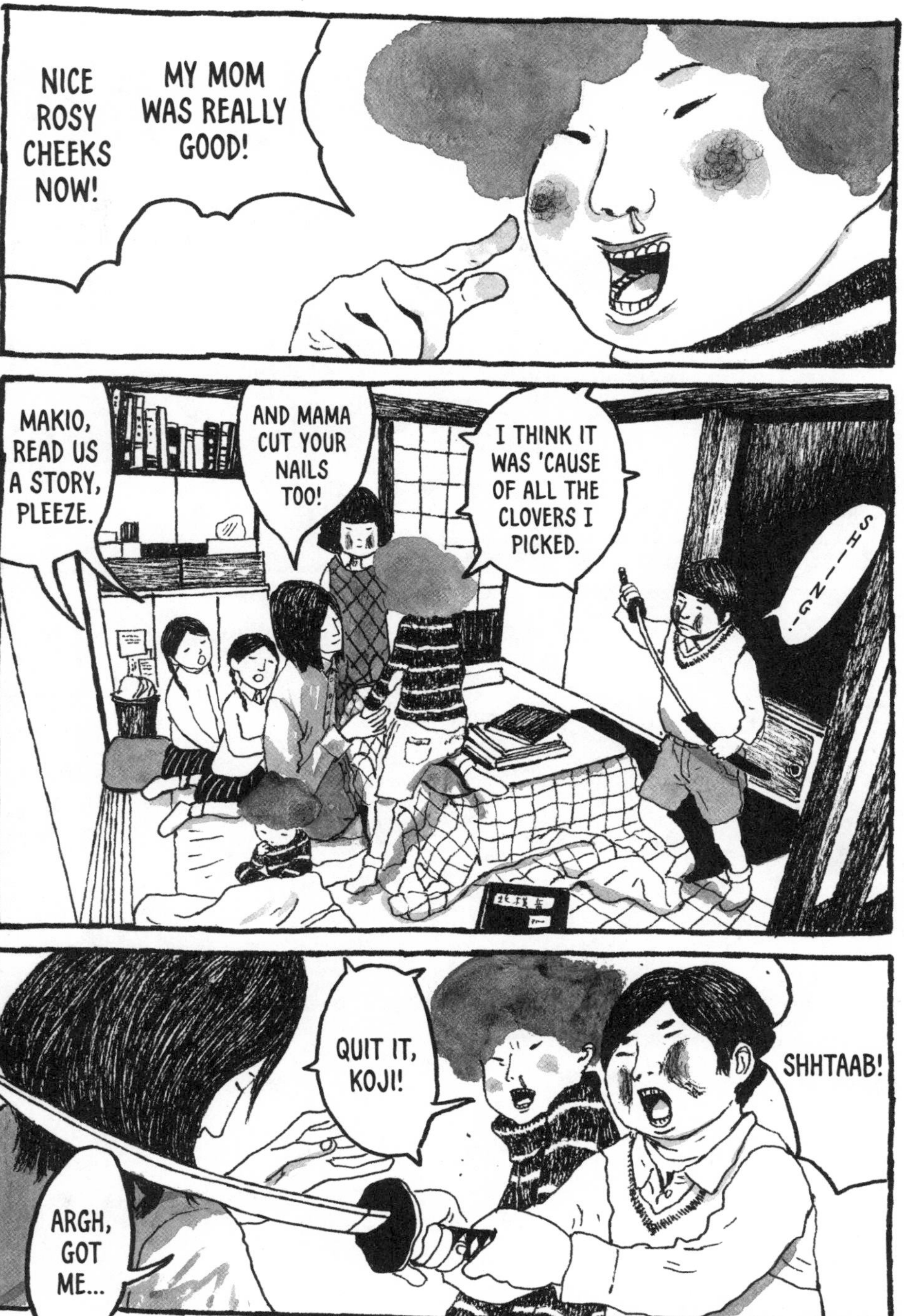
NICE ROSY CHEEKS NOW!
MY MOM WAS REALLY GOOD!
MAKIO, READ US A STORY, PLEEZE.
AND MAMA CUT YOUR NAILS TOO!
I THINK IT WAS 'CAUSE OF ALL THE CLOVERS I PICKED.
SH--I--N--G--!
QUIT IT, KOJI!
SHHTAAB!
ARGH, GOT ME...

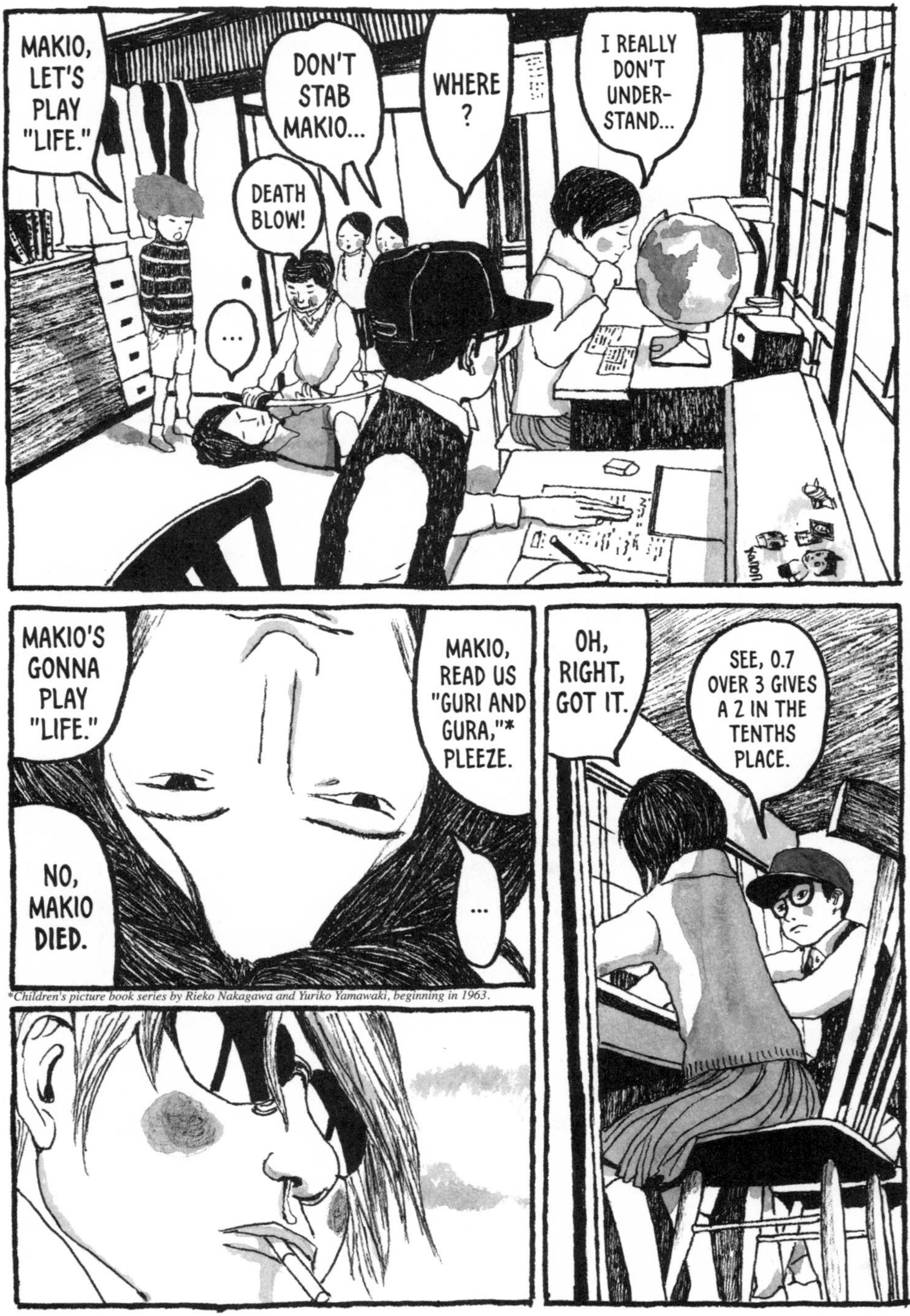
I REALLY DON'T UNDER-STAND...
WHERE ?
DON'T STAB MAKIO...
MAKIO, LET'S PLAY "LIFE."
DEATH BLOW!
...
SEE, 0.7 OVER 3 GIVES A 2 IN THE TENTHS PLACE.
OH, RIGHT, GOT IT.
MAKIO, READ US "GURI AND GURA,"* PLEEZE.
MAKIO'S GONNA PLAY "LIFE."
...
NO, MAKIO DIED.

*Children's picture book series by Rieko Nakagawa and Yuriko Yamawaki, beginning in 1963.

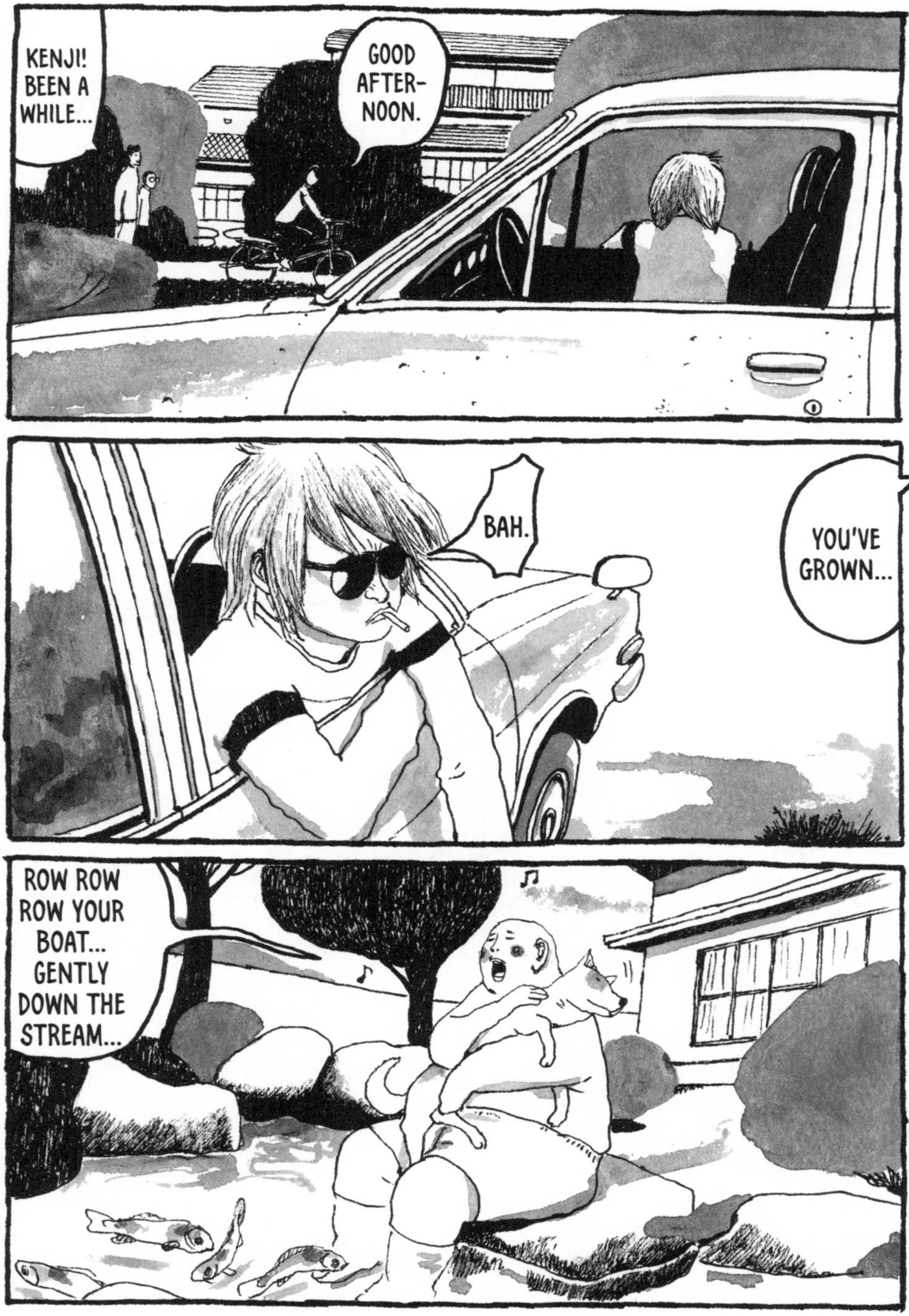
GOOD AFTER-NOON.
KENJI! BEEN A WHILE...
YOU'VE GROWN...
BAH.
ROW ROW ROW YOUR BOAT... GENTLY DOWN THE STREAM...

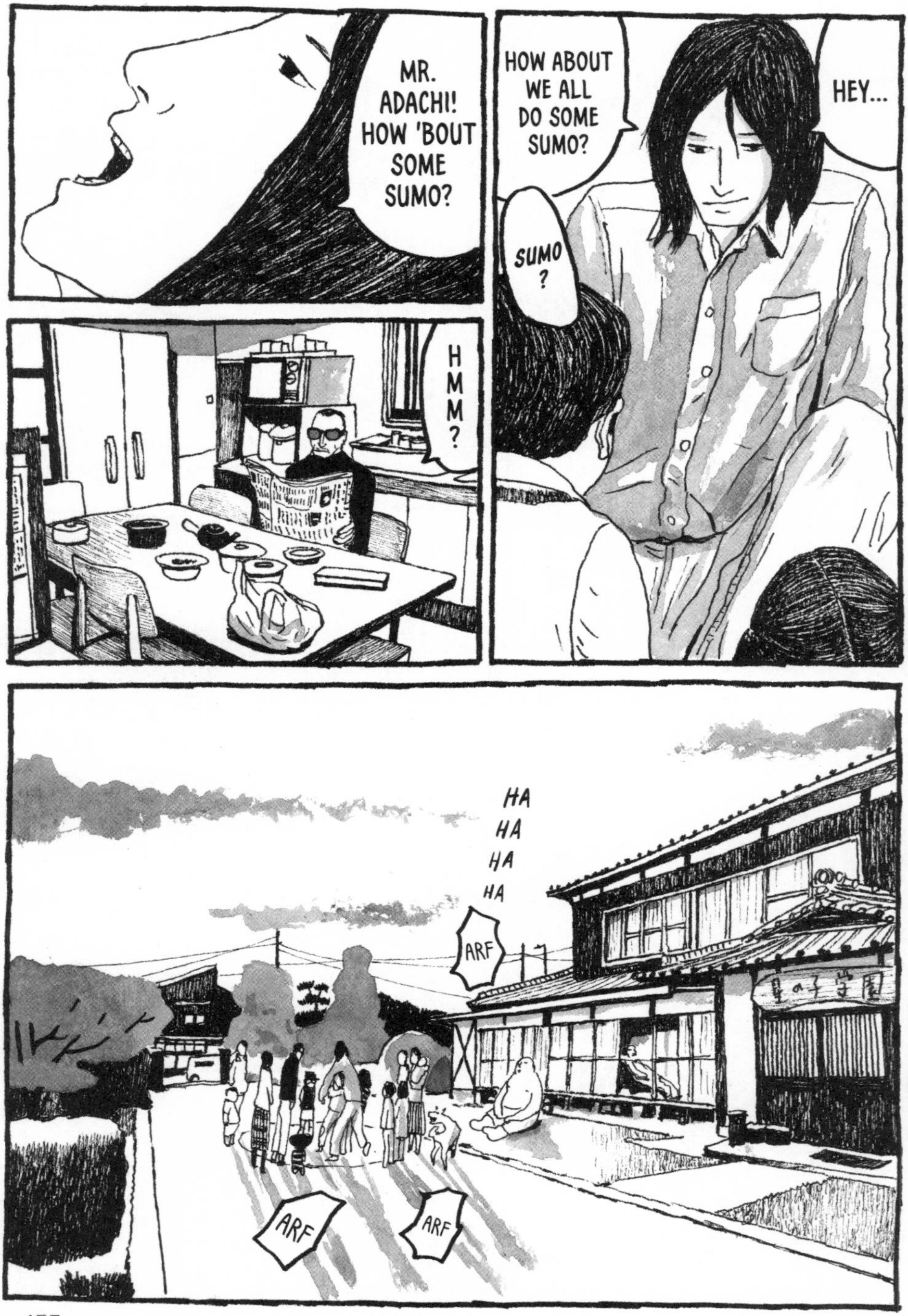
HEY...
HOW ABOUT WE ALL DO SOME SUMO?
SUMO?
MR. ADACHI! HOW 'BOUT SOME SUMO?
HMMM?
HA HA HA HA
ARF
ARF
ARF

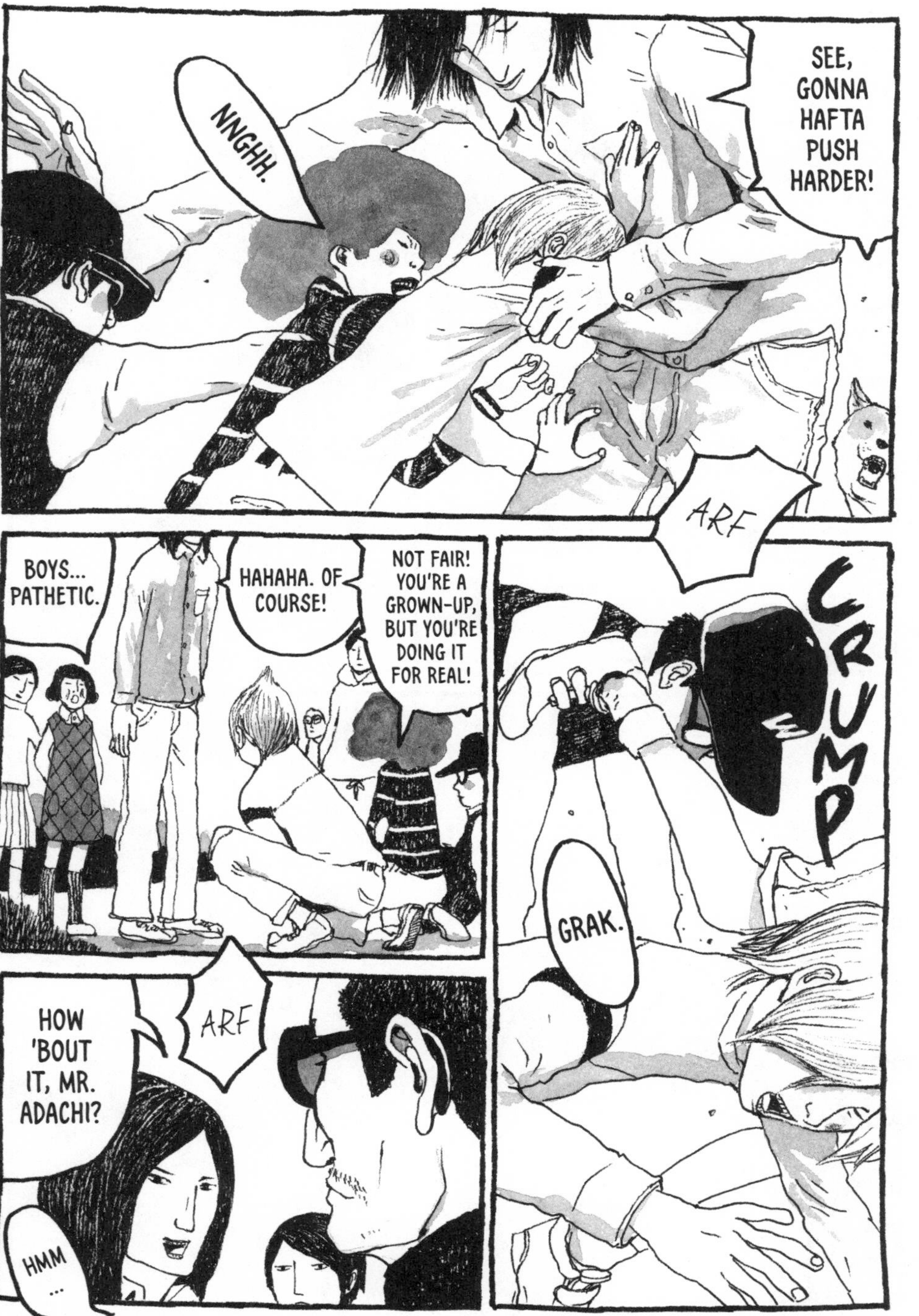
SEE, GONNA HAFTA PUSH HARDER!
NNGHH.
ARF
CRUMP
GRAK.
NOT FAIR! YOU'RE A GROWN-UP, BUT YOU'RE DOING IT FOR REAL!
HAHAHA. OF COURSE!
BOYS... PATHETIC.
ARF
HOW 'BOUT IT, MR. ADACHI?
HMM ...

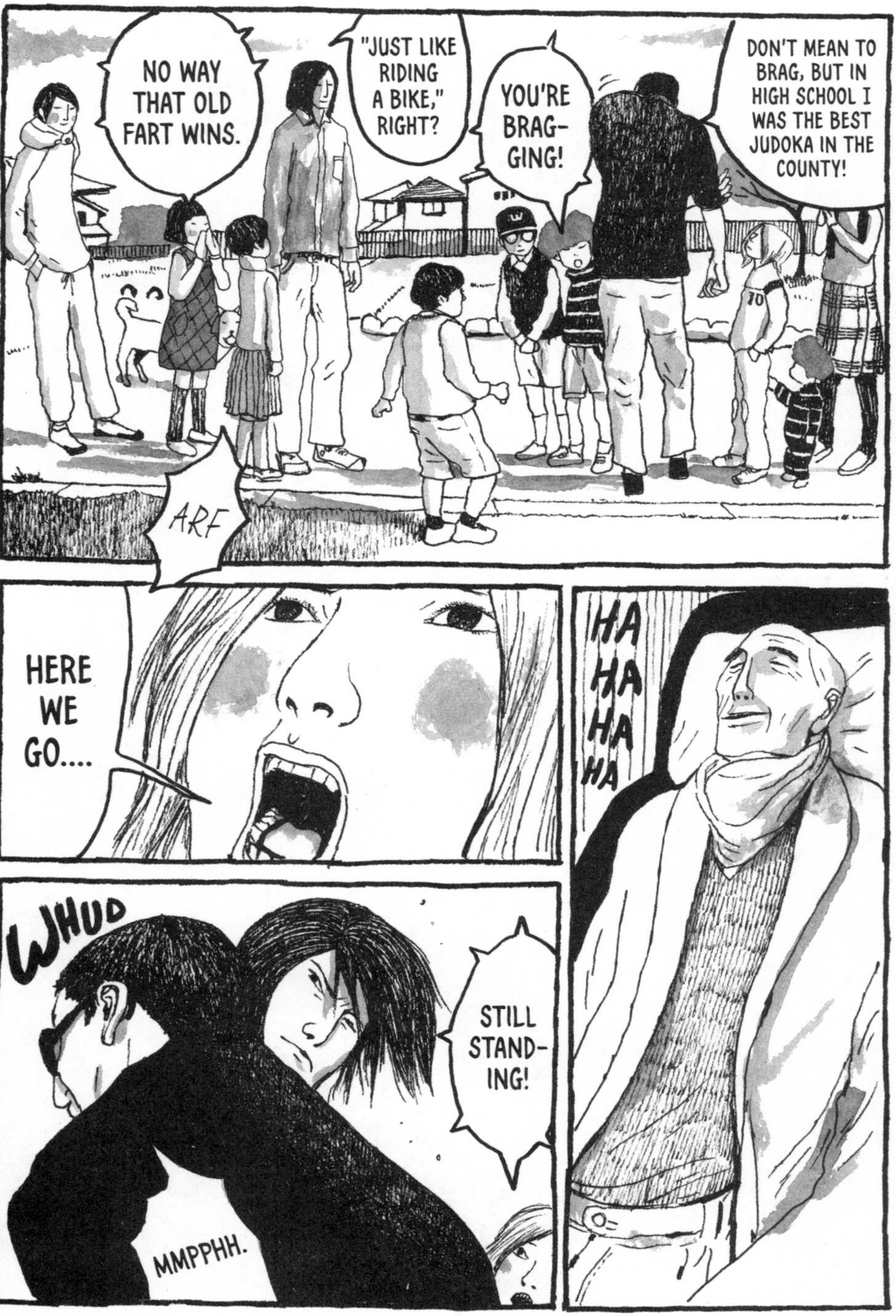
DON'T MEAN TO BRAG, BUT IN HIGH SCHOOL I WAS THE BEST JUDOKA IN THE COUNTY!
YOU'RE BRAG-GING!
"JUST LIKE RIDING A BIKE," RIGHT?
NO WAY THAT OLD FART WINS.
ARF
HA HA HA HA HA
HERE WE GO....
WHUD
STILL STAND-ING!
MMPPHH.

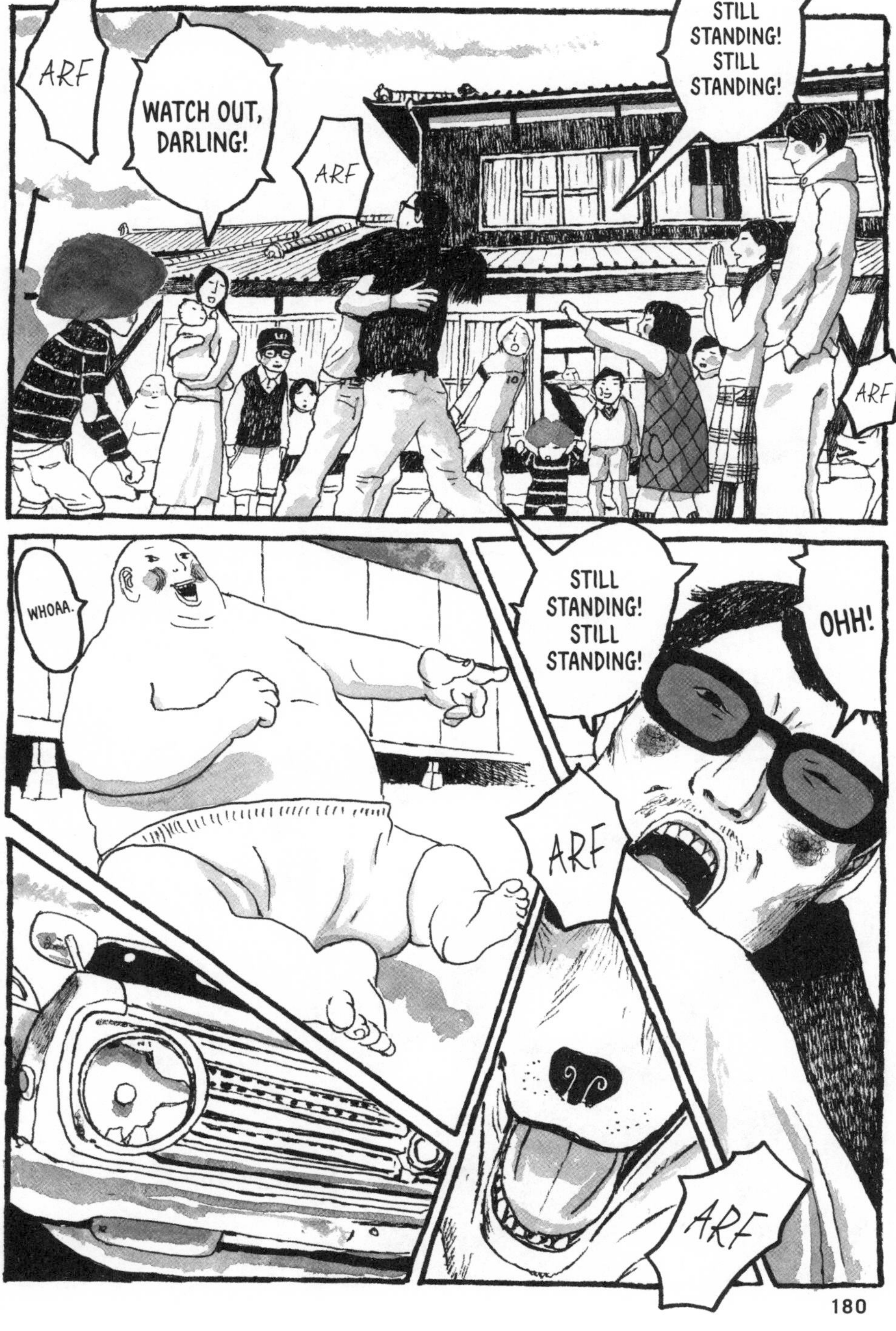
STILL STANDING! STILL STANDING!
ARF
WATCH OUT, DARLING!
ARF
ARF
OHH!
STILL STANDING! STILL STANDING!
ARF
ARF
WHOAA.

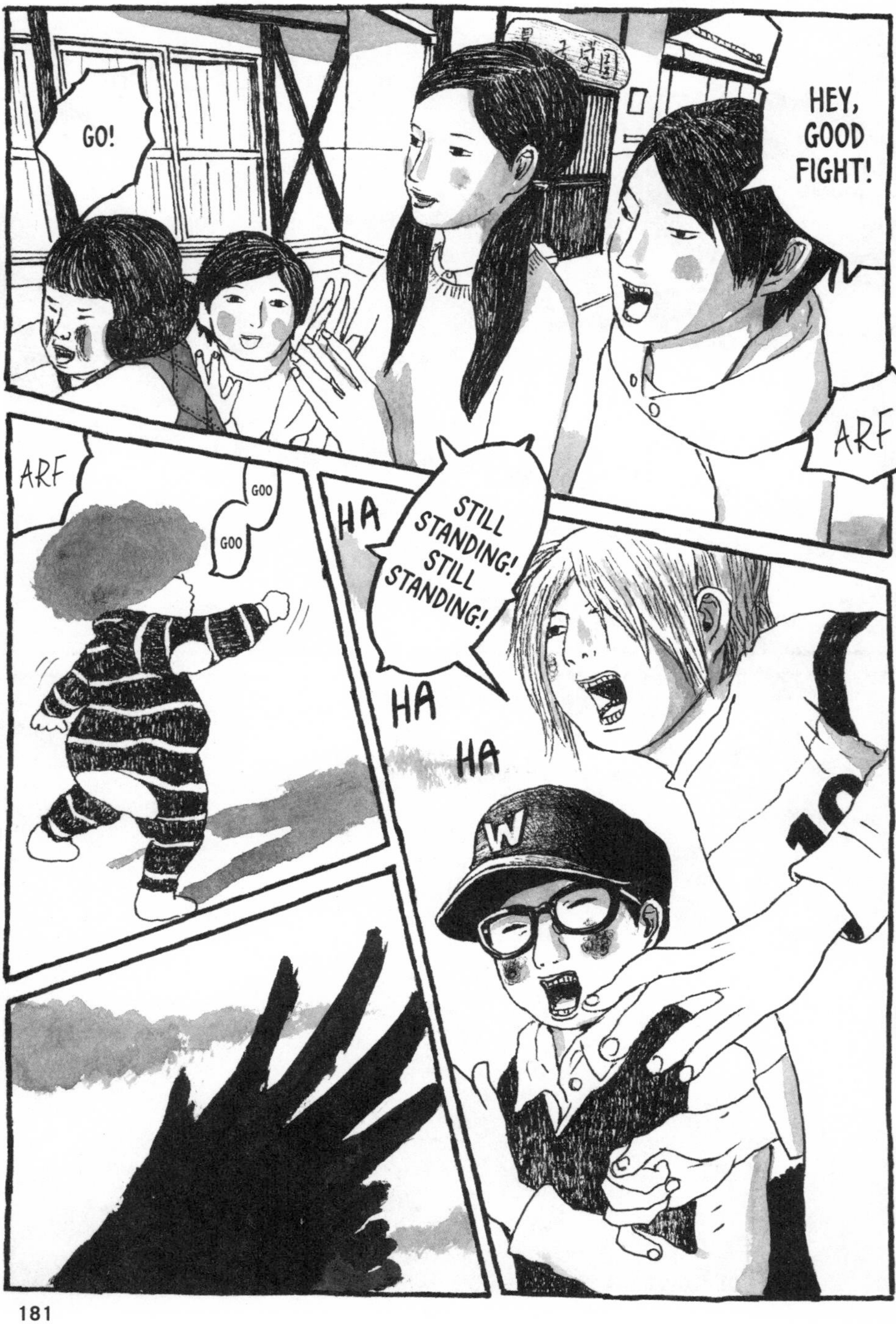
HEY, GOOD FIGHT!
GO!
ARF
HA
STILL STANDING! STILL STANDING!
HA
HA
ARF
GOO
GOO

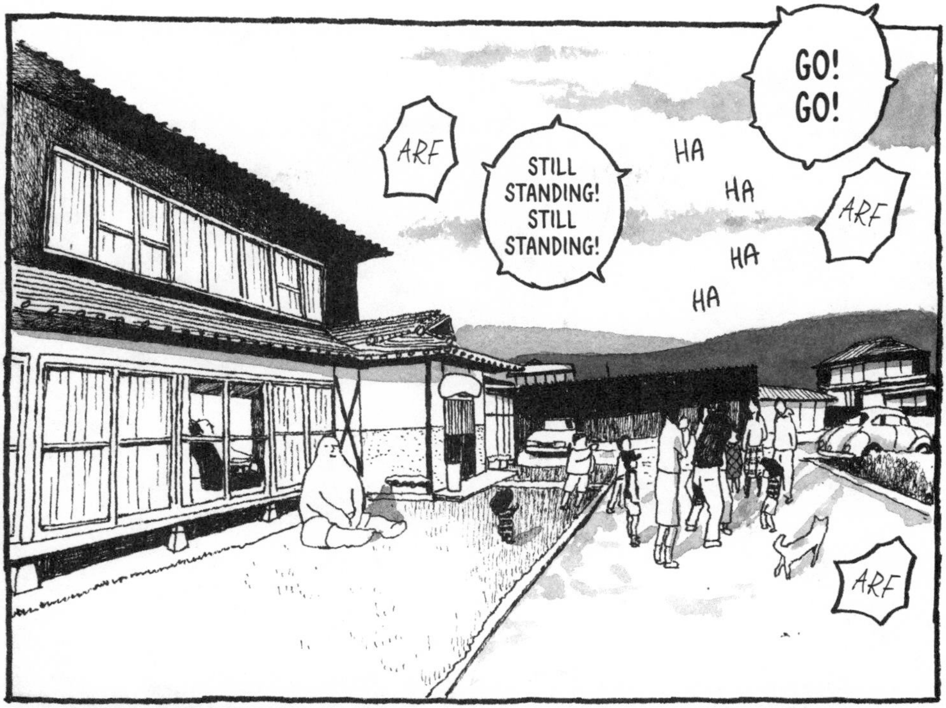
GO! GO!
ARF
HA
HA
HA
HA
STILL STANDING! STILL STANDING!
ARF
ARF

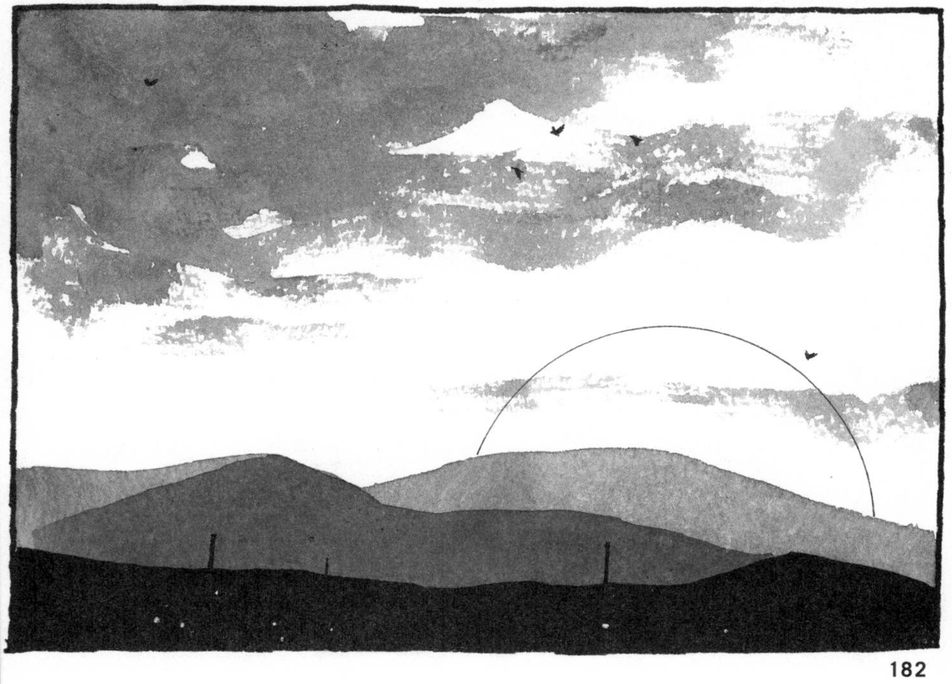

CHAPTER 6

"Whaddya
think's for
dinner
tonight?"

"Miss Mitsuko
said fritters."

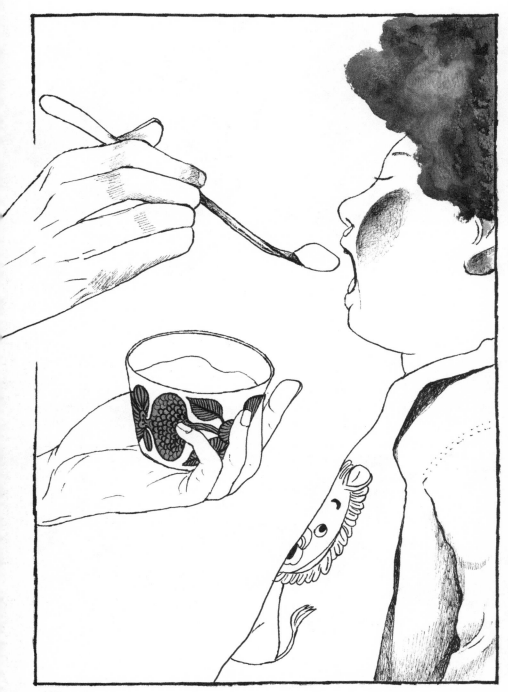

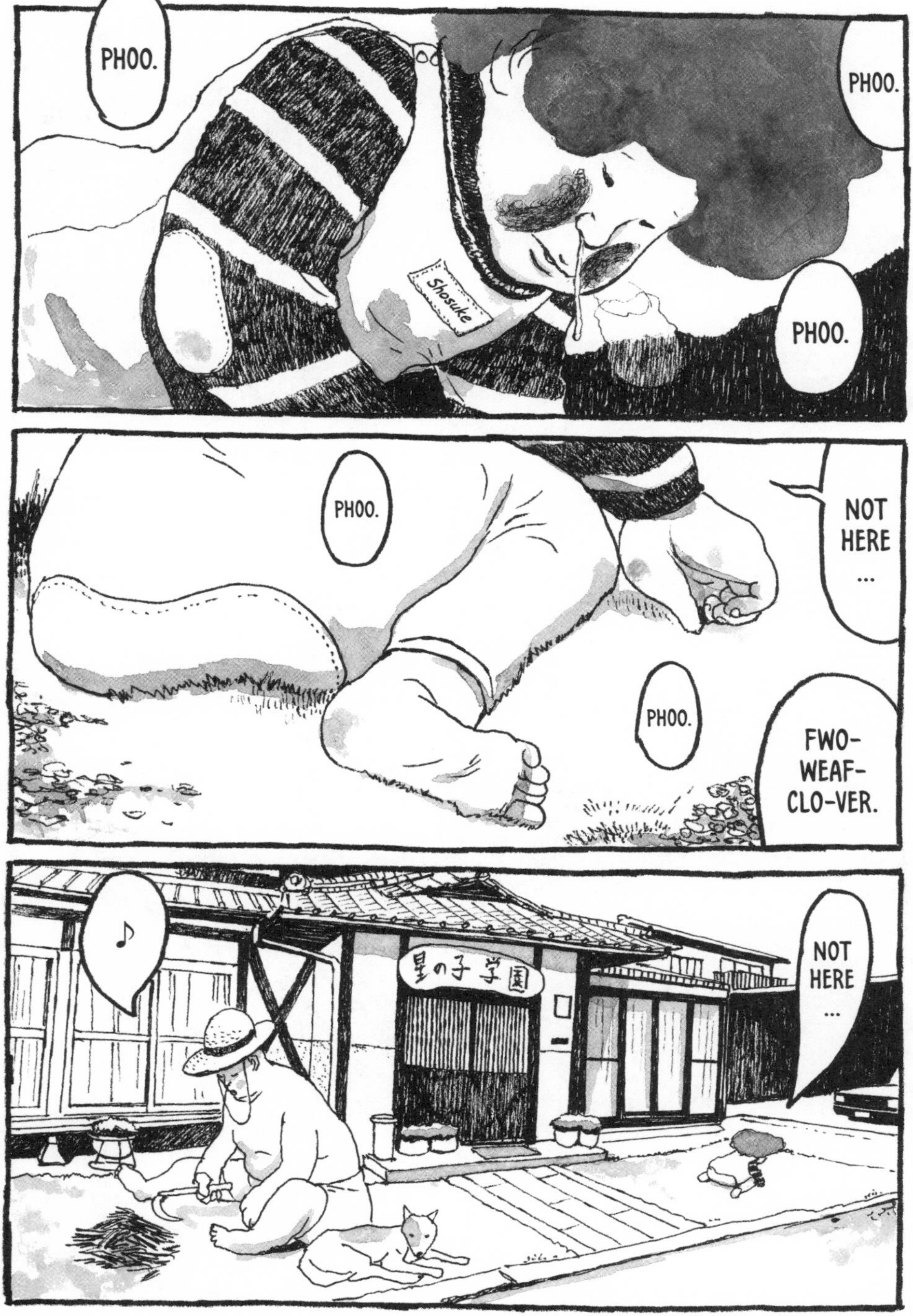
PHOO.
PHOO.
Shosuke
PHOO.
NOT HERE ...
PHOO.
PHOO.
FWO-WEAF-CLO-VER.
NOT HERE ...
星の子学園
♪

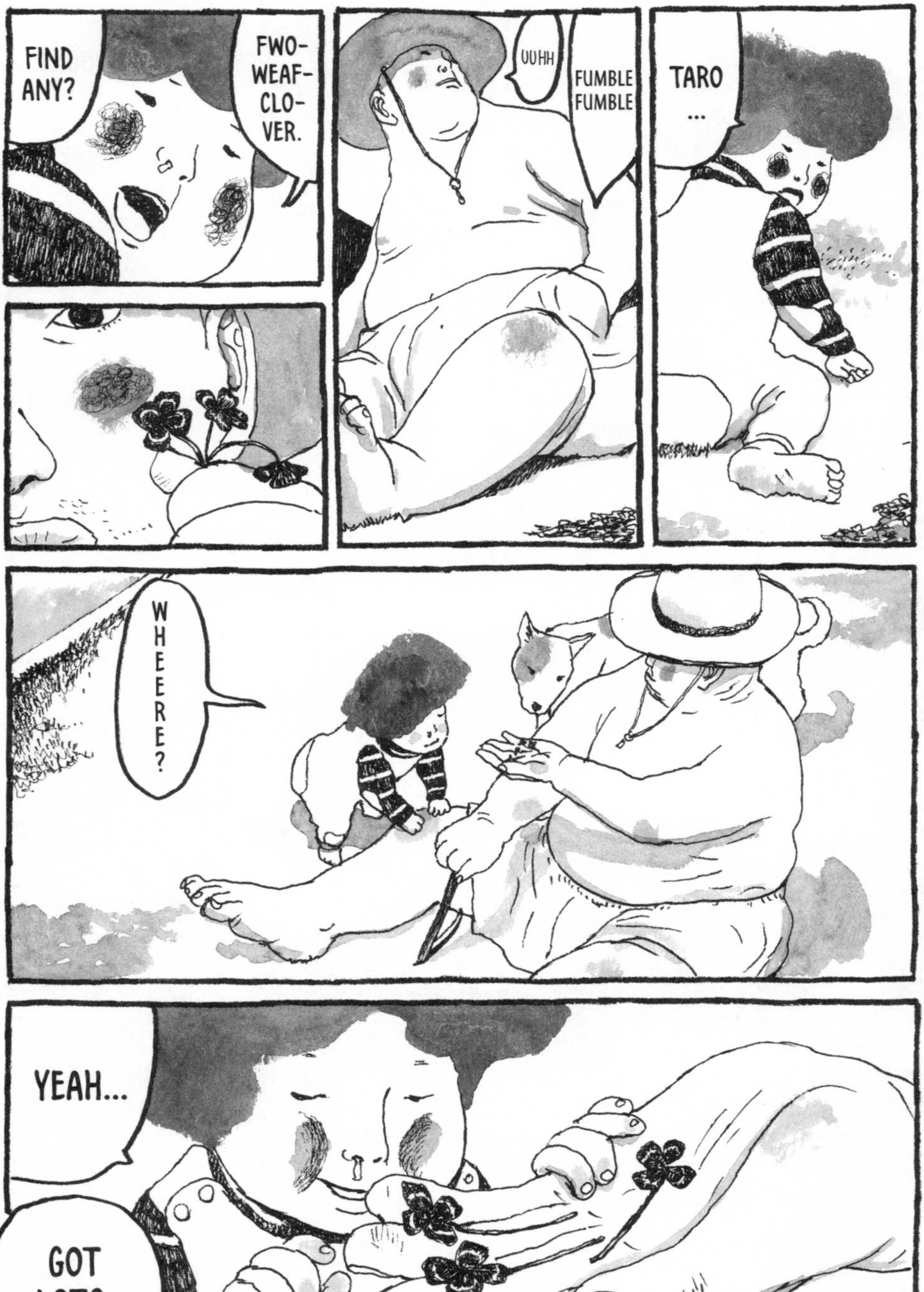
FIND ANY?
FWO-WEAF-CLO-VER.
UUHH
FUMBLE FUMBLE
TARO ...
WHEERE?
YEAH...
GOT LOTS.

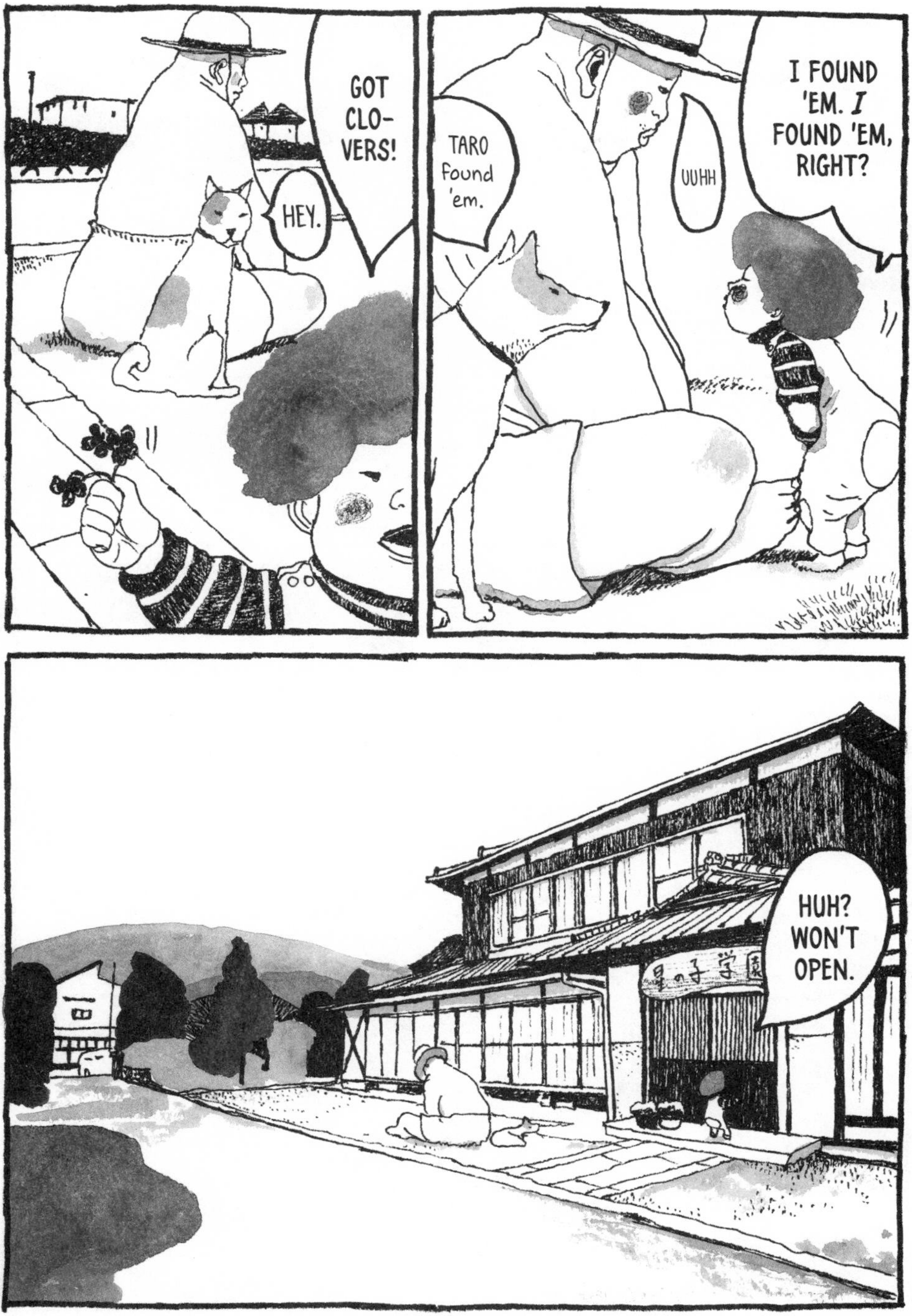
GOT CLO-VERS!
HEY.
TARO found 'em.
UUHH
I FOUND 'EM. *I* FOUND 'EM, RIGHT?
HUH? WON'T OPEN.

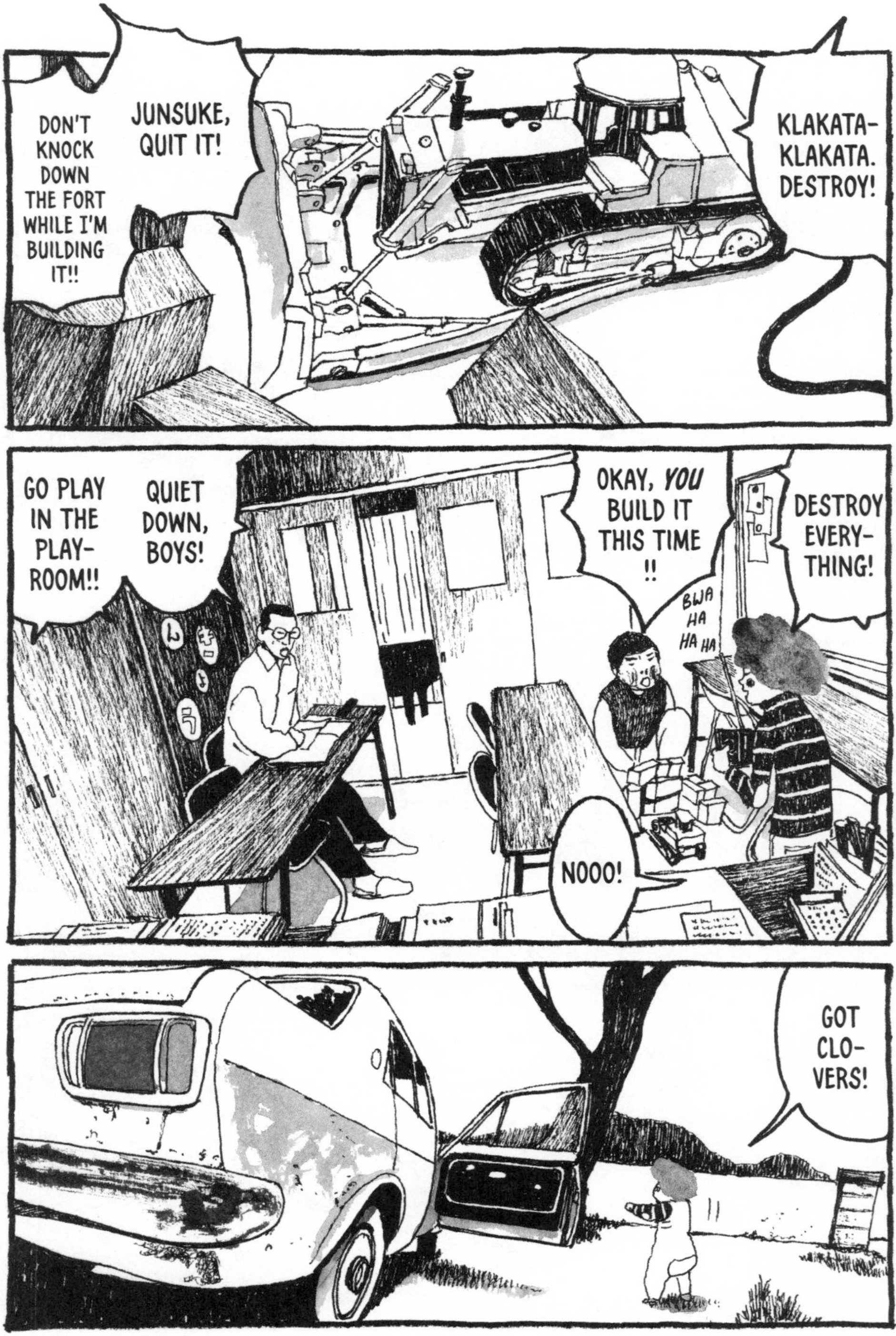
KLAKATA-KLAKATA. DESTROY!
JUNSUKE, QUIT IT!
DON'T KNOCK DOWN THE FORT WHILE I'M BUILDING IT!!
DESTROY EVERY-THING!
BWA HA HA HA
OKAY, *YOU* BUILD IT THIS TIME!!
NOOO!
QUIET DOWN, BOYS!
GO PLAY IN THE PLAY-ROOM!!
GOT CLO-VERS!

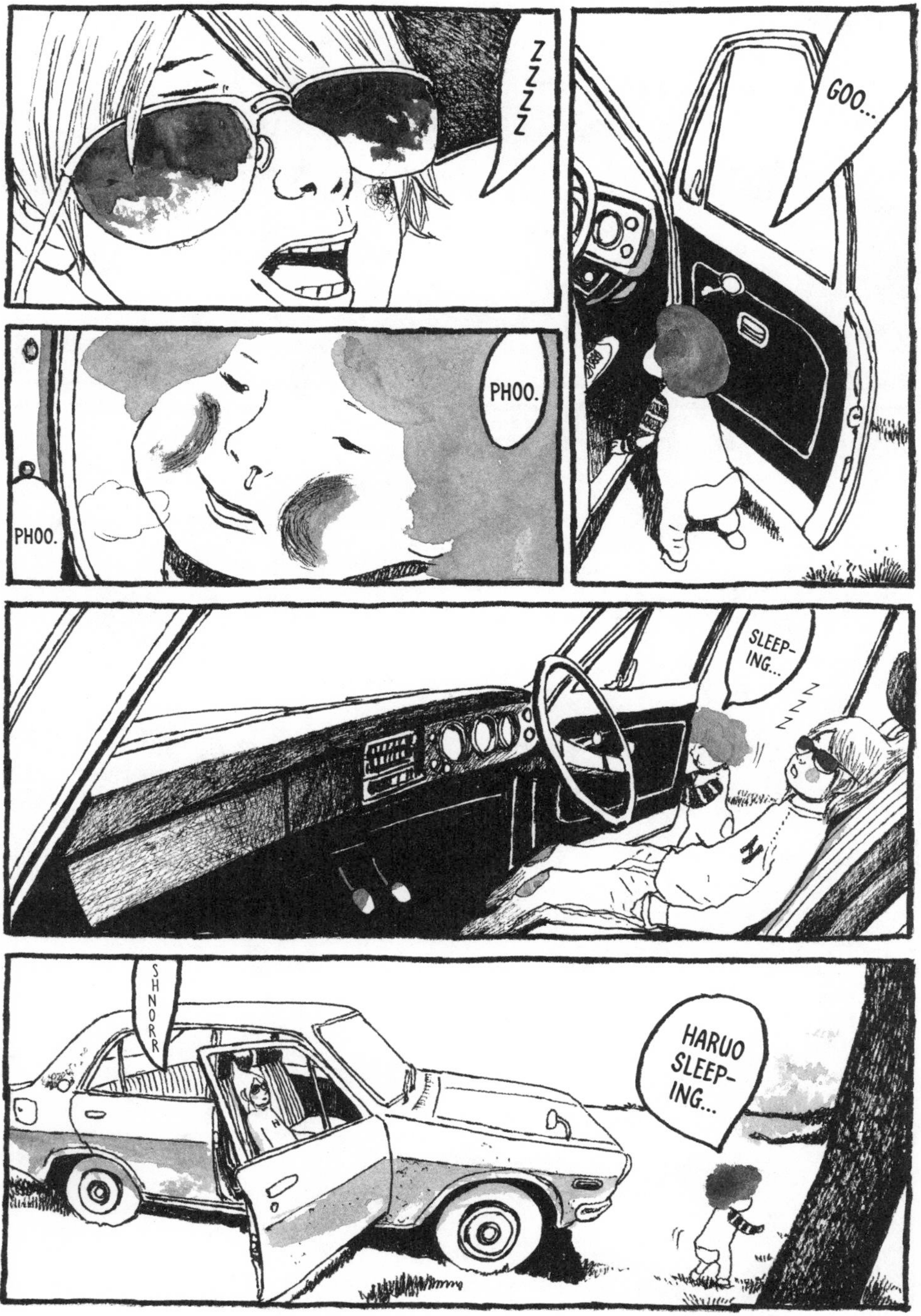
GOO...
ZZZZ
PHOO.
PHOO.
SLEEP-ING...
ZZZ
SHNORR
HARUO SLEEP-ING...

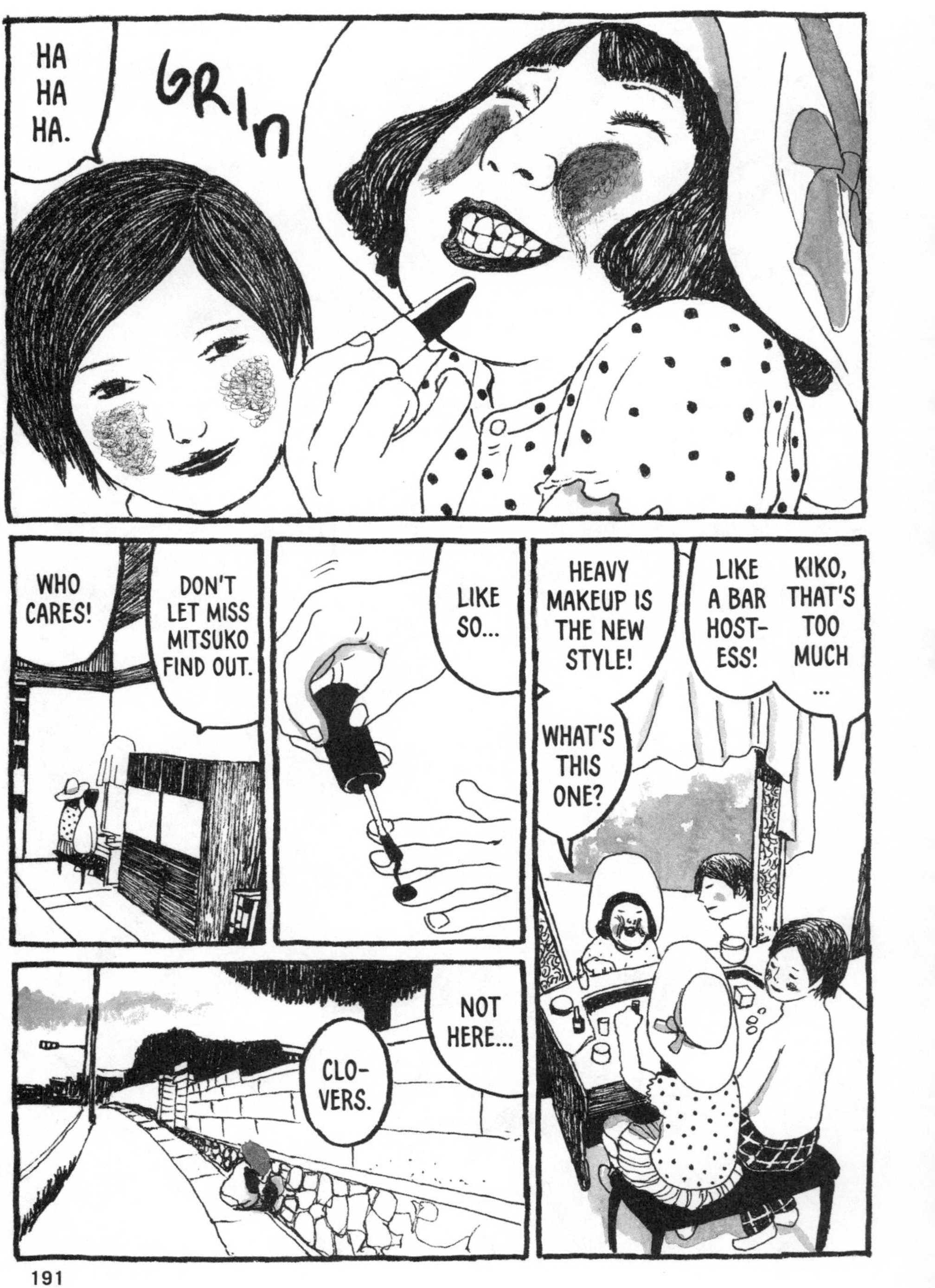
GRIN
HA HA HA.
KIKO, THAT'S TOO MUCH ...
LIKE A BAR HOST-ESS!
HEAVY MAKEUP IS THE NEW STYLE!
WHAT'S THIS ONE?
LIKE SO...
DON'T LET MISS MITSUKO FIND OUT.
WHO CARES!
NOT HERE...
CLO-VERS.

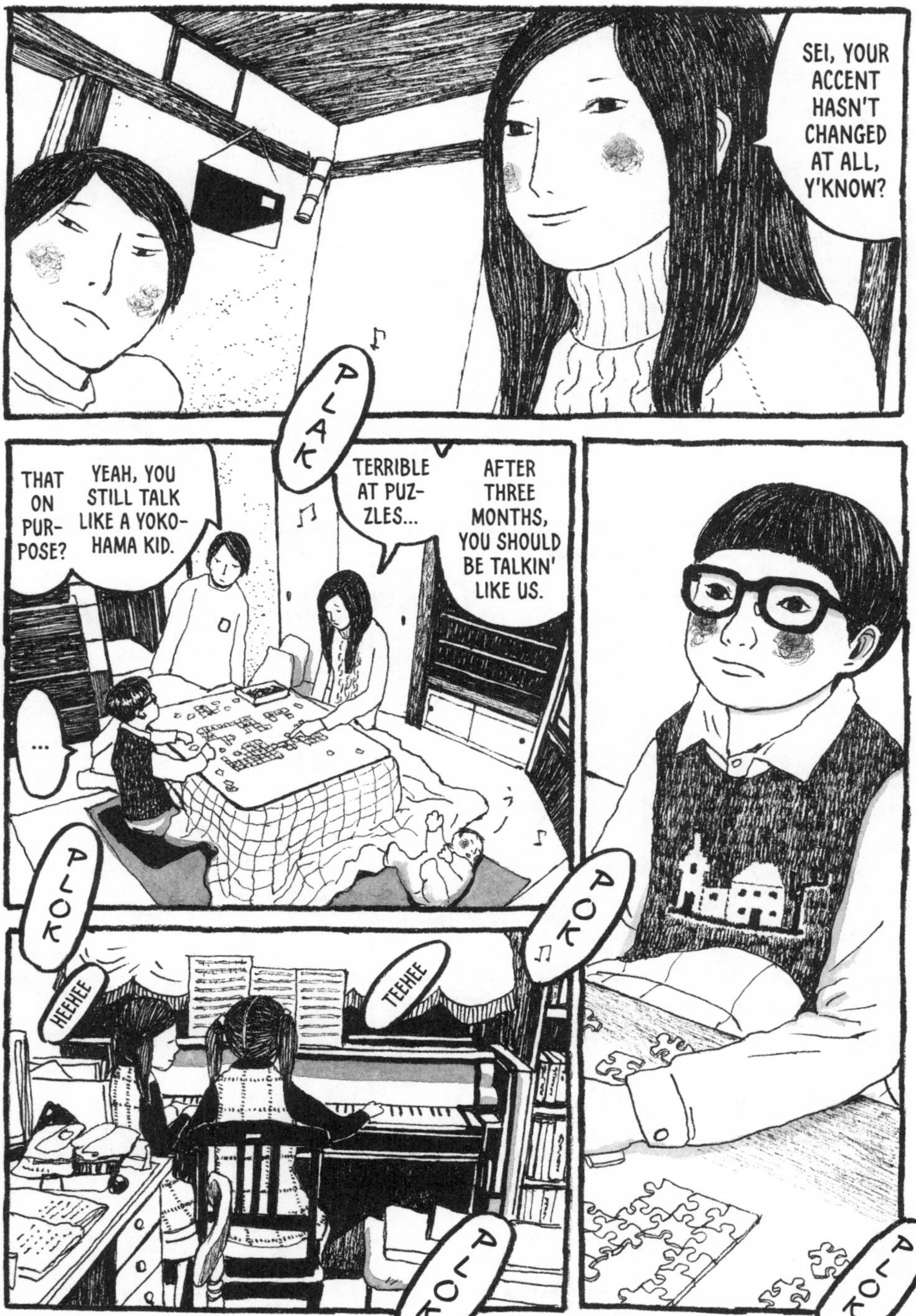
SEI, YOUR ACCENT HASN'T CHANGED AT ALL, Y'KNOW?
PLAK
POK
PLOK
AFTER THREE MONTHS, YOU SHOULD BE TALKIN' LIKE US.
TERRIBLE AT PUZZLES...
YEAH, YOU STILL TALK LIKE A YOKOHAMA KID.
THAT ON PURPOSE?
...
PLOK
TEEHEE
HEEHEE
PLOK

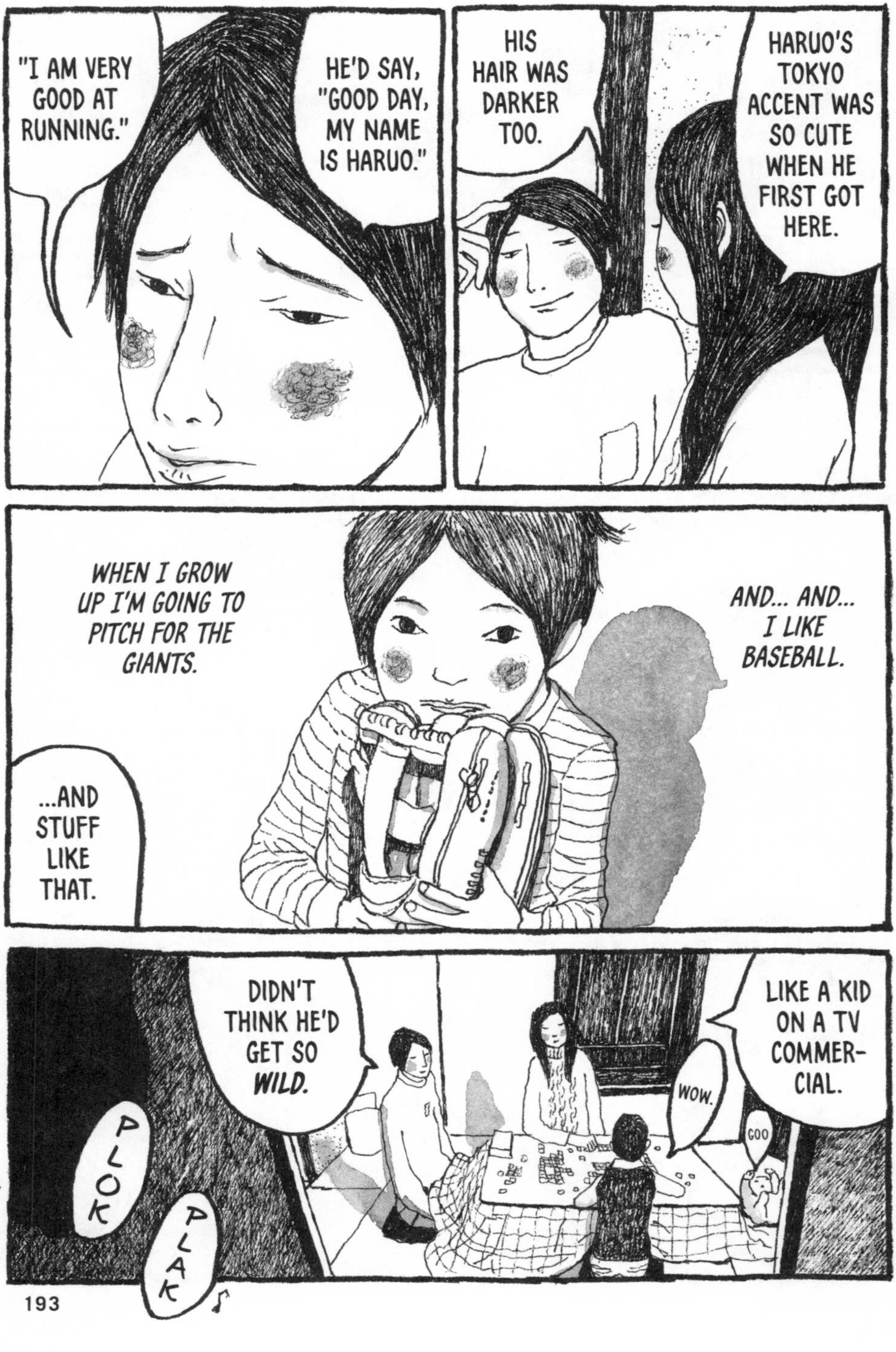
HARUO'S TOKYO ACCENT WAS SO CUTE WHEN HE FIRST GOT HERE.
HIS HAIR WAS DARKER TOO.
HE'D SAY, "GOOD DAY, MY NAME IS HARUO."
"I AM VERY GOOD AT RUNNING."
AND... AND... I LIKE BASEBALL.
WHEN I GROW UP I'M GOING TO PITCH FOR THE GIANTS.
...AND STUFF LIKE THAT.
LIKE A KID ON A TV COMMERCIAL.
GOO
WOW.
DIDN'T THINK HE'D GET SO WILD.
PLOK
PLAK

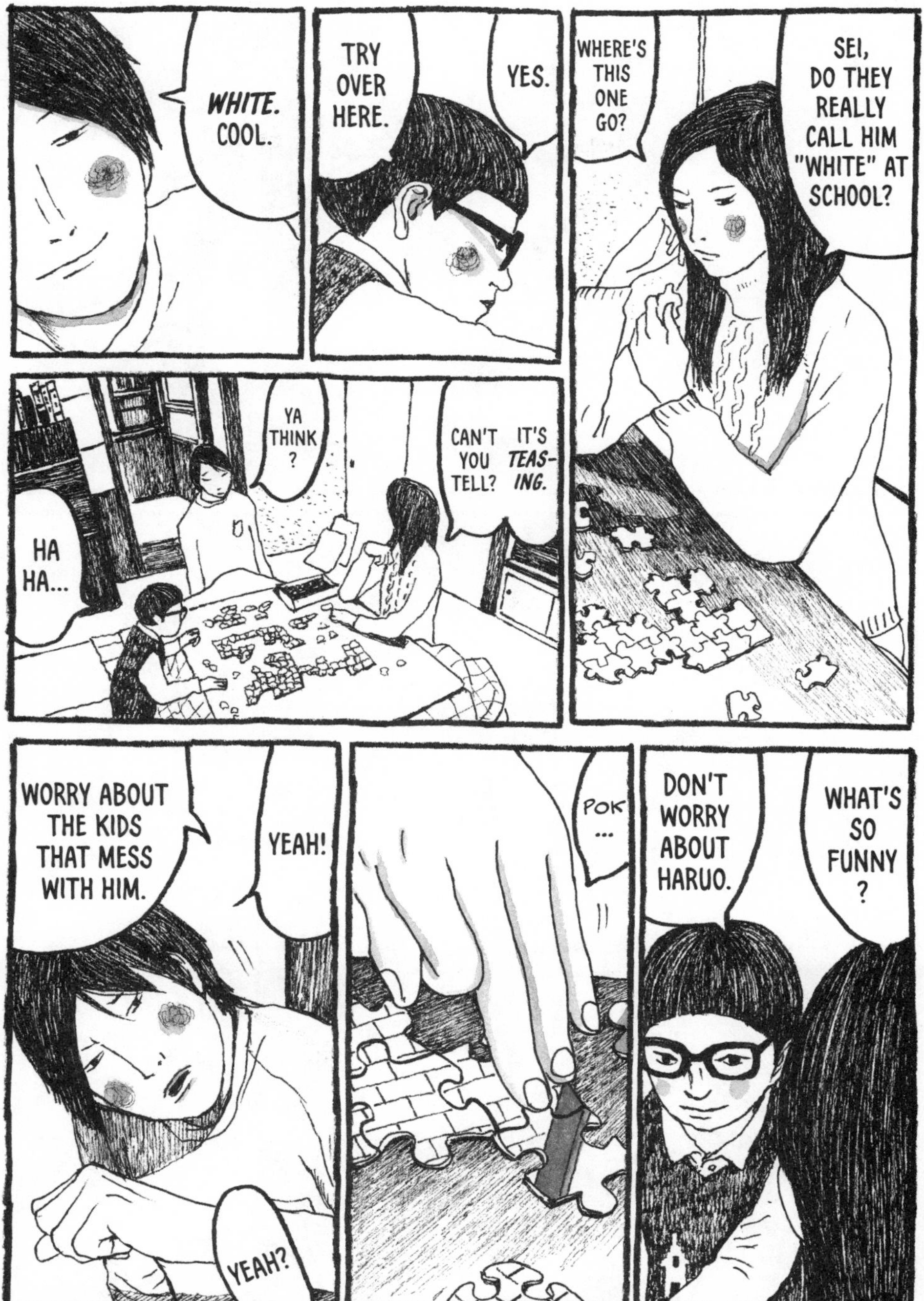
SEI, DO THEY REALLY CALL HIM "WHITE" AT SCHOOL?
WHERE'S THIS ONE GO?
YES.
TRY OVER HERE.
WHITE. COOL.
IT'S *TEAS-ING.*
CAN'T YOU TELL?
YA THINK?
HA HA...
WHAT'S SO FUNNY?
DON'T WORRY ABOUT HARUO.
POK...
YEAH!
WORRY ABOUT THE KIDS THAT MESS WITH HIM.
YEAH?

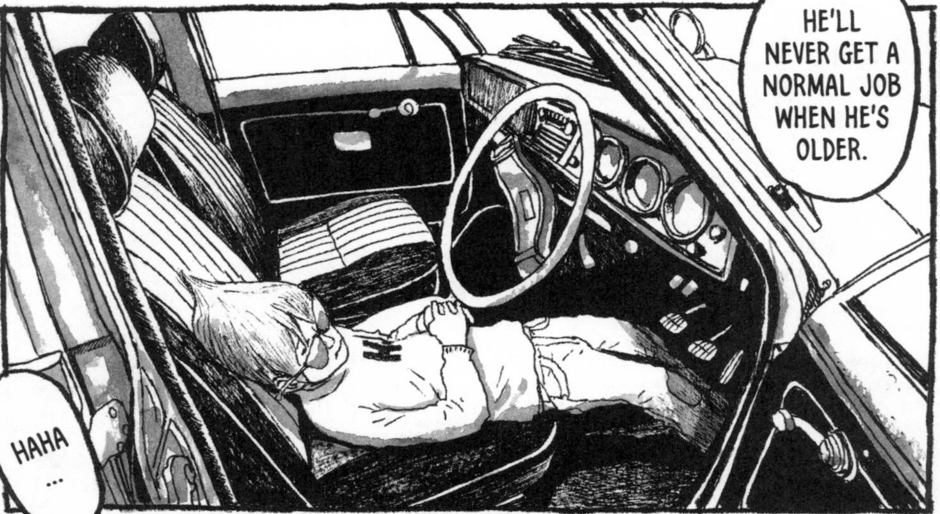
HE'LL NEVER GET A NORMAL JOB WHEN HE'S OLDER.
HAHA ...

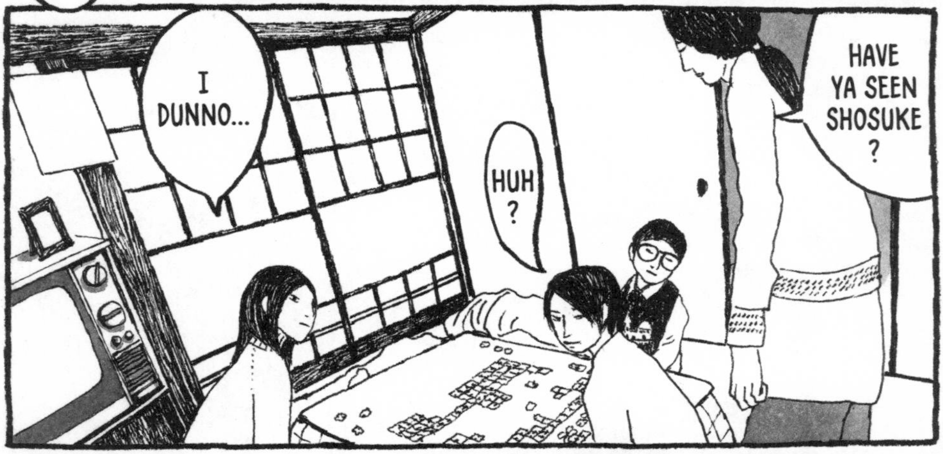
HAVE YA SEEN SHOSUKE ?
HUH ?
I DUNNO...

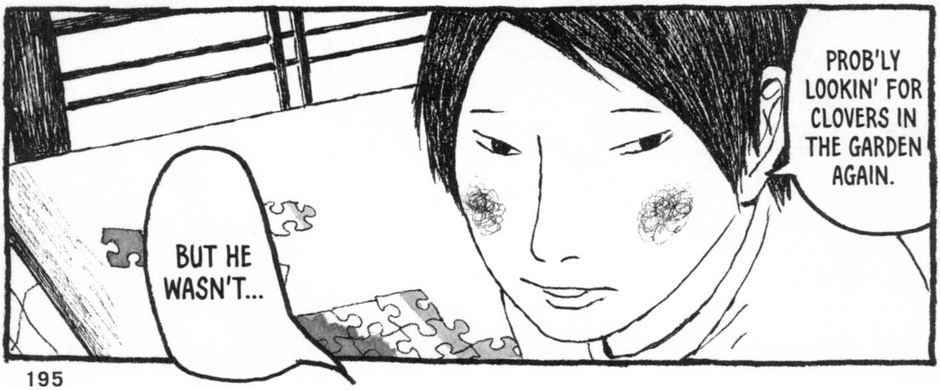
PROB'LY LOOKIN' FOR CLOVERS IN THE GARDEN AGAIN.
BUT HE WASN'T...

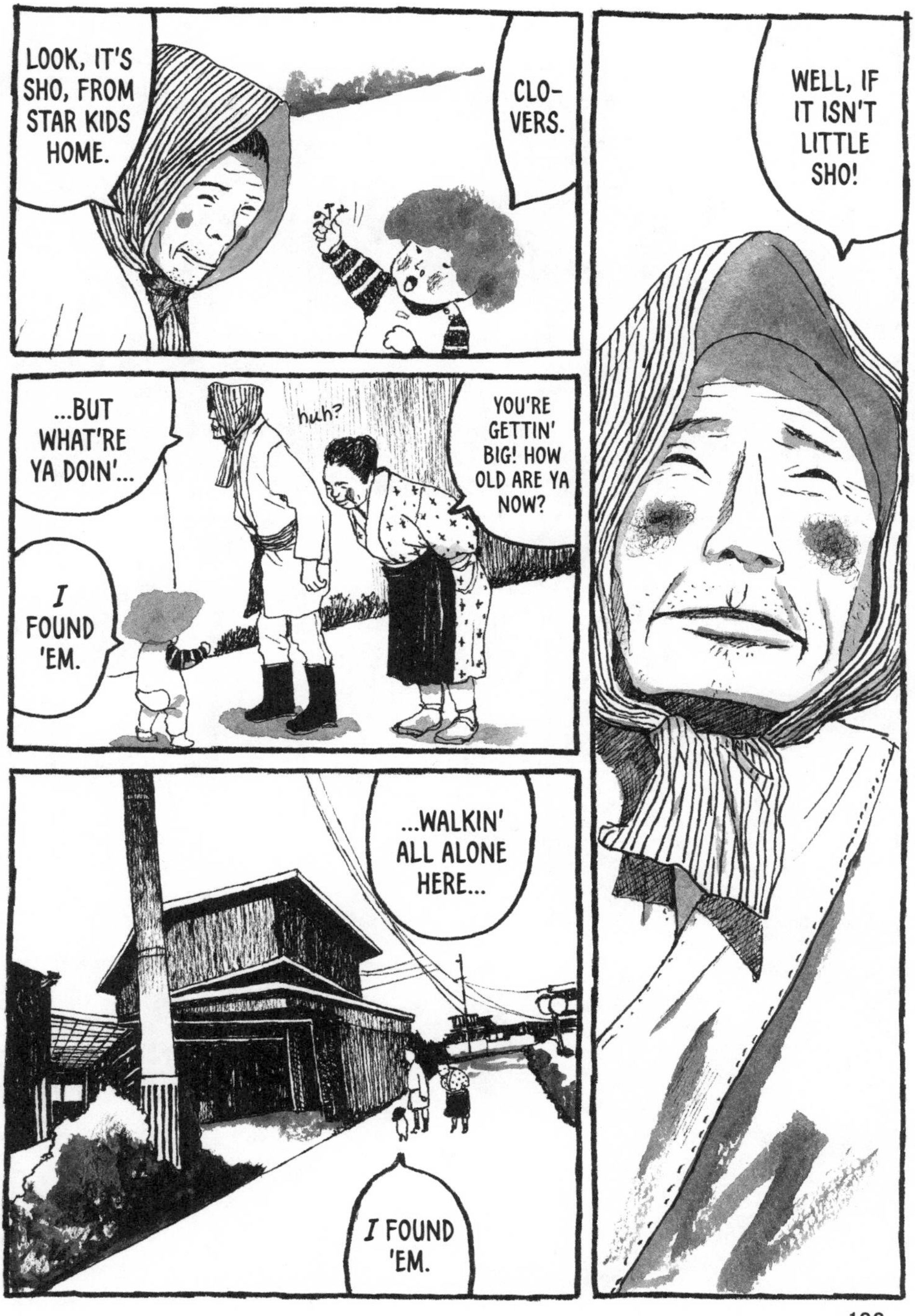
LOOK, IT'S SHO, FROM STAR KIDS HOME.
CLO-VERS.
WELL, IF IT ISN'T LITTLE SHO!
YOU'RE GETTIN' BIG! HOW OLD ARE YA NOW?
huh?
...BUT WHAT'RE YA DOIN'...
I FOUND 'EM.
...WALKIN' ALL ALONE HERE...
I FOUND 'EM.

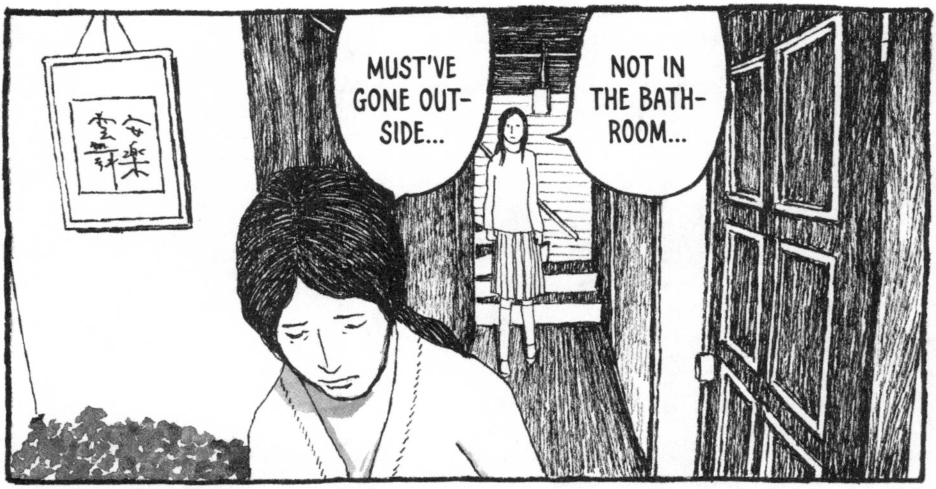
NOT IN THE BATH-
ROOM...
MUST'VE GONE OUT-
SIDE...

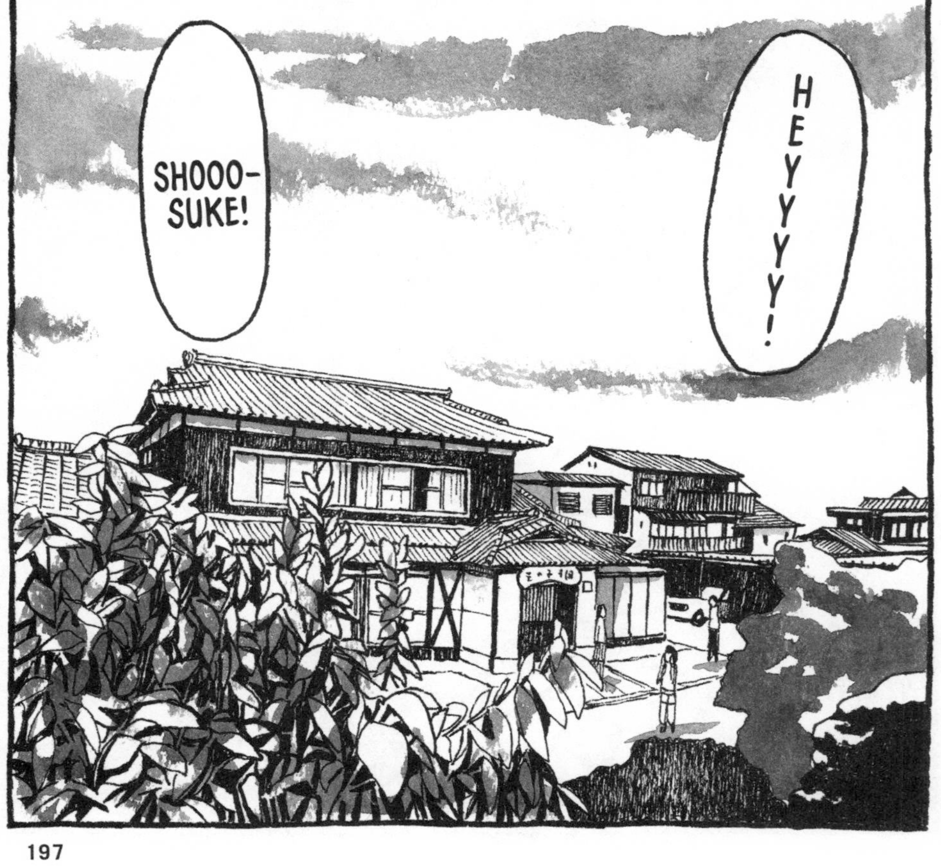
HEYYYYY!
SHOOO-
SUKE!

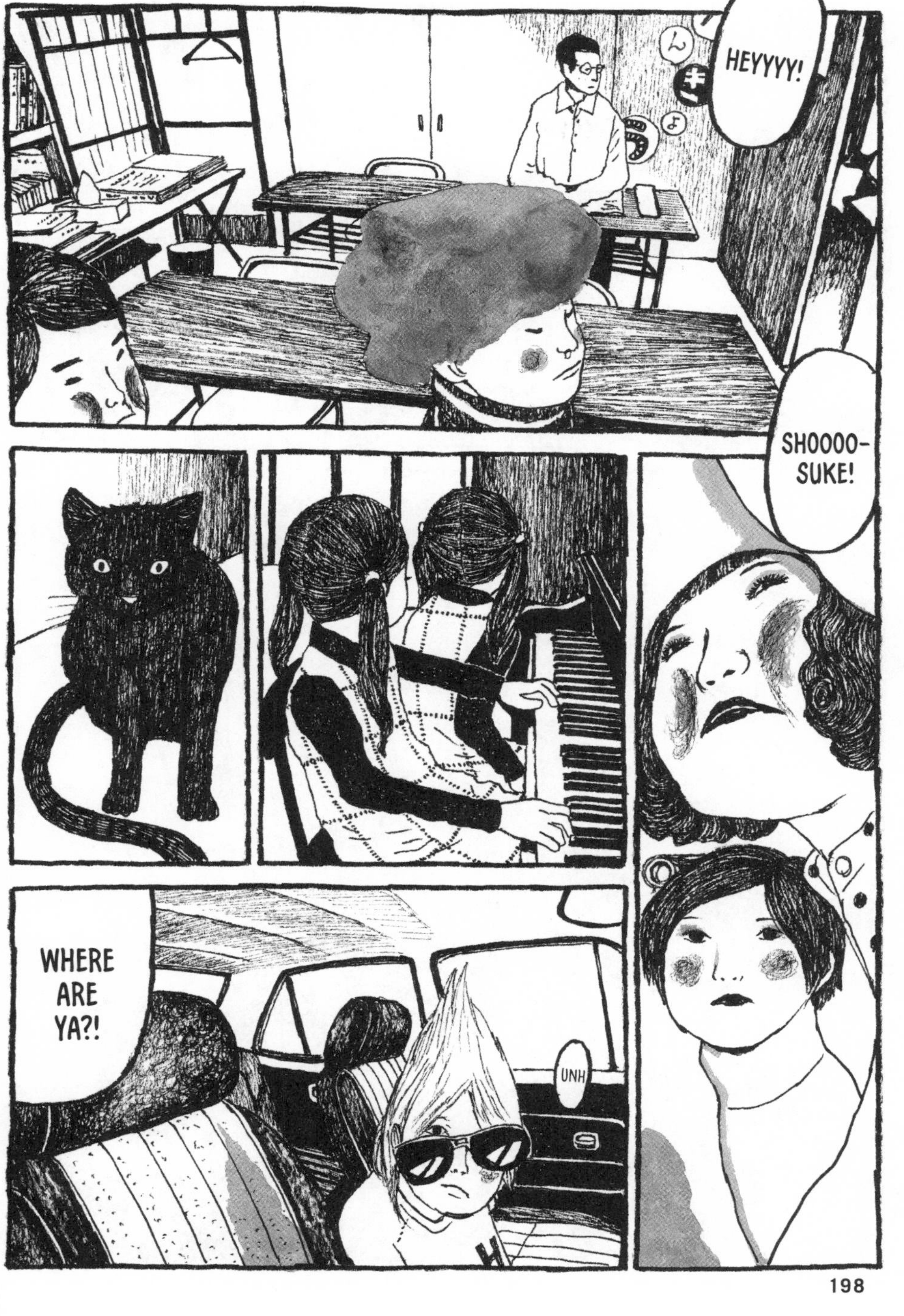
HEYYYY!
SHOOOO-SUKE!
WHERE ARE YA?!
UNH

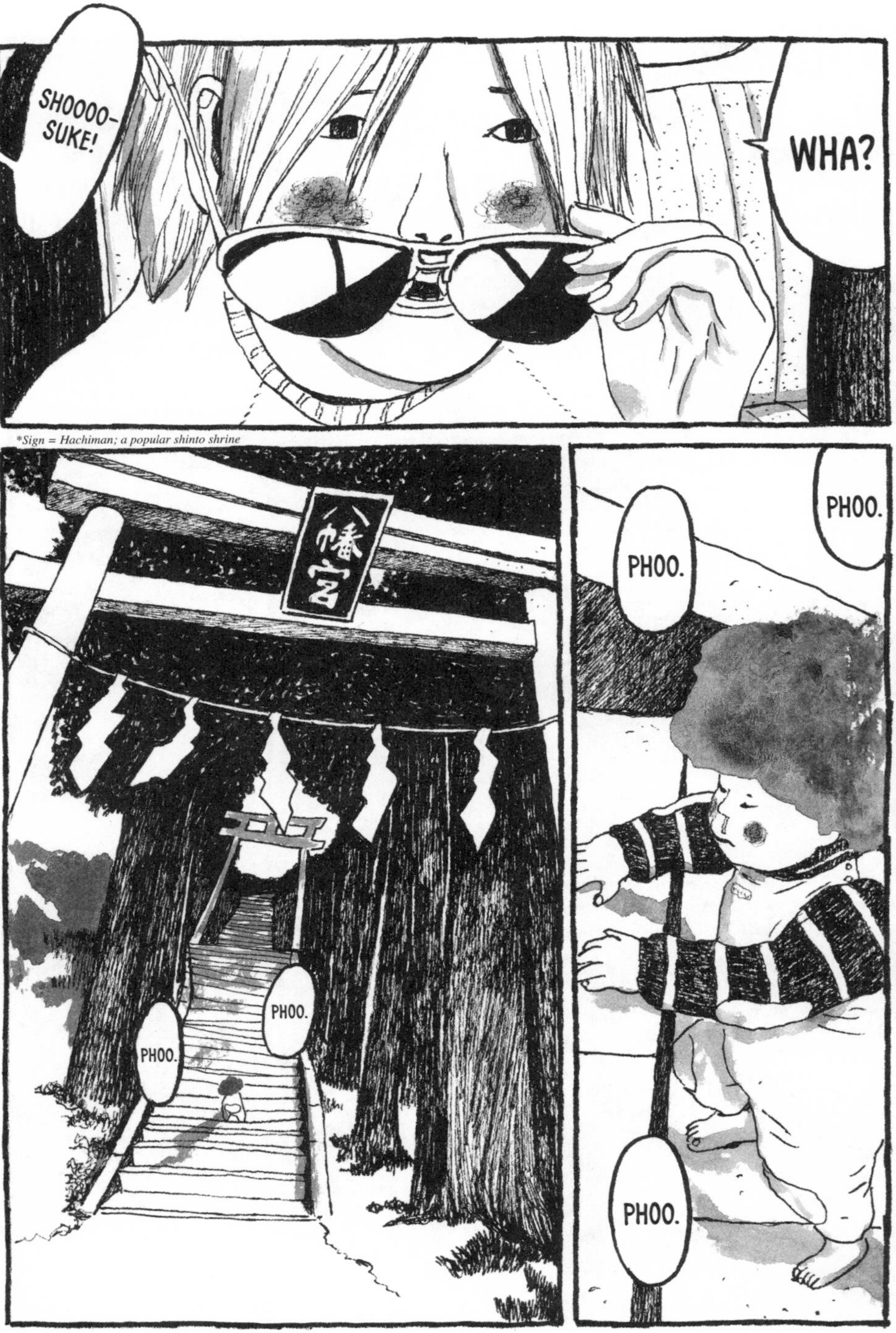
SHOOOO-SUKE!
WHA?
PHOO.
PHOO.
PHOO.
八幡宮
PHOO.
PHOO.
*Sign = Hachiman; a popular shinto shrine

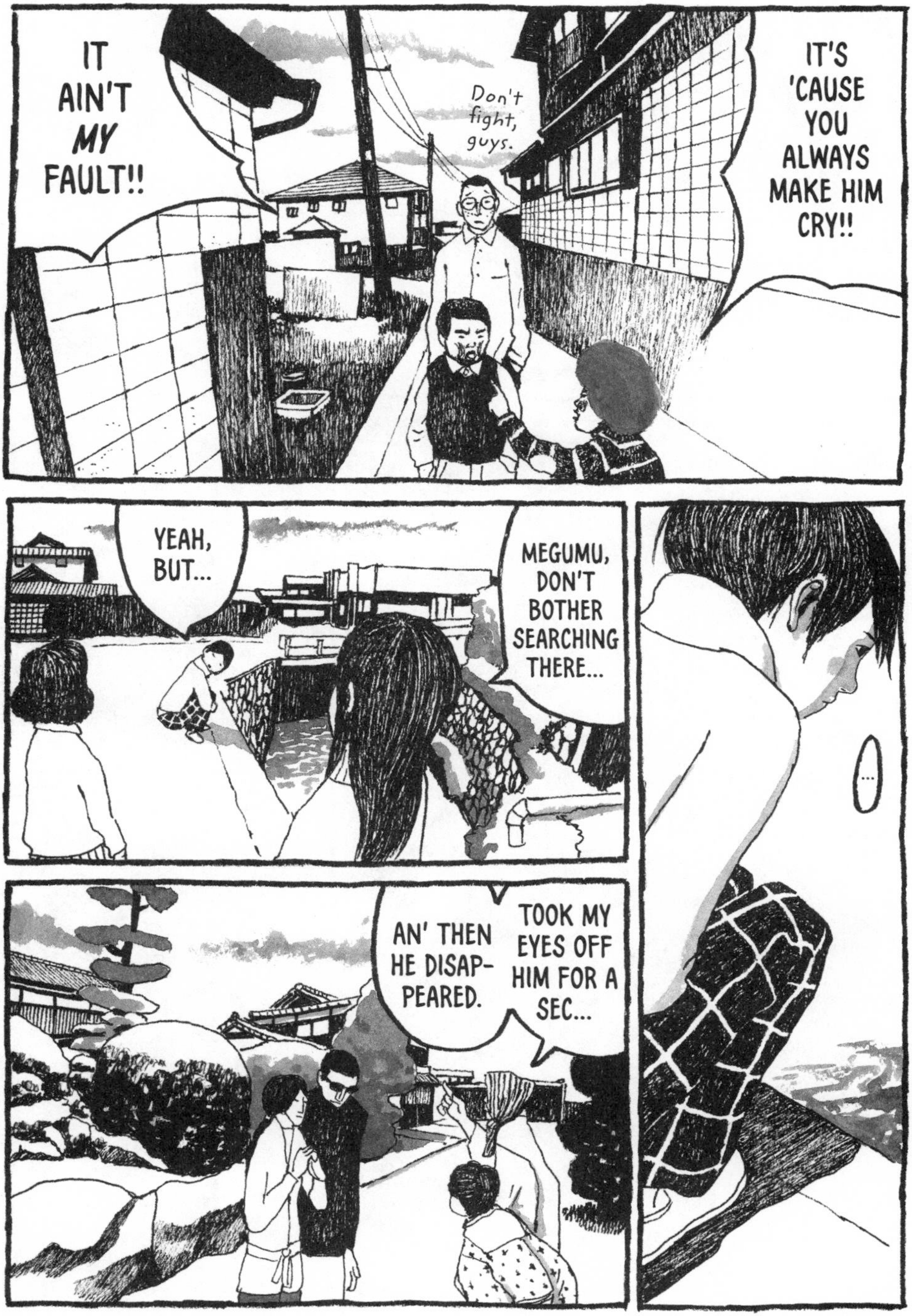
IT'S 'CAUSE YOU ALWAYS MAKE HIM CRY!!
IT AIN'T *MY* FAULT!!
Don't fight, guys.
...
MEGUMU, DON'T BOTHER SEARCHING THERE...
YEAH, BUT...
TOOK MY EYES OFF HIM FOR A SEC...
AN' THEN HE DISAPPEARED.

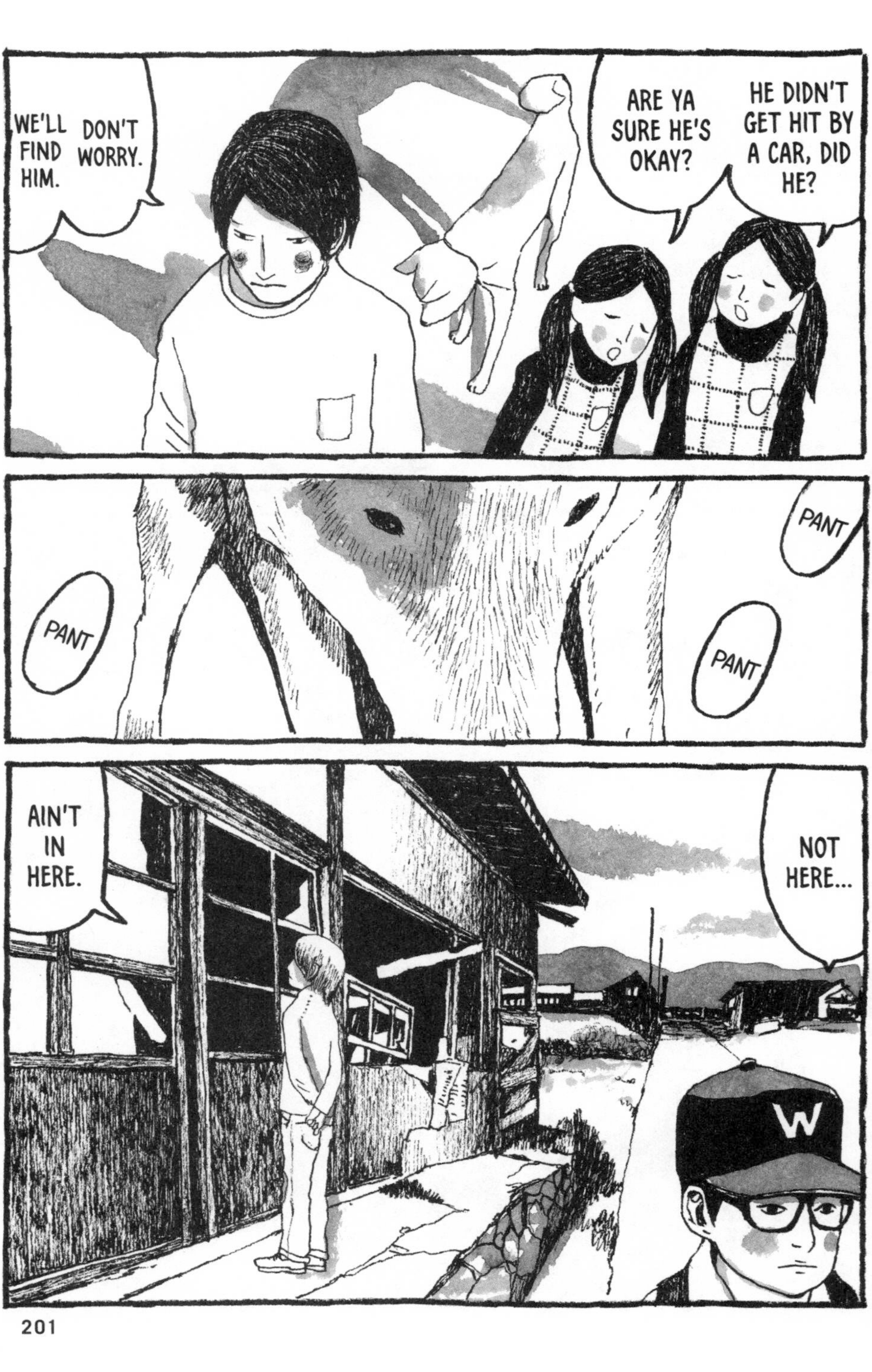
HE DIDN'T GET HIT BY A CAR, DID HE?
ARE YA SURE HE'S OKAY?
DON'T WORRY. WE'LL FIND HIM.
PANT
PANT
PANT
NOT HERE...
AIN'T IN HERE.

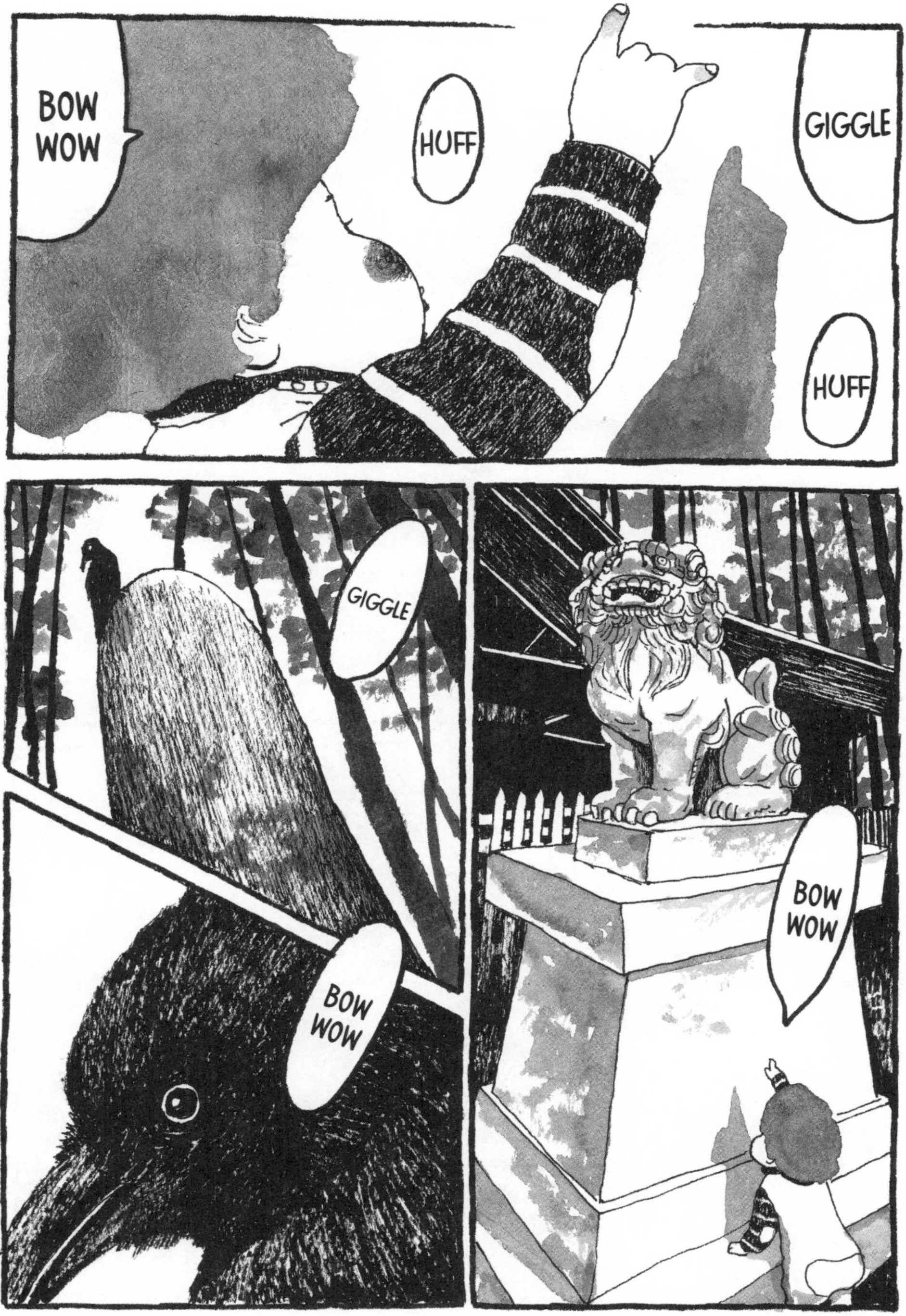
GIGGLE
HUFF
BOW WOW
HUFF
BOW WOW
GIGGLE
BOW WOW

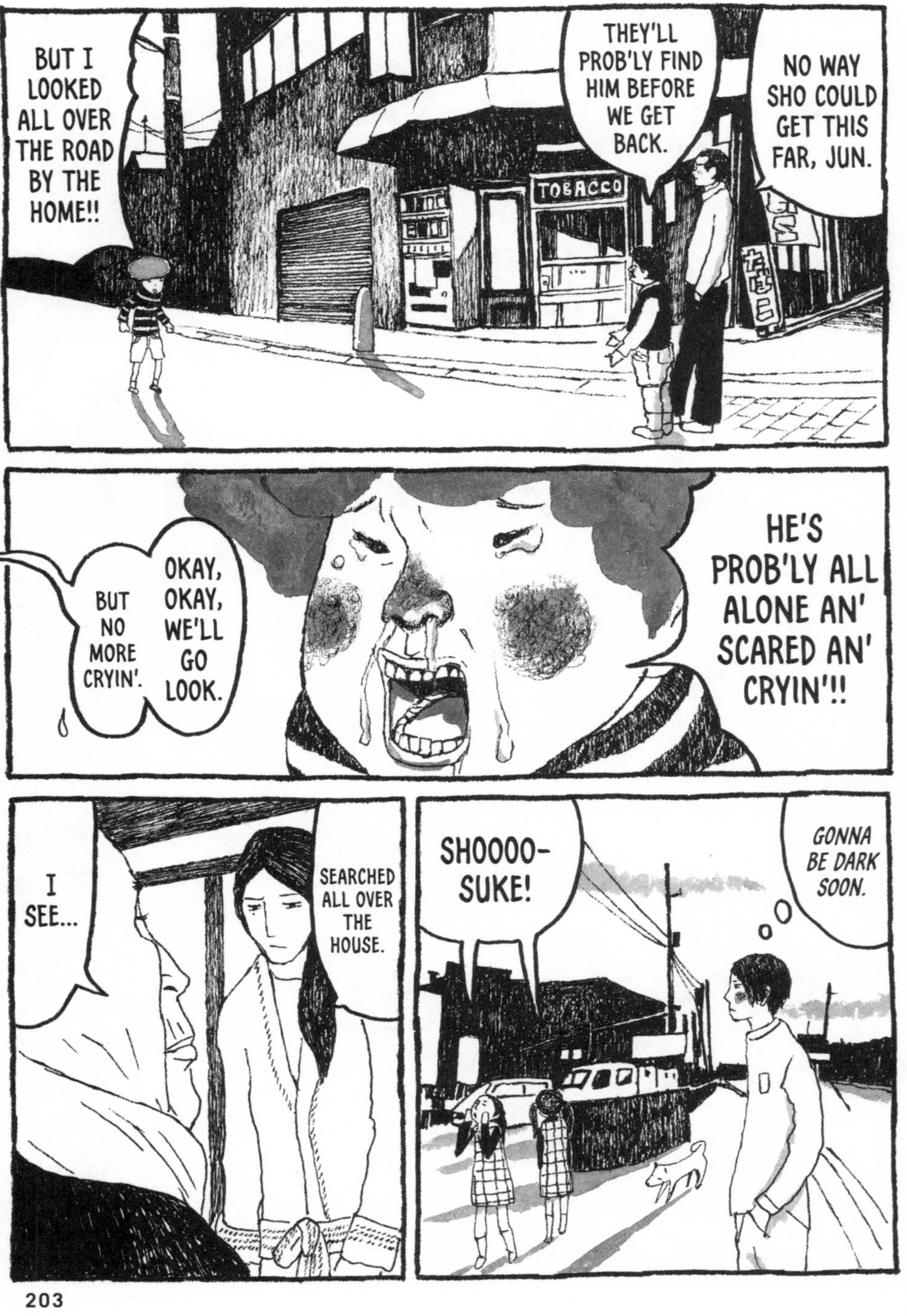
NO WAY SHO COULD GET THIS FAR, JUN.
THEY'LL PROB'LY FIND HIM BEFORE WE GET BACK.
BUT I LOOKED ALL OVER THE ROAD BY THE HOME!!
TOBACCO
HE'S PROB'LY ALL ALONE AN' SCARED AN' CRYIN'!!
OKAY, OKAY, WE'LL GO LOOK.
BUT NO MORE CRYIN'.
GONNA BE DARK SOON.
SHOOOO-SUKE!
SEARCHED ALL OVER THE HOUSE.
I SEE...

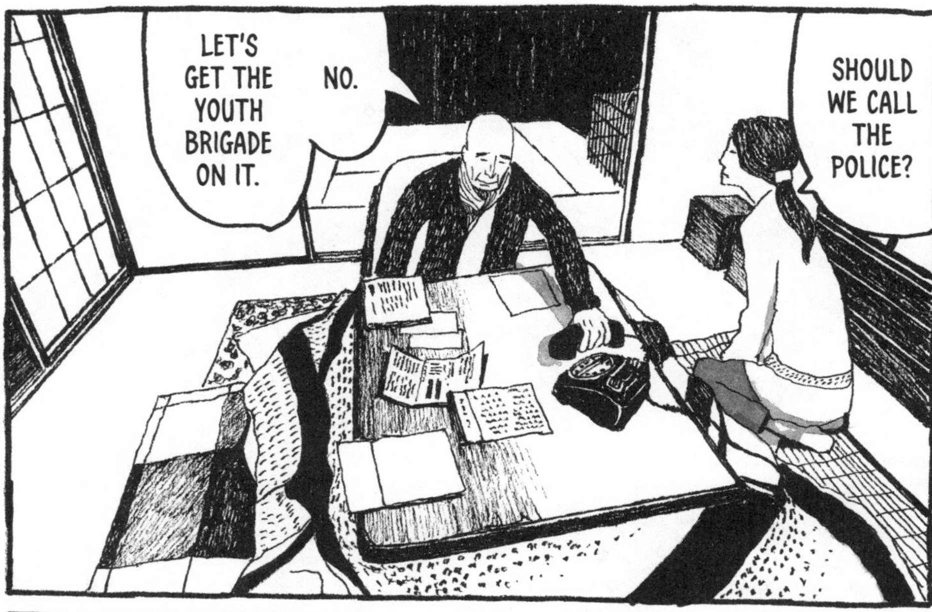
SHOULD WE CALL THE POLICE?
NO.
LET'S GET THE YOUTH BRIGADE ON IT.

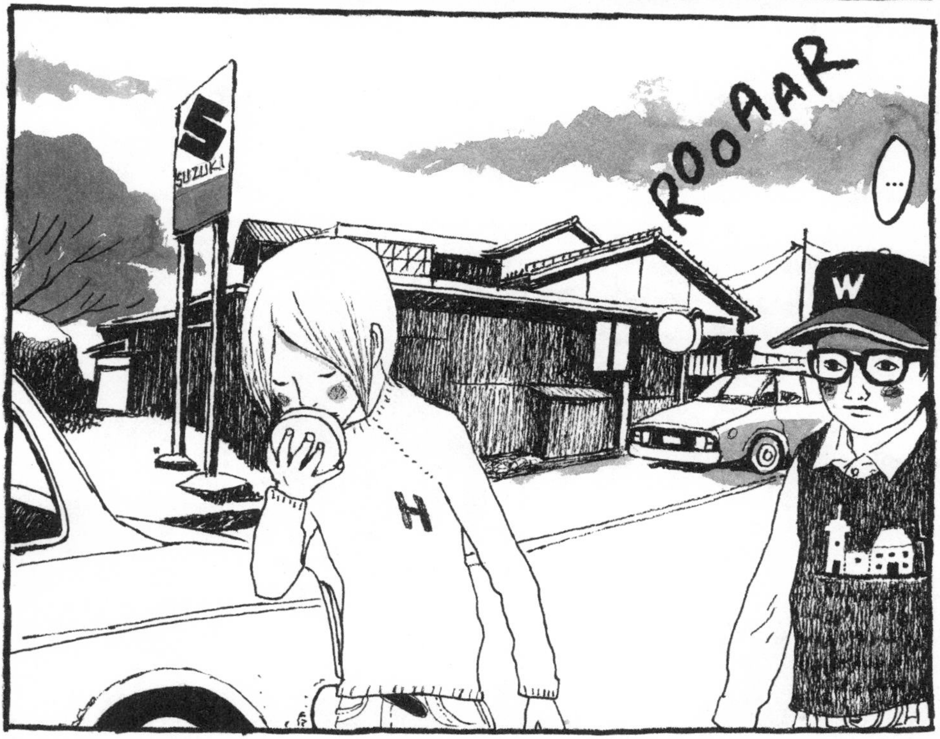
...
ROOAAR
SUZUKI

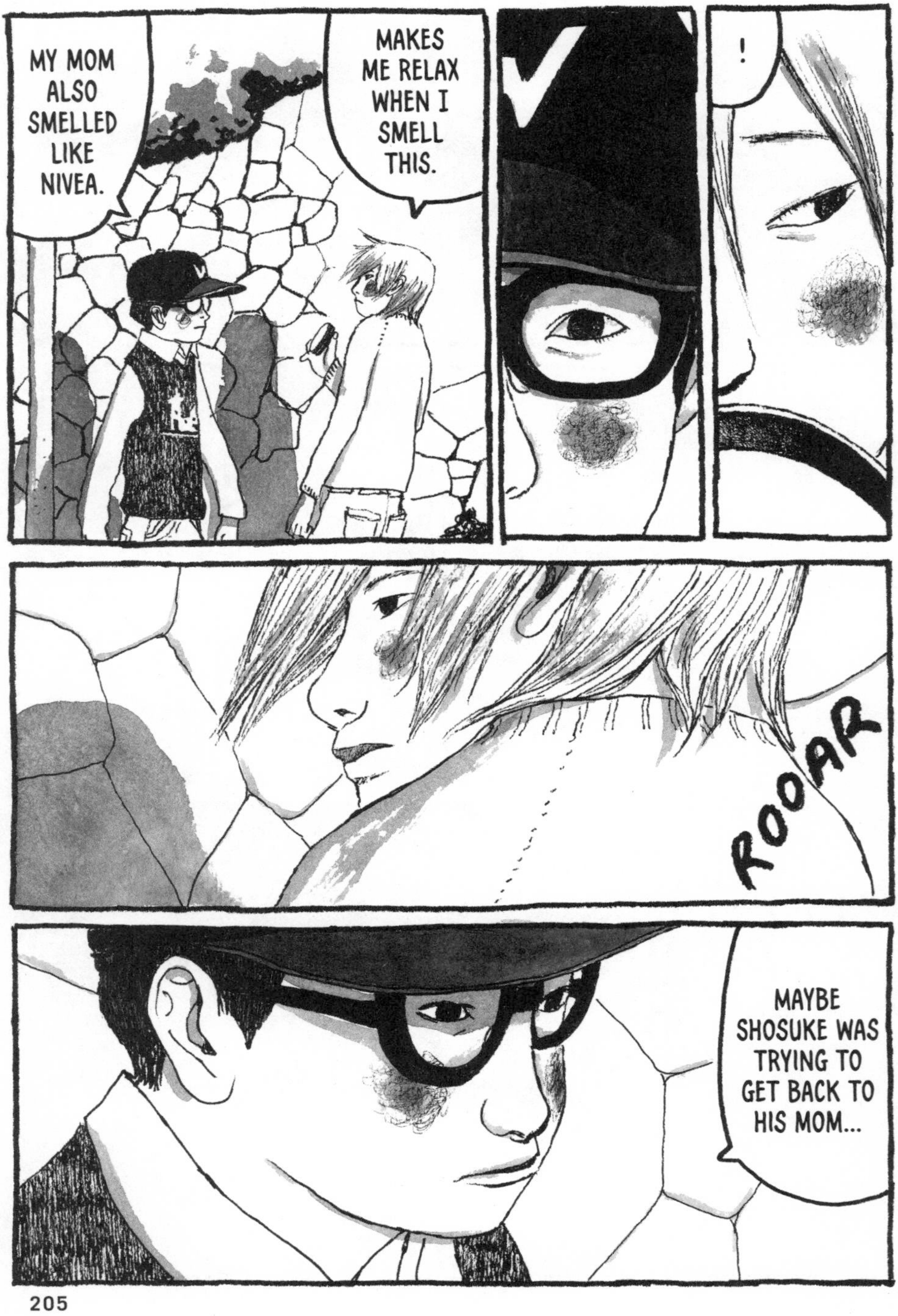
MY MOM ALSO SMELLED LIKE NIVEA.
MAKES ME RELAX WHEN I SMELL THIS.
!
ROOAR
MAYBE SHOSUKE WAS TRYING TO GET BACK TO HIS MOM...

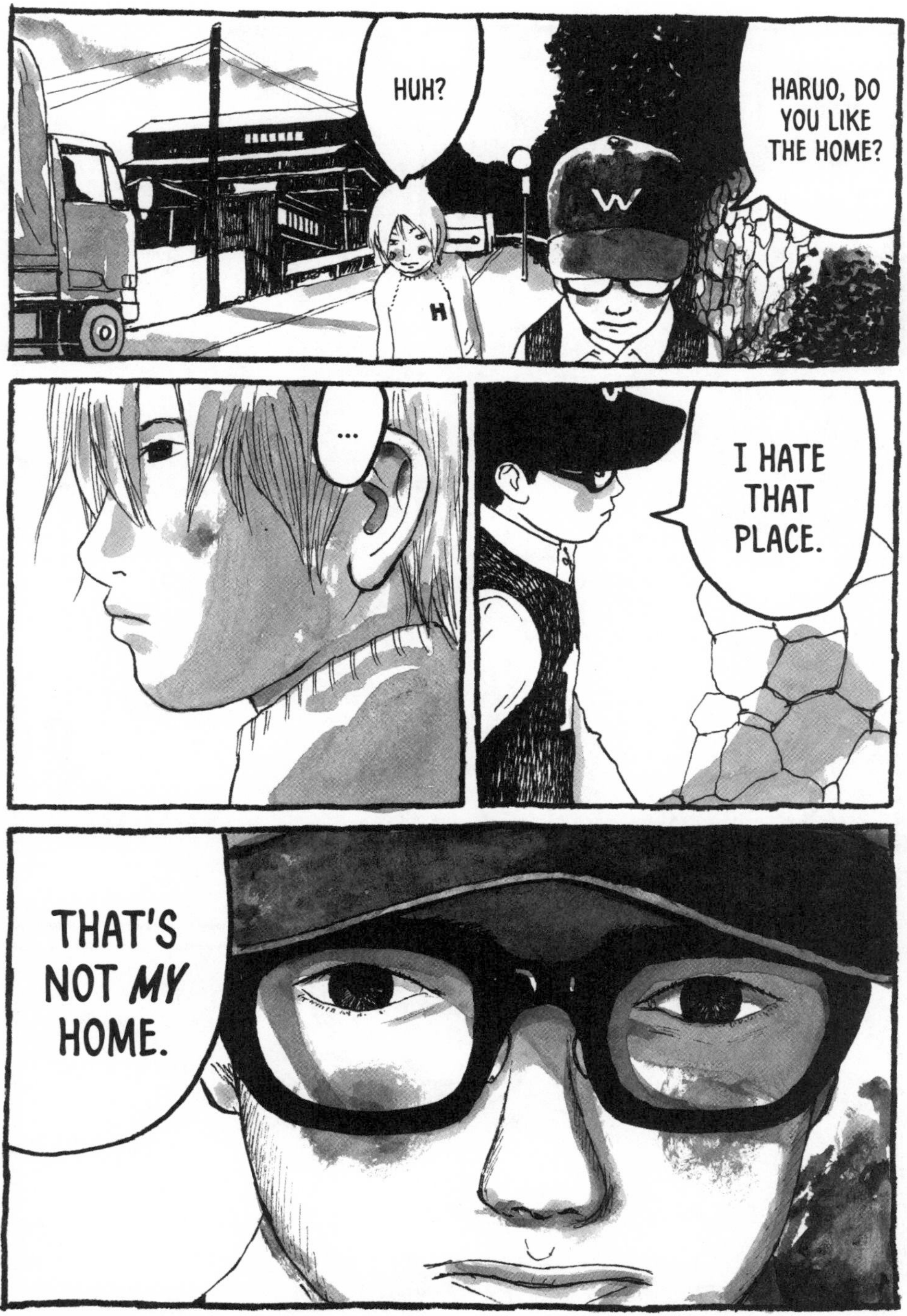
HARUO, DO YOU LIKE THE HOME?
HUH?
I HATE THAT PLACE.
...
THAT'S NOT *MY* HOME.

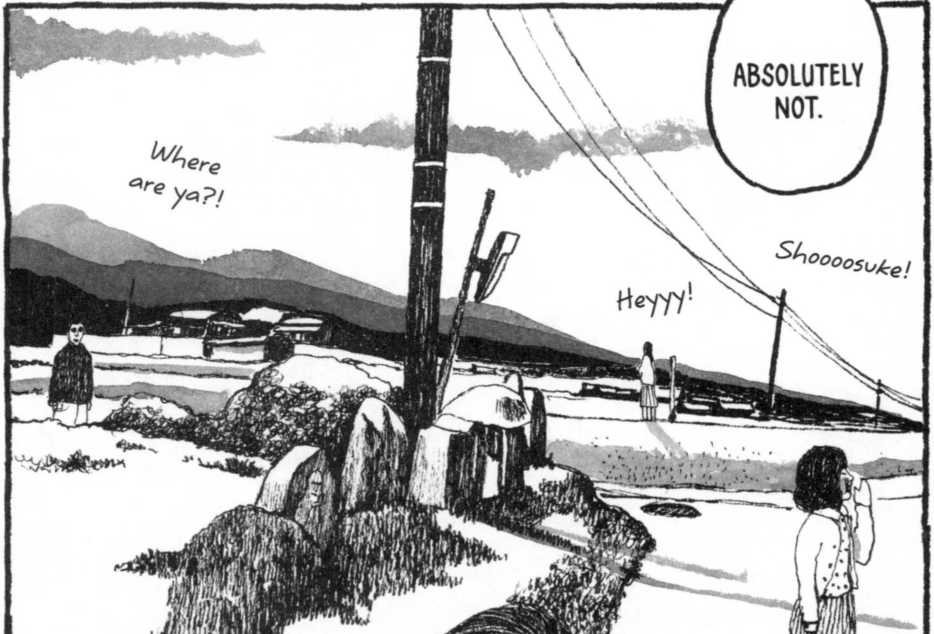
ABSOLUTELY NOT.
Shoooosuke!
Heyyy!
Where are ya?!

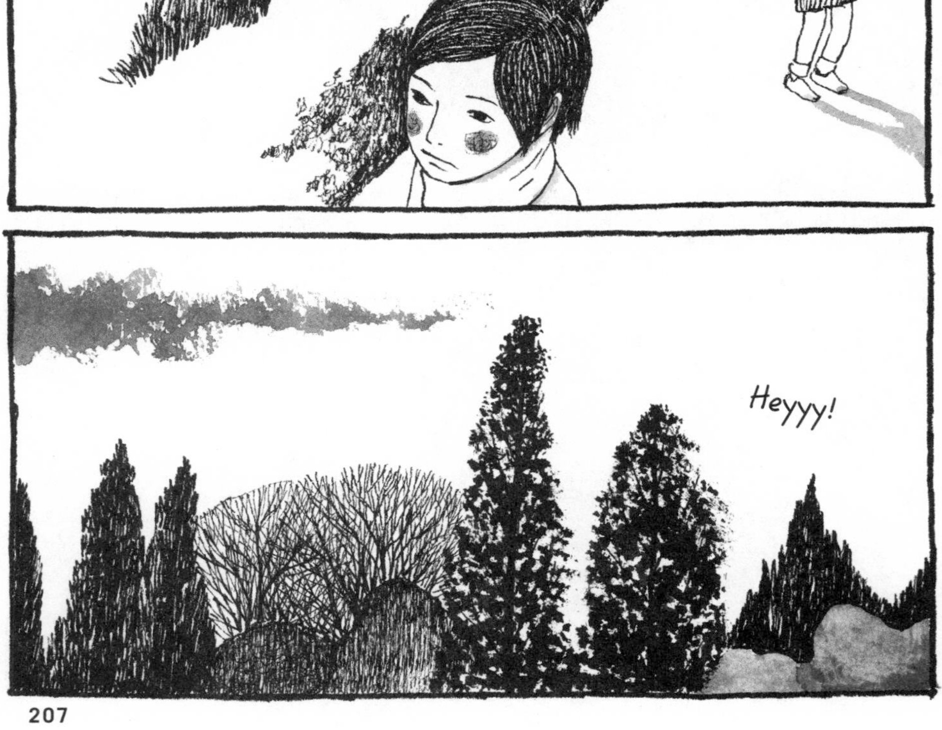
Heyyy!

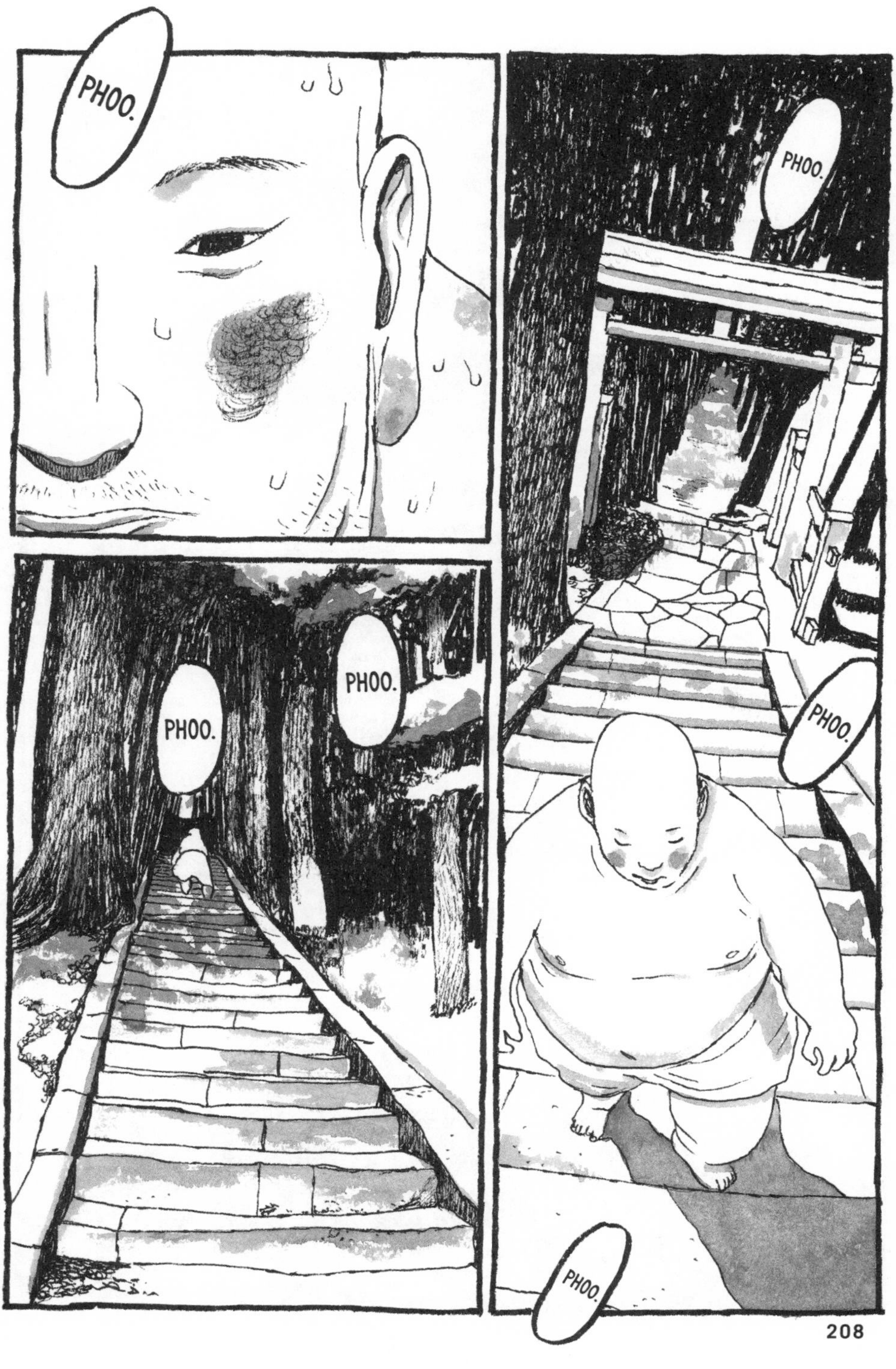
PHOO.
PHOO.
PHOO.
PHOO.
PHOO.
PHOO.

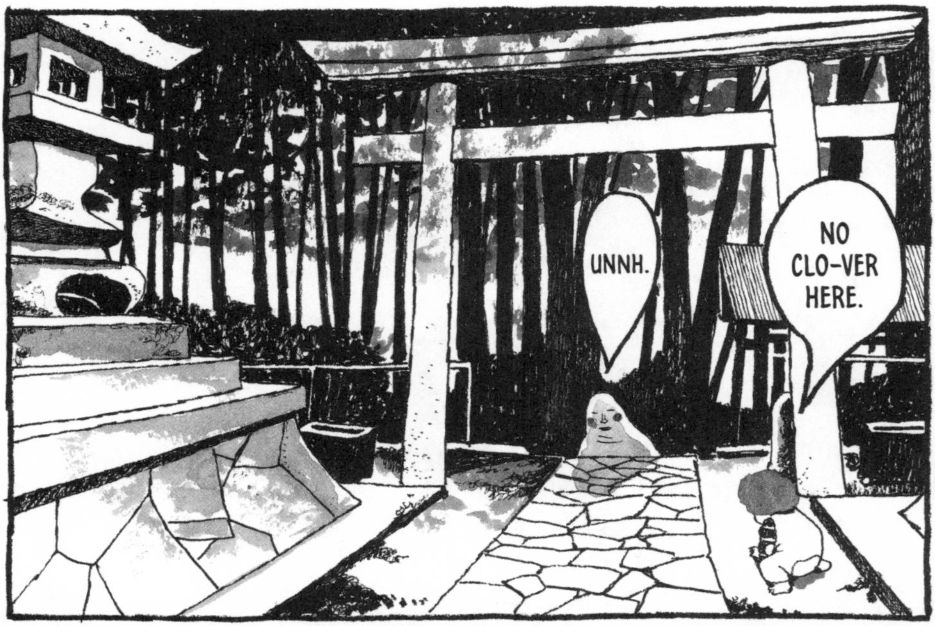
NO CLO-VER HERE.
UNNH.

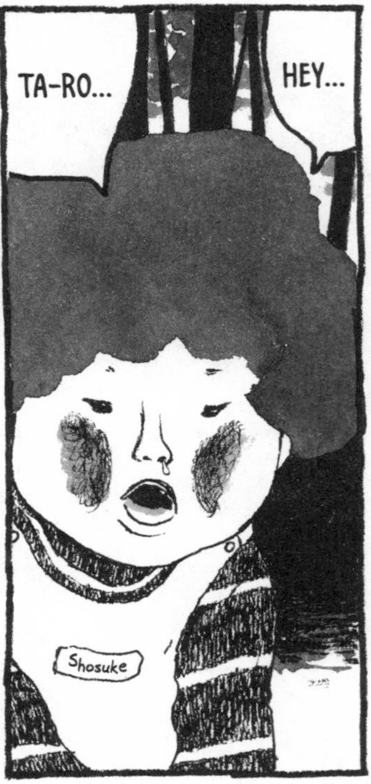
HEY...
TA-RO...
Shosuke

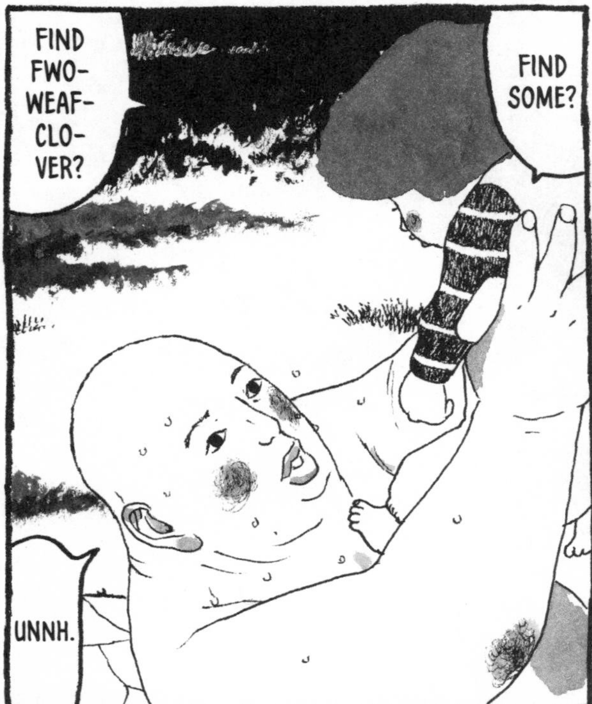
FIND SOME?
FIND FWO-WEAF-CLO-VER?
UNNH.

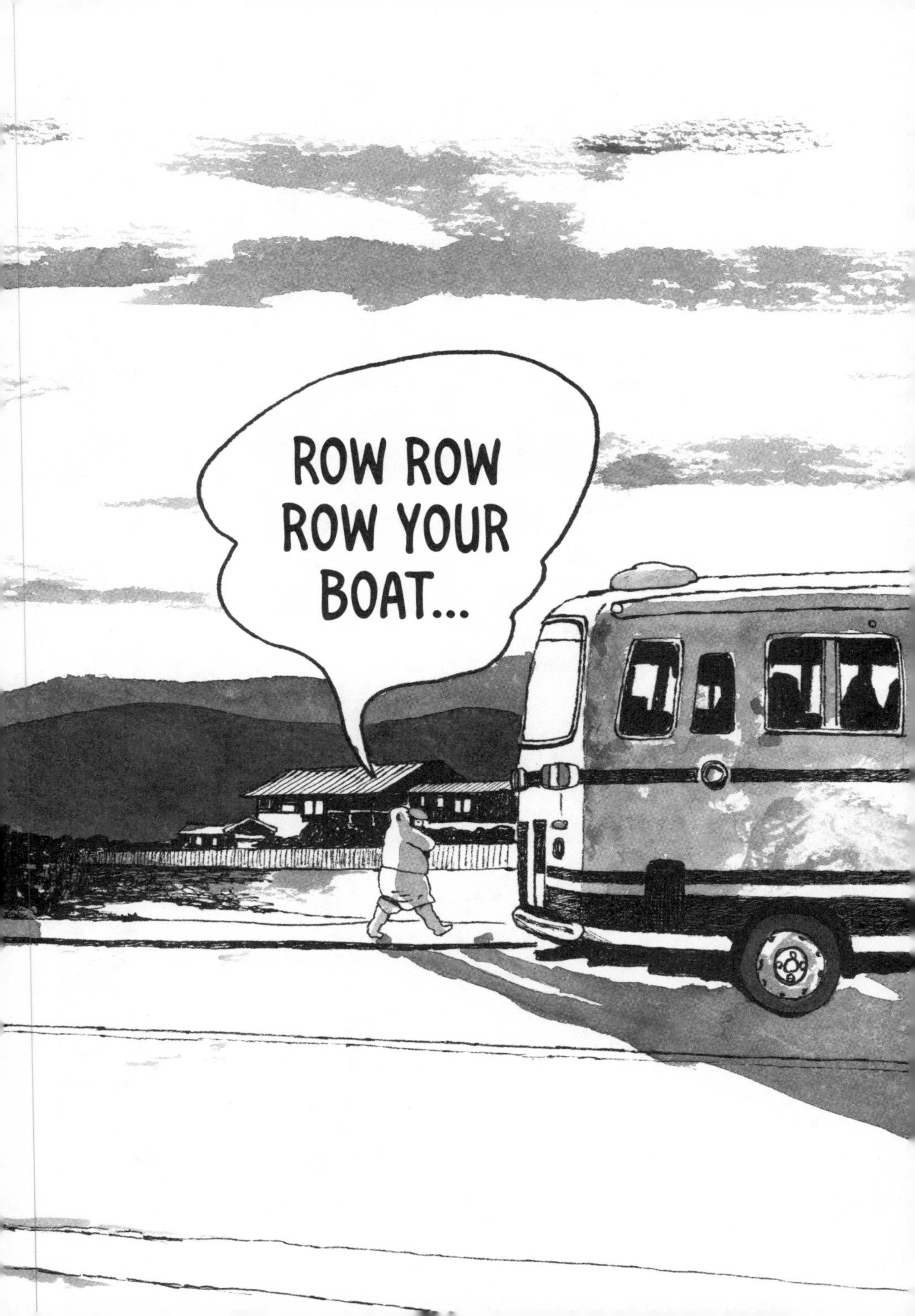
ROW ROW ROW YOUR BOAT...

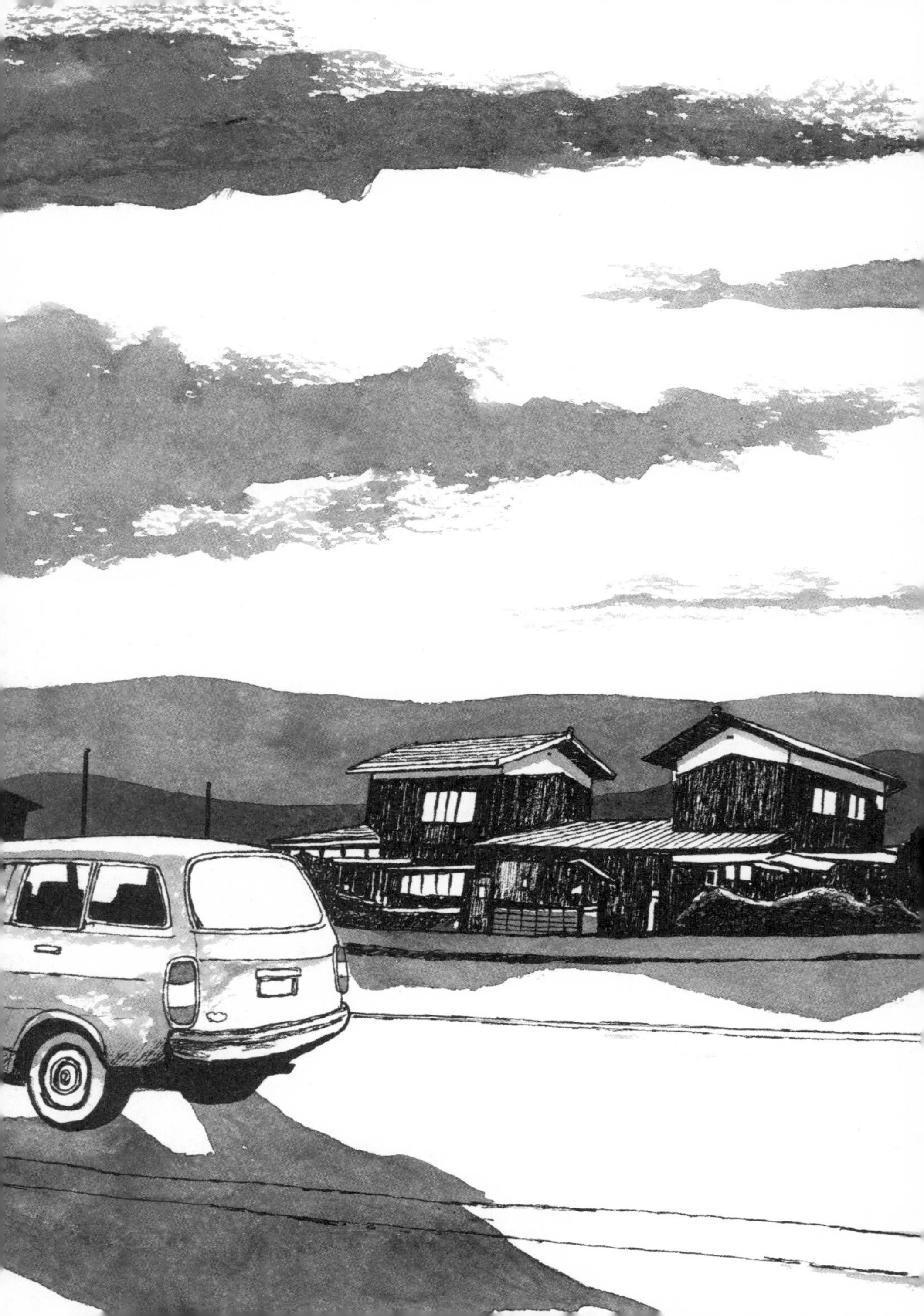

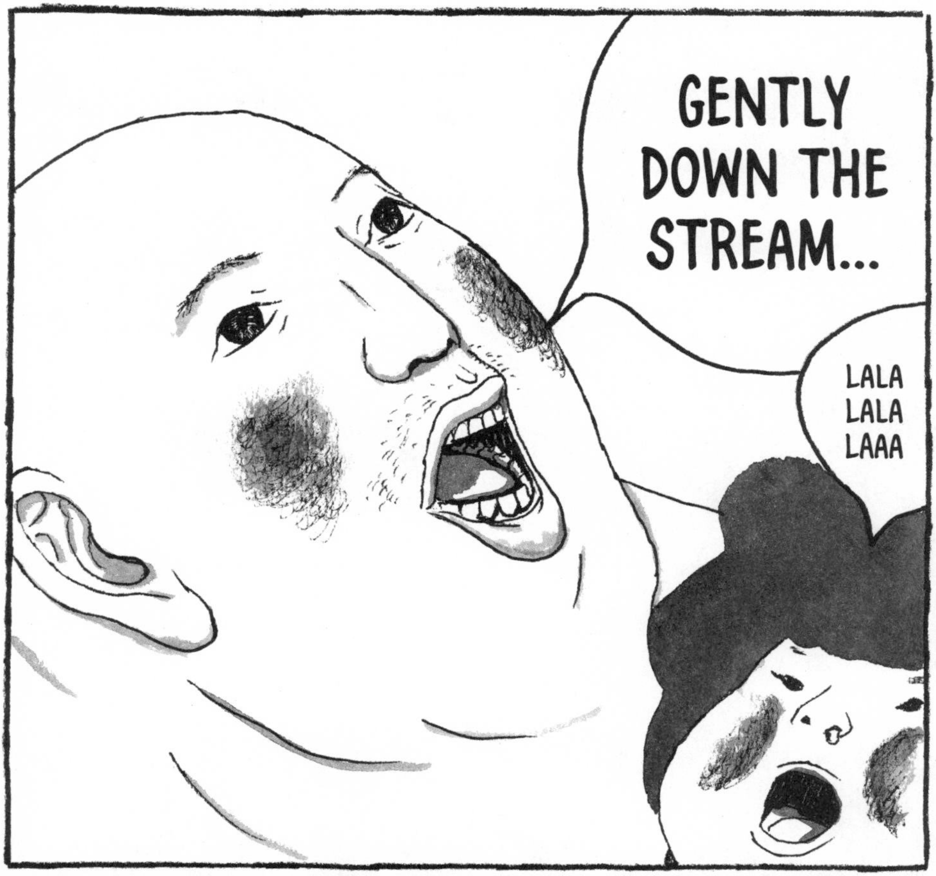
GENTLY DOWN THE STREAM...
LALA LALA LAAA

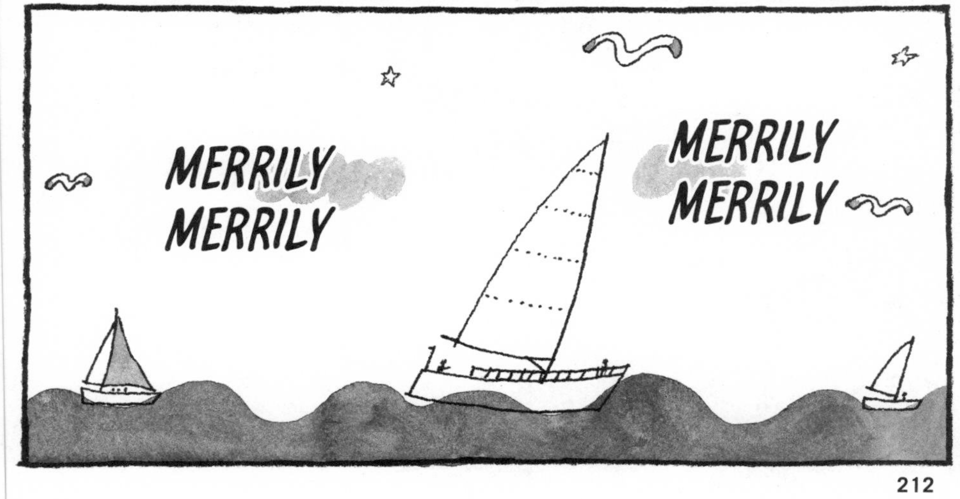
MERRILY MERRILY MERRILY
MERRILY MERRILY

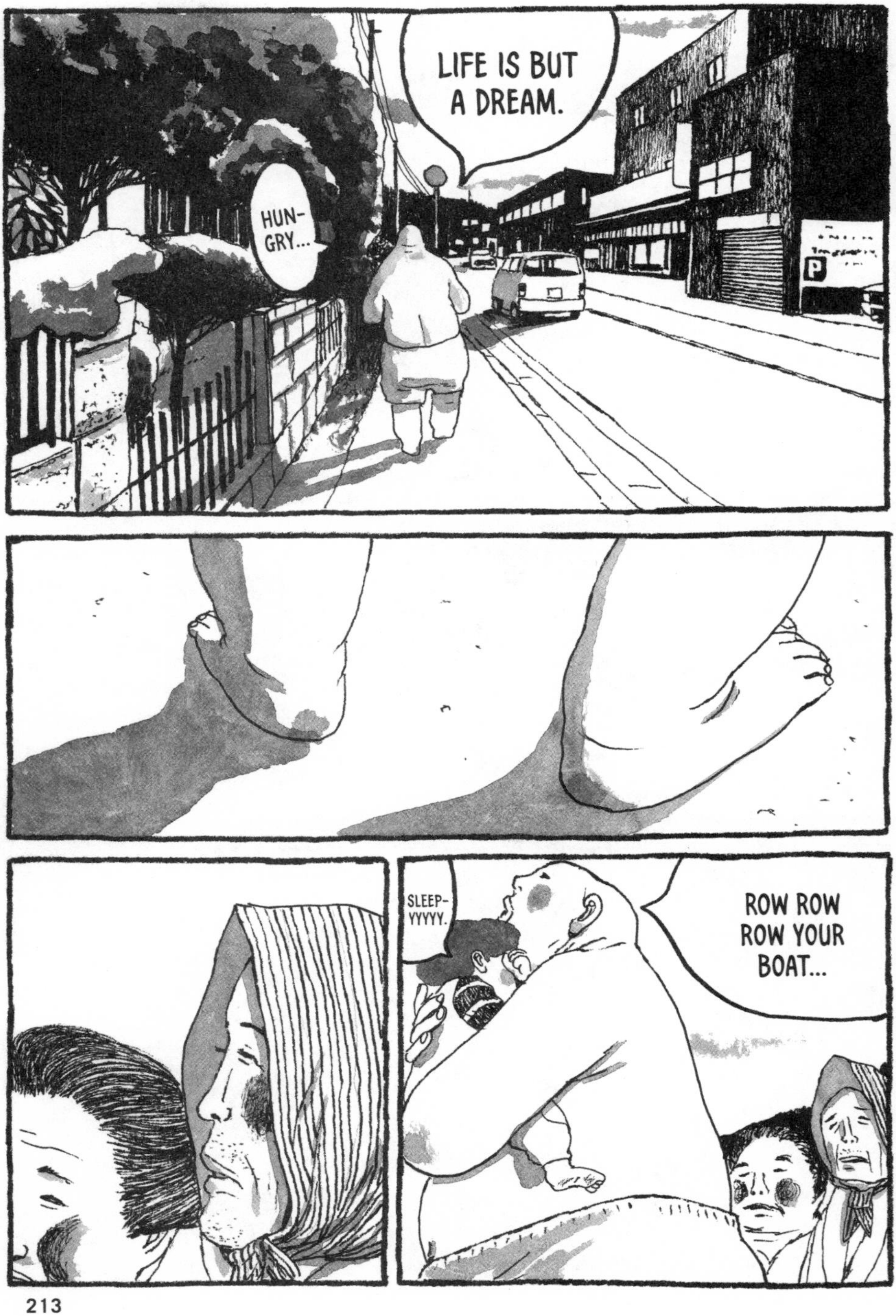
LIFE IS BUT A DREAM.
HUN-GRY...
ROW ROW ROW YOUR BOAT...
SLEEP-YYYYY.

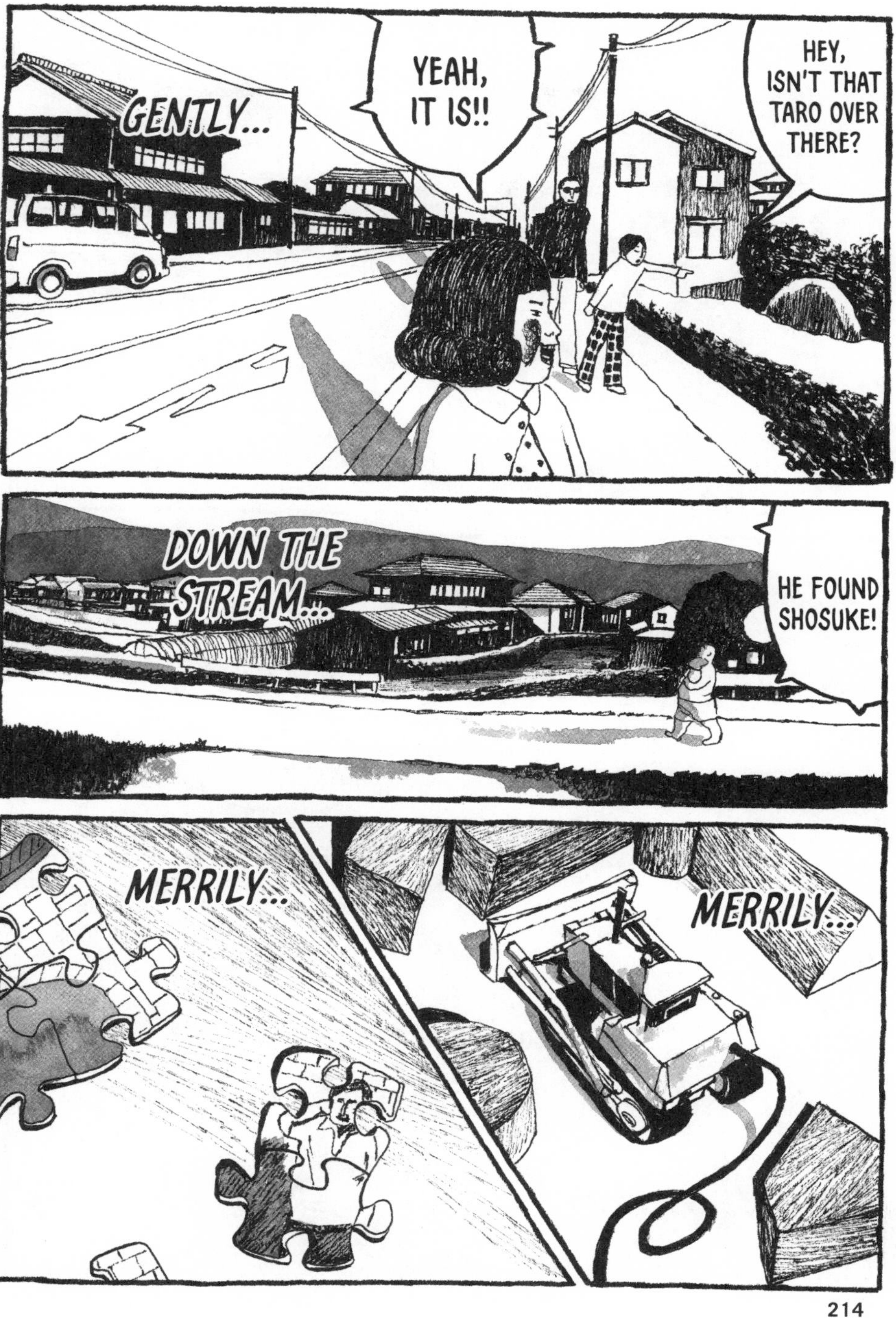
HEY, ISN'T THAT TARO OVER THERE?
YEAH, IT IS!!
GENTLY...
HE FOUND SHOSUKE!
DOWN THE STREAM...
MERRILY...
MERRILY...

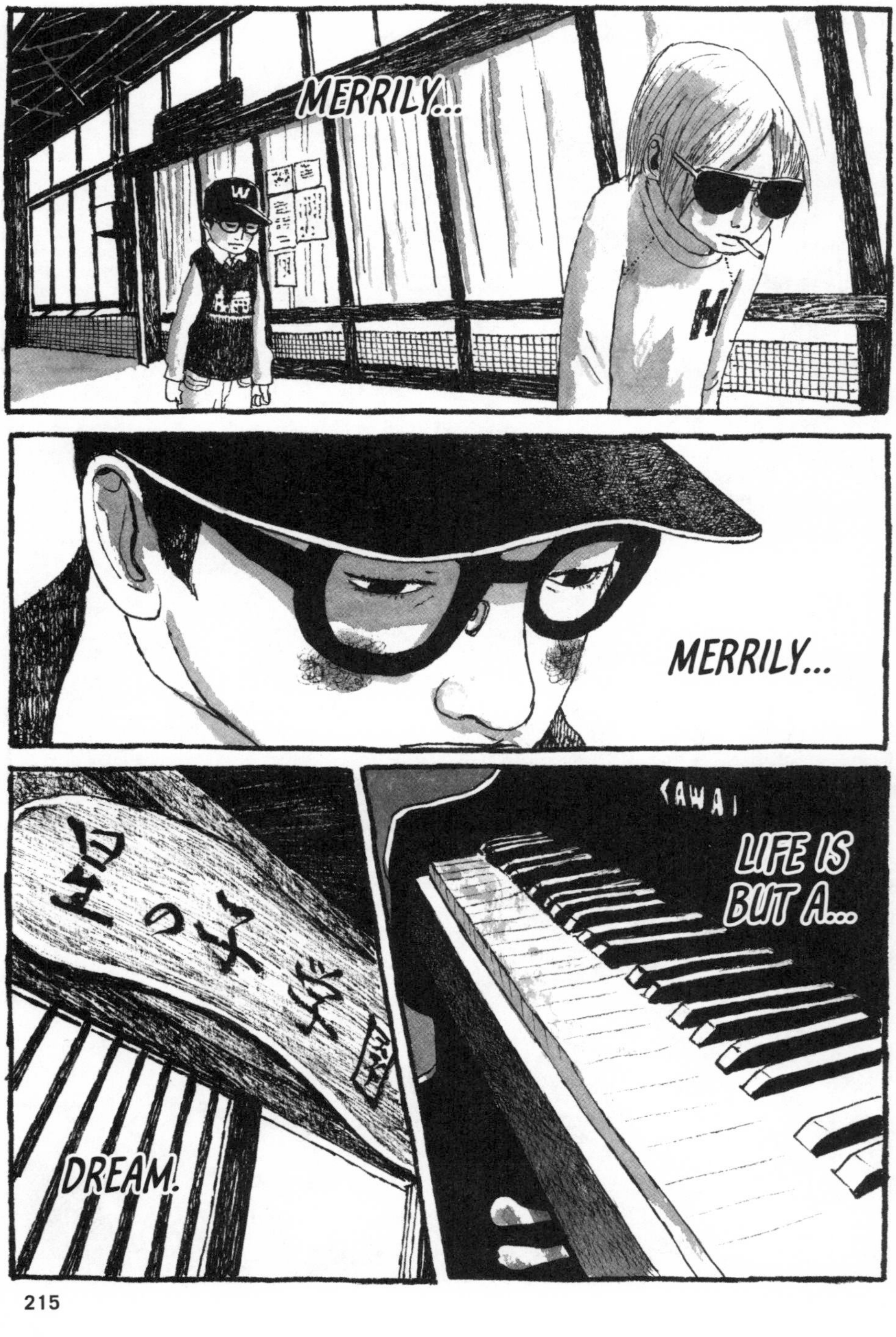
MERRILY...
MERRILY...
KAWAI
LIFE IS BUT A...
DREAM.

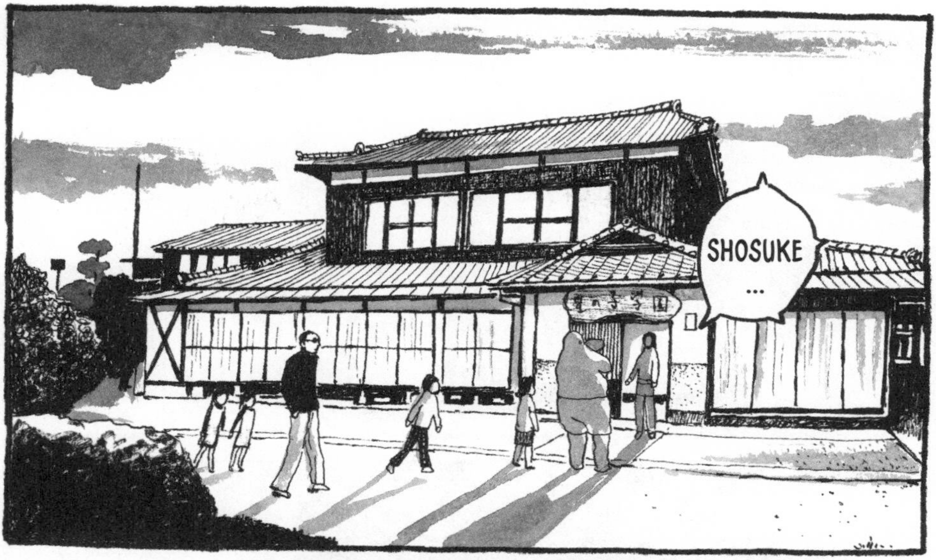
SHOSUKE ...
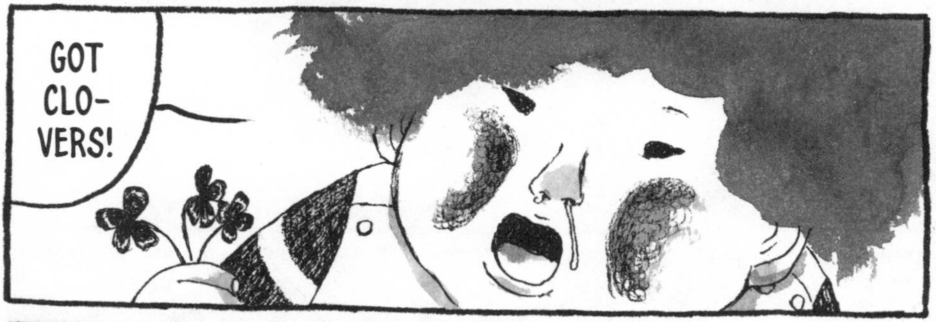
GOT CLO-VERS!
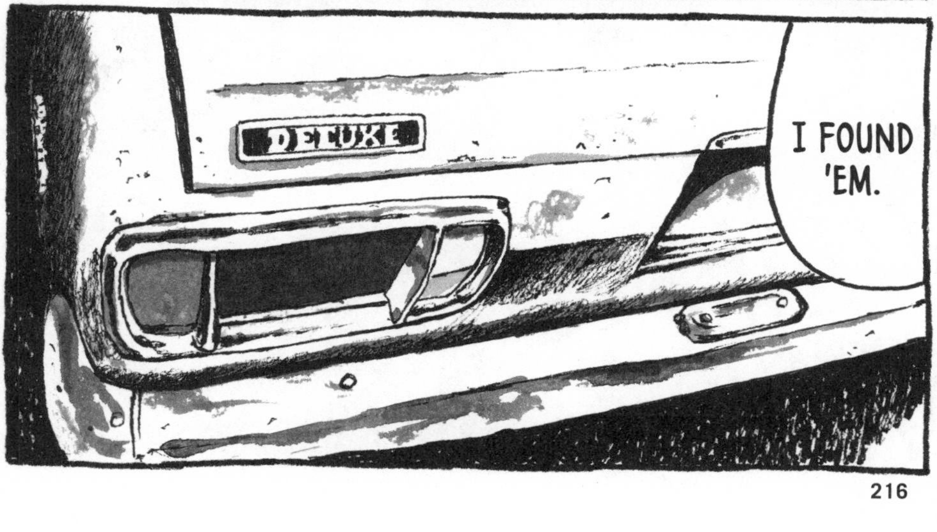
DELUXE
I FOUND 'EM.

Sunny

①

END

ny

Sun

First serialized in Japanese in *IKKI*, February, March, April, May, June, and July **2011**.

SUNNY

Volume 1
VIZ Signature Edition

Story and art by **Taiyo MATSUMOTO**

SUNNY Vol. 1
by Taiyo MATSUMOTO
© 2011 Taiyou MATSUMOTO
All rights reserved.
Original Japanese edition published by SHOGAKUKAN.
English translation rights in the United States of America and
Canada arranged with SHOGAKUKAN.

Original Japanese edition design by Sekine Shinichi Studio

With thanks to the Nissan Motor Co.,Ltd.

Translation by **Michael Arias**
Lettering by **Deron Bennett**
Book design by **Fawn Lau**

The stories, characters and incidents mentioned
in this publication are entirely fictional.

No portion of this book may be reproduced or
transmitted in any form or by any means without
written permission from the copyright holders.

Printed in Canada

Published by VIZ Media, LLC
PO Box 77010
San Francisco, CA 94107

10 9 8 7 6 5 4 3 2 1
First printing, May 2013

VIZ SIGNATURE
WWW.VIZ.COM

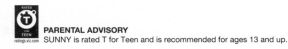

PARENTAL ADVISORY
SUNNY is rated T for Teen and is recommended for ages 13 and up.

TAIYO MATSUMOTO

is best known to English-reading audiences as the
creator of *Tekkonkinkreet*, which in 2006 was made
into an animated feature film of the same name,
directed by Michael Arias. In 2007 Matsumoto was
awarded a **Japan Media Arts Festival Excellence
Award**, and in 2008 he won an **Eisner Award** for
the English publication of *Tekkonkinkreet*.

Also available in **ENGLISH** by **TAIYO MATSUMOTO**
● *Blue Spring* ● *Tekkonkinkreet* ● *GoGo Monster*

WITHDRAWN

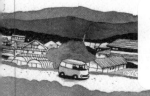

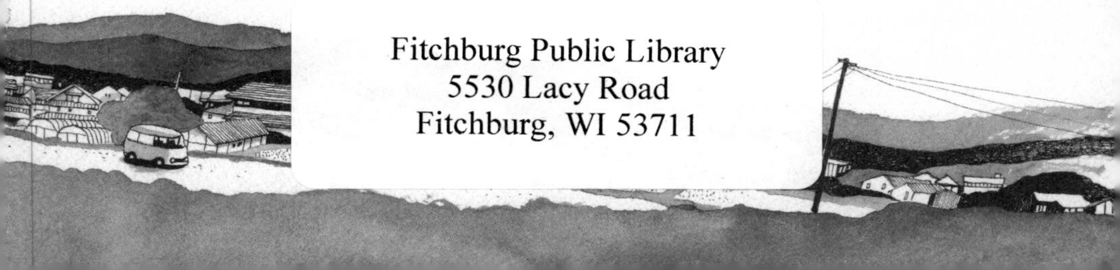

Fitchburg Public Library
5530 Lacy Road
Fitchburg, WI 53711

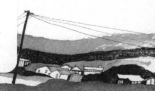

D0969019